The Byzantine Economy

This is a concise survey of the economy of the Byzantine Empire from the fourth century AD to the fall of Constantinople in 1453. Organized chronologically, the book addresses key themes such as demography, agriculture, manufacturing and the urban economy, trade, monetary developments, and the role of the state and ideology. It provides a comprehensive overview of the economy with an emphasis on the economic actions of the state, the productive role of the city, and the role of non-state economic actors, such as landlords, artisans and money-changers. The final chapter compares the Byzantine economy with the economies of western Europe and concludes that it was one of the most successful examples of a mixed economy in the pre-industrial world. This is the only concise general history of the Byzantine economy and will be essential reading for students of economic history, Byzantine history and medieval history more generally.

ANGELIKI E. LAIOU is Dumbarton Oaks Professor of Byzantine History, Harvard University, and Permanent Member of the Academy of Athens.

CÉCILE MORRISSON is Director of Research at the CNRS (National Center of Scientific Research) and Advisor for Byzantine Numismatics at Dumbarton Oaks.

Cambridge Medieval Textbooks

This is a series of introductions to important topics in medieval history aimed primarily at advanced students and faculty, and is designed to complement the monograph series *Cambridge Studies in Medieval Life and Thought*. It includes both chronological and thematic approaches and addresses both British and European topics.

For a list of titles in the series, see end of book.

THE BYZANTINE ECONOMY

ANGELIKI E. LAIOU
Harvard University
and
CÉCILE MORRISSON
National Center of Scientific
Research, Paris

CAMBRIDGE
UNIVERSITY PRESS

CAMBRIDGE UNIVERSITY PRESS

Cambridge, New York, Melbourne, Madrid, Cape Town, Singapore, São Paulo

Cambridge University Press
The Edinburgh Building, Cambridge CB2 8RU, UK

Published in the United States of America by Cambridge University Press,
New York

www.cambridge.org
Information on this title: www.cambridge.org/9780521615020

First published 2007

Printed in the United Kingdom at the University Press, Cambridge

A catalogue record for this publication is available from the British Library

ISBN 978-0-521-84978-4 hardback
ISBN 978-0-521-61502-0 paperback

CONTENTS

MAPS

——————— • ———————

FIGURES

———————— · ————————

TABLES

———————— • ————————

ACKNOWLEDGEMENTS

———————— • ————————

We would like to thank Dr Chris Lightfoot for generously discussing with us a number of the findings from the Amorion excavations, the importance of which will be obvious to the reader. Dr Demetra Papanikola-Bakirtzi helped us navigate through the intricacies of Middle Byzantine ceramics, and also contributed the image on the front cover. We are grateful to her. We thank Professor Jean-Claude Cheynet and the Centre d'Histoire et Civilisation de Byzance (CNRS), for the design of maps 1 and 5.

We are indebted to Professor Christian Morrisson who read the entire manuscript with the critical eye of the economist, and insisted on the use of proper terminology as well as on respect for economic logic. Not he but the authors are responsible for any defects in those realms.

Angeliki Laiou wishes to acknowledge with gratitude a grant from the Alexander S. Onassis Public Benefit Foundation, which allowed her to devote uninterrupted time to this project. The book would have been much longer in the writing, were it not for the generosity of the Foundation.

Angeliki E. Laiou
Cécile Morrisson

ABBREVIATIONS

———————— • ————————

AA	*Archäologischer Anzeiger*
AIBL	Académie des Inscriptions et Belles-Lettres (Paris)
AJA	*American Journal of Archaeology*
AnnalesESC	*Annales: Économies, sociétés, civilisations*
BCH	*Bulletin de Correspondance hellénique*
BMGS	*Byzantine and Modern Greek Studies*
BSA	*The Annual of the British School at Athens*
BSl	*Byzantinoslavica*
Byz	*Byzantion*
ByzForsch	*Byzantinische Forschungen*
BZ	*Byzantinische Zeitschrift*
CFHB	Corpus fontium historiae byzantinae
DOC	P. Grierson et al., *Catalogue of the Byzantine Coins in the Dumbarton Oaks Collection and in the Whittemore Collection*, 5 vols. (Washington DC, 1966–99)
DOP	*Dumbarton Oaks Papers*
EHB	A. Laiou, ed., *The Economic History of Byzantium From the Seventh through the Fifteenth Century*, 3 vols. (Washington DC, 2002)
Hommes et richesses	*Hommes et richesses dans l'Empire byzantin*, 2 vols. (Paris, 1989–91)
JÖB	*Jahrbuch der Österreichischen Byzantinistik*
JRA	*Journal of Roman Archaeology*
JRS	*Journal of Roman Studies*

MM	F. Miklosich and J. Müller, *Acta et diplomata graeca medii aevi–sacra et profana, 6 vols. (Vienna, 1860–90)*
OCP	*Orientalia christiana periodica*
ODB	*The Oxford Dictionary of Byzantium,* ed. A. Kazhdan et al., 3 vols. (New York–Oxford, 1991)
PG	Patrologiae cursus completus, series graeca, ed. J.-P. Migne, 161 vols. in 166 pts. (Paris, 1857–66)
PL	Patrologiae cursus completus, series latina, éd. J.-P. Migne, 217 vols. (Paris, 1844–55)
REB	*Revue des études byzantines*
RH	*Revue historique*
RN	*Revue numismatique*
SEG	*Supplementum epigraphicum graecum,* ed. P. Roussel et al. (Leiden, 1923–)
Skylitzes	I. Thurn (ed.), *Ioannis Skylitzae Synopsis* historiarum (Berlin-New York, 1973), 412 (hereafter, Skylitzes)
SuedostF	*Südost-Forschungen*
TM	*Travaux et Mémoires*
TRW	*The Transformation of the Roman World*, 14 vols. (Leiden, Boston, Cologne 1997–)
Villages	*Les villages dans l'Empire byzantin (Ve–XVe siècle),* eds. J. Lefort, C. Morrisson, J.-P. Sodini (Paris, 2006)
VV	*Vizantiiskii vremennik*
ZRVI	*Zbornik radova Vizantološkog instituta, Srpska akademija nauka*

INTRODUCTION

———————— • ————————

The Byzantine Empire was a state with extraordinary and enviable longevity. Formally, it may be said to have begun in 330, with the dedication of the new city of Constantinople, and to have ended in 1453. Even if one considers that the changes which occurred in the seventh century were substantive enough to signal a new era (and we think this argument can certainly be made with regard to the economy), that is still a period of eight hundred years. Certainly, society underwent considerable and continuous change over the centuries, and so did institutions. So, too, did the economy, which lay at the foundation of the society and the state. Neither the great wealth of tenth- or twelfth-century Byzantium, which so impressed Western European travelers and even Arab witnesses, nor the progressive impoverishment of the late period can be properly gauged without a deep understanding of how the economy developed.

It should not be necessary to justify the need to study the economy of the Byzantine Empire. The economic history of the Western Middle Ages is a well-established discipline, with a long pedigree and numerous practitioners of remarkable scholarship. The Byzantine state was an important and, for a long time, a highly developed part of Europe, yet its economy is only very rarely incorporated into studies of the Middle Ages,[1] and as a discipline it has developed only

[1] Chris Wickham is a major exception to this statement; Jean-Marie Martin and Jacques Lefort have studied the Byzantine agrarian economy with an awareness of developments in the Mediterranean region.

over the last few decades. In part, this is due to the relative dearth of source materials: we do not have the documentation available to Western medievalists, especially for the study of the urban economy and exchange, we do not have price series although we do have price information, the archaeological record is mixed. The problem of sources, however, no longer looks as forbidding as it did in the past. Scholars have exploited known but underused sources such as saints' lives; the archaeological evidence is mounting, both for the country-side and for the cities, and archaeologists are paying more attention to humble objects such as pottery, glass and metalwork; coins have been made to speak louder than ever by being subjected to scientific analysis. The evidentiary base for the economic history of Byzantium looks much larger now than it did a hundred years ago.

Another reason for the underdevelopment or, better, the skewed development of the economic history of Byzantium has to do with perceptions. The Byzantine state was powerful indeed, and had important functions in the economy, starting with fiscal policy. Most of the most obvious sources are fiscal. The state thus laid a trap for historians, who fell willingly into it. Since the nineteenth century and the work of Russian scholars the main object of study has been the fiscal system and the basis on which it rested, that is, the agrarian economy. The study of the urban economy, trade and everything else economic is a much more recent development. Another assumption, that the Byzantines generally, and the Emperor and the officials par-ticularly, had no interest in the economy and no understanding of its basic functions has had a much longer life, indeed has been reaf-firmed by one of the most eminent Byzantinists.[2] To some extent this argument stems from the idea that it was impossible for people in the ancient or medieval world to have had an awareness of the economy and of basic economic behavior. For Byzantium, this is belied by the ideas expressed by historians, commentators on Aristotle and legal commentators; an excellent description of how the market functions in oligopolistic conditions, and of the effect of grain price fluctua-tions on prices and wages is offered by Michael Attaleiates in the late eleventh century.[3] More generally, one might point at the famous

---

[2] M. Hendy, "The Economy: A Brief Survey," in Sp. Vryonis, Jr. (ed.), *Byzantine Studies: Essays on the Slavic World and the Eleventh Century* (New Rochelle, 1992), p. 149.

[3] See below, Chapter IV.

Chinese text of the first century BC, the *Debate on Salt and Iron*, a text imbued with Confucian values where, nonetheless, economic arguments are advanced on both sides of the debate; although they are not necessarily arguments that a modern economist would make, they show a real concern with practical economics.[4] The idea that the Byzantines had little interest in economic behavior has led, as a corollary, to a perhaps exaggerated interest in the actions of the state, primarily its fiscal policy, and a very underdeveloped interest in the behavior of other economic actors.

Much of this has been changing over the last fifty years or so, as new and old sources are exploited and as ideological or conceptual constraints are, much more slowly, evolving. A few important landmarks deserve special mention. A. P. Kazhdan and Clive Foss were among the first scholars to establish the fact of an urban decline in the seventh century, and the effects that had on Byzantine society.[5] This is now generally accepted, as is the "rehabilitation" of the eleventh and twelfth centuries as a period of economic growth despite territorial contraction. A. P. Kazhdan, M. Hendy, P. Lemerle and C. Morrisson were among the pioneers who escaped the iron hand of the preconception that political reverses necessarily mean economic failure, and recognized the signs of true economic growth in these centuries.[6] Alan Harvey's important book, published in 1989, was a major contribution in the development of this new position.[7]

It is not an exaggeration to say that over the last few decades a "new agrarian history" is being written, along with a new understanding of the economic role of the state. Michel Kaplan has studied both the economy and the society of the Byzantine countryside, and made extensive use of hagiographic sources, among others. Jacques Lefort

---

[4] E. M. Gale, transl., *Discourses on Salt and Iron: A Debate on State Control of Commerce and Industry* (Taipei, 1967).

[5] A. P. Kazhdan, "Vizantiiski goroda v vii–xi vekah," *Sovetskaya Arheologyia*, 21 (1954), pp. 164–83; among C. Foss' many works, see "Archaeology and the 'Twenty Cities' of Byzantine Asia," *AJA*, 81 (1977), pp. 469–86.

[6] Kazhdan, "Vizantiiski goroda;" M. Hendy, "Byzantium, 1081–1204: An Economic Reappraisal," *Transactions of the Royal Historical Society*, ser. 5, 20 (1970), pp. 31–52, reprinted in his *The Economy, Fiscal Administration and Coinage of Byzantium* (Northampton, 1989), Study II; C. Morrisson, "La dévaluation de la monnaie byzantine au XIe siècle: essai d'interprétation," *TM* 6 (1976), pp. 3–48, reprinted in her *Monnaie et finances à Byzance* (Aldershot, 1994), Study IX; P. Lemerle, *Cinq études sur le onzième siècle byzantin* (Paris, 1977).

[7] A. Harvey, *Economic Expansion in the Byzantine Empire, 900–1200* (Cambridge, 1989).

has combined a profound knowledge of documentary sources with knowledge of the topography of Macedonia and Bithynia in particular, to reach novel conclusions about settlement, land use and the production and productivity of Byzantine peasants. In the process, the economic, as opposed to the social, dimensions of the small independent peasant landholding and of the large estate have been placed in a new light.[8] The study of demography has also progressed significantly, so that the term no longer denotes, as it did until the 1970s, the study of the ethnic composition of the Empire. As for the state, the economic effect, if not always the intent, of government actions has been underlined by the late Nicolas Oikonomides, among others.[9]

Where the economy of exchange is concerned, there has been something of a revolution. Nicolas Oikonomides and Angeliki Laiou, working independently, established the existence of Byzantine merchants in the late period, and noted the constraints on their activities.[10] Oikonomides stressed the importance of the provincial merchant. David Jacoby's numerous studies have done a great deal to solidify and expand our knowledge of Byzantine trade, which now looks much more active and interesting than in the past.[11] The study of the urban economy has not yet seen such notable developments,

---

[8] M. Kaplan, *Les hommes et la terre à Byzance du VIe au XIe siècle* (Paris, 1992). Among the works of J. Lefort, see primarily his "Radolibos: Population et paysage," *TM* 9 (1985), pp. 195–234, and his syntheses in "Population et peuplement en Macédoine orientale, IXe–XVe siècle," in *Hommes et richesses dans l'empire byzantin*, II (Paris, 1991), pp. 63–82, and "The Rural Economy, Seventh–Twelfth Centuries," in A. E. Laiou (editor-in-chief), *The Economic History of Byzantium from the Seventh through the Fifteenth Century* (Washington, D.C., 2002), 1, pp. 231–310 (hereafter, this collective work will be referred to as *EHB*). See also Lefort's "Fiscalité médiévale et informatique: recherche sur les barèmes pour l'imposition des paysans byzantins au XIVe siècle," *RH* 252 (1974), pp. 315–56. All of Lefort's articles are being republished in his *Société rurale et histoire du paysage à Byzance* (Paris, 2006).

[9] N. Oikonomidès, *Fiscalité et exemption fiscale à Byzance (IXe–XIe siècle)* (Athens, 1996).

[10] N. Oikonomidès, *Hommes d'affaires grecs et latins à Constantinople (XIIIe–XVe siècle)* (Montreal, 1979); A. Laiou-Thomadakis, "The Byzantine Economy in the Mediterranean Trade System, 13th–15th Centuries," *DOP* 34/35 (1980/1), pp. 177–222, repr. in A. E. Laiou, *Gender, Society and Economic Life in Byzantium* (London, 1992), art. vii.

[11] References to these studies will be found in Chapter IV and Chapter V, pp. 134 ff., 200 ff. respectively.

because of the nature of the evidence. The work of Charalambos Bouras is an important contribution.[12]

Despite these advances, a comprehensive and general history of the Byzantine economy was long in coming. Two works, published in the late 1980s, deal at greater or shorter length with important aspects of the Byzantine economy over time.[13] It is fair to say, however, that the first work devoted exclusively to the history of the Byzantine economy and its development from the seventh through the fifteenth centuries was a three-volume collective work published very recently.[14] Since both authors of the present book were very closely involved with that publication, it would be inelegant for us to sing its praises here. However, we must clarify what the connections are between the volume at hand and the earlier work. The present volume was not conceived as either a summary or an abridged version of *The Economic History of Byzantium*. Certainly, we have made use of this work which in many areas represented and was based on the most recent research as it existed in the late 1990s. The reader will appreciate the degree to which we are indebted to the earlier publication simply by looking at the footnotes. However, this book has been written anew. The intended audience is different, and there are also substantive differences. Archaeological discoveries have made it possible to introduce nuances in agrarian history, and to rewrite, to some extent, the history of the urban economy. Both authors have engaged in new research, and recent bibliography has sometimes changed our interpretations. Some topics have become focal points, such as the productive role of cities. The material has been organized along chronological lines. This traditional organization in fact makes possible the linkage between production, distribution and demand, a great desideratum of medieval economic history generally.[15] Of course, given the format of the Cambridge Medieval Textbooks series, a great deal of material could not be incorporated, so

---

[12] Ch. Bouras, "Aspects of the Byzantine City, Eighth–Fifteenth Centuries," *EHB* 2, pp. 497–528.

[13] One is Michael Hendy's *Studies in the Byzantine Monetary Economy c.300–1450* (Cambridge, 1985); the other is the two-volume collective work, *Hommes et richesses dans l'empire byzantin* (Paris, 1989–91).

[14] *EHB*. The characterization is from the review by E. Patlagean in *Le Moyen Age*, 110 (2004), p. 659.

[15] On this, see below, Chapter VI, pp. 243–45.

that the earlier publication retains its importance. On the other hand, the present publication, the work of close collaboration between the two authors, is more cohesive and presents a clearer viewpoint than is possible in a collective work. We consider that the Dumbarton Oaks publication attained the maximum of cohesion and coherence to which such a work may aspire. But that is always less than can be achieved in a book with one or two authors.

Two further points should be made. The first is that the chronological division, adopted for its merits, also has disadvantages. Economic processes are slow and their maturation may be, and in this case is, reached at different points in time. A chronological division that works well for the agrarian economy may not be meaningful in terms of the urban economy, and vice versa. We certainly think that all economic sectors followed similar trajectories, but the point of substantive change may differ. Therefore, the periodization must not be taken as having precise and universal significance. In the text, we have indicated the nuances that must be brought to the chronological schema.

The second point has to do with our approach to economic history. There have been, and there still are, important debates as to the possibility of studying the economic history of any ancient or medieval society; the opponents of such a notion arguing that in these societies the "economic" is embedded in the "political," and the economy has no independent existence; therefore, modern economic concepts and rules cannot be applied. The debate is sometimes said to be between those who see the past as "Same," and those who see it as "Other." It affects primarily the distribution of commodities, and the role played by economic and non-economic factors. It has been a fruitful debate, which has enriched our understanding of the past. For our part, we consider, with Claude Nicolet, that societies of the past were different from our own, but were not from another planet.[16] We have given due weight to the role of the state that was clearly not always motivated by economic concerns. We have taken into account non-economic exchange to the degree possible: it is not possible to estimate the extent and effect of almsgiving, for example, but gift exchange, especially with Arab rulers, is well documented.

---

[16] C. Nicolet, *Rendre à César: Économie et société dans la Rome Antique* (Paris, 1988), p. 38: "Les Anciens ne sont pas des Modernes; mais ils ne sont pas, non plus, des habitants d'une autre planète."

However, we also believe that it is important to recognize both the existence of redistributive and "non-economic" factors, and also that of economic exchange that follows the rules of the market. We think that there are areas of the Byzantine economy where the laws of economics have high explanatory value. We further think that when one approaches production and distribution in tandem, and not as separate processes, the sharpness of the debate is reduced, and demand, an economic mechanism, plays a primary role.[17]

We have also consciously elected not to engage here in the discussion regarding the mode of production prevalent in Byzantium. In the hands of such scholars as Chris Wickham and John Haldon this has been an interesting and important discussion. To the degree that it centers around the role of the state, we have taken account of the different opinions, to the extent possible in a short book such as this. We have preferred, however, to give what seems to us due weight to the behavior of various actors in the economic process, the state very much included, and hope that we have shed new light on some of them. Perhaps the theoretical discussion will be somewhat affected by this. We note with interest that the scholar who has made the most powerful argument about the Byzantine Empire being a "tributary state" has, in a recent work, given an analysis that does not seem to depend on this concept, as is indicated by the choice of subtitles: "State-influenced patterns," "Non-state activity: the ceramic evidence," "Trade and commerce: the structure of demand."[18]

The two authors of this volume have collaborated closely, so that the book is a result of our joint efforts. There was, however, a division of labor in the writing. Cécile Morrisson is primarily responsible for Chapters I, II, III, and the discussion of monetary developments in Chapters IV and V. Angeliki Laiou is primarily responsible for the Introduction, the discussion of the state in Chapter III, and Chapters IV–VI.

---

[17] For a fuller discussion of the methodological questions, see A. E. Laiou, "Methodological Questions Regarding the Economic History of Byzantium," *ZRVI* 39 (2001–2), pp. 9–23. For a presentation of the problems involved in the concept of "same" as well as that of "other," see J. Moreland, "Concepts of the Early Medieval Economy," in I. L. Hansen and Ch. Wickham (eds.), *The Long Eighth Century* (Leiden–Boston–Cologne, 2000), pp. 1–34.

[18] J. Haldon, "Production, Distribution and Demand in the Byzantine World ca. 660–840," in Hansen and Wickham, *The Long Eighth Century*, pp. 225–64; cf. his earlier *The State and the Tributary Mode of Production* (London, 1993).

—— I ——

NATURAL AND HUMAN RESOURCES

———— . ————

LAND AND ENVIRONMENT: GEOGRAPHY, CLIMATE, NATURAL RESOURCES AND THEIR USE

The geographic area considered in this book is centered on the Mediterranean. This was not affected by the territorial changes that occurred as part of the transformation of the Late Roman Empire in the fourth century ($c.3.7$ million km^2) into the more restricted medieval entity which we call the "Byzantine" Empire: the fall of the *Pars Occidentalis* meant a decrease to a total area of $c.1.3$ million km^2. The reconquest of western provinces entailed only a partial and temporary recovery to $c.2.7$ millions km^2 under Justinian. After the Arab conquests and the long struggles of the Middle Byzantine period, the Empire consisted of only $c.1.2$ million km^2 at its height in the reign of Basil II, and $c.750\ 000$ km^2 in the mid-twelfth century. The fact that this territory was always centered on the Mediterranean and on the Black Sea does not imply that it enjoyed an exclusively Mediterranean or maritime climate. The Mediterranean climate with its dry and hot summers ($c.28°$ on average) and mild winters ($c.8°$ average in January) with irregular and varying rainfall, obtains only in the coastal regions on either side of the Aegean or the Ionian and Adriatic seas. Its area can be plotted against the isotherm of an average $3°$ in January which is the limit of olive culture.[1]

---

[1] B. Geyer, "Physical Factors in the Evolution of the Landscape and Land Use," *EHB* 1, pp. 31–45, especially map 2; J. Koder, *Vyzantio os choros: Eisagoge sten istorike geographia tes Anatolikes Mesogeiou ste Vyzantine Epoche* (Thessalonike, 2005), pp. 53–7.

Map 1. The Byzantine world

(The dotted line indicates the frontiers of the empire of Basil II in 1025)

© Centre d'Histoire et Civilisation de Byzance, CNRS Paris)

UMR 8167 - F. Tessier del. 2006

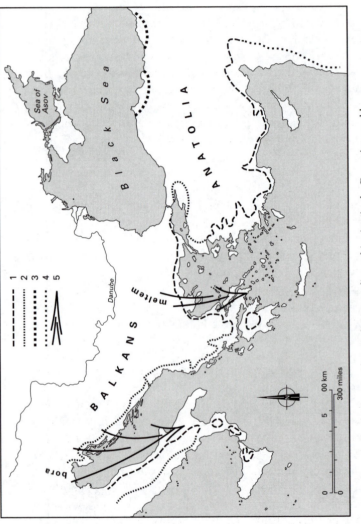

Map 2. Climatic limits to olive cultivation in the Byzantine world
(B. Geyer, *EHB* I, Ch. 3, fig. 2)

1. limit set by cold weather in winter; 2. limit set by cold weather in winter and damp weather in summer;
3. limit set by damp weather in summer; 4. limit set by aridity; 5. cold and dry wind

In the Balkans, successive mountain ranges oriented either north-west–south-east (Dinaric Alps, Pindos, Mani, Suva Planina, Plack-ovica between the Strymon and the Axios/Vardar Rivers) or west–east (Rhodope, Balkan/Stara Planina mountains) occupy two-thirds of the territory and bar maritime influence as well as inhibiting rain from penetrating further inland. These mountainous areas feature a continental climate with cold winters and extremely hot summers. In the eastern Balkans, a lower level of precipitation is generally observed than in the western parts. The only great plains are those centered on the valleys of the most important rivers (Danube or Marica/Hebros): Thrace and Valachia. Smaller coastal plains occupy the mouth of rivers like the Axios/Vardar or the Strymon and of smaller ones in Epiros or the Peloponnese.

The islands of the Ionian and above all the Aegean Sea are also mostly mountainous; Mount Ida in Crete reaches 2,456m, Mount Olympos in Cyprus 2,100m. Plains feature only in the larger islands, for example Sicily, Crete, Cyprus, Euboea. Smaller islands like Samothrake, Kos or Patmos often suffer from lack of water resources.

The core of Anatolia is a large elevated plateau (average: 1,000m) that occupies 90 per cent of the territory, plains being limited in size except in Bithynia, Cilicia and Pamphylia. Separated from the Mediterranean to the south-west by the Taurus mountains and bordered on the north-east by the Pontic chain (3,700m maximum), it often descends more or less abruptly into the sea, forming many anchorages. But in the western provinces, some large valleys (e.g., of the rivers Kaikos, Hermos, Kaystros and Meander) allow Mediterranean influences to penetrate and form a transition zone with the highland.

The Early Byzantine Empire included also the Danubian plain from the Sava and Drina confluence down to the Iron Gates, the Syrian plateau and the Syro-Palestine coastlands, as well as the Nile valley, Cyrenaica and eastern North Africa plus outposts on the coast to the Straits of Gibraltar. Of reconquered Italy, only Sicily and the southern regions of Apulia and Calabria remained long under Byzantine control, for three centuries or more. Here too, the mountainous character prevails (Abruzzi reaching nearly 3,000m, Calabria over 2,000m, north-eastern Sicily *c.*2,000m and Mount Etna 3,340m) and the relief divides western humid regions from eastern arid ones.

The existence in these regions of several rifts (the North Anatolian sliding rift at the encounter of the smaller Anatolian plaque and the

Eurasian plate, the Great rift marked by the Jordan and the Dead Sea
where the African and Arabian plates meet, the series of rifts created
by the encounter of the African and Eurasian plates in Italy) entails
chronic earthquakes or volcanic eruptions, with landslides and the
destruction of buildings. Seismic episodes regularly tested the reac-
tive capacity of social and political structures, but never affected the
economy as a whole except when combined with other disasters like
the plague and bad harvests as happened in the mid-sixth century.[2]

The geographic context had multiple consequences regarding land
use and settlement, natural resources and transport. Varied and complex climatic conditions permitted differentiated and complementary production: wine, even dates or cane, in sheltered coastal areas;
orchards and terrace cultivation in valleys; olive, fruit and mulberry
at intermediate altitude; timber exploitation as well as pig grazing
in the forests that grew on the mountains with greater precipitation
(Taurus, Calabria); winter cereals on plateaus with even a little rainfall (200–300mm) provided the rains are concentrated in the spring
season (e.g. in Galatia); stock raising in pasture lands.[3] Other livestock
grazed in Phrygia, Lykaonia and other Anatolian provinces as well as
in the Balkan highlands with poorer soils or dry continental climate.
In spite of these differences, marked specialisation was not the rule,
and whenever possible the Byzantine farmer tried to develop a dry
crop system based on cereals and often including orchards and vines.
Bithynia, Boeotia and Macedonia with their transitional temperate
climate are typical examples. They have been well studied, since
documents and archaeological surveys allow us to see the variety of
crops and vegetation.

Usually, land exploitation was carried out in concentric zones
around the village. Irrigated vegetable gardens and orchards were
cultivated near the inhabited nucleus, while dry land tilled for cereals, vineyards, or textile plants like hemp lay a bit further away:
since it sometimes took oxen as long as three hours to reach them,
their cultivation was less intensive and involved less frequent ploughing. Grazing lands and woodland were situated in the most remote

---

[2] I. G. Teleles, *Meteorologika phainomena kai klima sto Vyzantio*, (Ponemata 5/2)
(Athens, 2003), 2 vols. For a brief presentation in English, see I. G. Teleles,
"Medieval Warm Period and the Beginning of the Little Ice Age in the Eastern
Mediterranean: An approach of Physical and Anthropogenic Evidence," in
K. Belke et al. (eds.), *Byzanz als Raum* (Vienna, 2000), pp. 223–43.

[3] Cappadocia was renowned as the "land of beautiful horses" (*Anth. Graeca* 7.100).

locations.[4] Altitude and the quality of the soil entailed important differences: in the region of Brusa/Bursa in Bithynia, for instance, according to data derived from early Ottoman registers, the alluvial plain was devoted to cereal cultivation with a ratio of more than 1 hectare per person, while in the lower mountain area, a mainly pastoral zone, cereals were only cultivated for family consumption and the ratio fell to a third (0.36ha).[5]

Land exploitation was prone to abuse and the vegetal cover did not always find the favourable climatic conditions for its renewal that it did in "the beautiful province" of Bithynia even when its population was increasing. In more arid or fragile milieus, soils were easily eroded by violent downfalls and flooding. Byzantine farmers fought this constraint by building terraces and walls (often with stones extracted from the fields), irrigating whenever possible, ploughing, harrowing and manuring.[6] But in many areas the degradation of cultivable soil and of forests into *garrigue* or *maquis*, aggravated by human over-exploitation, led to irreversible land impoverishment.[7] The evolution of land use resulting from climatic fluctuations and human intervention will be considered in the following chapters.

MARITIME CONDITIONS

The maritime character of the Byzantine Empire lowered transportation costs[8] and fostered trade. This asset is recognized as essential to economic growth from Antiquity to modern times, as the modern British example demonstrates.[9] It also provided two essential elements

---

[4] J. Lefort (ed.), *Paysages de Macédoine: leurs caractères, leur évolution à travers les documents et les récits des voyageurs* (Paris, 1986), pp. 94–6; M. Kaplan, *Les hommes et la terre à Byzance du VIe au XIe siècle: propriété et exploitation du sol* (Paris, 1992), pp. 127–32.

[5] B. Geyer, Y. Koç, J. Lefort, Ch. Chataignier, "Les Villages et l'occupation du sol à l'époque moderne," in B. Geyer and J. Lefort (eds.), *La Bithynie au Moyen Âge* (Paris, 2003), pp. 419–20.

[6] A. Harvey, *Economic Expansion in the Byzantine Empire 900–1200* (Cambridge, 1989), pp. 125–8; Kaplan, *Les hommes et la terre*, pp. 65–9; J. Lefort, "The Rural Economy, Seventh-Twelfth Centuries," *EHB* I, pp. 233, 252–8.

[7] Geyer, "Physical Factors," pp. 36–44 (structural factors and evolution over time).

[8] In the fourth century, Gregory of Nazianzus (*Oratio* 43, ch. 43, J. Bernardi, ed. (Sources Chrétiennes, vol. 384), Paris 1992) contrasts Caesarea in Cappadocia with the "coastal cities which are able to bear times of need [famine] without difficulty, by an exchange of their own products for what is imported."

[9] See, among others, J. Sachs, *The End of Poverty* (New York: Penguin, 2005), pp. 32–5.

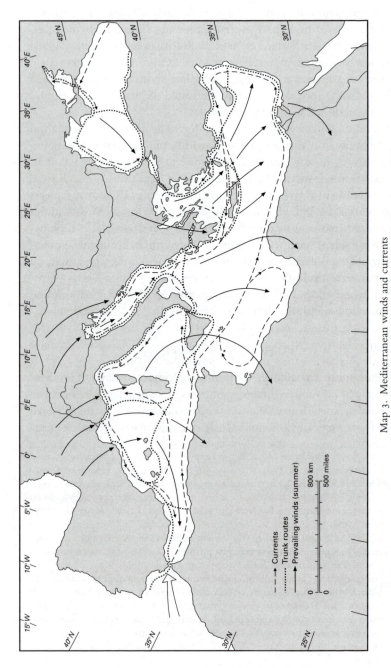

Map 3. Mediterranean winds and currents

(J. Pryor, *Geography, Technology and War: Studies in the Maritime History of the Mediterranean*, Cambridge, 1988, fig. 2)

800 km
500 miles

of provisioning: fish and salt. Fishing was an endless resource for the alimentation of cities, for exports (in the form of dried fish, garum or caviar) or autoconsumption, as texts and analyses of archaeological remains show.[10] Salt could be produced with little investment in many locations, and on a greater scale in the Thermaic bay near Thessalonica or in Cherson and other places on the Black Sea.[11]

The existence of steep or mountainous areas with rugged indented coastlines in southern Italy, part of Sicily, Dalmatia, Epiros or the Peloponnese, in many islands or in Lycia, to cite a few examples, far from being a handicap, proved essential to maritime activities. These features provided a combination of natural harbour facilities or anchorages, deep water close to land, proximity of forest resources, and a healthier climate as well as defense opportunities. Sailors found the indispensable water supply in a number of islands. This contrasts with the inhospitable flat coast of Palestine with its constantly moving dangerous sandbanks or the hostile lee shores of Egypt, Libya and North Africa from Gabes to Cape Bon.

As in early Antiquity, climatic conditions prevented normal sailing in winter, which was considered a period of "mare clausum" (closed seas) from October/November to March/April because of the frequent storms, northerly winds and reduced visibility.[12] The prevailing winds and currents in the Mediterranean which favoured navigation in the spring and summer are shown on the map (Map 3). Ancient and medieval ships unable to tackle head winds had to manage the prevailing north-western Mediterranean winds or the north-eastern ones in the Black Sea by using the counter-clockwise direction of the main currents, thus compensating for unfavourable wind directions

---

[10] Texts: see E. Chuliara-Raiu, *E alieia sten Aigypto ypo to phos ton ellenikon papyron* (Ioannina, 2003); archaeological references in C. Morrisson and J.-P. Sodini, "The Sixth-Century Economy," *EHB* I, p. 200.

[11] A. E. Laiou, *ODB*, *s.v.*; J. Koder, "Salz – Anmerkungen zu Wortbedeutung und Realie," in S. Kolditz and R. C. Mueller (eds.), *Geschehenes und Geschriebenes: Studien zu Ehren von G. S. Henrich u. K.-P. Matschke* (Leipzig, 2005), pp. 39–49 gives a detailed account of production processes on a comparative basis.

[12] D. Claude, "Der Handel im westlichen Mittelmeer während des Frühmittelalters," (*Abhandl. der Akad. d. Wiss. in Göttingen. Phil.-hist. Kl. III*, n. 144 = *Untersuchungen zu Handel und Verkehr der vor- und frühgeschichtlichen Zeit in Mittel- und NordEuropa*, vol. 2 [Göttingen, 1985]), pp. 31–4; M. McCormick, *The Origins of the European Economy: Communications and Commerce, c.300–c.900* (Cambridge, 2001), pp. 450–68. See also S. Medas, *De rebus nauticis: L'arte della navigazione nel mondo antico* (Rome, 2004).

for east–west or south–north travels. J. Pryor's analysis shows that this gave a clear advantage to the northern sea route for east–west voyages, hence to Byzantine seafarers and later to Italian ones, over the Muslims.[13]

THE HUMAN FACTOR

The importance of *population* as a source of manpower in a pre-industrial economy is well known. Many varying figures for the Byzantine population have been proposed: for the sixth century, for instance, they vary between 30 (E. Stein) and 21 million (J. Russell, more generally accepted). Recent methods of study combine the number of sites counted and the density of rural and urban population recorded by intensive regional surveys with pre-modern data (medieval *praktika*, that is, fiscal descriptions of property) and modern historic population records (e.g. Turkish registers – *defters*). On the basis of her analysis of peasant households in early fourteenth-century Macedonia, A. Laiou compares her estimate of a density of 34 persons per km² to the figure of 57.4 in the 1961 Greek census. She hazards another estimate of *c.*19 million people for the Empire at its maximum medieval extent under Basil II. This is close to the 18 million suggested on a similar basis by J. Koder, who makes a comparison with the 1890 census.[14] Surveys and other data provide a perspective on the evolution of settlement and land use, and the recurring peaks associated with high rural and urban population. The alternating cycles of intensification and abatement of population and land use will be considered in the relevant chapters.

Demography is subject to the same uncertainty, but for the fifth–sixth centuries or the fourteenth century there are reliable indications of low life expectancy (44.7 years for men and 42.4 for women at

[13] J. H. Pryor, *Geography, Technology and War: Studies in the Maritime History of the Mediterranean* (Cambridge, 1988), pp. 1–24. Useful summary on Roman Imperial harbours and ports – with emphasis on the Western Mediterranean – on http://www.ostia-antica.org/med/med.htm

[14] A. E. Laiou, "The Human Resources," *EHB* 1, pp. 47–55; J. Koder, *Lebensraum der Byzantiner* (Vienna, 2001), pp. 152–4; for density figures in Macedonia, see also J. Lefort, "Les villages de Macédoine orientale au Moyen Âge," in J. Lefort, C. Morrisson and J.-P. Sodini (eds.), *Les Villages dans l'empire byzantin (IVe–XVe siècle)* (Paris, 2005) (hereafter: *Villages*), p. 299, and n. 59; for Bithynia, see Geyer et al., "Les villages et l'occupation du sol," in Geyer and Lefort, *La Bithynie au Moyen Âge*, pp. 417–19.

5 years of age in Early Byzantine Egypt comparable to the 47.5 years at 5 years of age for females in fourteenth-century Macedonia).[15] The staple diet is exemplified in monastic documents that mention rations for *adelphata*[16] as well as in other monastic documents. It includes the usual Mediterranean foods: grains, pulses, olive oil – or butter in colder inland regions – wine, dairy products, fish and meat, fresh vegetables and fruit, and honey for sweetening, or cane sugar in some regions (southern Italy, Sicily, Cyprus) from the eleventh century onward. The military rations of the sixth century mention only the *annona* staples (wheat, wine and meat). Fiscal documents show the daily amounts delivered in kind to Gothic soldiers stationed in Egypt: 1.3kg bread (Cato gave as much to his slaves), 325g meat and 2 liters of (cheap) wine.[17] Leaving aside shortages and famines due to war or bad weather and other calamities, apparently the average peasant household produced enough for his subsistence, and more. In normal or good times, the Byzantine diet, whose constituent elements are confirmed by the archaeological evidence, was better and more balanced than that of Western Europeans, as is the "Cretan" diet today.

INTANGIBLE RESOURCES AND INSTITUTIONAL ENVIRONMENT

For a long time, economic historians insisted on the natural resource endowments of a given state or region. Over the past decades, more light has been thrown on the importance of political and social institutions and intangible resources on economic growth. Many of the factors considered below gave to Byzantium, at least till the turning point of the late twelfth century, a clear edge over the medieval West.

First of all, imperial political institutions ensured stability, provided protection and justice and, notably, ensured property rights, an

---

[15] R. Bagnall, W. Frier, *The Demography of Roman Egypt* (Cambridge, 1994); A. E. Laiou-Thomadakis, *Peasant Society in the Late Byzantine Empire: A Social and Demographic Study* (Princeton, 1977), pp. 276–9, 295; eadem, "Human Resources," pp. 51–2.

[16] A "fellowship" in a Byzantine monastery which entitled the holder to a living allowance for life (*ODB*, s.v.).

[17] See data and discussion in C. Zuckerman, *Du village à l'Empire: autour du registre fiscal d'Aphroditô* (Paris, 2004), pp. 160–70.

essential condition or incentive of economic investment.[18] In contrast to early medieval Western Europe or among the northern neighbours of the Empire, the elaborate Roman law never ceased to be enforced in Byzantium, transmitted and adapted over the centuries. It regulated contracts, transactions, commercial associations, loans and rates of interest, as well as dowries and inheritance.[19] Byzantium also maintained for more than a millennium a durable and flexible monetary system, which was responsive to fiscal and commercial needs. So, to a certain extent, the Byzantine state delivered (or aimed at delivering) "peace, [easy] taxes and a tolerable administration of justice." According to Adam Smith: "little else is requisite to carry a state to the highest degree of opulence from the lowest barbarism . . . all the rest being brought by the natural course of things."[20] But peace and political stability were not permanently maintained and the cost of security was high. Above all, state intervention, as will be seen below, did not always protect all property rights or encourage productive activities.

The role of family structures

The strengthening, starting in the fifth–sixth centuries, of the nuclear family unit under the pressure of the Church can be considered as a positive factor for the peasant economy and society in general, as has been pointed out by P. Toubert for the West since the Carolingian era and by D. P. Lal for Western Europe.[21] So can the equal treatment of women in inheritance and the recognition of some property rights to them.[22] The nuclear family creates greater incentives than

---

[18] The landmark book by D. North and R. Thomas, *The Rise of the Western World: A New Economic History* (New York, 1973), rarely cited by historians, is still fundamental reading in this respect. But it hardly considers the early Middle Ages and not at all the Byzantine world.

[19] See the various contributions on "Legal Aspects of the Economy," in *EHB* 3, pp. 1059–1120.

[20] A famous quote from a 1755 lecture recorded by D. Stewart.

[21] P. Toubert, *L'Europe dans sa première croissance* (Paris, 2004), pp. 260–81 and 321–56; D. Lal, *Unintended Consequences: The Impact of Factor Endowments, Culture and Politics in Long-Run Economic Performance* (Cambridge, Mass., 1998).

[22] For the status of women in Byzantium, among many studies by A. E. Laiou, see for inheritance, "Marriage Prohibitions, Marriage Strategies and the Dowry in Thirteenth-Century Byzantium," in J. Beaucamp and G. Dagron (eds.), *La transmission du patrimoine: Byzance et l'aire méditerranéenne* (Paris, 1998), pp. 129–60; for women and work, see eadem, "Women in the Marketplace of

kinship groups (or the Slavic extended family) for investment and production.

Literacy

Byzantium is generally assumed to have maintained the Graeco-Roman classical tradition, possibly "democratizing" it in the process of christianization.[23] Literacy is thought to have been more widespread than in the West, at least down to the late Middle Ages, although ideas about literacy in the Carolingian period, for example, are being revised upward.[24]

Most studies, however, have been primarily concerned with the literary aspects of the phenomenon and not with the economic implications of what might be called 'practical literacy and numeracy' (reading ability and elementary writing and calculating abilities).[25] 'High' Byzantine literacy presupposes and indicates prosperity combined with the leisure of a wealthy, generally urban, elite, as it existed in the early period down to the sixth century and again from the tenth century onward. There can be no reliable quantitative measure of either 'high' or 'basic' literacy or their evolution over time. But for the early period, one may stress the numerous examples of the

Constantinople, 10th–14th Centuries," in N. Necipoğlu (ed.), *Byzantine Constantinople: Monuments, Topography and Everyday Life* (Leiden–Boston–Cologne, 2001), pp. 261–73.

[23] See J.-M. Carrié, "Antiquité tardive et 'Démocratisation de la culture': un paradigme à géométrie variable," *Antiquité tardive* 9 (2001), pp. 27–46, with an evaluation of the debate and reference to S. Mazzarino, "La democratizzazione della cultura nel 'basso impero'," in *Antico, tardoantico ed èra costantiniana*, I (Rome, 1974), pp. 74–98. When N. Wilson, *Scholars of Byzantium*, 2nd edn. (London, 1996), p. 1, writes: "literacy was less widespread and the average level of culture less high than had been the case in the ancient world," he has in mind the impoverished Byzantium of the seventh–ninth centuries.

[24] R. McKitterick, *The Carolingians and the Written Word* (Cambridge, 1989).

[25] R. Browning, "Literacy in the Byzantine World," *BMGS* 4 (1978), pp. 39–54 provides a balanced introduction to the subject. See also A. Kazhdan in *ODB s.v.* The Dumbarton Oaks Symposium of 1971 questioned these conclusions but was more focused on élite literacy: *Byzantine Books and Bookmen* (Washington, D.C., 1975). See also N. Oikonomides, "Literacy in Thirteenth-Century Byzantium: An Example from Western Asia Minor," in J. S. Langdon, J. Allens and S. Kyprianides (eds.), *TO EΛΛHNIKON; Studies in Honor of Speros Vryonis, Jr.* (New York, 1993), pp. 223–65 with references to his and other scholars' earlier publications. All of Oikonomides' articles on literacy have been reprinted in his *Society, Culture and Politics in Byzantium* (Aldershot, 2005).

posting of imperial decisions in public places,[26] and the survival of many inscriptions on stone or pottery, or transactions, accounts or contracts recorded on papyri, ostraka or wooden tablets.[27] Even in the eighth and ninth centuries, although Leo VI — like Justinian I in Novel 73 — complains about the lack of instruction (*paideia*) and knowledge (*mathesis*) in the countryside and authorizes wills to be witnessed by "ignorant" people (*amatheis*), saints' lives show the survival of elementary and more advanced education, the former accessible to modest families.[28] In 867, Basil I ordered that fiscal documents should have fractional figures written in full so that they could be more easily read by the *agroikoi* (peasants, countryside dwellers).[29] The ubiquitous inscribed lead seals (more than 50,000 survive today), the signatures on archival documents, the writing implements found on many sites,[30] even graffiti on a few buildings and on a significant number of gold coins testify to the essential role of writing in Byzantine daily life. From this picture an educated guess would suggest a 30 per cent rate of basic literacy and numeracy among men, comparable to that in eighteenth-century China and superior to that in eighteenth-century France. Literacy is recognized as an important factor in economic development for societies of the past as well as the present.[31]

---

[26] Not only in important trading places like Abydos, but also in secondary ones like Anazarbos or Karalis (Cagliari) and more remote inland cities like Didymae (D. Feissel, "Un rescrit de Justinien découvert à Didymes (1er avril 533)," *Chiron* 34 [2004], 285–365), or in *chorai* like Amastris where a decision protecting the villagers of Ziporea from offenses committed by passing soldiers was set up in "the most prominent place of the village": D. Feissel and J. Gascou (eds.), *La pétition à Byzance* (Paris, 2004), citing *SEG* 43.904.

[27] Cf. J. P. Conant, "Literacy and Private Documentation in Vandal North Africa: The Case of the Albertini Tablets," in A. H. Merrills (ed.), *Vandals, Romans and Berbers, New Perspectives on Late Antique North Africa* (Aldershot, 2003).

[28] Leo VI, Nov. 43, ed. and transl. P. Noailles and A. Dain, *Les Novelles de Léon VI le Sage* (Paris, 1944), pp. 175–7; saints' lives: see P. Lemerle, *Le premier humanisme byzantin* (Paris, 1971), pp. 74–5 and 97–103; Browning, "Literacy," pp. 47–9.

[29] Theophanes Continuatus, ed. Bekker, p. 261; N. Oikonomidès, "Byzance: À propos d'alphabétisation," in J. Hamesse (ed.), *Bilans et perspectives des Études médiévales en Europe* (Louvain-la-Neuve, 1995), pp. 35–42.

[30] See, for example, D. Papanikola-Bakirtzi (ed.), *Everyday Life in Byzantium*, exhibition catalogue (Thessalonike, 2004).

[31] For the Middle Ages see, for example, J. Moreland, "The Signifiers of Production in Eighth-Century England," in I. L. Hansen and C. Wickham (eds.), *The Long Eighth Century: Production, Distribution and Demand* (TRW, 11) (Leiden, 2000), pp. 96 ff.

Science and technical knowledge

Despite their importance, Byzantine science and technical knowledge have been much debated and little studied. The role of Byzantium in the preservation and transmission, even the enrichment, of the Classical and Hellenistic scientific heritage, has long been recognized.[32] Elementary arithmetic and geometry were part of the education of the Byzantines. Many literate clerks, notaries and *logariastai* (accountants) were able to keep accounts and fiscal or cadastral registers throughout the Byzantine period. Even if officials were ignorant of philosophy and Euclid, as Michael Italikos scolds them for, surveyors of the fiscal services knew enough to measure land with a small margin of error.[33]

Little is known of technology and the application of scientific concepts since literary sources despise practical topics and mention only spectacular achievements: the loan of Byzantine mosaicists to Abd-al-Malik for decorating the Dome of the Rock in Jerusalem, the automata of Theophilos' palace, or the system of fire beacons, devised by Leo the Mathematician in the ninth century, that relied on synchronized clocks, the "export" of other mosaicists to Córdoba in the tenth century,[34] the abduction of the Theban silk workers by Roger II in 1147, for example. But extant Byzantine buildings like Saint Sophia, public works like aqueducts, luxury and craft objects (silks, glass, ceramics etc.), even coins and the sophisticated processes of their purification or debasement, testify to the training in geometry, mechanics and alchemy and to the know-how of engineers or craftsmen.[35] The survival of the Empire and its prestige owed much to the continuation of such high added-value production and to the

---

[32] K. Vogel, "Byzantine science," in *The Cambridge Medieval History*, vol. 4.2 (Cambridge, 1967), pp. 267–305, remains valuable reading. On astrology, see now P. Magdalino, *L'orthodoxie des astrologues: entre science et divination* (Paris, 2006).

[33] Sources cited in C. Morrisson, "La puissance économique de Byzance avant la IVe Croisade," *Comptes Rendus, Académie des Inscriptions et Belles-Lettres* (Paris, 2003), pp. 843–54. On the surveyors, see J. Lefort et al., *Géométries du fisc byzantin* (Paris, 1991).

[34] Below, p. 77.

[35] On the scientific knowledge of Anthemios of Tralles and Isidore of Miletus, architects of Saint Sophia, see *ODB, s.v.*, and R. Rashed, "De Constantinople à Bagdad: Anthémius de Tralles et al-Kindí," in P. Canivet and J.-P. Rey-Coquais (eds.), *La Syrie de Byzance à l'Islam* (Paris, 1992), pp. 165–70.

efficient military organization and techniques used in terrestrial and naval warfare: not only the Greek fire devised in the seventh century, but also fortifications, siege-engines and possibly horse transportation in ships.[36] Beyond our fragmented documentation, the Byzantine edge over its northern neighbors and the West till some time in the twelfth century is indisputable: there lay the reason for its wealth.

[36] See J. H. Pryor and E. M. Jeffreys, *The age of the dromōn: the Byzantine navy ca. 500–1204* (Leiden, Boston, 2006).

II

THE LATE ANTIQUE ECONOMY AND THE SHIFT TO MEDIEVAL STRUCTURES (SIXTH–EARLY EIGHTH CENTURIES)

In the first half of the sixth century, the Byzantine economy went through the last flourishing period of the Late Antique Roman civilization. It stood in sharp contrast with the West where most of the regions were severely affected by invasions, civil wars and social unrest in the fifth century, while the former imperial unified government was replaced by fragmented, often unstable and competing, barbarian kingdoms which maintained only partly the administrative and legal Roman traditions. The longer resilience of the Roman institutions and economy in the East was due to a virtuous circle of political stability and economic prosperity that enabled it to buy off or fight enemies in the Balkans while maintaining a by and large peaceful equilibrium in the east with Persia. These general comments are not applicable to every region and will be qualified below, when we examine the considerable differences in wealth and settlement between Illyricum and the eastern prefectures. Following Justinian's reconquest of North Africa and Italy, part of the Roman West was reunited with the East, a development which created a revival of Mediterranean trade. The costly long war against the Ostrogoths (535–55) and the devastation it caused in Italy have long been considered a major error of policy and a waste of state resources. Such criticism, however justified by the Byzantines' inability to defend the greatly extended territory, does not take into account the benefits which accrued to Byzantium in the long run from the recovery of the resources of southern Italy and Sicily.

From the middle of the sixth century, signs of economic decay begin to be more and more apparent. Demographic losses resulting from the plague (541–42) and its recurrences reduced both production and demand and consequently the imperial finances. The state was unable to withstand the invasions of Slavs and Avars that began in the 560s, while war resumed with the Sassanians in 572 and the Empire was forced to fight on two fronts. The weakening of the economy is particularly evident in the Danubian provinces but was also felt, to a lesser degree, in the east, and in the western provinces of Italy and Africa.

Herakleios (610–41) led a desperate struggle against the combined attacks of the Slavs, Avars and Persians which culminated in their joint siege of Constantinople in 626. By mustering all available treasures, including sacred vessels, by his alliance with the Turkish kaghanate north of the Caucasus and through his astute strategy, he managed to protect Constantinople and recover the rich territories of Syria, Palestine and Egypt which had been occupied by the Persians for some twenty years. These successes were short-lived. The swift and unexpected Arab conquest, starting in the 630s, reduced imperial territory by half within fifty years or so, depriving it of its more prosperous provinces. While Syria, Palestine and Egypt – together with the conquered former Persian territories – enjoyed a prolonged prosperity under Umayyad rule, Byzantium witnessed a clear deurbanization with a related decline in production and trade. The result was a major transformation of economic and social structures.

WEALTH AND PROSPERITY OF THE EARLY BYZANTINE ECONOMY IN THE FIRST HALF OF THE SIXTH CENTURY

The vast extension of the Byzantine Empire in the 530s resulted in a powerful demand from a numerous *population* (30 million people according to Stein and Mango), and offered access to abundant factors of production such as labour, natural resources and capital: both fixed capital (tools, mills, presses, transport devices, livestock, weaponry) and working capital (stocks of raw materials, including coined and uncoined metals and goods). The organization of production was sufficiently varied to suit local economic or geophysical conditions. The institutional framework, including material structures (roads, public buildings) and institutional ones (education, legal system), provided a stable environment which fostered economic activity. The following sketch outlines these factors as well as the primary and secondary production and exchange in this flourishing period.

The density of population differed widely: its distribution followed roughly the same pattern in the Middle Ages down to the nineteenth century, with few exceptions.[1] The more densely populated areas were those in coastal regions and plains (especially the north-west Peloponnese, Attica, western Asia Minor and Campania), or in fertile valleys like those of the Nile, the Vardar or the Hebros, or in large islands like Sicily, Crete and Cyprus. These patterns are partly reflected in differential *urbanization*: the inner Balkans, and northern and eastern Anatolia had far fewer cities than the above-mentioned regions, but on the whole Byzantium was more urbanized than the West.[2]

Rural settlement increased in the fifth and early sixth centuries in many regions: surveys and excavations plot this ascendant in the Peloponnese as well as in the Near East (Cyprus, the Lebanese hinterland, northern and southern Syria, the Roman provinces of Palestina I/II and Arabia). The number of documented sites increases significantly but attention has been drawn to the fact that this multiplication of villages may have been quite short-lived and that "prosperity" was an illusion. Notwithstanding, ample evidence shows that in the east from the fifth to the early sixth century there was a peak in the number of settlements, from villages of several hundred inhabitants to hamlets or farmsteads, and marginal lands were exploited.[3] This can be attributed not only to security but also in part to a certain climatic change with warmer winters in the northern Mediterranean and a

---

[1] See the map of population distribution in the eastern Mediterranean in 1890 in J. Koder, *Lebensraum der Byzantiner* (Vienna, 2001), p. 150.

[2] Official records such as Hierocles' Synekdemos list cities according to an administrative definition, and the names of some episcopal sees in later Conciliar lists may be those of abandoned cities. But with limitations, their geographic distribution gives a proxy of urban density: see M. F. Hendy, *Studies in the Byzantine Monetary Economy* (Cambridge, 1985), pp. 67–85, 90–100 and corresponding maps, especially on p. 71, 74, 95.

[3] See, among others, the reports by Avraméa, Gatier, Hirschfeld and Walmsley, in J. Lefort, C. Morrisson and J.-P. Sodini (eds.), *Les Villages dans l'Empire byzantin IVe–XVe siècle* (Paris, 2005), the data of C. Dauphin, *La Palestine byzantine: peuplement et population* (Oxford, 1998) or G. Tate, *Les campagnes de la Syrie du Nord* (Paris, 1992) and his summary in *Hommes et richesses dans l'empire byzantin*, I (Paris, 1989), pp. 63–77. For evidence of short-lived villages and a critique of the "myopic view" of long-term prosperity, see Walmsley, in Lefort et al., *Villages*, p. 516. This applies only to Jordanian sites.

little more rain in the south, a trend attested by various paleobotanical or paleogeographical indexes.[4] The pattern of settlement was far from uniform: in the Balkans, villas, which had played an important role in the development of the Late Antique countryside, were abandoned in the fifth century. In Thrace and the Illyricum, archaeological surveys highlight the multiplication of settlements in ancient hilltop fortresses or new sites in moderately elevated zones (300–900m); these settlements were due to the insecurity which began again in the 540s.[5] A few villas survived in coastal areas like the Argolid, Corinthia or Messenia. In Palestine, similar rural complexes do not constitute villas in the Roman sense, but, rather, agricultural productive compounds. On the whole, village and farmstead dominated the countryside with varying balance between the two depending on the geographic and political context.[6]

The prosperity of early Byzantine *cities* in the eastern Mediterranean is well known. A few points must be recounted: Constantinople, the most populous city in the world at that time, numbered at least 400,000 inhabitants,[7] Antioch attained 200,000, Alexandria and Thessalonike 100,000. The urban network inherited from the Roman period included numerous middle-sized cities of around 50,000–100,000 souls, such as Apameia, Ephesus, Caesarea or Jerusalem. The population of provincial capitals was in the range of 15,000–50,000 and big villages like Aphrodito had around 5,000 inhabitants.

From the qualitative point of view, a certain decline in the monumental character and public amenities of the Roman heyday (second century AD) occurred; but abundant archaeological remains

---

[4] Koder, *Lebensraum*, and revised Greek edition, *To Vyzantio os khoros* (Thessalonike, 2005), pp. 57–65; K. Randsborg, *The First Millenium* (Cambridge, 1991), pp. 22–30. More specifically: J. Koder, "Climatic Change in the Fifth and Sixth Centuries?" in P. Allen and E. Jeffreys (eds.), *The Sixth Century: End or Beginning?* (Brisbane, 1996), pp. 270–86.

[5] A. G. Poulter, *Nicopolis ad Istrum: A Roman, Late Roman and Early Byzantine City: Excavations 1985–1992* (London, 1999).

[6] C. Morrisson and J.-P. Sodini, "The Sixth-Century Economy," *EHB* 1, pp. 177–8; Lefort et al., *Villages*, passim and notably P.-L. Gatier, "Les villages du Proche-Orient protobyzantin", *ibid.*, pp. 101–19.

[7] C. Mango, *Le développement urbain de Constantinople, IVe–VIIe siècle* (Paris, 1985), p. 51; D. Jacoby, "La population de Constantinople à l'époque byzantine: un problème de démographie urbaine," *Byzantion* 31 (1961), pp. 81–109 (= D. Jacoby, *Société et démographie à Byzance et en Romanie latine* (London, 1975), art. 1). A much higher estimate of about 700,000 is now proposed by C. Zuckerman, *Du village à l'empire: autour du registre fiscal d'Aphroditô* (Paris, 2004).

and inscriptions in the capital and in the provinces give evidence of great *building activity*. New construction was still undertaken in the sixth century. It included religious buildings like the famous Saint Polyeuktos, Saint Sergius and Bacchus and Saint Sophia in Constantinople with their costly decoration. Many other churches were built in provincial cities – 160 churches in Arabia and the two Palestines date from the sixth and early seventh centuries. New construction also included, to a certain extent, public buildings. Aqueducts, cisterns, baths, porticoes, and agoras were still maintained in many cities or rebuilt after earthquakes; a few were newly established. The fortification program of Anastasios I and Justinian was carried out on a massive scale in the Balkans, from the Danubian frontier to the Long Walls of Dyrrachium or Thrace, in Africa and above all in northern Syria where the walls of Resafa, Dara, and Antioch, for example, remain as masterpieces of military architecture.[8] From the economic point of view, this is undoubtedly an index of wealth and available surplus. More than a million gold coins (*solidi*) were spent on Saint Sophia; Julianus Argentarius, the banker, spent 26,000 *solidi* on San Vitale in Ravenna. Even if these buildings are deemed a non-productive investment, which was not the case for defence works that maintained security, all represented high demand from the state and the Church and mobilized considerable reserves, providing a living for many workers and craftsmen in cities and in the countryside.

Craftsmen were mainly active in the *urban economy*. They often combined production and sale in the same location, as may be seen in the shops of Sardis.[9] Funeral and other inscriptions document the variety of existing trades and sub-trades. In construction there were masons, sculptors, stone-cutters, mosaicists, plasterers, contractors and architects. In textiles, there were fullers, weavers, dyers. Makers of metalwork (*chrysochooi, chalkitai*) and glass or pottery produced both luxury objects – silk, gold and silverplate, jewelry – or copies in cheaper materials with less refined execution for poorer customers; potters also produced containers (amphoras) and building materials (bricks, tiles). Carpentry and above all shipbuilding deserve special mention. Archaeology supports the epigraphic and literary evidence of urban activity: workshops for glass and *opus sectile*, purple dye production,

---

[8] Morrisson and Sodini, "Sixth-Century Economy," pp. 185–9; W. Liebeschuetz, *The Decline and Fall of the Roman City* (Oxford, 2001), with references.

[9] J. S. Crawford, *The Byzantine Shops at Sardis* (Cambridge, Mass., 1990).

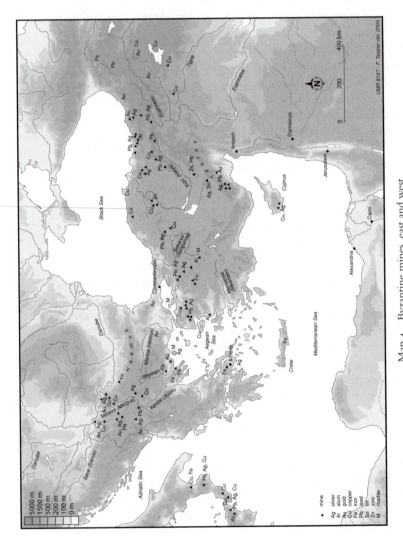

Map 4. Byzantine mines, east and west

(© Centre d'Histoire et de Civilisation de Byzance, CNRS Paris)

▲ Mine; Ag : silver; Al : alum; M: marble; Pb : lead

Au : gold; Sn : tin; Cu : copper; Zn : zinc; Fe : iron

fishponds, and storage areas have been excavated in Caesarea, met-
alworks and glassworks in Sardis and in several Balkan locations like
Caričin Grad or in Cherson among other places.[10]

Craft activity relied on the exploitation of *natural resources* which
still abounded in the Empire: timber, marble, clay and metals. *Timber*
was available in several coastal mountainous regions (Dalmatia,
Calabria, northern Greece, Bithynia, Pontus, Lycia, Cilicia, Crete,
Cyprus). It was an essential input for fuel, construction and shipbuilding. *Marble* was exploited in Thasos and other islands, in Proconnesos,
in Asia Minor at Dokimeion and other Phrygian or more coastal
locations, often in imperial quarries.[11] *Mines* and mineral resources
were widely, if unevenly, distributed (Map 4). The analysis of written
sources, mainly legal ones in our period,[12] can be supplemented with
some archaeological data. In the Balkans, the scattered gold mines
were controlled by the *comes metallorum per Illyricum* and the municipal decurions (later often the bishops) that he chose as mine con-
trollers (*procuratores metallorum*), while silver, copper and iron were left
to private managers delivering part of the production to the state. The
loss of Noricum, Pannonia (respectively in present-day Austria and
Hungary) and Dalmatia entailed increased exploitation of the mines
or rivers of Illyricum and Thrace in the fifth–sixth centuries.[13] Gold

---

[10] See A. Raban and K. Holum (eds.), *Caesarea Maritima: A Retrospective after Two Millennia* (Leiden, 1996) and other sources cited by S. Kingsley, "'Decline' in the ports of Palestine in Late antiquity," in *Recent Research in Late-Antique Urbanism* (*JRA* Suppl. Series 42) (Portsmouth, RI, 2001), pp. 69–88, at pp. 77–83 (J. Patrich holds a less optimistic view and dates the apogee of Caesarea to the late fourth century). Comprehensive survey by J.-P. Sodini, "L'artisanat urbain à l'époque paléochrétienne," *Ktèma* 4 (1979), pp. 71–119 and other data in Morrisson and Sodini, "Sixth-Century Economy," pp. 201–4.

[11] J.-P. Sodini, "Marble and Stoneworking in Byzantium," *EHB*, I, pp. 129–32 (with map).

[12] S. Vryonis, "The Question of the Byzantine Mines", *Speculum* 37 (1962), pp. 1–17 (= S. Vryonis, *Byzantium: Its Internal History and Relations with the Muslim World* (London, 1971)), art. VI. See, now, A. G. C. Savvides, "Observations on Mines and Quarries in the Byzantine Empire," *Ekklesiastikos Pharos* 82/2 (2000), pp. 130–55.

[13] See B. Bavant in C. Morrisson (ed.), *Le Monde byzantin*, I (Paris, 2004), pp. 331–2, based on S. Dušanić, "Aspects of Roman Mining in Noricum, Pannonia, Dalmatia and Moesia Superior," *Aufstieg und Niedergang der Römischen Welt*, 2. 6 (1977), pp. 52–94. See also S. Dušanić, "Late Roman Mining in Illyricum: Historical Observations," in B. Jovanović et al. (eds.), *Ancient Mining and Metallurgy of Southeast Europe* (Belgrade, 1995), pp. 219–25 and the valuable old study by C. Jireček, "Archäologische Fragmente aus Bulgarien," *Archaeologisch-Epigraphische Mitt. aus Österreich-Ungarn* 10 (1886), pp. 43–104, 129–209.

was also found in Nubia and in central Egypt where excavations in Bir Umm Fawakhir have brought to light extended installations.[14] The eastern Egyptian desert also yielded emeralds, beryls, malachite and marble from the Mons Porphyrites. Cyprus had scores of small mining camps in the Troodos region. In the upper Vasilikos valley in Cyprus, many temporary or permanent encampments were situated around large copper mines.[15] The gold resources of Armenia were a recurring bone of contention with Persia in our period, often the cause of war. Asia Minor is best known today thanks to surveys; ancient or early medieval sites are concentrated in Bithynia and the west (copper, zinc, lead, silver and iron), in northern Phrygia (mainly copper), in the Pontus (argentiferous lead) and in the Taurus range (silver, lead and tin).[16]

As in most pre-industrial economies, *agriculture* accounted for the greatest part of production (some two-thirds of the GNP). In this period, it could rely on a large supply of arable land per capita, still unlimited except in highly fertile areas like Egypt. As in Antiquity, hard and soft wheat was produced in Sicily, Africa, Egypt, the plains of Asia Minor, and Thrace. Barley, rye, millet, and oats and various pulses (peas, vetch, and lentils), which dominated the diet of the poor, were widespread both as items of self-consumption and on the market. Wheat yields varied on average between 1:5 to 1:7, with higher figures in Egypt (up to 1:10) because of the specific conditions in the Nile valley. Oil and wine, though common in many areas as staples of daily consumption, were also privileged, but not exclusive, cash crops in some regions like, respectively, Africa and northern Syria or Gaza. Textile plants like hemp or flax are attested in Egypt, for instance, and various fruits are ubiquitous. The mulberry tree, which grows in moderate and not too humid climates, served for the feeding of silk worms after some time in the sixth century in Syria and Asia Minor. According to Procopius,[17] "in order that the Romans should no longer buy their silk from the Persians," Justinian asked certain monks who had learned about sericulture to smuggle

[14] C. Meyer et al., *Bir Umm Fawakhir, Survey Project 1993: A Byzantine Gold-mining Town in Egypt* (Chicago, 2000).

[15] M. Rautman, "The Villages of Byzantine Cyprus," in Lefort et al., *Villages*, pp. 453–63, at p. 455.

[16] B. Pitarakis, "Mines anatoliennes exploitées par les Byzantins: recherches récentes," *Rev. Num.* 153 (1998), pp. 141–85.

[17] Procopius, *Wars*, VIII.17.1–8.

out silk moth eggs in the 550s from *Serinda* (China). Whatever the truth of the anecdote, it indicates that moriculture for the feeding of silkworms spread at that period (see below for silk industry).[18]

The combined testimony of palaeobotanical studies of materials from excavations or surveys along with papyri and textual data makes it possible to outline the variety of rural production. The *Geoponika*, commissioned by Constantine VII (913–59), relying on an Early Byzantine source, report agrarian practices in the sixth century and shows the variety of products, including fresh vegetables grown around large cities for urban consumption. Agricultural *implements* and *tools* appear rather rudimentary. In fact, the sole ard with asymmetrical ploughshare, the spade-fork (*lisgari*), the two-pronged drag-hoe (*dikelli*) for turning the soil, the sickle (*drepanon*) used instead of the scythe for harvesting, were adapted to Mediterranean conditions, and fragile and often lighter soils.[19] The use of water mills spread during the sixth century. Although their horizontal wheel was less efficient than the vertical one, they were not a later Western medieval innovation, as once thought. One should not therefore underestimate the effectiveness of Byzantine techniques used, for instance, in quarrying, in irrigation and in wine and oil extraction: oil presses with levered counterweights and rolling stones are found in the Pontus, Bithynia, Phrygia, Caria and Judaea. But production was mostly carried out on a small scale and the few concentrated installations of the Roman period are no longer present.

Stock raising was important and extensive in plateaus or mountainous areas. Pasture also occurred in villages territory in special enclosures or nearby woodland as shown by traces of stables and

---

[18] A. Muthesius, "Essential Processes, Looms, and Technical Aspects of Production of Silk Textiles," *EHB* I, pp. 50–1 with references to her other studies. R. S. Lopez, "The Silk Industry in the Byzantine Empire," *Speculum* 20 (1945), pp. 1–42, reprinted in R. S. Lopez, *Byzantium and the World Around it* (London, 1978), art. III, is still indispensable reading in spite of subsequent studies.

[19] A. Bryer, "The Means of Agricultural Production: Muscle and Tools," in *EHB* I, pp. 101–13. For adaptation, see M. Kaplan, *Les hommes et la terre à Byzance du VIe au XIe siècle: propriété et exploitation du sol* (Paris, 1992), and J. Lefort, "The Rural Economy, Seventh–Twelfth Centuries," *EHB* I, pp. 232–6. For archaeological evidence (mostly tenth–eleventh century): B. Pitarakis, "Objets métalliques dans le village médiéval," in Lefort et al., *Villages*, pp. 247–65. For a wide-ranging appraisal in Mediterranean and non-Mediterranean contexts, see F. Sigaut, "L'évolution des techniques," in M. Barceló and F. Sigaut (eds.), *The Making of Feudal Agricultures* (*TRW*, 14) (Leiden, 2004), pp. 1–31. See also below, ch. IV, pp. 98–100.

archeozoological studies of bone remains of oxen, goats, sheep, pigs and poultry.

The *landholding* pattern was an articulated one in which the state, great and smaller landlords and peasants interacted but in which possessions were usually scattered and large plots the exception. The state and the Church possessed great estates derived from imperial and confiscated lands or from imperial and private donations respectively. Imperial estates were run by specialized managers of the so-called *domus divinae* (imperial domains); they were dominant in Cappadocia and eastern Asia Minor, and are documented in Egyptian papyri. The estates of senatorial families were smaller in the east than they had been in the west, but the paradigmatic Apions' holdings amounted to 31,000ha in the Antaeopolis district alone. Papyri enable us to analyse the distribution of property in the village of Aphrodito in Egypt: one estate owned some three-fifths of total land, the remaining two-fifths being divided between city-dwellers (*astika*: 25 per cent of taxpayers, among whom a monastery owned a third of the land) and villagers (75 per cent of taxpayers). Inequality was higher among urban owners than among villagers. Among smallholders, there was still in the early sixth century a "broad base of landholders . . . most landowners had enough land to support a family and there was a broad band of middle-range men capable of bearing public obligations."[20] The great landowners were able to exact part of the agricultural surplus by lending money to peasants who sold their crops for future delivery. But the economic independence of the small freeholder, the working out of share-cropping contracts with tenants and the weight of taxation are still much debated.[21] And there is no way of estimating the proportion of landless peasants and the inequality of *income*.

The same fiscal documents record in villages *craftsmen* grouped in guilds much as they were in bigger cities: carpenters, bakers, fullers, undertakers, tailors, boatmen and smiths. Craftsmen were also

[20] R. Bagnall, "Landholding in Late Roman Egypt: The Distribution of Wealth," *JRS* 82 (1992), pp. 285–96, reprinted in R. Bagnall, *Later Roman Egypt: Society, Religion, Economy and Administration* (Aldershot, 2003), art. XII. For Aphrodito, data from the cadaster are compared to those from the fiscal register by Zuckerman, *Du village à l'empire*.

[21] J. Banaji, *Agrarian Change in Late Antiquity: Gold, Labour and Aristocratic Dominance* (Oxford, 2002), and the critical assessment by D. Kehoe, *JRA* 16 (2003), pp. 711–21; A. K. Bowman and E. Rogan, (eds.), *Agriculture in Egypt from Pharaonic to Modern Times*, reviewed by R. Bagnall, "Egyptian Agriculture in Historical Perspective," in *JRA* 13 (2000), pp. 707–11.

employed on great estates. Archeology, epigraphy, papyri, saints' lives and Talmudic sources provide evidence of free wandering peddlers, craftsmen and workers based in villages, especially in the crafts of building, metalwork, glass and ceramic production.[22]

The actors of the urban and the rural economy participated in complex *exchanges* to which we now turn, starting with the most important of its actors: *the state*. Not only was the state a producer in its numerous estates, mines (*metalla*), quarries and workshops (textile ones for weaving: *gynaecea, lyniphia*, or dyeing: *baphia*; arms factories: *fabricae*), it also controlled the trade of sensitive materials like silk, murex (purple dye), alum and salt over which it wielded total or partial monopolies.[23] It played a major role in trade through the system of the *annona*, and it regulated credit and banking as well as coinage. The assessment of the state's influence and participation in the Early Byzantine economy and trade has been much debated: "primitivists" ("substantivists") ascribe an enormous weight to the state, combined with extended self-sufficiency in the rural sector and limited commercial trade "tied" to public transportation. Speaking of an entirely trade-based economy would be anachronistic; a more balanced view emerges when one combines legal and textual evidence (in part biased in favour of high-level tied exchange) with that from ceramics and coins recovered from excavations of urban and rural sites all over the Empire, which points to important private exchanges.[24]

In the sixth century, the *annona* consisted, on the one hand, of the military rations issued to soldiers, now generally commuted to cash and being part of their pay, and, on the other, of the *annona civica*: commodities (wheat or bread, oil, wine, lard and pulses in Constantinople), destined for distribution in the capital and in a few

---

[22] See e.g. R. Bagnall, "Village and City: Geographies of Power in Byzantine Egypt," in Lefort et al., *Villages*, pp. 553–65; F. R. Trombley, "Town and Territory in Late Roman Anatolia", in L. Lavan, ed., *Recent Research in Late-Antique Urbanism* (Portsmouth, R.I., 2001), pp. 217–32.

[23] A. H. M. Jones, *The Later Roman Empire 284–602: A Social, Economic and Administrative Survey* (Oxford, 1964), pp. 834–7; R. Delmaire, *Largesses sacrées et res privata: l'aerarium impérial et son administration du IVe au VIe siècle* (Rome: École française de Rome, 1989), pp. 443–525.

[24] J.-M. Carrié, "Les échanges commerciaux de l'État antique tardif," in *Économie antique: Les Échanges dans l'Antiquité: le rôle de l'État* (Saint-Bertrand-de-Comminges, 1994), pp. 175–211 with references to previous literature. S. Kingsley, "The Economic Impact of the Palestinian Wine trade in Late Antiquity," in S. Kingsley and M. Decker (eds.), *Economy and Exchange in the East Mediterranean during Late Antiquity* (Oxford, 2001), pp. 44–68.

other cities. Although the government tried thus to "ensure that . . . bread shortages and consequent riots should not occur", not all Constantinopolitans were on the dole. Free distributions were limited to the 80,000 "political breads," i.e. rations, assigned to heads of household, supplemented by the *panes aedium* attached to houses built in the capital before 390. The existence of only 21 big (*pammegetheis)* public bakeries versus some 120 smaller private ones, probably provisioned by wheat sold at its fiscal price by the state, show that only part of the population (*c.*120,000 people) relied on public distributions. The *arca frumentaria*[25] acted as a stabilization office, selling wheat at moderate prices in times of dearth. The size of the imports of Egyptian wheat sent annually as taxes (the so-called *embole* amounting to 234,000 tons reduced to *c.*175,000 by losses in transportation and warehousing) has given rise to many calculations of the population of Constantinople.[26]

The shipping of these huge quantities required some 500 ships in three rotations between Egypt and the capital. Down to the time of Justinian it was entrusted to a guild of shipowners (*naukleroi*), who were exempted from the land tax on specially assigned lands and from indirect taxes (*vectigalia*). Later, it was transferred to paid transporters who could likewise complement the official cargo with other commodities.[27] *Long-distance trade* was clearly not only the affair of the state and of great landowners who shipped products from their estates to the market. Many independent traders of different status traveled along a complex network of routes. Ceramics and metalware finds, the classification and dating of which has made continuous progress over the last decades, have contributed to a new, less impressionistic and more positive, picture of Mediterranean exchanges. In the fifth century, as Constantinople flourished and the Western Empire

---

[25] A civic fund for buying grain.

[26] Jones, *The Later Roman Empire*, pp. 696–8; G. Dagron, *Naissance d'une capitale, Constantinople et ses institutions de 330 à 451* (Paris, 1974), pp. 530–41; J. Durliat, *De la ville antique à la ville byzantine: le problème des subsistances* (Rome, 1990). Like Durliat, C. Zuckerman (*Du village à l'empire*, pp. 194–206) favors the thesis of a mainly public wheat trade and transportation. J.-M. Carrié, "L'institution annonaire de la première à la deuxième Rome: continuité et innovation," in B. Marin and C. Virlouvet (eds.), *Nourrir les cités de Méditerranée: antiquité – temps modernes* (Paris, 2003), pp. 153–212 with references.

[27] M. McCormick, "Bateaux de vie, bateaux de mort, maladie, commerce, transports annonaires et le passage économique du Bas-Empire au Moyen Âge," *Morfologie sociali e culturali in Europa fra tarda antichità e alto medioevo* (Settimane 45) (Spoleto, 1998), pp. 35–122, at pp. 68–93.

decayed, a "re-routing" of commerce toward the East is manifest. The main maritime route was the *annona* one which brought wheat shipments to Constantinople from Egypt through Cyprus, Chios, the Lycian coast, Tenedos, and Abydos. A secondary route linked the capital to Italy, Sicily and Africa. Justinian's reconquests revived its importance, although it had not been interrupted by the Vandals or the Ostrogoths – in the ancient and medieval context, chronic or permanent military conflicts never entirely stopped commercial exchange. The ports of call circle the Peloponnese where finds of African Red Slip act as tracers of imports.

Proof of '*non-annona*', *private trade* is given by the existence of direct routes that bypass Constantinople. They link Africa and Syria-Palestine, via Crete. Exports of Gaza wine and other eastern wines (Laodicea), mapped by finds of Palestinian amphorae (LRA 1 and 4), reached Cyprus, the whole Aegean, the Crimea and the Danube, Italy and southern Gaul, even, further north, the south-west coast of England.[28] Phocaean pottery (Late Roman C), produced in Phocaea itself and in coastal workshops nearby, increasingly competed with African production in the sixth century, especially in the East, and is attested widely from Spain and Britain to the Red Sea to the Black Sea, even reaching inland areas in Asia Minor, Greece and the East in a 'capillary' distribution.[29] Glass, produced from local sands in Syria and Palestine, is less easily traceable, but analyses confirm that it was exported as cullett to the West where it was worked and marketed. Many eastern and Byzantine wares were still exported to Gaul and beyond. The combined evidence of ceramics, coins and texts allows

[28] Kingsley and Decker, *Economy and Exchange*, pp. 44–68; S. Kingsley, "Late Antique Trade: Research Methodologies and Field Practices," in L. Lavan and W. Bowden (eds.), *Theory and Practice in Late Antique Archaeology* (Late Antique Archaeology 1) (Leiden–Boston, 2003), pp. 113–38; D. Piéri, *Le commerce du vin oriental à l'époque byzantine (Ve–VIIe siècles): le témoignage des amphores en Gaule* (Beyrouth, 2005).

[29] C. Abadie-Reynal, "Céramique et commerce dans le bassin égéen du IVe au VIIe siècle," in *Hommes et richesses*, I, pp. 143–60; C. Panella, "Gli scambi nel Mediterraneo Occidentale dal iv al vii secolo," *ibid.*, pp. 129–41 and eadem, "Merci e scambi nel Mediterraneo tardoantico," in A. Momigliano and A. Schiavone (eds.), *Storia di Roma*, vol. 3, *L'età tardoantica*, part 2, *I luoghi e le culture*, ed. by A. Carandini, L. Cracco-Ruggini and A. Giardina (Turin, 1988), pp. 613–97; J.-P. Sodini, "Productions et échanges dans le monde protobyzantin (IVe–VIIe s.): le cas de la céramique," in K. Belke et al. (eds.), *Byzanz als Raum: zu Methoden und Inhalten der historischen Geographie des oestlichen Mittelmeerraumes* (Vienna, 2000), pp. 181–208.

us to draw a map of the location of Syrian traders (*Syri*, i.e. Byzantine traders, from Syria or other provinces as well) in the Merovingian period.[30] It calls to mind the description of Saint Jerome:

there remains in the Syrians an inborn zeal for transacting business; they go about the whole world with a desire for money . . . the business people of Tyre . . . trade damask, purple, and checked garments; linen also, and silk and cotton they place in their trade (*polymita, purpuram et scutulata mercantur: byssum quoque et sericum, et chodchod proponunt*). (In Ezechiel 27:15, 16; *PL* 25, 255B–C)

In the Far East, fine bleached glass found its way to China. Other commodities, with hardly any physical remains, like textiles or spices fuelled long-distance exchanges with the Far East: raw silk, pearls, spices and gems were imported from India and China and reached the Empire either in Syria through Arabia and the caravan routes, or in Egypt from the Red Sea, where Clysma and Adoulis still flourished in the sixth century. The often-cited anecdote of the merchant Sopatros and his contest with a Persian competitor in front of the king of Taprobane (Ceylon) reported by Cosmas Indicopleustes (the 'Indian sailor') is indirectly confirmed by the coins and ceramic finds on the coasts of south India and Sri Lanka.[31]

Long-distance trade was a mainly maritime one supplemented by fluvial navigation in Egypt where wheat was easily shipped on the Nile, or on the northern frontier where provisions and materials were sent on the Danube to Byzantine garrisons up to Pannonia. A few other rivers, like the Marica or the Halys, Iris and Acampsis in the Pontic area, were navigable for part of their length and served regional trade. *Land transport* was much more costly and slower, but less hazardous and constant over seasons; on long distances it was generally reserved for expensive, high-profit commodities.[32] However, it played a great role in regional or local commerce, facilitated by the continued maintainance of the Roman roads (6 to 9m wide) and bridges. This network included the "Imperial route" crossing the Balkans through the Morava–Vardar (Axios) valleys, the Via Egnatia

[30] See R. Hodges and D. Whitehouse, *Mahomet, Charlemagne et les origines de l'Europe* (Paris, 1996), pp. 78–80, fig. 29.

[31] W. Wolska-Conus (ed.), *Topographie chrétienne* (Sources Chrétiennes 197), III (Paris, 1967), pp. 350–1. R. Walburg, "Antike Münzen aus Sri Lanka/Ceylon," in M. R.-Alföldi (ed.), *Studien su Fundmünzen der Antike*, 3 (Berlin, 1985), pp. 27–260.

[32] Jones, *Later Roman Empire*, pp. 840–1.

from Dyrrachium to Thessalonike, and the roads in Asia Minor leading to Antioch or Armenia and the upper Euphrates frontier.[33] Although intended mostly for military and administrative purposes, these roads served regional exchanges as well. Goods were carried by a variety of ox- or horse-driven carts and pack animals (donkeys, mules, camels), whose loads depended on the distance travelled.[34]

Local exchange involved larger rural sites (the *komai*) of several thousand inhabitants, which functioned as minor central points, attracting wares from a radius of one day's return walk. These were rural markets, serving a number of small villages of a few hundred people. The combination of local and more far-flung inter-regional exchanges is being more and more researched in many areas like Cyprus or Palestine.[35] In this chapter, cities are separated from the countryside for the sake of clarity. The two were in fact deeply intertwined in bi-directional relations, not necessarily the parasitical one emphasized in previous scholarship. Recent studies on Alexandria show, for instance, the multifaceted relationship and two-way flow of goods and services between the *megalopolis*, its immediate hinterland (the *chora* and the Mareotis) and more remote destinations.[36] Constantinople entertained the same kind of mutual dependence with its various hinterlands and the rest of the Empire.[37]

All transactions could be carried out in an articulated *coinage*[38] which provided the means for payments of widely differing value, from the *solidus* (which could circulate in sealed bags of one to a hundred pounds, 72 to 7,200 gold pieces), its fractions of $\frac{1}{2}$ and $\frac{1}{3}$, to the copper coin (*follis*) and its divisions down to the tiny *nummus*, a few of which could buy a loaf of bread or a handful of pulses. Texts and coin finds point to a high level of monetization. Cities and smaller towns, as well as the rural contexts recently studied, yield coins in numbers proportional to their relative population. They even point to an increased diffusion of new issues in the

---

[33] A. Avramea, "Land and Sea Communications," *EHB* 1, pp. 57–90.

[34] McCormick, *Origins*, pp. 76–7.

[35] M. Rautman, "Rural Society and Economy in Late Roman Cyprus," in T. S. Burns and J. W. Eadie, *Urban Centers and Rural Contexts in Late Antiquity* (East Lansing, MI, 2001), pp. 241–62.

[36] C. Haas, "Alexandria and the Mareotis Region," in Burns and Eadie, *Urban centers*, pp. 47–62.

[37] G. Dagron and C. Mango (eds.), *Constantinople and its Hinterland* (Aldershot, 1995).

[38] C. Morrisson, "Monnaie et prix du Ve au VIIe siècle," in *Hommes et richesses* I, pp. 239–60 and Morrisson and Sodini, "Sixth-Century Economy," pp. 212 ff., with references to major works.

countryside in some regions in the early sixth century, indicating a rise in the commercialization of the agricultural surplus.[39] *Banking* was in the hands of moneylenders and changers whom the state controlled and protected. Lending was regulated: 12 per cent for sea-loans and 4 to 8 per cent for other loans, depending on the lender's status and profession. Alexandrian bankers, often acting in partnerships, could wield considerable power. They made written transfers based on compensation but also supervised large physical transfers of coins, even tons of them, and were instrumental in the issue of copper coinage to the public and in exchanges between gold and copper.[40] There is no doubt any more that trade and exchange in sixth-century Byzantium were still comparable with those in the Early Roman Empire even if the quantities had decreased because of the decline of the West in the fifth century. But decay and crisis was to hit the East very soon.

"DECAY," CRISIS AND THE TRANSFORMATION OF THE ECONOMY (*c.* 550–EARLY EIGHTH CENTURY)

The *Great Plague*,[41] which occurred in 541/2, and its cyclical return (notably in 558, 573/4), which persisted, at increasingly longer intervals, until the beginning of the eighth century, is clearly a turning point in the economic history of Byzantium. The population may have decreased by as much as 30 per cent, the pandemic striking all age groups and weakening survivors since no immunity was developed by exposure. The plague was spread by rats, which travelled on boats with staples, and thus hit the West a year later. It affected cities more than the countryside, villagers more than nomads and contributed to de-urbanization. It occurred in conjunction with other diseases, like smallpox, several disrupting earthquakes, and long-lasting wars, the

---

[39] See the various contributions assembled in Lefort et al., *Villages*.

[40] S. J. B. Barnish, "The Wealth of Julianus Argentarius: Late Antique Banking and the Mediterranean Economy," *Byzantion*, 55 (1985), pp. 5–38; Bagnall, *Egypt*, pp. 74–8 and Gascou's review in *Topoi* 6 (1996), pp. 333–49. On gold and copper, see now Zuckerman, *Du village à l'Empire*, pp. 57–114.

[41] D. Stathakopoulos, *Famine and Pestilence in the Late Roman and Early Byzantine Empire* (Aldershot, 2004) with references; idem, "The Justinianic Plague Revisited," *BMGS* 24 (2000), pp. 256–76. The proceedings of a 2001 conference in Rome, *The Justinianic Plague: the Non-Literary Evidence*, ed. L. K. Little, were published after the completion of this book.

"Gothic" war in Italy 535–55, the wars with Persia 540–5, 572–91 and 605–28, the struggle against the Arab forces from 636 onward, while Avars and Slavs penetrated more and more deeply into the Balkans. This conjunction of factors and not the sole "catastrophe" of the plague prevented a recovery in the normal 100–130 years time observed after the Black Death. A climatic deterioration beginning in the 530s, with cold and arid winters leading to poor harvests and the "dust veil" episode entailing severe drought, had perhaps contributed to the diffusion of the disease by weakening the population. Variations in the level of lakes and inland seas and increased alluvial deposits have been taken as signs of this climatic episode. But anthropogenic influence in the process leading to an extension of woodland and scrubland from the late sixth and early seventh century was also an important factor.[42]

It is in this context that signs of general impoverishment must be considered. With some regional differences, Illyricum and Thrace being affected much earlier, while public buildings and facilities were still being maintained or built in the islands or the Levant, the area occupied by cities progressively decreased. The remaining occupied surface was degraded by spoliation and robbing. Ancient monuments served for housing or industrial purposes: oil presses or lime kilns were established in churches or theaters, slaughterhouses, metalwork and glass workshops were housed in baths, as, for example, at Leptiminus and Carthage. The debris of monuments were used for building walls around smaller centres.[43] Former residential houses were transformed into workshops or divided into smaller and poorer dwellings.[44] The middle class of landowners who resided in cities had been progressively pressured by the increased rate of taxation in the 550s.[45] The

---

[42] D. Stathakopoulos, "Reconstructing the Climate of the Byzantine World: State of the Question and Case Studies," in J. Laszlovszky and P. Szabó (eds.), *People and Nature in Historical Perspective* (Budapest, 2003), pp. 247–61. Geyer's insistence on the anthropogenic factor (*EHB* 1, p. 44) is questioned by A. Dunn (review of *EHB*, *Speculum* 80/2 (2005), pp. 616–21).

[43] Among innumerable other examples of this general transformation (references in Ch. Bouras, "Aspects of the Byzantine City, Eighth–Fifteenth Centuries," *EHB* 2, pp. 497–528), see Corinth (G. D. R. Sanders, *EHB* 2, p. 648), Sardis (C. Foss and J. A. Scott, *EHB* 2, pp. 615–22), and Anemourion (J. Russell, *EHB* 1, pp. 221–8).

[44] J.-P. Sodini, "Archaeology and Late Antique Social Structures," in Lavan and Bowden, *Theory and Practice* (Leiden, 2003), pp. 25–56.

[45] Zuckerman, *Du village à l'Empire* , pp. 215–19.

encroachment of shops on public spaces characterizes the transformation of the ancient city. This break and ruralization of the "Late Late"
ancient city, called "de-urbanization" by others, has been dated to
the seventh century and principally attributed to the Persian invasion
of Asia Minor,[46] but can be traced, even in Sardis, somewhat earlier.

Impoverishment is also evident in the *countryside*. Building shifted
massively from cut stone to drystone or to wood and cob, rubble and
mud bricks. Tiles disappeared in favour of wooden planks or thatch
for roofing, and beaten floors replaced stone ones. The transformation occurred earlier in the Balkans which had never recovered after
the settlement of the Goths (in the fourth century); renewed insecurity there led to the abandonment of villages in the plains in favor
of upland settlements and to a dramatic decline in the monetization
of the countryside.[47] A general decline in the number of settlements
is assumed to have taken place in many other areas (Asia Minor,
Cyprus and Northern Syria from 650 onward). In other regions like
Calabria, the development of hilltop and secure villages starting in
the 550s helped maintain the export of agricultural staples to Rome
as well as craft activities.

The decline of urban markets occasioned by demography and war
(public wheat distribution ceased in 618 and never resumed) led to
a downsizing of trade at all levels. A decrease in long-distance trade
can be assumed from several converging indicators. The number of
shipwrecks[48] in the seventh century is less than half that of the sixth
century and becomes a mere tenth in the eighth century. Most ships
were now middle-sized ones like the Dor D wreck (20m) or the Yası

---

[46] See the seminal article by C. Foss, "The Persians in Asia Minor and the End of
Antiquity," *The English Historical Review* 90/357 (Oct. 1975), pp. 721–47 and other
studies by the same author.

[47] Agathias mentions the *deserted villages* of Moesia and Scythia Minor as early as 558.
A. Poulter, "Cataclysm on the Lower Danube: The Destruction of a Complex
Roman Landscape," in N. Christie (ed.), *Landscapes of Change: Rural Evolutions
in Late Antiquity and the Early Middle Ages* (Aldershot, 2004), pp. 223–53. Decline
of rural monetization: E. Oberländer-Târnoveanu, in Lefort et al., *Villages*,
pp. 382–3.

[48] A. J. Parker, *Ancient Shipwrecks of the Mediterranean and the Roman Provinces* (Oxford,
1992); F. van Doorninck, Jr., "Byzantine Shipwrecks," *EHB* 2, pp. 899–905 with
references; S. Kingsley, *A Sixth-century AD Shipwreck off the Carmel Coast, Israel:
Dor D and Holy Land Wine Trade* (Oxford, 2002). On the limitations of current information and its potential, S. Kingsley, "Late Antique Trade. Research
Methodologies and Field Practice," in Lavan and Bowden, *Theory and Practice*,
pp. 25–56.

Ada ship (21m and 50 tons capacity, carrying some 800 amphoras). The construction technique shifted to the medieval skeleton one (where wales are assembled first and planking is more loosely joined) which made them less expensive to build than in Roman times and appropriate to shorter distances.

The number of African tableware ceramics finds dwindles dramatically,[49] while their distribution becomes more and more restricted to coastal areas or privileged centres where a few wealthy customers remained. Downsizing did not mean a complete halt; trade within or beyond the imperial frontiers continued across the Mediterranean down to the eighth century, as shown by finds of eastern wine amphoras in excavations in Marseilles, of African ones in the Fos shipwreck (Saint-Gervais 3), and of oriental glass in the late seventh-century levels of the Crypta Balbi in Rome. Trade routes in Western Europe were progresssively beginning to shift to the north. The increase in amphoras and fine ware finds in Cherson in the early seventh century and the continued imports from the Mediterranean point to the emergence of a new commercial centre connected to new partners.[50] Constantinople now depended chiefly on Thrace, Paphlagonia, the Pontic area and Bithynia for the provisioning of its much reduced population.[51]

New types of ceramic products point to this regionalization of trade: Constantinopolitan 'Glazed White Ware' beginning in the early seventh century had a limited distribution, like Sicilian *ciabatta* lamps or gray *sigillata* in the West. Entire inland zones in the remaining Byzantine territories had been abandoned by the former populations and a new rudimentary type of economy emerged. In the Balkans, Slavic populations, originally nomadic, progressively settled in the deserted plains where they lived in hamlets of semi-buried log huts and practised rudimentary agriculture, raising stock and beginning to cultivate wheat. They engaged in small-scale exchanges with the local populations, which had moved to cities or fortified upland settlements or remained in the few cities that survived thanks to their fortifications, like Thessalonike. The *Miracles* of Saint Demetrios hint at relations between the city and surrounding Slavic settlements which

[49] See Fentress–Perkins graph of African Red Slip finds on western sites in *Cambridge Ancient History*, XVI, p. 372.

[50] A. Bortoli and M. Kazanski, "Kherson and its Region," *EHB* 2, p. 660.

[51] J. L. Teall, "Byzantine Agricultural Tradition," *DOP* 25 (1971), pp. 35–59.

must have resembled the earlier ones on the Danubian frontier: city-dwellers providing metalwork, from jewelry or buckles to agricultural implements, or functional pottery, beads, etc. in exchange for provisioning, probably on a barter basis, since the Slavs had no monetary tradition.[52] Small-scale local exchanges were more easily practised on such a basis even in provinces where no such change in population had taken place. Evidence for a decline in monetization comes from all regions and is a well-attested phenomenon.[53]

The shrinking of Byzantine territory with the loss of its richest southern provinces, the dramatic decline in the state's fiscal resources, the decrease of population, not only in absolute numbers, but also in density, introduced a period of smaller, insecure markets with very limited specialization; trade reached a low ebb in the early eighth century. But Byzantium had human (political, cultural and military) and material assets on which it could draw to adapt and survive. Not all cities nor all riches were gone, hoarded metals could be mobilized, advanced crafts like silk production could even increase, and some provinces were still yielding wheat and taxes, while in others agriculture and defense were probably reorganizing around communities of smaller landholders. A few strongholds and small centers of production, most of them in the coastal or island territories, could still communicate with the capital and among themselves. The administration, too, adapted to meet the needs of the survival of the Empire. These were the bases from which the medieval Byzantine economy would launch its progressive recovery in the late eighth century, as we will see.

---

[52] Bavant (as above, n. 13), p. 340.

[53] Summarized in C. Morrisson, "Byzantine Money: Its Production and Circulation," *EHB* 3, pp. 954–7, and her "Survivance de l'économie monétaire à Byzance (VIIe–IXe s.)," in *Dark Centuries in Byzantium* (Athens, 2001), pp. 377–97.

III

RESTRUCTURING, RECOVERY AND CONTROLLED EXPANSION (EARLY EIGHTH TO TENTH CENTURIES)

By 700 the Empire had lost Africa, the last of its wealthiest provinces (Carthage fell in 698), and ceded the plains between the Danube and Haemus to the Bulgars (681). It was reduced to fragmented holdings in Italy, to coastal outposts around the Balkan peninsula and isolated ones on the Black Sea. Its core consisted now of two "pillars": the islands – Sicily, Crete and the Aegean ones – and Western Asia Minor. No part of the territory was immune from hostile incursions. Only its powerful walls, fleet and Greek fire prevented Constantinople, besieged four times in 100 years, from falling into the hands of its strongest enemy, the Arab caliphate.

Undoubtedly the eighth century in Byzantium, was a difficult one, characterized by depopulation, de-urbanization, diminished production and reduced trade, accompanied by a marked decrease in monetization as we saw above. The economy was now based on different urban centres, smaller fortified *kastra* with downsized hinterland and decreased demand for primary and secondary products, and on different relations between peasants and landowners. Society evolved accordingly with the replacement of the former senatorial and municipal elites by a new ruling class.[1] The hard times lasted until the end of the eighth century when the improvement on the military front, the restoration of control in the Balkans and stabilization of the

---

[1] J. Howard-Johnston, "Social Change in Early Medieval Byzantium," in *Lordship and Learning: Studies in Memory of T. Aston*, R. Evans (ed.) (Woodbridge: Boydell Press, 2004), pp. 39–50.

frontier in Asia Minor in conjunction with a turn in the demographic trend signal the beginning of recovery. The role of the Isaurian dynasty (717–802) in this process of restructuring was instrumental. The process of "revival," which extended over a period longer than the 62 years assigned to it in the most detailed – if debated – survey of this early period,[2] led to continuous territorial expansion in the tenth century which culminated in the reign of Basil II (976–1025). In the tenth century, signs of economic expansion abound as will be seen below.

The paucity of our sources on the economy is particularly acute for the early part of the period considered in the present chapter: papyri, inscriptions, multiple historical sources and reliable archeological tracers are gone and the Greek monastic or Italian commercial archives are still to come. Not only are chronicles, as usual, very short of economic information, but the few, highly important data they give on financial and fiscal measures are all biased by the prejudice of their authors against the great iconoclast emperors.[3] However, texts like the *Farmer's Law*, the *Rhodian Sea Law* dating to the late seventh–eighth centuries and the *Ecloga* (741) offer information on the rural and urban economy. We do not know how representative they are, although saints' lives and a few correspondences throw some light on these matters. Ceramic evidence loses part of its pertinence since other, less traceable, containers are gaining ground in the period and because it is an age of more regionalized and coarse fabric; but the typology of ceramics is making continuous progress and surveys contribute pertinent outlines of regional development. Documentary evidence increases in the tenth century and, together with Leo VI's Novels, the *Book of the Prefect* and other texts, helps us to perceive in greater detail the functioning of the economy.

Compared to the mid-sixth century, *population* in the early eighth century had decreased in absolute numbers because of territorial losses. Density was low and land plentiful. Consequently, there were no great obstacles to the many *migrations* or "encouraged" settlements observed in this period: either the migration of Slavs in the Balkans, whose demographic impact has been greatly exaggerated, or the flux

---

[2] W. Treadgold, *The Byzantine Revival 780–842* (Stanford, 1988).

[3] General up-to-date account by M.-F. Auzépy, "Byzantium in the Iconoclast period, c. 700–c. 850," in *The New Cambridge Byzantine History*, J. Shepard (ed.), forthcoming.

of refugees fleeing the invasions in the West (for example the people from Patras migrating to southern Italy;[4] the 200,000 Slavs fleeing the Bulgars and settling in Bithynia under Constantine V, Greeks from Sicily taking refuge in Calabria after the Arab conquest of the island) and in the East (12,000 Armenians and their families in the 790s settling in Cappadocia, Armenians or Jacobite Syrians settling in the late tenth century in Cilicia and Northern Syria).[5]

Various *deportations* documented in the eighth, ninth and tenth centuries had political and military motivations. Emperors would displace troublemakers or unreliable groups from frontier zones (Slavs deported in Bithynia, Phrygia, Cappadocia, Lycia and Caria by Justinian II in 694–6; restless soldiers of the Armeniac theme sent to Sicily and other islands by Constantine VI), while manning the frontier with more reliable groups, such as the Mardaites from Lebanon, probably good sailors, settled in Pamphylia by Justinian II.[6] Resettlements also aimed to stimulate agriculture, for what mattered most from the seventh century was the labour force. Devastated Thrace was thus progressively repopulated by transplantations of Armenians and Syrians under Constantine V and Leo IV. Greeks were sent to the *Sklaviniai* by Constantine V probably in order to introduce a more advanced mode of land exploitation and to facilitate the hellenization and christianization of the Slavs. The figures given by sources run from tens to several hundred thousand. They are not necessarily reliable. Undoubtedly, however, the various movements and measures, combined with the relative restoration of security, had a positive influence in the long run on production and on state finances.[7]

It is generally assumed that a general demographic increase followed the end of plague recurrence in the 740s. The evidence for demographic growth comes primarily from *settlement patterns* (especially the creation or growth of villages) and the expansion of cultivated and exploited areas. Palynological and carbon 14 studies show,

---

[4] *Chronicle of Monemvasia*, cited by P. Charanis, *DOP* 5 (1960), pp. 145–6 (= idem, *Studies in the Demography of the Byzantine Empire* (London, 1972), art. XIV).

[5] Charanis, *Studies*, art. V, p. 197 and art. II, p. 28; G. Dagron, "Minorités ethniques et religieuses dans l'Orient byzantin à la fin du Xe et au XIe siècle: l'immigration syrienne," *Travaux et Mémoires* 6 (1976), pp. 177–216.

[6] H. Ahrweiler, *Byzance et la mer* (Paris, 1967), pp. 399–400.

[7] H. Ditten, *Ethnische Verschiebungen zwischen des Balkanhalbinsel und Kleinasien vom Ende des 6. bis zur zweiten Hälfte des 9. Jahrhunderts* (Berlin, 1993); J. Lefort, "Population et démographie," in J.-C. Cheynet (ed.), *Le monde byzantin*, II (Paris, 2006), pp. 203–19.

already in the ninth century, the expansion of agriculture into areas that were previously wooded: examples are known from both Macedonia and Thessaly. In the eighth century many zones remain depopulated:[8] some, like northern Thrace or Eastern Asia Minor, were consciously considered as no man's land frontier zones separating the Empire from its main enemies. In the ninth and tenth centuries there is a net increase in the number of settlements. In Bulgaria, villages grew along the Byzantine–Bulgarian frontier in the tenth century.

In Byzantine southern Italy, the population of Apulia recovered in the ninth and tenth centuries. Archaeology shows that in the Peloponnese people began to resettle deserted areas of the Pylos region in the tenth century, and of the southern Argolid around the year 1000. Areas unoccupied for almost two centuries were resettled: so the Mani after 812. Generally in Thessaly, central Greece and the Peloponnese there was expansion of both the population and cultivation after the ninth century; the same may be said of south-eastern Anatolia.[9] In Bithynia too there is higher population density. Macedonia and southern Italy have been most extensively studied, in terms of both demography and the rural economy, thanks to the path-breaking work of Jacques Lefort and Jean-Marie Martin. Here, the demographic curve was on an upward slope, though with different starting

[8] On the seventh–ninth-century break see J. Bintliff, "Frankish Countryside in Central Greece: The Evidence from Archaeological Field Survey," in P. Lock and G. D. R. Sanders (eds.), *The Archaeology of Medieval Greece* (Exeter, 1996), pp. 1–18, J. Vroom, *After Antiquity: Ceramics and Society in the Aegean from the 7th to the 20th Century: A Case Study from Boeotia, Central Greece* (Leiden, 2003), and P. Armstrong, "The Survey Area in the Byzantine and Ottoman Periods," in W. Cavanagh et al. (eds.), *Continuity and Change in a Greek Rural Landscape: The Laconian Survey*, I (London, 2002), pp. 339–402.

[9] A. Dunn, "The Exploitation and Control of Woodland and Scrubland in the Byzantine World", *BMGS* 16 (1992), pp. 244–47, with reference to earlier studies; B. Geyer, "Physical Factors in the Evolution of the Landscape and Land Use," *EHB* I, pp. 42–3; A. E. Laiou, "The Byzantine Village (5th–14th century)," in J. Lefort, C. Morrisson, J.-P. Sodini (eds.), *Les Villages dans l'Empire byzantin (IVe–XVe siècle)* (Paris, 2005), pp. 31–54. See also A. Avramea, "Les villages de Thessalie, de Grèce centrale et du Péloponnèse (Ve–XIVe siècle)," J. Lefort et al., *Villages* (pp. 213–23); J. M. Moore, *Tille Hoyuk 1: The Medieval Period*, British Institute of Archaeology at Ankara, Monograph No. 14 (Oxford, 1991); S. Redford, *The Archaeology of the Frontier in the Medieval Near East: Excavations at Gritille, Turkey*, Archaeological Institute of America, Monographs, New Series no. 3 (Boston, 1998); cf., for Bulgaria, R. Rašev, V. Dinčev, B. Borissov, "Le village byzantin sur le territoire de la Bulgarie contemporaine," in Lefort et al., *Villages*, pp. 351–62.

points, in the period under discussion.[10] The population increase may be seen not only in the documents but also in the expansion of cultivated land and the retreat of pasture lands and woodlands. The increase in the number of settlements accompanies the annexation and revived exploitation of new territories, such as Apulia or southern Bulgaria or the intensification of land use in ancient ones like Bithynia. It is also possible that the change from "the little ice age" of the early Middle Byzantine period to a warmer and moister phase in the ninth–eleventh centuries was a favorable factor in this transformation.

The *urban settlement* pattern had also changed significantly. Demand decreased dramatically in the eighth century. Constantinople around 700 was a shadow of its former self with as few as some 40,000–70,000 inhabitants, partly ruralized like other centres.

In the eighth century, a few ancient cities remained, such as Thessalonike, Athens, Corinth, Thebes, Nicaea, Smyrna, Ankyra, Chalcedon, Cherson and Trebizond, but their occupied area was greatly reduced. A number had been abandoned (e.g. Olympia, Aphrodisias, Anemourion).[11] The shrinking of this network has been plotted using the rough index attested in the conciliar lists and the *Notitiae Episcopatuum* since in this period bishops had replaced the former councils (*curiae*) in representing their cities. Most of those that survived were located near the sea.[12] The Cretan city and capital of Gortyna, embellished by Herakleios, offers a well-excavated example of the

---

[10] References to the numerous works of J. Lefort may be found in his "The Rural Economy, Seventh–Twelfth Centuries," *EHB* 1, pp. 231–310 and in n. 8 of the Introduction to this volume. For Italy, see J.-M. Martin and G. Noyé, "Les villes de l'Italie byzantine (IXe–XIe siècle)," in *Hommes et richesses*, II, pp. 27–62; J. Lefort and J.-M. Martin, "L'organisation de l'espace rural: Macédoine et Italie du Sud (Xe–XIIIe siècle)," *ibid.*, pp. 11–26; cf. J.-M. Martin and G. Noyé, "Les villages de l'Italie méridionale byzantine," in Lefort et al., *Villages*, pp. 149–64.

[11] References in Ch. Bouras, "Aspects of the Byzantine City," *EHB* 2, 502–3. On Olympia see T. Völling, "The Last Christian Greeks and the first Pagan Slavs in Olympia," in Kontoura-Galake (ed.), *Dark Centuries*, pp. 303–23; on Anatolian cities, see the studies of C. Foss on Sardis and Ephesos and his articles in *History and Archaeology of Byzantine Asia Minor* (Aldershot, 1990) as well as the case studies surveyed in *EHB* 2.

[12] J. Haldon, "The Idea of the Town in the Byzantine Empire," in G. P. Brogiolo and B. Ward-Perkins (eds.), *The Idea and the Ideal of the Town between Late Antiquity and the Early Middle Ages* (Leiden, 1999), pp. 1–23; W. Brandes, "Byzantine Cities in the Seventh and Eighth Centuries – Different Sources, Different Histories," *ibid.*, pp. 25–57 with references to their respective earlier studies.

transformation of a classical city into a much smaller ruralized center but a still active one, linked to the capital thanks to its administrative and religious role. Although most of the new urban centers were, like villages, located on elevated, easily defendable and fortified sites, following an aptly named evolution "from *polis* to *kastron*," the latter becoming a synonym of polis,[13] "lower" towns mentioned in texts continued to be inhabited. In Amorion, excavations demonstrate economic activity in the lower city throughout the Dark Ages before the siege and destruction in 838, and its resumption later on.[14] In such cities, administrative and military functions, now united in the same hands, dominated over those of a regional market and production centre.[15] The new "city" of the Byzantine Middle Ages clearly derived much of its economic activity from the incentive and supportive role of the state to which we will turn below.

The re-establishment of security, which took place piecemeal, slowly in the eight century, more systematically in the ninth and tenth, was important in the growth, in number and size, of cities like Amorion. A number of urban agglomerations were created anew by the state, and older urban sites began to expand, first in Asia Minor, then in Thrace, Macedonia, Thessaly and the Peloponnese.[16] In tenth-century Constantinople, the number of new foundations

---

[13] W. Müller-Wiener, "Von der Polis zum Kastron," *Gymnasium* 93 (1986), pp. 435–75.

[14] C. Lightfoot, "The Survival of Cities in Byzantine Anatolia: The Case of Amorium," *Byzantion* 68 (1998), pp. 56–71 and idem, "Trade and Industry in Byzantine Anatolia – the Evidence from Amorium," *Dumbarton Oaks Papers*, 59 (2006), pp. 173–81. We are grateful to the author for communicating his text to us before publication.

[15] W. Brandes, J. Haldon, "Towns, tax and transformation. State, cities and their hinterlands in the East Roman World, *c.* 500–800," in Brogiolo and Ward-Perkins, *Idea and Ideal of the Town*, pp. 141–72 with reference to the authors' earlier studies. See also J.-M. Spieser, "L'évolution de la ville byzantine de l'époque paléochrétienne à l'iconoclasme," in *Hommes et richesses*, I (Paris, 1989), pp. 97–106 (repr. in an updated version in his *Urban and religious Spaces in Late Antiquity and Early Byzantium* (Aldershot, 2001), pp. 1–15 under the title, "The City in Late Antiquity)."

[16] Dagron, "Urban Economy," *EHB* 2, pp. 398–400 and maps 15 and 20–3 in M. F. Hendy, *Studies in the Byzantine Monetary Economy* (Cambridge, 1985), pp. 74, 90–5, with comment on their distribution pp. 69–85 and 90–100; E. Ivison, "Urban Renewal and Imperial Revival in Byzantium (730–1025)," *Byzantinische Forschungen* 26 (2000), pp. 1–46. See the case studies in *EHB* 2.

and monasteries attracting new residences points to the revival leading to the twelfth-century apogee of the capital.[17]

STATE INTERVENTION AND ECONOMIC DEVELOPMENT

Policies of economic integration and articulation

The Byzantine Empire, unlike most Western European political units in this period, had a powerful and centralized state; the exception to this statement is the state at the time of the strong Carolingians, and even there the resemblances are superficial. This fact had major consequences in the economic realm. The state provided a vast integrating framework not only through the fiscal system but also through the monetary mechanism as well as through the institutions that governed economic relations or created the conditions for them. Furthermore, the state was the largest landlord, and also functioned as a major pole of demand. Finally, the economic ideology held by the state and expressed in administrative action had significant effects on the economy.

The role of the state was not the same throughout the long period examined in this chapter. As elsewhere in the economy, there was a period of restructuring until the late eighth century, when the framework was set for the economy of the Middle period. The economic recovery and expansion which began at about the same time took place within this framework.

Traditionally, scholars have focused on the fiscal role of the state, and for good reason. The Byzantine state was a major motor force in the economy, certainly until some time in the eleventh century. It retained exclusive rights over taxation, from which it drew most of its revenues; that is, it collected, in the form of tax, the part of the added value that did not remain with the producers. It redistributed its revenues primarily in salaries of officials, military and civil, in defense and military campaigns, and in public and infrastructural works. The money thus distributed trickled down the various economic strata, and some eventually reached the producer, who paid taxes. Thus, not only did the government concentrate surplus wealth into its own

[17] P. Magdalino, *Constantinople médiévale* (Paris, 1996) and idem, "Medieval Constantinople," in *EHB* 2, pp. 532–3.

hands, it also was the moving force behind the circulation of money. Its economic role was varied, but since much of the state's possibility of intervention derived from fiscality, one should start there.[18]

The fiscal system of the middle Byzantine period developed over the centuries, starting probably with Herakleios (610–41), and undergoing reforms during the reigns of the Isaurians (717–97) and the economist-emperor Nikephoros I (802–11); it was solidly in place by the ninth century, and began to change again in the middle of the tenth century, the changes becoming evident in the eleventh.[19] At the time of its highest efficiency, the system was designed to bring to the state coffers as much gold as possible, without, at the same time, overly burdening the peasant. More than lip service was paid to the principle of equity that formed the foundation of Byzantine economic ideology in this period.

The base tax, and the most important one, was the land tax, paid by all owners of land; indeed, payment of the tax was itself proof of ownership. Since the early eighth century, perhaps earlier, the tax was estimated on the value of the land each person owned. Land had a fiscal value, established by the financial services: one *modios* (*c*.889 m², somewhat less than 1/10 of a hectare) of first-quality land was reckoned to be worth one gold coin; second-quality land was worth half a gold coin, and third-quality land, essentially pasture land, was worth one third of a coin. Vineyards had considerably higher value. The tax was 1/24 of this fiscal value. When it becomes possible to estimate the proportion of tax on annual cereal production,

[18] As we stated in the Introduction, we do not engage in the discussion on the Byzantine mode of production. We note that although we have different premises from those of John Haldon, the statements made in this chapter regarding the state and the economy are not, in their essence, very different from what may be found in his most recent statements; many differences on specifics remain: J. Haldon, "Production, Distribution and Demand in the Byzantine World ca. 660–840," in I. L. Hansen and Ch. Wickham, *The Long Eighth Century* (Leiden–Boston–Cologne, 2000), pp. 225–64.

[19] The most extensive studies on the fiscal system have been done by N. Oikonomides. Reference is here made only to two major studies of his, *Fiscalité et exemption fiscale à Byzance (IXe–XIe s.)* (Athens, 1996), and "The Role of the Byzantine State in the Economy," *EHB* 3, pp. 972–1058, in both of which the reader will find the earlier bibliography. What follows is largely based on his work, but also on Haldon as well as on C. Zuckerman, "Learning from the Enemy and More: Studies in 'Dark Centuries' Byzantium," *Millennium: Jahrbuch zu Kultur und Geschichte des ersten Jahrtausends n. Chr.*2 (2005), pp. 79–135.

that is found to be approximately 23 per cent.[20] This type of tax system depended on a cadastre, which was brought up to date every thirty years. The village community was an important unit for fiscal purposes: the land of each peasant household was registered, and the total fiscal value formed the basis for estimating the quantity of money owed by the village, which was collectively responsible for its payment.

Peasants paid other taxes as well. A personal tax, originally levied on males, was introduced in the 660s. It subsequently became a household tax (*kapnikon*). In its developed form, it was estimated on the basis of the productive capacity of the household, represented by its head. The *kapnikon* was calculated as 1/24 of the fiscal worth of the peasant.

Other taxes, on domestic animals, bees and so on, were also collected, as well as relatively limited taxes for the administration of the fiscal system. Peasants were subject to state corvées, for defense, road building, bridge construction and fortifications. On the other hand, significant categories enjoyed a limited tax exemption. The most important such category consisted of the peasant households that were responsible for military service, the peasant soldiers who have been credited with the survival and expansion of the Byzantine state. The part of their land which was considered necessary for the discharge of their military obligations was inalienable, and they were relieved of secondary taxes and corvées. Such peasant soldiers may have existed since the late seventh century.[21]

During much of this period, the state insisted on the payment of taxes in cash, and specifically in gold. In 769, the emperor Constantine V asked that the base tax be paid in cash, a measure that resulted in

---

[20] Oikonomides, "The Role," pp. 1154, and below, Chapter IV.

[21] This follows the interpretation of N. Oikonomides, "Middle-Byzantine Provincial Recruits: Salary and Armament," in J. Duffy and J. Peradotto (eds.), *Gonimos: Neoplatonic and Byzantine Studies Presented to Leendert G. Westerink at 75* (Buffalo, N.Y., 1988), pp. 121–36 (reprinted in his *Social and Economic Life in Byzantium* (Aldershot, 2004), art. X); see the different conclusions of J. Haldon, "Military Service, Military Lands and the Status of Soldiers; Current Problems and Interpretations," *DOP* 47 (1993), pp. 1–67, esp. pp. 11–29; he thinks that such lands were not given to soldiers as a general policy until the tenth century; this position was argued much earlier by P. Lemerle, *The Agrarian History of Byzantium from the Origins to the Twelfth Century* (Galway, 1979), pp. 140 ff., based on his "Esquisse pour une histoire agraire de Byzance: les sources et les problèmes," *RH* 219 (1958), pp. 33–74, 254–84; 220 (1958), pp. 43–94; M. Hendy, *Studies*, pp. 634 ff., disagrees.

a glut of agricultural products on the marketplaces and discontent on the part of the farmers. While it is possible, indeed probable, that this reform was not immediately all-inclusive, it is perfectly clear that the tax system was almost entirely monetized by the tenth century.[22] This necessarily brought about a degree of monetization in the country-side. Although monetization that is due to fiscal exigencies is always shallow, it is an important feature of the countryside as well as an important factor in its development. Its importance is indicated by the fact that when the province of Bulgaria, which had been annexed in 1118 and been allowed to pay its taxes in kind, was forced in the 1140s to make the payments in cash, a revolt ensued.[23]

The state also taxed commercial transactions. The tax was called *kommerkion*, a term that appears in the late eighth century, and was, according to later sources, a 10 per cent *ad valorem* tax on transactions at fairs and markets. Merchandise entering Constantinople, a special commercial zone, paid the *kommerkion* at the entry points, at Aby-dos and Hieron.[24] Unfortunately, it is not possible to estimate the importance of the *kommerkion* for state revenues in the period under consideration.

The tax system, as organised by the late eighth century, was super-vised by a competent civil service based in Constantinople, although the registering of the population and the land was done locally, as was the collection of taxes. On the whole, it was well administered in this period. Tax-farming was very limited, tax increases were not excessive, and the administration made an effort to be seen to be fair. These aspects of the system began to change in the middle of the tenth century, when territorial expansion necessitated great expenses; tax-farming with abusive collection, tax increases and arbitrary taxa-tion eroded the system and changed it by the first half of the eleventh century.[25]

---

[22] Haldon argues that both taxes and army pay were chiefly in kind until the mid-ninth century: *Byzantium in the Seventh Century* (Cambridge–New York, 1990), pp. 147 ff., repeated in his "Production," p. 232.

[23] I. Thurn (ed.), *Ioannis Skylitzae Synopsis historiarum* (Berlin–New York, 1973), p. 412 (hereafter, Skylitzes).

[24] On Constantinople as a special economic region, see N. Oikonomides, "The Eco-nomic Region of Constantinople: From Directed Economy to Free Economy and the Role of the Italians," in G. Arnaldi and G. Cavallo (eds.), *Europa medievale e mondo bizantino: contatti effettivi e possibilità di studi comparati* (Rome, 1997), pp. 221–38.

[25] Oikonomidès, *Fiscalité*, pp. 146–7. Cf. below, Chapter IV.

In the period under discussion, the state redistributed a large portion of its revenues through the payment of salaries to civil, military and ecclesiastical officials, through investments in infrastructures and through expenditures for military campaigns or gifts, whether voluntary or forced, to foreign rulers. Salaries were the largest annual expenditure. In part, they were financed through the sale of offices. A number of administrative posts and honorific titles could be purchased, for the lifetime of the holder. This represented a considerable investment on the part of the title holder, especially since he never recovered the capital; he did get an annual salary which amounted to 2.5–3.5 per cent of the original sum, or, in the case of high titles, 5.55–8.33 per cent. But the majority of salaries were pure expenditure on the part of the state. High officials received their salaries from the hand of the emperor, once a year, in gold and silk garments; Liutprand of Cremona has left an unforgettable description of the scene at the palace on Palm Sunday of the year 950. Soldiers were paid in cash only once every four years, when they went on campaign outside their province.

The expenditures involved in non-economic exchange, primarily in gifts and disguised tribute, could be enormous. Those sent to foreign rulers included gold coins, high-quality silks and works of art made of gold, silver and precious stones, as well as luxury manuscripts. Arab sources discuss such gifts in loving detail. The emperor Theophilos (829–42) is said to have sent the caliph al-Mamun a gift of 1,000 kentenaria of gold (100,000 lbs, or 7,200,000 gold coins, a grossly exaggerated figure), while Leo VI (886–912) is reported to have sent to the governor of Azerbaijan and Armenia purple brocade garments, each worth 2,000 dinars, and a bejeweled gold girdle worth 10,000 dinars.[26] Military campaigns, however, were much more expensive. In the tenth century, two campaigns against Muslim-held Crete cost 234,732 and 127,122 gold coins respectively. Diplomacy was much cheaper than war, but the Byzantines were at war for most of the period. In the tenth century these wars, being mostly successful, repaid their expenses through the increase of territory and the influx of booty. When Basil II died in 1025, he is said to have left in the imperial treasury 14.4 million gold coins. This, of

[26] A. E. Laiou, "Exchange and Trade, Seventh–Twelfth Centuries," *EHB* 2, pp. 716–17.

course, represents money taken out of circulation, which is not so
good for the economy.

The Byzantine state was poor in the eighth century and very rich
indeed in the tenth. Its economic role went beyond mere wealth and
was more than fiscal. The state functioned as a force of economic
integration in other ways. In macroeconomic terms, it provided the
framework for the functioning of the economy as a whole, thus
making it possible for us to speak of the *Byzantine* economy, that is,
the economy of a unit that was contained within the borders of the
state. To be sure, all production was local, and distribution could take
place locally or within regions. But the institutional framework was
the same everywhere; and economic integration was a function of
institutions on the one hand and, on the other, of the existence of a
very large administrative center that was also a center of production
and consumption, that is, the capital city, Constantinople. First of
all, the fact that the state retained the monopoly of issuing coinage
and that the coinage it issued was the same throughout the Empire
not only is *prima facie* evidence of the existence of a large economic
sphere, it is also a factor that helps create this sphere. A unique coinage
also reduces the transaction costs of businessmen and merchants, since
it makes irrelevant the costs associated with currency exchange. The
state had a monopoly of issuing legislation which, in theory, was valid
throughout the Empire. Certain modifications must be made to this
statement, to the extent that Constantinople was, in some respects,
an economic unit within a unit, so that special conditions existed: for
example, the guild system such as we know it in Constantinople was
not necessarily the same throughout the Empire, while it appears that
in the tenth century imperial legislation limiting the acquisition of
land by the "powerful" did not apply to land within the city limits.[27]
Still, this legislation was valid everywhere else, and purely economic
legislation, such as that on interest rates, for example, was applicable
universally.

State legislation regarding exports served to create a distinction
between one region, the Byzantine Empire, on the one hand, and,
on the other, the foreign or international market. While there were no
import prohibitions, a number of prohibitions applied to exports. The
category of goods called "forbidden" (*kekolymena*) included important alimentary products (cereals, salt, wine, olive oil, fish sauce),

---

[27] Oikonomides, "The Economic Region," 224.

precious metals, especially gold, strategic commodities like iron and arms, and silks of very high quality. The prohibitions were motivated not only by economic reasons but also by political ones, but they still had economic effects. Thus, while the legislation was sometimes breached, and began to become attenuated by the early tenth century, it nevertheless signals the concept, as well as the reality, of a domestic market, where goods traveled freely, as opposed to the foreign market which was subject to controls. In that sense, the state created a "national" market.

Within the Empire, the state also provided some of the material conditions necessary for economic development. Recent scholarship on Western Europe has stressed the role of security in the demographic increase and the resettlement of the countryside. This phenomenon is well studied in Latium, where the work of Pierre Toubert has shown how the *incastellamento* of the countryside, in the period 920–1030, was a major factor of the restructuring of agricultural activity.[28] There, it was private warlords who carried it out. In the Byzantine Empire, on the other hand, it was the state that slowly restored conditions of security, by creating, from the eighth century onwards, not fortified villages as in Western Europe but rather refuges and networks of fortified towns, most of which were walled in the course of the ninth century.[29] The cities and towns, where the army was stationed and fiscal services were located, provided an important focus for the countryside. A perfect example, although an extreme one, is Bithynia, important because it was situated across the straits from Constantinople. Because of the interest of the state, Bithynia did not suffer as much as the rest of the Empire from the economic downturn of the seventh and eighth centuries, while recovery here

---

[28] P. Toubert, *Les structures du Latium médiéval*, 2 vols. (Rome, 1973); cf. the important observations of Chris Wickham, "L'incastellamento e i suoi destini, undici anni dopo il *Latium* di P. Toubert," in *Castrum 2. Structures de l'habitat et occupation du sol dans les pays méditerranéens: les méthodes et l'apport de l'archéologie extensive* (Actes de la rencontre de Paris, 12–15 Novembre 1984), ed. G. Noyé (Rome-Madrid, 1998), pp. 411–20, regarding the use of the term *incastellamento* for places outside Italy.

[29] See A. E. Laiou, "The Byzantine Village (5th–14th Century)," in Lefort et al., *Villages*, pp. 41–2, based on J. Lefort, "Habitats fortifiés en Macédoine orientale au Moyen Âge," in *Castrum I. Habitats fortifiés et organisation de l'espace en Méditerranée médiévale*, ed. A Bazzana, P. Guichard and J.-M. Poisson (Lyons, 1983), pp. 99–103 and J. Lefort and J.-M. Martin, "Fortifications et pouvoirs en Méditerranée (Xe–XIIe siècle), *Castrum* 1, pp. 197–207.

started early, and is clearly visible already in the early ninth century. As the population grew, and state needs with it, local authorities intervened to lower the water level of the lake of Nicaea, in order to make more lands available for cultivation.[30] Amorion, too, where important excavations are currently taking place, emerges not only as a city with a major military role, but also as a center of artisanal and commercial activity.

Constantinople itself should be seen as part of the state's role in the economy. It was a *megalopolis*, with all that implies, because it was the center of government. At the time of economic retraction, it remained relatively well populated, in part because of concerted government action. Constantinople exercised a major demand role, and demand was variegated. The state, and the civil service that it engendered and which served it, created demand for services and luxury goods, feeding the industries of the capital and generating trade: the emperor himself purchased Syrian silks in the marketplace of Constantinople. Where the industries of art are concerned,[31] the pull of Constantinople was such that the provinces followed its styles and probably imported its artisans. Whether that concentrated demand delayed the development of other cities is debatable; historians take it as axiomatic that it did, but the experience of other economies shows that such is not necessarily the case.

Constantinople, with its large population, was also a great center of consumer demand for alimentary products and raw materials. In the case of alimentary products, the state had a particular interest in keeping the population adequately supplied at accessible prices, for the fear of rioting was never far away. Hence the protection of the consumer through the regulation, for example, of a maximum profit on bread, items sold in general stores, and fish. Hence also the fact of a limited but real interference of the state in the grain trade. The available evidence is ambiguous. One supposes that in the eighth century the grain trade was regulated, although not entirely. In the ninth–tenth centuries, there seems to be a mixture of government-regulated and private ships carrying grain to Constantinople. But the grain trade was not organized by the state, nor was the price of grain

---

[30] Bithynia is now a well-studied province, thanks to the collective volume edited by B. Geyer and J. Lefort, *La Bithynie au Moyen Âge* (Paris, 2003). References to the statements made above will be found on pp. 173–4, 318 ff., 323, 329–30, 392 ff., 408, 487, 538–45.

[31] For the term, see A. Cutler, "The Industries of Art," *EHB* 2, pp. 555–87.

entering Constantinople regulated, which is why there were short-term fluctuations in its price. The state did intervene by ensuring supplies: for example, requiring the owners of grain ships in Bithynia to transport, once a year, grain for the imperial treasury. In times of crisis, when there was scarcity of grain, the emperors would have grain brought in from other parts of the Empire. And they would certainly open the imperial warehouses to distribute grain and keep the price down. This, as well as imperial legislation which aimed at preventing stockpiling and profiteering, doubtless had an influence on price formation. But it is important to note that as far as we know this interference was limited to Constantinople, and did not constitute true regulation.[32]

Apart from the fact that it created the institutional framework for economic activity, the state also intervened to shape economic activity in Constantinople and to give a particular form to economic development throughout the Empire. In ninth- and tenth-century Constantinople, this was done through the regulation of profits on some transactions. More generally, there was an effort to impede the accumulation of resources in the hands of individuals. Both of these subjects are much debated and complex, for they involve political, economic and ideological factors.

In Constantinople, according to the *Book of the Prefect*, the state imposed maximum profit rates on the sale of some commodities or on some economic activities: the retail sale of food, the profit on the resale of Bulgarian commodities, the profit realized by rich silk merchants who resold to poorer artisans are specifically mentioned, but it is possible that maximum profits were imposed on other transactions as well. The government certainly did not fix prices, since there is no evidence that the price of commodities entering Constantinople was in any way controlled. Fixing the profit margins, however, apart from its impact on the final price, also affects the way merchants conduct their business: since they cannot maximize profits by buying cheap and selling dear, they have to maximize turnover and keep their capital costs low. Their response to market fluctuations may

---

[32] For Bithynia, see M. Gerolymatou, "Le commerce, VIIe–XVe siècle," in Geyer and Lefort, *La Bithynie*, p. 487; for the rest, see Laiou, "Exchange and Trade," *EHB* 2, pp. 719–21; G. C. Maniatis, "The Wheat Market in Byzantium, 900–1200; Organization, Marketing and Pricing Strategies," *BS* 62 (2004), pp. 103–24, must be used with caution.

be dampened. There is no evidence of regulated profit rates outside Constantinople, nor do they seem to apply after the tenth century.

Government efforts to prevent the accumulation of resources and economic activities in the hands of individuals is, by contrast, visible everywhere. In Constantinople, they may be seen in the guild structure. The activities of guilds were overseen by the government, which also issued important regulations. Among other things, the regulations strictly delineated the activities of each guild to ensure that none could encroach upon the activities of another. Thus, both vertical and horizontal integration were impossible, and so was the creation of large enterprises that might control the manufacturing or trade of particular commodities.[33] The government did not prevent competition among members of the same guild to capture a larger market share; but regulations made it difficult for anyone to corner the market.[34]

Similar is the tenor of the legislation of a number of tenth-century emperors regarding the sale or donation of land by the "poor" or "weak" to the "powerful", who were military, civil or ecclesiastical officials, or monasteries, and thus could exercise both economic and non-economic pressure on peasants. The legislation was triggered by massive land sales after the great famine of 927–8. In a Novel issued in 934, the emperor Romanos I Lekapenos (920–44) tried to reverse the situation that had resulted from the crisis and to restore, to the degree possible, the earlier patterns of land ownership. The Novel envisaged various scenarios, depending on the purchase price of the land. The most interesting of these is the case in which the peasant had been forced by need to sell at a price lower than half the "just value" of the land. In such a case, the buyer lost the land, with no compensation at all for the price he had paid. This is a highly expansive interpretation of the law regarding the "excessive damage" (*laesio enormis*) done to the seller who sells, albeit with his full knowledge and uncoerced consent, at an excessively low price, that

---

[33] G. Dagron, "The Urban Economy, Seventh–Twelfth Centuries," *EHB* 2, pp. 413–14.

[34] On the question of government regulation of the guilds see now the various articles by G. C. Maniatis, especially his "Organization, Market Structure, and Modus Operandi of the Private Silk Industry in Tenth-Century Byzantium," *DOP* 53 (1999), pp. 263–332, and "The Domain of Private Guilds in the Byzantine Economy, Tenth to Fifteenth Centuries," *DOP* 55 (2001), pp. 339–69. He provides a useful antidote to earlier ideas of the very close regulation of the Byzantine economy by the state, but goes too far in claiming that the tenth-century state aimed to safeguard free competition.

price being less than half the just price. The Emperor's motives were undoubtedly fiscal in the first instance. It remains the case that this legislation and that of subsequent emperors, if put into full effect, would have delayed a process whose origins were economic. In a period of rising population, good, productive land was at a premium, and wealthy or powerful individuals sought to accumulate it. Imperial legislation went against this trend. There are some cases in which it is known to have been implemented. Ultimately, it was unsuccessful, since the economic reasons for pressure on land continued to exist and even increased.[35]

The impact of the state on the economy was much greater in the early part of this period. In fact, the state had virtually no competitors in the eighth century. As a landlord, it was by far the largest; the aristocracy does not appear as a competitor until the ninth century. Although the property of the state kept increasing through the first part of the eleventh century, as a proportion of total landholding it was very significant in the eighth century as well. It is likely, though unattested, that the products of imperial estates were marketed by state agents. And a considerable part of the economy, including the army, was, according to some interpretations, outside the market system altogether.[36] The little that is known about this early period, when the economy was still in deep decline, indicates that, although individual, professional merchants and sea-captains did, indeed, exist, the state was much more important than the marketplace as an economic force. Individual wealth, such as it was, derived from state office. Monetary circulation was limited, especially in the provinces, and thus the role of money as a factor of articulation was correspondingly lower. All of these conditions changed after the late eighth or early ninth century, as the recovery of the economy began.

The state, then, played an important and complex role in the economy of this period. It did not, however, wield the deadly hand of monopoly and asphyxiating control with which it has been credited. It provided the framework, institutional and to some degree

[35] On this, see A. E. Laiou, "E diamorfose tes times tes ges sto Vyzantio," in *Vyzantio, kratos kai koinonia: Mneme Nikou Oikonomide* (Athens, 2003), pp. 339–48, and Laiou, "Koinonike dikaiosyne: to synallatesthai kai to euemerein sto Vyzantio," *Praktika tes Akademias Athenon*, 74 (1999), pp. 103–30.

[36] This is the interpretation of J. Haldon, *Byzantium in the Seventh Century*, pp. 147 ff., 223 ff., and his "Production," p. 232. Oikonomides, "Middle Byzantine Provincial Recruits," assumes the participation of soldiers in the market economy where, according to him, they bought their equipment.

moral, in which economic activities took place, it controlled certain aspects of production, and collectively it was by far the most weighty consumer. In other words, it put in place all the material and institutional conditions in which the economy could function. Within that framework, and with the constraints already discussed, market forces operated. The land market was active. Prices were nowhere controlled. The peasants selling their wares to pay their taxes received whatever price the market would bear, and the same is true for the artisans, at least where no ceilings on profits existed. Merchants circulated with a large degree of freedom. One of the two most important commodities in the medieval economy, grain, seems to have been marketed freely after an early period, in the seventh century, when state officials probably played an important role. The other important commodity, silk, was regulated in terms of the process of production, but, except for imperial silks, its sale was in the hands of individuals. Finally, imperial decisions often depended for their implementation on acceptance by collective actors, that is, on the market. That is to say, the state had created the conditions that were necessary in a large domestic market; the extent and efficiency of the market depended on economic conditions: effective demand and the response of the productive forces. One example will serve by way of illustration. In the middle of the tenth century, the Emperor Nikephoros II (963–9) issued a light-weight gold coin, the *tetarteron*, weighing 22 instead of 24 carats, and issued a law ordering that it be preferred, in transactions, to the older and heavier coin. For the Fisc to profit from this measure, he depended on two mechanisms. The first was that of taxation, for he insisted that the taxes be paid in the old coin. The other, however, was the marketplace. He expected that commercial transactions would be effected using his coin only, and that he would profit from the resulting *seignorage*. His measure may well have been due to fiscal and military reasons, as has been argued. But for its implementation it depended on the market, which behaved in ways unexpected perhaps by the emperor but fully in accordance with economic laws. The merchants passed the cost on to the consumer by raising prices, and thus the measure had inflationary results.[37] Thus,

---

[37] For this, see Zonaras, M. L. Dindorf and M. Buettner-Wobst (eds.), *Epitome historiarum*, 6 vols. (Leipzig, 1868–97), vol. 3, p. 507; M. Hendy, *Studies*, p. 507; H. Ahrweiler, "Nouvelle hypothèse sur le tétartèron d'or et la politique monétaire de Nicéphore Phocas," *ZRVI* 8.1 (1963), pp. 1–9 (=Ahrweiler, *Études sur les structures administratives et sociales de Byzance* (London, 1971), art. III).

the state did, in specific matters, exercise strong influence, but did not truly control the marketplace, where market forces operated.

Ideology

The system described here was based on a specific ideological base. Ideology can become a factor of production, and it was so in Byzantium. Economic ideology, if one sets aside the concept that considers all economic activity unnecessary because what matters is the Kingdom of Heaven, revolves around the rich and multifaceted idea of justice in exchange. All medieval European societies were profoundly concerned with justice; justice in exchange is a concept that belongs to the heirs of Aristotle. It was partly incorporated in Roman law, and was certainly adopted by the fourth-century Greek Fathers of the Church, notably, Saint Basil of Caesarea, who defined justice as "distributing [to each] what is equitable." When speaking of distributive and corrective justice, Aristotelian concepts both, he also wrote of the "judge," whose duty was to restore equality between those who have much and those who have little, by giving to one what he takes away from another.[38] Until some time in the twelfth century, ideology was based on the implicit concept that the economy is a zero-sum game, where resources can only be redistributed. It is only in Aristotelian and legal commentaries of the twelfth century that the possibility of creating value through the investment of capital appears with any clarity, in advance of similar developments in Western Europe. At the time of the profound crisis that followed the Slavic invasions and Arab conquests, the state assumed the role of the Aristotelian "judge," and until the late tenth century concepts of justice are inextricably connected with equity in the specific definition of protection of the poor and weak members of society. Like the Aristotelian judge, who acted as living justice (*dikaion empsychon*), the state aimed at correcting the inequalities that resulted from exchange.[39] The Prologue to the *Ecloga*, the law code issued by the first two Isaurian emperors in 741, copies almost verbatim the words of Saint Basil regarding the duty to redistribute resources according to justice and equity. The Preface to the *Book of the Prefect*, issued in its surviving form in 912, states that God had inscribed the Law on the tablets so that "the more powerful should not injure the less powerful, but that everything should be weighed by a just measure," and that the ordinances contained in this

---

[38] PG 31, 401–5.   [39] See Laiou, "Koinonike dikaiosyne," pp. 105–11.

regulatory document had the same purpose.[40] The land legislation of the tenth century expressed similar ideas. These were not merely pious sentiments. The regulations regarding guilds and the land legislation are two notable examples of economic measures where ideas of equity are important, even though the measures also served fiscal or other purposes.

Ideas of equity also underlay the concepts of just price, just value, and just profits, which were given legal or regulatory expression. Here, there was a constant tension between the moral idea of corrective justice on the one hand and, on the other, the freedom of transactions carried out between competent persons, and the resulting sanctity of contracts, established by Roman law. These principles, which returned in full with the *Basilics* in the early tenth century, reflect the idea that justice in exchange derives from free negotiation, and that price formation results from this process. In the period up to the tenth century, the tension was partially resolved through an emphasis on the just price and just profit. The just price was not legislated: even the fiscal price of land was established through a mixture of fiscal estimation and the "customs of the area," that is, the market value of the land. Just profit, however, meaning the margin which could be reached through negotiation, was another matter. Already in the early ninth century, the patriarch Nikephoros of Constantinople had stated that the profit of the merchant was "just" if it did not exceed 10 per cent. The regulations in the *Book of the Prefect* spoke of "unreasonable profit," and established "just profit" margins for a number of commodities and transactions; it is through this means that the state carried out its role of issuing corrective justice. Thus the final price, at least in Constantinople, was formed through a mixture of market and moral principles. Furthermore, the tenth century saw an extremely expansive interpretation of the idea of *laesio enormis*, a clear example of corrective economic justice. Not only was it extended far beyond the original legislation in the case of land sold to the powerful by the "poor," it was also implemented in the case of contracts in the building trade, where all contracts in which

---

[40] *Ecloga*, 164; J. Koder (ed.), *Das Eparchenbuch Leons des Weisen* (Vienna, 1991), pp. 72 (hereafter, *EB*). Much of this section depends on Laiou, "Koinonike dikaiosyne." G. C. Maniatis' "Operationalization of the Concept of Just Price in the Byzantine Legal, Economic and Political System," *Byzantion* 71 (2001), pp. 131–93, lacks historical depth; among other things, it misinterprets a law of Michael VIII: p. 174 and n. 108.

the builder agreed to a wage below the just wage were invalid; there is a clause in the relevant ordinance that suggests that the same held true for all commercial transactions, which would be a truly immense extension of the original legislation.[41] Similarly, interest rates, that is, the profit of capital (a definition that does not seem to have existed before the twelfth century), incorporated a non-economic concept, since social position was a factor in the establishment of the rates: the aristocracy was obliged to ask for much lower rates than anyone else. For the concept of just price (or just profit) to have any meaning at all, a market and free negotiation must exist. What happened in the period through the tenth century is that the state placed limits on the results of free negotiation. It is a system static in conception, in which individual economic action is limited by the needs of society as a whole. All of this was to change in the course of the twelfth century and after, although the ideas underlying it were too powerful ever to disappear.

PRIMARY PRODUCTION

Natural resources: loss and recovery

In Byzantium, as in Western Europe at that time, land was available at a constant marginal cost, the cost of clearing land. It is only in the thirteenth century that diminishing returns to labor employed in agriculture manifested themselves. But the territorial losses incurred by Byzantium in the seventh century had entailed the loss of many other natural resources, including an essential and important one: *mines*, notably in the northern Balkans, Armenia and the Taurus Range. But the Empire fought hard for them and must have regained control of the Macedonian mines in the ninth century, of the Cappadocian and Taurus ones in the tenth, and kept control during most of the period of those in Bithynia, the Pontus, Calabria, and possibly Cyprus. Although we have little definite information on the chronology of mine exploitation (there is some archaeological evidence, e.g. at Sulucadere in the Bolkardag, of mining in the ninth century),[42] metallurgical analyses of Byzantine coins prove that some quantity of newly mined gold and silver was available for striking coins and

---

[41] *EB*, 22.3.   [42] see above, Chapter II, p. 30, and n. 16.

renewing the monetary stock. Whether this source of new metal was inside or outside Byzantine territory or a combination of both, is unfortunately not determined.[43] Owing to impoverishment, the smaller scale of buildings and the decline of demand for luxury materials, marble was apparently no more quarried in our period and was mainly reused.[44]

Timber remained abundant in many regions: Calabria, Macedonia, Bithynia, the Pontus, Crete, Cyprus, south-eastern Anatolia. Oak for the framework of ships and pine resin for caulking, together with pitch derived from heated resins or tar were valuable assets for the Byzantine fleet which developed from the late seventh century onward (*Karavisianoi* and later thematic fleets like the Kibyrrhaeots).[45] On the other hand, wood was already scarce in the lands of the Caliphate, and the Arabs often raided the Lycian coast in order to avail themselves of shipbuilding material; wood hunger was certainly a compelling reason for the capture of Crete by the Arabs in the 820s. This was a welcome gain for the Arabs, added to the resources available from the ongoing condominium in Cyprus (late seventh–late tenth). But the territorial gains of the tenth century and recovery of the big islands (Crete in 961, Cyprus in 965) restored completely the Byzantine edge in this matter.

Agriculture: tools, techniques and products[46]

Rural population and production remained the most important sector of the economy and its share was probably greater than in the sixth century, at least in the eighth and ninth centuries, before slowly returning in the tenth–eleventh centuries to a ratio between primary and secondary production roughly similar to that of the sixth century.

The main tools, techniques of tilling, and crops were by and large the same as previously, sericulture excepted, and the most important change lay in the distribution of land, as will be seen below. The

---

[43] C. Morrisson et al., *L'or monnayé*, I: *De Rome à Byzance* (Paris, 1985); A. A. Gordus, D. M. Metcalf, "The Alloy of the Byzantine Miliaresion and The Question of the Reminting of Islamic Silver," *Hamburger Beiträge zur Numismatik* 24/26 (1970/72) [1977], pp. 9–36.

[44] J.-P. Sodini, "La sculpture médio-byzantine: le marbre en ersatz tel qu'en lui-même," in G. Dagron and C. Mango (eds.), *Constantinople and its Hinterland* (Aldershot, 1995), p. 289.

[45] Dunn (as above, n. 9), pp. 258–61.

[46] Lefort, "The Rural Economy," *EHB*, pp. 231–310 provides the best account.

Farmer's Law, probably "a practical guide for the benefit of the coun-try judge" dating to the early eighth century,[47] records the normal *tools* of a peasant: spade, mattock, pruning-knife, sickle and axe; this list is indirectly confirmed by the chronicles which mention the use of such tools as weapons by peasants to defend themselves, and the tools are directly attested in the growing material from rural exca-vations.[48] *Production techniques* are mainly known from indications in the *Geoponika*, compiled in the tenth century, combined with scat-tered later mentions in monastic and other documents. A two-year rotation cycle was partly applied and fields were given over to graz-ing (and consequently manuring) after harvest and before ploughing. Sowing legumes on part of the fallow land increased its fertility. The same result was also obtained by the well-known practice of select-ing seeds. *Yields*, of course, varied greatly according to the quality of land and climate. In modern Greece, yields per hectare varied from *c*.5 quintals in Chios to 9.8 in Macedonia and 11.5 in Arcadia. In the early twelfth century, in the Macedonian village of Radolibos, documents suggest a minimum cereal yield of 5.1:1, that is around 5.3 quintals per hectare.[49]

Better climatic conditions from the ninth century onward may have fostered *agricultural production*; it benefited also from increased security and new settlement. Cereals were cultivated in Thessaly, Thrace, Macedonia, Bithynia and the Pontus,[50] which accounts for the emperors' constant interest in the repopulation of these areas. These areas hold a dominant position in the distribution of preserved seals of "*annonarioi*" or "*horreiarioi*," officials in charge of imperial granaries.[51] No information is available on the relative ratio of wheat

---

[47] W. Ashburner, "The Farmer's Law," *Journal of Hellenic Studies* 30 (1910), pp. 85–108 (Greek text) and 32 (1912), 68–95 (English translation and commentary, to be used with caution); P. Lemerle, *The Agrarian History of Byzantium* (Galway, 1979), pp. 27–67.

[48] A. Harvey, *Economic Expansion in the Byzantine Empire, 900–1200* (Cambridge, 1989), 123–5; M. Kaplan, *Les hommes et la terre à Byzance du VIe au XIe siècle* (Paris, 1992), pp. 46–52; B. Pitarakis, "Témoignage des objets métalliques dans le village médiéval," in Lefort et al., *Villages*, pp. 247–65.

[49] See the accounts in Kaplan, *Les hommes et la terre*, pp. 80–4; Harvey, *Economic Expansion*, p. 139 and Lefort in *EHB* 1, p. 259.

[50] J. Teall, "The Grain Supply of the Byzantine Empire, 330–1025," *DOP* 13 (1959), pp. 89–139, at pp. 117–28; Hendy, *Studies*, pp. 46, 49–50.

[51] J.-C. Cheynet, "Un aspect du ravitaillement de Constantinople aux Xe/XIe siècles d'après quelques sceaux d'hôrreairioi," *Studies in Byzantine Sigillography* 6 (1999), pp. 1–26, map, p. 10.

to barley; rye and oats were apparently introduced or reintroduced later. The cultivation of legumes acquired great importance owing to their efficacy in restoring the soil and their role in everyday diet, especially that of the poor in the cities. Dry vegetables (*ospria*: lentils, peas, vetches, etc.) were cultivated in all peasant gardens according to saints' lives of the period and later monastic documents. In the suburbs, and even in urban gardens, they coexisted with a great variety of fresh vegetables.[52]

The *olive* tree was cultivated in most coastal areas from southern Italy to the Peloponnese, the islands and Bithynia or Lydia.[53] Vines must have remained ubiquitous wherever mild winters and altitude permitted their cultivation. But the quality of the wines certainly declined and only in the tenth century do the names of a few vintages reappear, which implies wider distribution than the local trade of ordinary wines. The variety of other *fruit* – species adapted to temperate Continental or Mediterranean climates: apple, pear, plum, quince, cherry, peach, walnut, chestnut, pomegranate, almond, pistachio etc. – was a specificity of Byzantine (and Islamic) agriculture compared to the West. Not only did fruit play a part in the peasant's diet; it was also a source of profit for farmers near great or smaller cities or for areas that could export them as dry fruits.[54] In Macedonian and southern Italian forests, the chestnut was cultivated or simply collected in the ninth century.[55]

Industrial textile plants like hemp and flax, essential for the rigging and sails of ships, are documented in Thessaly, Macedonia, Thrace, and Anatolia.[56] Red *dyes* could be extracted from the kermes and cochineal, parasites on oak trees, madder could be mixed with indigo to fake expensive murex purple, sumach (*rhus*) was a source of yellow, while various leaves, bark, acorn-cups and roots would serve for tanning and dyeing leather.[57] The *mulberry*, whose leaves feed silkworms,

---

[52] J. Koder, "Fresh Vegetables for the Capital," in Dagron and Mango, *Constantinople and its Hinterland*, pp. 49–56.

[53] Hendy, *Studies*, pp. 49–57; Harvey, *Economic Expansion*, pp. 145–7.

[54] Kaplan; *Les hommes et la terre*, p. 36.

[55] G. Noyé, "Byzance et Italie méridionale," in L. Brubaker (ed.), *Byzantium in the Ninth Century: Dead or Alive?* (Aldershot, 1998), pp. 229–43; Eadem, "Économie et société dans la Calabre byzantine," *Journal des Savants* (juillet–décembre 2000), pp. 209–80.

[56] Teall, "Grain Supply," pp. 117–28; Hendy, *Studies*, pp. 46, 49–50.

[57] Dunn (as above, n. 9), pp. 256, 279–95. There is no general study of Byzantine dyes. On natural dyes and medieval pigments, see now B. Guineau, *Glossaire des*

could grow in many regions and must have spread in this period: N. Oikonomides plotted the diffusion of sericulture by connecting it to the distribution of seals of *kommerkiarioi* into Anatolia in the seventh and eighth centuries.[58] From the ninth century onward reference to the Peloponnese as 'Morea' (the land of mulberries) and the well-known report on the *sidonia* (silk cloth) and other precious textiles given to Basil I in 880 by the widow Danelis, a great landowner with possessions near Patras,[59] point to mulberry cultivation being widespread in the region. The importance of a well- and apparently long-established silk industry in tenth-century Constantinople speaks for the availability of indigenous, Byzantine raw silk. When the transformation of the cocoon into silk yarn was undertaken in the producing regions it constituted a labor-intensive and profit-yielding activity. But the presence of Syrian merchants selling raw silk in Constantinople in the tenth century points to a shortage of material in Byzantium.[60]

On untilled waste land as well as on fertile meadows *cattle raising* was widely practiced on a varying scale. Every village needed to raise a few oxen for ploughing or transport, as well as donkeys, sheep for wool and meat, and other animals, such as cows, goats, pigs, and poultry for provisioning and trading. Bithynia is known to have provided Constantinople with animals for slaughter in the tenth century.[61] On great domains such as those in Cappadocia, the imperial stud farms raised horses of all types, from expensive war or riding horses to packhorses and other pack animals (mules and the like) for the imperial baggage train which was described in the treatises on

---

matériaux de la couleur et des termes employés dans les recettes de couleurs anciennes (Turnhout, 2005); for a short introduction, B. Guineau and F. Delamare, *Colors: The Story of Dyes and Pigments* (New York, 2000).

[58] N. Oikonomides, "Silk Trade and Production in Byzantium from the Sixth to the Ninth Century: the Seals of Kommerkiarioi," *DOP* 40 (1986), pp. 33–53, reprinted in his *Social and Economic Life*, art. VIII.

[59] *Vita Basilii*, V.74.

[60] D. Jacoby, "Silk in Western Byzantium before the Fourth Crusade," *BZ* (1991/2), pp. 452–500 (= idem, *Trade, Commodities and Shipping in the Medieval Mediterranean* (Aldershot, 1997), art. VII), p. 454. On the process and its complex operations, see Muthesius, *EHB* I, p. 150. Possible shortage: J. Shepard, 'Silks, Skills and Opportunities in Byzantium: Some Reflexions,' *BMGS* 21 (1997), pp. 246–57 (stimulating review article of Muthesius' studies).

[61] *EB*, chs. 15, 16 and other texts assembled in Geyer and Lefort, *La Bithynie*, pp. 75 f.

imperial expeditions.[62] But the organization of these stud farms is
not known. In spite of its exaggerations, the *Life of Philaretos* hints
at the importance of herds on a big private estate of the late eighth
century; the saint is supposed to have owned 600 cows, 200 oxen,
800 horses, 80 mules and packhorses and 12,000 sheep.[63] Philaretos'
domain, a possible forerunner of many other aristocratic estates in
tenth-century Anatolia, leads us to consider the relationship between
villages and estates in the rural economy of this period.

Landlords and peasants: village (chorion) *versus estate* (proasteion)

The eighth and ninth centuries and part of the tenth are generally
described as dominated by village communities consisting of peasant
landowners, who were collectively responsible for paying taxes to the
state.[64] It is the fiscal role that primarily defines the Byzantine rural
community. In terms of settlement, these were grouped habitations,
characteristic of Mediterranean landscapes to the twentieth century,
and certainly constituted the dominant form of both settlement and
land use. Only from the late tenth century onward did the creation of
many hamlets on their outskirts modify this pattern. The functioning
of the early medieval village community (*chorion*) is described in the
Farmer's Law.[65] The status of the peasant (*georgos*) had improved over
that of the *colonus*, certainly because of the scarcity of manpower:
he could move and sell his products freely, and owned or possessed
land which he could alienate or exchange with no restrictions. The
availability of land explains the fact that uncultivated land, whether
long deserted or recently abandoned, could be either put to common
use, or divided among the members of the village community. The
law alludes specifically to land clearance. However, social relations
between the members of the village were less pacific and egalitar-
ian than some scholars want them to be. A few slaves (*douloi*) were
employed as shepherds and are mentioned later on estates, but the

---

[62] Haldon, *Three Treatises*, pp. 118–19; idem, *Warfare, State and Society in the Byzantine World 565–1204* (London, 1999).

[63] M. H. Fourmy and M. Leroy (eds.), "La vie de saint Philarète," *Byzantion* 9 (1934), pp. 113–15.

[64] See p. 51.

[65] Ashburner, "The Farmer's Law"; Lemerle, *Agrarian History*, pp. 27–67; Harvey, *Expansion*, pp. 15–19; Laiou, in Lefort et al., *Villages*, pp. 36–9.

sources do not reveal any more of their role.[66] Peasants would also leave the village and its fiscal obligations and go elsewhere.[67] Some are mentioned as working a lessor's (*chorodotes*) land on a share-cropping (*morte*) basis of 1/10.[68] This ratio apparently implies that the lessee met the fiscal obligations. But it is not certain that this 1/10 rate always applied and later contracts show a higher figure of 1/4 in the eleventh century.[69] One may ask whether this could be due to the demographic increase and to a less favourable situation of rural manpower in the later period.[70]

The estate does not feature in the *Farmer's Law* but had by no means disappeared. In the eighth and ninth centuries the state and the Church were already maintaining or developing their property: Nikephoros I restored to the imperial *kouratoreia* the management of lands he had confiscated from religious institutions richly endowed by Irene.[71] The correspondance of Ignatios the Deacon shows the economic power of the metropolitan see of Nicaea in the 820s, its dependent peasants (*paroikoi*), its harvests that had to be protected from the claims of the authorities of the Opsikion, and the relationship of the nearby metropolitan see of Nicomedia with the imperial domains (*kouratoreia*). At the same time, in the ninth century, the romanced life of Saint Philaretos can be taken as offering an example of extended private property and exploitation on the Anatolian plateau. Even if it is exaggerated, the mention of his original wealth in Paphlagonia (48 estates, large and irrigated, numerous slaves, and immense herds)[72] must have conveyed some impression of reality to the contemporary audience. Progressively, provincial military commanders were able to accumulate land, specially in frontier or insecure zones. Great military families already held large estates in the East: the Maleïnoi, Argyroi and Phokades in Cappadocia, the Skleroi near Melitene, the Doukai in Paphlagonia, the Melissenoi near Dorylaion.[73] That the trend was a general one is confirmed by the tenth-century imperial legislation

---

[66] Lefort, *EHB* I, pp. 241–2.   [67] Kaplan, *Les hommes et la terre*, pp. 383–6.

[68] *Ibid.*, p. 262 and cf. idem, "Quelques remarques sur la vie rurale à Byzance d'après la correspondance d'Ignace le Diacre," in Kontoura-Galake (ed.), *Dark Centuries*, pp. 365–76.

[69] Lefort, "Rural Economy," in *EHB* I, pp. 306–7.   [70] See Chapter IV.

[71] Theophanes, ed. De Boor, I, pp. 486–7; C. Mango and R. Scott, *The Chronicle of Theophanes Confessor* (Oxford, 1997), pp. 668–70.

[72] Above, n. 63.

[73] See J.-C. Cheynet, *Pouvoir et contestations à Byzance* (Paris, 1990), pp. 207–37.

limiting the acquisition of land by the "powerful."[74] This accelerated
in the next century as will be seen in Chapter IV, where we discuss
the economic implications of the shift to estates from the landowning, tax-paying peasant who was prevalent till some time in the tenth
century.

SECONDARY PRODUCTION

As opposed to most of Western Europe in the same period,[75] secondary production in eighth–tenth-century Byzantium was, in our
opinion, predominantly urban and will be examined in this context. There is virtually no evidence that production might form part
of a domanial economy.[76] This is not to say that villages, estates
and the countryside were entirely devoid of specialized craftsmen,
notably blacksmiths or coppersmiths, indispensable for mending tools
or shoeing animals, or potters making coarse ceramic for everyday use
in storage,[77] cooking, eating and lighting,[78] but this activity did not
reach the importance it attained in the later period. And, as always,
peasants would build or maintain their houses themselves while their
wives would spin, weave and sew clothes, make simple pots or tan
the skins of slaughtered animals.[79]

[74] Lefort, *EHB* I, pp. 286–7. However, Cheynet ("L'aristocratic byzantine (VIIIe–
   XIIIe siècle)," *Journal des Savants* [July–Dec. 2000], 281–322), referring to the novel
   of 996 (E. McGeer, *The Land Legislation of the Macedonian Emperors: Translation
   and Commentary* (Toronto, 2000), pp. 112, 117), considers this legislation to have
   been partly inspired by the need to check the increasing power of the Anatolian
   aristocracy and their menacing rebellions.

[75] At least in Carolingian and post-Carolingian period, see A. Verhulst, *The Carolingian Economy* (Cambridge, 2002), pp. 72 f.

[76] Characteristically, such evidence is adduced by Harvey only for the Peloponnese
   in the ninth century (the case of textile production on the vast estates of the
   widow Danelis), and in the monastic community of Mt Athos. He adds that as
   the urban economy expanded, production became concentrated in the cities and
   towns: *Expansion*, p. 235.

[77] Buried *pithoi* are characteristic of excavated Byzantine villages (Bouras, "Aspects
   of the Byzantine City," p. 522; Lightfoot, "Evidence from Amorium," (see
   n. 14)); for an illustration of *pithoi* in the Boeotian village of Panakton, see the
   front cover of Lefort et al., *Villages*.

[78] Rašev et al. in Lefort et al., *Villages*, pp. 360; Vroom, *After Antiquity*. On coarse
   ceramics, see C. Bakirtzis, *Vyzantina Tsoukalolagena* (Athens, 1989).

[79] On the indoor activities of Byzantine women, see M. Fulghum Heintz, "The Art
   and Craft of Earning a Living," in I. Kalavrezou (ed.), *Byzantine Women and their
   World* (Cambridge, Mass. 2003), pp. 139–47.

Following the transformation of the medieval Byzantine cities, demand had reached a nadir in the early eighth century, but did not disappear and recovered slowly before expanding steadily in the tenth century. It was met by supply from traditional crafts which evolved but had never been interrupted. They operated under the supervision of the state and in the framework of stable institutions. We will consider these crafts and their context first before turning to the production of the capital and the provincial cities. Although a few texts give important information on the subject, mainly for Constantinople, the study both of manufacture and of cities is hampered by the limited nature of archaeological evidence. While parts of a number of cities have been excavated, the excavations usually encompass only a small segment of the medieval site. Unfortunately, this is the case with the major production centers like Constantinople, Thessaloniki, Thebes and Corinth.[80] Rescue excavations connected with the Athens subway system have yielded quantities of material which awaits study and publication.

Urban economy: actors and institutions

Taxation, profit and market regulations have already been considered above in their general economic implications. The focus here is on the mechanisms of the urban economy and relations between its various actors: craftsmen, traders and their customers, the elite and the people, and the state representatives dealing with economic matters.

Craftsmen and traders (*ergasteriakoi*) were organized in *corporations* (*somateia*) following Justinian's law (CJ 1.28.4), repeated in the *Basilics* (B 6.4.13); they were subject to the Eparch of Constantinople. We know them primarily in Constantinople. In the eighth–ninth centuries, only a few mentions of them survive.[81] We have detailed information from the *Book of the Prefect* issued in 912, but incorporating ninth-century regulations. It applies to Constantinople only.[82]

---

[80] For a discussion of these problems, see Bouras, "Aspects of the Byzantine City," pp. 497–500.

[81] P. Schreiner, "Die Organisation byzantinischer Kaufleute und Handwerker," in H. Jankuhn and E. Ebel (eds.), *Untersuchungen zu Handel und Verkehr der vor- und frühgeschichtlichen Zeit in Mittel- und Nordeuropa, 6, Organisationsformen der Kaufmannsvereinigungen in der Spätantike und im frühen Mittelalter* (Göttingen, 1989), pp. 44–61.

[82] Edited and translated by J. Koder, *EB*, who has commented upon it in many articles.

The state regarded the guilds (called *systemata* in the *Book of the Prefect*) as an instrument of control and fiscal apportionment. But these guilds acted principally as representatives of their members, providing mutual help and controlling admission of new members in the *koinotes*, as well as training the apprentices. Membership was granted to the craftsmen (not necessarily the owners) or to persons responsible for the *ergasteria*, even to slaves guaranteed by their masters. The internal organization of guilds and state control over them were varied and depended partly on the relevance of each trade to public concerns: most had selected leaders (*prostatai*) of their own supervised by an official of the Prefecture (*exarch*), but a few (like the sellers of silk garments and the saddlers) apparently fell under the direct authority of the Eparch. Specific rules aimed at ensuring fair conditions of trade and relative competition, the quality of the products and the protection of the buyers. Weights and measures were, as in the six century, controlled by the Eparch. It was forbidden for guild members to participate in two trades at the same time, to poach a competitor's employee, or to hoard staples like grocery items, while fraud (like mixing soap with tallow, clipping, filing, faking or gilding coins) was prosecuted. Not all trades are mentioned in the *Book of the Prefect*, which is not a comprehensive law. It deals only with the trades pertaining to items of high value or strategic products of interest to the state and finance (among them, goldsmiths, silk producers and traders, saddlers, spice sellers, notaries, bankers and moneychangers), or pertaining to common products and services for daily life (chandlers selling wax and soap, grocers, bakers, sheepsellers, butchers, porksellers, fishmongers, innkeepers, etc.). Although they are mentioned in the text, builders do not seem to have belonged to a guild.[83]

The *Book of the Prefect* also lists bankers (*argyropratai*) ahead of moneychangers (*trapezitai* or *katallaktai*), artisans and merchants, which points to their higher status. They worked and traded in precious metals, gems and objects which they were allowed to purchase from private persons. Very probably, as in Late Antiquity, they were also involved in pawning and lending. Funding and credit were certainly available from other sources (notably from wealthy aristocratic circles). Credit was available to some extent, in spite of the variations of legislation over time (interdiction of interest-bearing loans by Basil

[83] Dagron, "Urban Economy," *EHB* 2, pp. 407–17.

I in 886, abrogation of this legislation by Leo VI, who permitted a single rate of 4.2 per cent).[84]

The financing of trade and industry was facilitated by *partnerships* which Byzantine law regulated. Since at least the eighth century a form of business partnership (*chreokoinonia*), attested in both the *Ecloga* and the *Rhodian Sea Law*, was available. It resembled the later Italian *commenda* or *colleganza*, both in its unilateral form (where one partner contributes money and the other labor) and the bilateral form where both partners contribute funds and one of the two also contributes his labor. The partners shared the profits and losses proportionately, whereas in maritime loans the creditor was not a partner and, if the voyage did not end well, could not recover his capital, hence the higher rate of interest for this risky loan (*c.*16.6 per cent).[85] This highly important innovation was clearly a major advantage for the Byzantine traders before the developments of the so-called "commercial revolution" in the West in the eleventh century.

Urban economy: production

Cities with a reduced population now relied on their immediate hinterland, from one to a few days walk or sailing, for their provisioning, and on themselves for the satisfaction of elementary demand for manufactured objects, while some primary staples like wine and oil could be processed, and gardening and intensive fishing could be practiced within or near their walls.[86] More elaborate needs in most instances had to be served by imports from further afield.

Constantinople, on which we are better informed, was much ahead of the provincial cities with a high level of artisanal and commercial specialization. Its craftsmen not only could respond to basic demand for goods and services, as in most provincial towns; some highly skilled ones made luxury and refined wares in imperial or private

---

[84] Gofas, "The Byzantine Law of Interest," *EHB* 3, pp. 1099–1102.

[85] O. Maridaki-Karatza, "Legal Aspects of the Financing of Trade," *EHB* 3, pp. 1111–20. It could also apply to non-maritime trade; N. Oikonomides considers the 1,500 *nomismata* mentioned as trading capital in a hagiographic source to have been assembled this way: "Le marchand byzantin des provinces," in *Mercati e mercanti nell'altomedioevo* (Spoleto, 1993), p. 650.

[86] J. Koder, "Fresh Vegetables for the Capital," in Dagron and Mango, *Constantinople and its Hinterland*, pp. 49–56; G. Dagron, "Poissons, pêcheurs et poissonniers de Constantinople," *ibid.*, pp. 57–73.

workshops, which were sought in the whole Empire and beyond, even before the tenth century. The concentration of elite demand in the capital had stimulated these *"industries of art."*[87] They demonstrated a technical advance in comparison to the West, a level of know-how going back to uninterrupted ancient eastern tradition, which compares with that of the Muslim world. This situation contrasts with that in the West where decline in technique and fall of craft and manufacturing, except in isolated sites like Rome, is undeniable.[88]

Imperial workshops: the Late Roman tradition which reserved to the emperor the use of precious materials like gems, gold and above all purple silks, was still in force. Owing to the political and prestige role of these sumptuary objects, given to high officials or foreign potentates, their production was still either controlled or carried out in imperial workshops (*ergodosia*). Most of the early Byzantine workshops for arms (*fabricae*), dyeing (*baphia*) or weaving (*gynaecia*) which provided arms and textiles for the army and the court all over the Empire disappeared in the seventh–century crisis. The official production of special textiles and jewelry, as of coins[89] and arms, was now reduced in scope and concentrated in the capital inside, or near, the Palace, since it was an imperial monopoly. The state arsenals (*armamenton*) feature in a number of texts and seals of our period. Like the mint (*kharage*), they were directed by an official (*arkhon*), who reported to the logothete of *eidikon*, but private industry was also resorted to for equipping the army. Imperial workshops for textiles (*basilike istourgia*) and goldsmithing are mentioned sporadically in eighth–tenth-century sources.[90]

Pottery was made in a large number of cities. The downsizing of its manufacture explains why the old interdiction of location *intra muros* was no longer respected. By far the commonest type of finds consists of coarse wares, that is, unglazed pottery, whose geographic

---

[87] A. Cutler, "The Industries of Art," *EHB* 2, pp. 555–87.

[88] R. Hodges and D. Whitehouse, *Mahomet, Charlemagne et les origines de l'Europe* (Paris, 1999), postface, p. 168.

[89] C. Morrisson, "Moneta, *kharagè*, zecca: les ateliers byzantins et le palais impérial," in *I luoghi della moneta: le sedi delle zecche dall'antichità all' età moderna* (Milan, 2001), pp. 49–58.

[90] Dagron, "Urban Economy," *EHB* 2, pp. 429–32; Oikonomidès, *Les listes de préséance byzantines des IXe et Xe siècles* (Paris, 1972), p. 317. The *khrysoepsetes* (gold refiner) or the arkhon of the *khrysokheion* (gold smelter) must have acted not only for imperial goldsmith commissions, as usually stated, but mainly for preparing refined metal to be minted.

distribution was more limited than that of glazed wares, and is not yet fully understood.[91] Contrasting with earlier decorated fine wares imitating silverware, a new regionalized production of a more functional and non-decorative character emerged which dominated poorer markets: Sicilian Ware, the various mono-fired glazed (*vetrina pesante*) potteries of early medieval Italy produced in several centers, not necessarily urban,[92] or the possibly Middle Byzantine red micaceous water jars.[93] The pottery that has been most studied, however, is glazed pottery, consisting essentially of tableware, like the Constantinople Glazed White Ware, identified in the Saraçhane excavations. Starting from the seventh century it replaced the earlier Red Slip tableware, but its diffusion in the eighth century was limited.[94] In fact, glazed pottery was not necessarily a luxury item; there are gradations in its quality as well as differences in decoration, which make it particularly useful for any effort to establish both the type of demand and the commercialization of production.[95] The second major center of production was Corinth. Glazed pottery was made here from at least the end of the seventh century. Kilns and wasters found in the excavations at Amorion now prove that a red glazed ware was being produced locally before 838.[96] Glazed pottery of the very early period (seventh-eighth centuries) has also been found in Samos, Thasos, Crete, Cyprus, Sardis, Anemourion and Italy, but it is not entirely certain that all of these resulted from local production.[97]

[91] See Ch. Bakirtzis, *Vyzantina Tsoukalolagena* (Athens, 1989). This study is of great importance for the systematic way in which it categorizes coarse wares according to shape, name and function.

[92] S. Gelichi, "Ceramic Production and Distribution in the Early Medieval Mediterranean Basin (Seventh to Tenth Centuries AD): Between Town and Countryside," in Brogiolo et al., *Idea and Ideal of the Town*, pp. 115–39.

[93] M. Whittow, "Decline and Fall? Studying Long-Term Change in the East," in L. Lavan and W. Bowden (eds.), *Theory and Practice in Late Antique Archaeology* (Leiden–Boston, 2003), pp. 413 and plates 1–2.

[94] J. W. Hayes, in R. M. Harrison (ed.), *Excavations at Saraçhane in Istanbul* (Princeton, 1992), pp. 3–4 ff.

[95] J.-M. Spieser and V. François, "Pottery and Glass," *EHB* 2, p. 599; V. François, "La céramique byzantine et ottomane," in Geyer and Lefort, *La Bithynie*, p. 293.

[96] We thank Beate Böhlendorf-Arslan for sharing with us this still unpublished information. See also her *Die glasierte byzantinische Keramik aus der Turkei* (Istanbul, 2004), pp. 222–3.

[97] A Yangaki, *La céramique des IVe–VIIIe siècles ap. J.-C. d'Eleutherna* (Athens, 2005), 131–3; N. Poulou-Papametriou, "Vyzantine keramike apo ton Elleniko nesiotiko choro kai apo ten Peloponneso (7os–90s ai.): Mia prote proseggise," in Kontoura-Galake, *Oi skoteinoi aiones tou Vyzantiou (7os–90s ai.)* (Athens, 2001), 231–66.

A special type of very high-quality pottery consists of a subcategory of Glazed White Ware, the Polychrome Ware of Constantinople, brightly-painted polychrome ceramics in fine white clay used for icons, architectural decorations and revetments for the templon screens of churches. They were produced in Constantinople and Nicomedia, or, possibly, Nicaea, and date from the mid-ninth to the mid-twelfth century, with the highest concentration around the year 1000. Elite demand of the highest order may have been at the very origins of these polychrome wares. It has been suggested that these were introduced from Baghdad around 830 as "a fashion novelty at imperial level."[98] Production required craftsmen of the highest skills. Polychrome Ware has been found in many and disparate places (Corinth, Cherson, Tmutarakan), suggesting commercialized diffusion. It has been found also, although in very small quantities, in out-of-the way places, such as Crete and Sparta, in the tenth century, signaling "elite" demand there.[99]

Polychrome ceramics were also manufactured in a few places outside the Constantinople area and outside the Byzantine Empire. They were status items that stimulated elite demand and imitative production outside the frontiers of the Empire. In Bulgaria, Preslav, Patleina and Tuzlalaka produced Polychrome Wares. It is possible that they were manufactured by Constantinopolitan artisans. Preslav was the capital of Tsar Symeon (893–927), whose greatest desire was to become Byzantine Emperor, and it is likely that the Preslav production is associated with imperial dreams.[100]

---

[98] M. Mango, in Sh. Gerstel and J. Lauffenberger (eds.), *A Lost Art Rediscovered: The Architectural Ceramics of Byzantium* (Baltimore, 2001), p. 39; cf. A. Cutler, "Tiles and Tribulations: A Community of Clay across Byzantium and its Adversaries," *ibid.*, pp. 159–69. On Polychrome Ware, see also Hayes, in Harrison *Excavations*, pp. 35–7, G. D. R. Sanders, "Byzantine Polychrome Pottery," in J. Herrin, M. Mullett and C. Otten-Froux (eds.), *Mosaic: Festschrift A. H. S. Megaw* (BSA Suppl., 2002), pp. 89–103.

[99] Spieser and François, pp. 600–1; Papanikola-Bakirtzi, "Ergasteria efyalomenes keramikes sto Vyzantino kosmo," in *VIIe Congrès international sur la céramique médiévale en Méditerranée* (Athens, 2003), pp. 49–50; Gerstel and Lauffenberger, *Lost Art*; R. B. Mason and M. Mundell Mango, "Glazed 'Tiles of Nicomedia' in Bithynia, Constantinople, and elsewhere," in Mango and Dagron, *Constantinople and its Hinterland*, pp. 313–31; See also the articles by A. Bakourou et al., and N. Poulou-Papademetriou, in *VIIe Congrès international*, pp. 233–6, 211–26 respectively.

[100] On the Bulgarian production see T. Totev, *The Ceramic Icon in Medieval Bulgaria* (Sofia, 1999).

Glass-making was apparently more common than hitherto assumed, as archeological evidence from Amorion and Corinth begins to indicate. Middle Byzantine mosaic decoration is in itself proof of the continuous production of coloured glass and it is now known that there was, indeed, glass production in Constantinople in the ninth–tenth centuries, where the *Miracles of Saint Photeine* (9th–10th century) cite a "glass smelting workshop" located near the Strategion.[101] The tenth-century mythological dark red glass bowl, gilded and enamelled in various colours, from the treasure of San Marco is an example of the exceptional craftsmanship of the imperial artisans.[102] Glass served not only for tableware but also for window panels and of course mosaics. The Byzantines would sometimes export their renowned mosaicists (some were sent to the Caliph for the decoration of the Dome of the Rock in the late seventh century) or their precious materials: Nikephoros II gave forty loads of tesserae to the Caliph al-Hakim II for the great mosque of Córdoba.[103] Sometimes, lack of precious glass tesserae obliged the craftsmen to resort to ersatz colors or stone cubes or spoliation of earlier mosaics. Anyway, together with ivories, cameos, enamels, gold and silver objects like those preserved in the treasure of San Marco or the famous golden plane tree, with singing birds, and a moving throne and Pentapyrgion of Theophilos described in several texts,[104] they displayed the "glory of Byzantium" and its ability to produce high-value-added objects, with no equivalent in the Christian world of the time.

[101] J. Henderson and M. Mundell Mango, "Glass at Medieval Constantinople: Preliminary Scientific Evidence," in Mango and Dagron, *Constantinople and its Hinterland*, pp. 333–56 (reference to the *ergasterion uelopsestikon*, p. 346).

[102] Illustration in H.C. Evans and W. D. Wixom (eds.), *The Glory of Byzantium: Art and Culture of the Middle Byzantine Era*, AD 843–1261 (New York, 2003), p. 221; commentary by A. Cutler, "The Mythological Bowl of San Marco," in D. K. Kouymjian (ed.), *Near Eastern Studies in Honour of George C. Miles* (Beyrouth, 1974), pp. 94–110.

[103] P. Jaubert (transl.), *La géographie d'Idrisi* (Paris, 1836), vol. 2, p. 60. See also R. B. Mason and M. Mundell Mango, "Glazed 'Tiles of Nicomedia'," in Mango and Dagron, *Constantinople and its Hinterland*, p. 315, n. 3 for references to a publication by H. Stern of the mosaics themselves and the presence of Byzantine ceramic tiles in the cornice of the dome of the mihrab.

[104] Leo Grammaticus, ed. Bekker, p. 215; Theophanes Continuatus, ed. Bekker, p. 173; Liutprand, *Antapodosis*, VI. 5. See C. Mango, *The Art of the Byzantine Empire 312–1453* (Toronto, 1986), pp. 160–1.

Metalwork and leatherwork   Copperworkers (*khalkitai*) produced both items for daily life like nails, especially for shoeing horses, cauldrons, locks and keys etc. Their molds for the production of ordinary bronze jewelry, and their tools and artifacts, as well as those of ironworkers/blacksmiths (*sidereis*) have been found in many sites from the Balkans to the Euphrates. These artisans were active in many cities, for example, in Constantinople near the church of Chalkoprateia, which had taken its name from them in the early period.[105] *Leather* workers, known in the capital from texts, were also active in the provinces where remains of tanneries are usually found outside the city enclosure, as at Amorion. Common textiles could be imported but were also produced in cities, as the mention of "those who produce linen in the City" in the *Book of the Prefect* proves.

Textile industry   The importance of the textile industry is highlighted by the *Book of the Prefect* which provides much information on the organization of the *silk industry* of Constantinople, even though scholars disagree on details. In the tenth century, two pivotal guilds were involved in the manufacturing of silk cloth: first, the *metaxopratai*, who bought, as a cartel, raw silk or cocoons, and sold these on to the *katartarioi* who dressed them, then bought the silk yarn back from the *katartarioi* and sold it to the *metaxarioi*. The latter formed the second pivotal guild since they wove the silk, dyed it and cut it. They were in charge of the most important and lucrative part of the production process, and the one which necessitated the heaviest investment. It is possible and indeed probable that members of the Constantinopolitan aristocracy invested in this part of the process, but their involvement was in no way a monopoly. Gilbert Dagron has argued that the guild of the *metaxarioi* would have been able to dominate the industry, except that, in the highly controlled environment of the silk industry in tenth-century Constantinople, they could neither purchase raw materials nor sell the finished product except to the silk cloth merchants (*vestiopratai*).[106]

---

[105] For archaeological and textual evidence, see B. Pitarakis, *Les croix reliquaires pectorales en bronze* (Paris, 2006), pp. 165–77.

[106] Dagron, "Urban Economy," pp. 439–41. Cf. the useful remarks of G. C. Maniatis, "Organization" (as above, n. 34), pp. 270–1, 285 ff.

The demand for silk cloth ran along a spectrum, since a number of different varieties of silk existed.[107] The highest-quality silks, purple in hue and often dyed with the expensive porphyra, extracted from the mollusk *murex*, were for a long time restricted to the needs of the imperial court. In the tenth century, they seem to have been manufactured primarily by the imperial workshops, which, however, did not fill all of the needs of the imperial court; when the emperor set out on campaign he also bought silks in the marketplace, as eventual gifts to lesser potentates. It is clear from the *Book of the Prefect* that silks were also produced in private workshops. But their sale and export was tightly controlled and a distinction was made between the *kekolymena*[108] prohibited to "outsiders" (*exotikoi*) and other garments which could be sold under the eparch's supervision provided the price of the garment did not exceed 10 *nomismata* (in terms of purchasing power the price is similar to that of a kimono nowadays).[109]

In the tenth century, it is clear that the increase in urban demand and economic expansion were fostering secondary production in cities at all levels, although we are relatively better informed on luxury ones. A variety of trades, shops and open-air stands would cater to the needs of all classes of the population. Bakeries, and likewise taverns and groceries would be situated throughout the city in larger centers like Constantinople. *Metata* (inns or hostels for merchants) may have been closer to the trading places or harbours.[110] Other *services* (physicians and institutions like hospices) were available more easily in a big city where more people could afford their prices or wealthy patrons subsidized them.[111] It is clear that there was by that

---

[107] There is a vast bibliography on their nature and nomenclature: see Muthesius, *EHB* 1, pp. 158–65, with references to her *Studies in Byzantine Weaving* and to Haldon, *Three Treatises*, commentary on the different denominations of silks according to their dyes or weaving. Some names in the *Book of Ceremonies* allude to iconographic motives.

[108] *Egoun oxeon kai porphyraerion megalozelon* (*EB*, 4.1).

[109] R. S. Lopez, "Silk Industry in the Byzantine Empire," *Speculum* pp. 20 (1945), 20–42, repr. in idem, *Byzantium and the World around it* (London, 1978), art. II.

[110] M. Mundell-Mango, "The Commercial Map of Constantinople," *DOP* 54 (2000), 189–99. See also P. Magdalino, "The Maritime Neighborhoods of Constantinople: Commercial and Residential Functions; Sixth to Twelfth Centuries", *DOP* 54 (2000), pp. 209–26.

[111] G. Maniatis, "The Personal Services Market in Byzantium," *Byzantion* 74 (2004), pp. 25–50.

period a sufficient degree of specialization and division of labour to fuel an articulated exchange system.

EXCHANGE AND TRADE

Though fragmentary, there is evidence in the mainly literary sources for merchants and marketplaces, a proof in itself of the persistence of this activity throughout the period. Merchants, called *emporoi* or *naukleroi*, sometimes *pragmateutai*, were not the only agents; often churchmen and occasionally members of the aristocracy engaged in commerce. So did officials, notably when it came to provisioning the cities, and craftsmen or peasants could sell directly the production of their shops or farming lots.

The combination of imperial office and mercantile activity may be seen in the activities of the *kommerkiarioi*. It has been hypothesized by N. Oikonomides that these state officials were authorized to carry out trade in silk (on which they had the monopoly) and other goods.[112] Part of the demonstration relies on the established relation between these customs officials and the control of the silk trade in the seventh century when a *kommerkiarios* was called "lord of the silk cloth," and the ninth century when the new "general *kommerkiarios*" is also often "lord of the purple" (*arkhon tou blattiou*), implying that they had the monopoly of trade in silk. His arguments have not been universally accepted and a great debate ensued.[113]

The responsibilities of the merchants and shipmasters (*naukleroi*) are described in the *Rhodian Sea Law* (late seventh–eighth century) which documents both common staples carried in bulk (wheat, oil, wine, cloth) and valuable items (silk and pearls), and shows the merchants holding cash and contracts (*grammateia*).[114] Foreign traders were allowed in Constantinople but their residence and activities

---

[112] Oikonomides, *Mercati* (as above n. 85), pp. 639–41; idem, "The Role of the Byzantine State in the Economy," *EHB* 3, pp. 984–7; Laiou, "Exchange and Trade," p. 706.

[113] N. Oikonomides, "Silk Trade and Production in Byzantium from the Sixth to the Ninth Century: The Seals of Kommerkiarioi," *DOP* 40 (1986), pp. 33–53 (reprinted in *Social and Economic Life*, art. VIII); *contra* Haldon, *Byzantium in the Seventh Century*, pp. 232–8, following on Hendy, *Studies*, pp. 628–30. The constructive criticism by A. Dunn, "The *Kommerkiarios*, the *Apotheke*, the *Dromos*, the *Vardarios* and *The West*," *BMGS* 17 (1993), pp. 3–24 was taken into consideration by Oikonomides himself in *EHB* 3, p. 984.

[114] Laiou, "Exchange and Trade," p. 707.

were limited. The Rus were first prohibited from residing within the city walls, then quartered near Saint Mamas. Muslims were assigned to a special *mitaton* near the Golden Horn. Foreign traders were not allowed to stay for more than three months.

Markets Trade took place either in permanent shops lining a main street (like the *Mese*), or in temporary stalls in marketplaces (like the Amastrianon or the Strategion in Constantinople), still called *agorai*, without the ancient political function, and also in free open spaces outside city walls. The latter location was usual for periodic markets, often annual fairs (*panegyreis*) which took place on the feast day of the city's patron saint, as in Thessalonike or Ephesos. The fairs declined in number with de-urbanization in the seventh century but some did continue. There is evidence for other such fairs in Nicomedia, Trebizond, Euchaita, Chonai, Myra, Charax, i.e. Parthenius (Bartín) in Paphlagonia,[115] catering for regional and inter-regional, indeed international trade. The number of local or regional fairs increased from the late tenth century onward.[116]

Local and regional exchanges By local exchange we understand here short distances under 50km on the land route or a day's sailing in small ships, that involved direct exchange between producers and customers. Regional exchange would extend over larger areas (from 50 to *c.* 300km) and would involve transactions on a larger scale. Some of the ancient roads had been abandoned in favour of shorter more direct trails, reflecting a shift from carts to smaller pack animals like donkeys or mules. The state took pains to maintain bridges and ensure communications for military considerations, which also benefited the economy.

Here again, evidence can be found in the *Book of the Prefect* and other texts for regional trade: the capital's market received cattle driven overland from Bithynia or Paphlagonia; Thessalonike in the ninth and tenth centuries got wares and staples from Bulgarian and Slavic areas or from Thessaly, which arrived along the river routes, or by sea and land. Trade in Thessalonike involved wheat, woolen

---

[115] C. Mango, "A Journey Round the Coast of the Black Sea in the Ninth Century," *Palaeoslavica* 10 (2002/1), pp. 255–64 (the fair is mentioned in the ninth-century life of Saint Andrew).

[116] Bouras, "Aspects of the Byzantine City," pp. 512–15; Laiou, "Exchange and Trade," pp. 709–10, 730–2; Haldon, "Production," pp. 258–9.

textiles, metalwork and glass, and brought to the city much wealth in gold, silver and silk.[117] Other centers of trade appear in the sources: Sparta and Thebes, which developed from the ninth century probably in connection with local sericulture, Demetrias in Thessaly, Preslav in Bulgaria, Develtos, Cherson, Amastris and Trebizond on the Black Sea. These cities traded not only with their immediate hinterland as Niketas Paphlagon relates of people living south of Amastris and flocking to the city "as to a common *emporion*," but also with much more remote destinations, like Attaleia, port of call on the route between Alexandria and Constantinople.[118]

Inter-regional and long-distance trade   Except for valuable items like spices or silks which traveled easily on the land routes, most of Byzantine inter-regional and long-distance trade was maritime. Merchant ships were smaller in size (*c.*14 to 20m) and built more economically than in the past: a shift from the traditional plank-first oriented manner to the skeleton, frame-first model, occurred some time in the sixth–seventh centuries. The ninth-century shipwreck from Bozburun and the Serçe Liman shipwreck (eleventh century) were built this way.[119] However, the cost of construction involved an important investment: applying the *Rhodian Sea Law* rate of 50 *nomismata* per sea *modios*,[120] gives them a value of *c.*6 pounds of gold (432 *nomismata*), half the amount of the forced loan imposed on *naukleroi* by Nikephoros I.[121] Their performance capabilities were rather low, their speed varying between 2 and 4 knots on average depending on the winds. Their water-carrying capacity was limited. Under these constraints, ships would in most cases make coastal runs and inter-island hops of a few days, putting into beaches and ports for supplies and overnight stops.[122] This port-to-port sailing applied to both inter-regional and long-distance trade which took place on trunk routes.

---

[117] N. Oikonomidès, "Le kommerkion d'Abydos, Thessalonique et le commerce bulgare au IXᵉ siècle," in *Hommes et richesses*, II, pp. 241–8.

[118] Laiou, "Exchange and Trade," pp. 725–8, with bibliography.

[119] See Chapter II, n. 48.   [120] Equivalent to a volume of 17.084 liters.

[121] On the costs, sailing and routes of ships, see also McCormick, *Origins*, pp. 404–30, 483–91 (slower speeds in the eighth century; increase in the ninth, attributed to sailing at night), pp. 502–8 (trunk route from Italy to the Aegean).

[122] J. H. Pryor, "Types of Ships and their Performance Capabilities," in R. Macrides (ed.), *Travel in the Byzantine World* (Aldershot, 2000), pp. 33–55, at p. 38.

The *military ships* to which the state devoted much effort and money from the seventh century onward for the defense of the Empire against the Arabs, were quite different. The *dromones* were oar-powered vessels, with two masts and sails that had only an auxiliary function. They improved on the Roman tradition and became long biremes of around 32 meters with 100 oarsmen (25 per side, one below deck, one above) on average and up to 230 in some cases, armed with the *siphon* in order to spray Greek fire. In favorable conditions, they would sail at some 3 to 4 knots, exceptionally 7 knots.[123] Thousands of horses were transported in maritime expeditions to Crete in 949 and 960 but probably not more than a dozen or so per ship.[124] The existence of specialized warships – a creation of the seventh century – at a time when the West had no such distinction is a testimony to the advanced level of the Byzantine navy. Warships could sometimes accommodate traders carrying only limited and valuable wares.

Only a few examples can be given here of complex relations in which naturally Constantinople played a central, pivotal role, symbolized by the description of its lively port by Masudi. Schematically speaking, the capital was related to the Black Sea on the one hand, and on the other to the Aegean, and from there either to Syria or Egypt or to the West, Italy and further.[125] However, commerce was not only center-oriented; direct inter-regional exchanges took place between Bithynia and the Pontus, or Synada in Phrygia and Attaleia in Lydia, or between the northern and southern coasts of the Black Sea. In the Black Sea, trade linked Byzantium with the steppes and central Asia, through several successive partners such as the Khazars and the Rus.[126] Two main outlets were involved. One was Trebizond, where spices and textiles arrived from northern Syria or central Asia; in the tenth century, Ibn Hawqal reports that its *kommerkion* (transactions duty)

---

[123] H. Ahrweiler, *Byzance et la mer* (Paris, 1967), pp. 408–18; G. Makris, "Ships," *EHB* I, p. 92; Zuckerman (as above, n. 19), pp. 107–25; Pryor, "Types of Ships," pp. 39–55.

[124] J. H. Pryor, "Transportation of Horses by Sea during the Era of the Crusades: Eighth Century to 1285. Part I: To *c* 1225," in idem, *Commerce, Shipping and Naval Warfare in the Medieval Mediterranean* (London, 1987), art. V.

[125] McCormick, *Origins*, pp. 588–91.

[126] See the contributions by J. Howard-Johnston, I. Sorlin, E. de la Vaissière, T. Noonan, I. Konovalova and M. Espéronnier, in M. Kazanski *et al.* (eds.), *Les centres protourbains russes entre Scandinavie, Byzance et Orient* (Paris, 2000), pp. 301–424.

yielded 72,000 *nomismata* annually; the second was Cherson, which exported its salt fish and amphoras to the north, or Crimaean wine to Dalmatia and south-west Asia Minor. It also acted as an intermediary in the export of Byzantine luxury objects and in imports from the Caucasian silk route, on which Russian archeology is bringing much new information.[127] The Rus, first involved in trade in furs, swords and slaves mostly with the Islamic world through Khazaria, turned in the tenth century to direct trade with Constantinople. They also raided the city several times, which explains the restrictive clauses in the treaties of 911 and 944.

Commerce on the Aegean route to the West had reached a low ebb in the 770s and regained importance in the tenth century when the Venetians, who had already developed their relations on the Dalmatian coast, engaged in commerce with Egypt and Constantinople, as did the Amalfitans. In 968, Liutprand of Cremona mentions both cities as exporting silk to Italy, illegally. Unfortunately it is difficult to distinguish clearly between Byzantine and Arab products among the pieces surviving in the West. In any case, their number had increased already in the late ninth century.[128] Since these developments are the early signs of the new orientation of trade and routes related to the Fatimid conquest of Egypt in 969, and further Fatimid expansion in the eleventh century, they are considered in the next chapter. But one must mention here that Byzantine traders were not sedentary, expecting goods to be brought to them in the capital, but were active in the outside world.[129] Byzantine exports (precious metalwork, silk, slaves, timber) are mentioned in Arab literature of the tenth century.[130] The balance of this trade may have been positive for the Empire.

MONETARY DEVELOPMENTS

Naturally, in the above outline, coins and money have been constantly mentioned. As a major instrument of economic activity they

---

[127] Laiou, "Exchange and Trade," pp. 726–7. On the Khazars, see T. S. Noonan, *The Islamic World, Russia and the Vikings, 750–900.: The Numismatic Evidence* (Aldershot, 1998) (for a short outline, see idem, "Les Khazars et le commerce oriental," in *Dossiers d'archéologie* 256 (2000), pp. 82–5) and C. Zuckerman (ed.), *La Crimée entre Byzance et les Khazars (VIIe–IXe siècle)* (Paris, 2006).

[128] McCormick, *Origins*, pp. 719–28.

[129] Laiou (see Chapter IV), contrary to the views of R. S. Lopez.

[130] D. Jacoby, "Byzantine Trade with Egypt from the Mid-Tenth Century to the Fourth Crusade," *Thesaurismata* 30 (2000), pp. 25–77.

deserve the brief special treatment that follows, which will outline an evolution reflecting that of the general economy.[131] The seventh-century crisis affected also the coinage: the alloy and weight of the gold denominations (the *solidus* and its fractions of $\frac{1}{2}$ and $\frac{1}{3}$) were slightly reduced in the 680s; the issues of silver coins, limited to special distribution issues in the sixth century, which had resumed with the creation of the hexagram in 616, soon declined again from 675 onward, while the copper coinage underwent a constant decline in weight and value, its badly and hastily struck, often overstruck, pieces showing the inflationary context of their production. Several causes contributed to this transformation, among them a difference in the silver:gold ratio between Byzantium and the Caliphate, and the loss of control over the gold and silver mines in the Balkans and in eastern Anatolia.

This was corrected by the Isaurians with the creation of a new silver coin, the *miliaresion*, which competed with, even partly copied, the Arab *dirhem*, being a thin and large coin with a religious inscription around the cross on one side, and the name of the emperors, not their portrait as before, on the other. It replaced the fractions of the gold coin (*solidus*, called *nomisma* in Greek) which disappeared in the eighth century, served as the intermediary coin for mid-value exchanges, and lasted until the eleventh century, varying in value between $\frac{1}{12}$ and $\frac{1}{14}$ of the gold unit. The divisions of the copper coin (*follis*) progressively disappeared as well. Therefore the monetary system of the eighth–tenth centuries resulted in a simplified structure with one denomination per metal: the gold *nomisma* with an average high purity of 97 per cent, the silver *miliaresion* with a more irregular fineness varying between 98 per cent and 83 per cent,[132] and the copper *follis*. This last coin underwent important changes in weight, which the lack of textual sources prevent us from contextualizing properly; at least it is clear that Michael II and Theophilos stabilized it for a long period. This unit of everyday exchanges was valued at 1/24 of the *miliaresion* and the *miliaresion* at 1/12 of the *nomisma*.

[131] Fundamental reading: Ph. Grierson, *Catalogue of the Byzantine Coins in the Dumbarton Oaks Collection and in the Whittemore Collection*, vols. II (*602–717*) and III (*717–1081*) (Washington, D. C., 1968, 1973); Hendy, *Studies*. Shorter outlines by C. Morrisson: "Byzantine Money: Its Production and Circulation," *EHB* 3, pp. 909–66 and in J.-C. Cheynet (ed.), *Le monde byzantin*, vol. 2, *641–1204* (Paris, 2006), Chapter 7.

[132] Data assembled in T. Bertelè, *Numismatique byzantine*, C. Morrisson (ed.) (Wetteren, 1978), pp. 61–8.

A major restructuring of the *mint organization* had also taken place in the seventh century. The old Diocletianic pattern implied in the sixth century that gold was issued in the capital and in the prefectures of Thessalonica, Rome, later, Ravenna, and Carthage, and bronze in the same cities as well as in the diocesan capitals (Antioch, Kyzikos, Nikomedeia, Alexandria). They were supplemented by a few others for special regions (Catania for Sicily, Constantia for Cyprus and Cherson) or for temporary, military purposes (Alexandretta, Seleukia and Isaura in Isauria under Herakleios). This hierarchized and regionalized scheme was disrupted in the Balkans and in the East by the Slavic and Persian conflicts and finally dismantled between 627 and 695 when Nikomedeia, Kyzikos, Thessalonike, Constantia and Cherson successively ceased striking. In the eighth century minting for the eastern provinces, from the Balkans to Asia Minor, was centralized in Constantinople. In the West, the regional mints which survived (Rome till 776, Ravenna till 751, Syracuse till 879), or had been created to cope with local needs (Sardinia, as a replacement for Carthage, from 695 to 741, Naples, from 660 to 842; Reggio, as a replacement for Syracuse, from 879 to 912), were increasingly autonomous, and diverged more and more from the metropolitan standards until they disappeared. Lack of support from the capital and decrease of fiscal resources left them to their own devices; gold and smaller denominations (silver and copper in Rome and the North, $^1/_2$, $^1/_3$ *nomismata* and copper in Sicily) were now issued in very limited quantities, except in Sicily. Gold was more and more debased, following a pattern which also affected the Lombard coinages of Tuscany and Benevento in the same period.

In Sicily, this evolution is related to the political context: the fall of gold fineness from 97 per cent before 695 to 70–80 per cent in 695–c.710 coincides with the creation of the "theme" of Sicily in 695, while the stabilization at 82 per cent from the 720s to 820 certainly results from the fiscal reforms of Leo III and the confiscation of the papal domains in the island. The aggravated alteration under Theophilos and Michael III (from 80 to 40 per cent, even a mere 10 per cent under Basil I) reflects the impoverishment of the island due to the Arab raids.[133] In Rome, debasement affected gold as well as the little silver coins with the emperor's effigy and the monogram

---

[133] C. Morrisson et al., in eadem, *Monnaies et finances* (Aldershot, 1994), art. X.

of the popes, which were replaced by *denarii* in Carolingian style in 796.[134]

The loss of most Italian possessions, except for Calabria and part of Apulia, resulted in a near-complete centralization of imperial mints from the ninth century onward. Following the creation of new themes, the two provincial mints at Cherson and Thessalonike resumed activity under Theophilos. Cherson issued cast bronze coins of peculiar fabric and limited local circulation from 842 to 989, Thessalonike was active only in the ninth century. Coin finds prove that Constantinople was in fact able to provide the provinces from reconquered Apulia to the Danubian or the eastern provinces with the necessary circulating medium. We have, however, no information on the concrete means of cash transportation other than scattered mentions of sums from tax collecting or intended for military pay being robbed or seized by enemies or rebels.

Coin hoards together with random or excavation coin finds give some information on the *monetization* of the Byzantine economy. The decrease in the number of gold coin hoards from around 95 in the sixth and seventh centuries to only 11 in the period 700 to 850 is more than proportional to Byzantium's territorial losses; it reflects the impoverishment of the period. They contain fewer coins on average, which also points to diminished wealth. The chronology of copper coins found in excavations has long served as an illustration of the general collapse of coin circulation in the eighth and early ninth centuries. The annual frequency index, obtained by dividing the number of bronze coins discovered and arranged in phases by the number of years for each of them, shows a general dramatic decrease in the period 668–829 or 886 on most sites.[135] It reveals in any case the limited influx of newly minted currency into the circulating medium, which consisted now of a majority of old and worn coins. In a few important cities or in better-favored regions, the decrease was not as severe: Constantinople (St Polyeuktos excavations), Sicily, Calabria, Amorion, or Albania and Bithynia to a lesser extent, received a significant quantity of new coins in the eighth and ninth centuries.

---

[134] C. Morrisson et al., *ibid.*, art. XII; on Lombard, early Papal and Carolingian coinages in Italy, P. Grierson and M. Blackburn, *Medieval European Coinage* I, *The Early Middle Ages* (Cambridge, 1986), pp. 55–73, 210, 259–66; see also A. Rovelli, "Emissione e uso della moneta: le testimonianze scritte e archeologiche," in *Roma nell'alto Medioevo* (Spoleto, 2001), pp. 821–52.

[135] See figs. 6.1 to 6.15 in *EHB* 3, pp. 912–13.

Ongoing research will certainly increase evidence in this direction.[136] As stated above, taxation and the fact that the government had managed to keep sizeable cash revenues, go far to explaining the resilience of the Empire and of its economy. It is nonetheless clear that many inland areas in the eighth–ninth centuries were marginally or little monetized.

Things change from the 830s in relation to the increase in population, rural and urban settlement and production. In Athens and Corinth the annual growth of the index of coins found is respectively 1 and 4 per cent, leading to a fourfold or sevenfold increase in 969 versus 820; in Sparta it is four times more in 867–969 than in 829–67. Recent studies show the penetration of coinage in rural areas, as in the Peloponnese, Apulia or southern Dobrudja and north-western Bulgaria, while the shorter span of coin hoards suggest a higher velocity of circulation.[137]

This implied an increase in the number of coins struck which concerned not only copper coins, whose issues burst out in the 980s with the so-called "Anonymous folles", but also gold coins. The numbers issued show a clear increase starting from the 950s, as the estimates of the original number of dies drawn from the exemplary statistical analysis of a sample of 4,600 *nomismata* of the period demonstrate.[138] At the same time the alloy of the *nomisma* began to drift from the 97 per cent average of the ninth century to 95 per cent in 920–69, 94 per cent in 969–76, and even 92.1 per cent in 977–1001. This "creeping devaluation" was carried out by simply abstaining from refining the newly mined gold available to the Treasury and made possible a slight increase in the money supply, in the order of some 0.2 per cent annually. The failed attempt by Nikephoros II Phokas to impose the circulation of his light-weight *nomisma tetarteron* must be considered in this context of the growing financial needs of the state.[139] At the same time, the economic expansion led to an increase of monetized

---

[136] See the contributions by A. Lambropoulou et al., C. Morrisson, and V. Penna in Kontoura-Galake, *The Dark Centuries of Byzantium*, and Whittow, "Decline and Fall?" pp. 404–23.

[137] V. Penna, "Life in Byzantine Peloponnese: The Numismatic Evidence (8th–12th Century)," *Mneme Martin Jessop Price* (Athens, 1996), pp. 265–88; E. Oberländer-Târnoveanu, "Les échanges dans le monde rural byzantin de l'est des Balkans (VIe–XIe siècle)," in Lefort et al., *Villages*, pp. 363–401.

[138] F. Füeg, Vom Umgang mit Zufall und Wahrscheinlichkeit in der numismatischen Forschung, *Revue Suisse de Numismatique* 76 (1997), 135–60.

[139] See p. 60.

transactions which prevented debasement from having the negative impact that would happen later, in the second half of the eleventh century, as we will see in the next chapter.

CONCLUSION

In this period, Byzantium had a mixed economy, characterized by the coexistence of state regulation and a market-based economy. The role of the state was heavier in the beginning of the period. As the economic situation improved, its role was tempered, although it was still much more significant than it would be in the future. There was a well-functioning state economy but market mechanisms were also in place. It is precisely because the economy was mixed that it had the possibility of evolving. The system that we see in its clearest form in the early tenth century had underwritten the beginnings of economic recovery and the slow and measured expansion that began in the late eighth century, and is visible in all sectors by the tenth. The situation, however, had contradictions, and the system was under stress. Already in the tenth century the pressures are evident: rich and powerful people strain to accumulate landed resources, while the limitations on trade begin to come up against the demands of opening markets. The Emperor Leo VI, the same one who redacted the regulatory *Book of the Prefect*, also issued a Novel permitting the sale of small pieces of highest-quality purple silk to private individuals, thus lifting the prohibition, "so that they may acquire a measure of dignity."[140] It is a first dent in the restrictive export policy, which would collapse by the twelfth century. Already in the second half of the tenth century, illicit exports of highest-quality silks to Western Europe seem to have been common. The economic system was evolving into one where the role of market forces in economic integration would be on the ascendant.

The reign of Basil II (976–1025) spans the tenth and eleventh centuries. The Emperor himself stands as a Janus between two economic systems. In his persecution of the powerful and the protection of the "poor" he is the apex of the tenth-century tradition. But in many other ways his policies are the harbinger of a new era, and will be discussed in the next chapter.

---

[140] P. Noailles, A. Dain, *Les Novelles de Léon VI le Sage* (Paris, 1944), no. 80.

— IV —

THE AGE OF ACCELERATED GROWTH
(ELEVENTH AND TWELFTH CENTURIES)

——————— • ———————

There is no question that the Byzantine economy experienced secular growth in the period after the late eighth century. What is argued in this chapter is that growth accelerated over a period which extended from sometime in the tenth century until a point that varies considerably for the various sectors of the economy as well as in terms of the factors that influence growth. The demographic upward swing continued until some time in the early or mid-fourteenth century.[1] The rural population was in a Malthusian bind by the late thirteenth–early fourteenth century, as the land constraint appears to have been reached, diminishing returns set in and, as a result, the economic condition of the population worsened.[2] The urban economy reached

[1] See the somewhat different views of J. Lefort, "Population et peuplement en Macédoine orientale, IXe–XVe siècle," *Hommes et richesses dans l'Empire byzantin, II, VIIIe–XVe siècle* (Paris, 1991), pp. 73–5, who argues that the demographic increase continued until the great upheavals of the 1340s, which include the Black Death; and A. E. Laiou-Thomadakis, *Peasant Society in the Late Byzantine Empire* (Princeton, 1977), Chapters VI and VII and A. E. Laiou, "The Agrarian Economy, Thirteenth-Fifteenth Centuries," *EHB* 1, pp. 312–17, who thinks that the population decline had already set in early in the fourteenth century.

[2] For various ideas regarding the demographic behavior of pre-industrial populations and the results of economic growth without very significant technological change, and taking into account the fact that land is, in the long run, a fixed resource, see G. Clark, *The Conquest of Nature: A Brief Economic History of the World* (accessed through the Internet; publication by Princeton University Press announced for 2005), Part I; D. Lal, *Unintended Consequences: The Impact of Factor Endowments, Culture and Politics in Long-Run Economic Performance* (Cambridge, Mass., 1998), passim; K. Pomeranz, *The Great Divergence: China, Europe and the Making of the Modern World Economy* (Princeton and Oxford, 2000). For the decline in the economic position of the peasantry, see below, Chapter V.

its heights in the twelfth century; and the economy of exchange, which certainly attained high levels in the twelfth century, functioned under significantly different terms in the period after the fall of Constantinople to the crusaders in 1204. That there was extensive growth in this period is quite clear. The question will also be raised whether one may also speak of what D. Lal has called a "Smithian intensive growth," with a secular increase in the per capita income that, however, in the long run comes up against the land constraint and diminishing returns set in.[3]

DEMOGRAPHY

In examining the growth patterns of the age of accelerated growth one must, once again, begin with demography and population movements, for a number of reasons. In a pre-industrial economy that is heavily agricultural, labor constitutes a very important factor of production: land is useless without labor. Bringing under-exploited or unexploited land into production requires, in the first instance, a sufficient labor force.[4] It has further been argued that where there is evidence of population rise in a given economy, extensive (as distinguished from intensive) economic growth, that is, an increase in production sufficient to maintain the population at subsistence levels, may be predicated; in that sense, population growth is in itself an indicator of increased production, though not necessarily of increased productivity.[5] Finally, our argument here is that, although trade and exchange were the dynamic factors in the economy, increase in

[3] Lal, *Unintended Consequences*, p. 20. The idea here is that in a pre-industrial economy, such as Adam Smith's, trade, especially free trade, leads to division of labor, rise in productivity in all sectors, and, by lowering the cost of consumption, to a rise in per capita income: A. Smith, *An Inquiry into the Nature and Causes of the Wealth of Nations*, ed. E. Cannan (Chicago, 1976), vol. I, pp. 7–21 and passim. Obviously, the concept would apply only partly to the medieval period.

[4] On the importance of labor as a factor of production in medieval Europe, see D. C. North and Robert P. Thomas, *The Rise of the Western World* (Cambridge, 1973), Chapters 5–6; they argue that in a period of underpopulation (ninth century) labor was the most valuable factor of production; and that a rising population was the dynamic element that led to economic growth.

[5] E. Jones, *Growth Recurring* (Oxford, 1988), as reported by Lal, *Unintended Consequences*, p. 21. The theoretical underpinnings of this argument, that otherwise the population would die off, should perhaps be modified in view of the observation that subsistence levels are not necessarily near-starvation levels, but rather the level at which the population just reproduces itself: Clark, *The Conquest of Nature*, pp. 6–7.

agricultural production was essential, as making possible both product differentiation and differentiation in economic activity; and agricultural production, in the conditions outlined here, depended on an adequate supply of labor.

The idea that the demographic growth which had started in the late eighth century[6] persisted and intensified in the eleventh and twelfth centuries, despite inevitable chronological and geographic fluctuations, has become generally accepted over the last forty years or so. Earlier, some scholars had argued that the Byzantine Empire had suffered a demographic decline in the tenth century, or at some point in the eleventh, whether early or late.[7] The relatively recent consensus on a sustained and long-term demographic growth is based on archeological, scientific and documentary evidence. The political disasters of the late eleventh century, with the loss of the Anatolian plateau to the Seljuk Turks, were not sufficient to reverse the overall trend, since that part of the Empire was less well populated than the coastlands and the Balkan provinces. The areas that remained were constituent parts of a cohesive state and economy.

Both archeology and archival documents allow us to plot the increase in settlements and population in this period. In Bulgaria, after the annexation of the territory by the Byzantines (1018), there was dense reoccupation of the countryside south of the Haemus Mountains. In Byzantine southern Italy, there was a population explosion in Calabria in the eleventh century. In south-western Boeotia, archeological evidence points to an increase in settlements and expansion of cultivation in the course of the twelfth–fourteenth centuries as

---

[6] W. Treadgold, *The Byzantine Revival, 780–842* (Stanford, 1988), p. 30; J. Lefort, "The Rural Economy, Seventh-Twelfth Centuries," *EHB* I, p. 269.

[7] N. Svoronos, "Société et organisation intérieure dans l'empire byzantin au XIe siècle: les principaux problèmes," *Proceedings of the Thirteenth International Congress of Byzantine Studies, Main Papers XII;* (Oxford, 1966), pp. 12–17, reprinted in his *Études sur l'organisation intérieure, la société et l'économie de l'empire byzantin* (London, 1973), art. IX. Modified in his "Remarques sur les structures économiques de l'Empire byzantin au XIe siècle," *Travaux et Mémoires* 6 (1976), pp. 49–67, which places demographic stagnation in the late eleventh century; H. Antoniadis-Bibicou, "Démographie, salaires et prix à Byzance au XIe s.," *Annales*, 27 (1972), pp. 217–22; it was refuted by P. Charanis, "Observations on the Demography of the Byzantine Empire," *Thirteenth International Congress of Byzantine Studies, Main Papers XIV* (Oxford, 1966), pp. 456–61 (= Charanis, *Studies on the Demography of the Byzantine Empire* (London, 1972), art. I), who posited demographic growth in the Balkan provinces until the late twelfth century. N. Oikonomidès, "Terres du fisc et revenue de la terre aux Xe–XIe siècles," *Hommes et richesses*, II, pp. 336–7, wonders whether Svoronos might be right.

well as during the Frankish conquest. The Land Register of Thebes, which dates to the second half of the eleventh century, shows evidence of increase in the fiscal units, that is, households, together with a reduction in the size of plots and intensification of land exploitation.[8] In Macedonia, the demographic curve continued to grow until, by the thirteenth century, the shepherds and woodcutters of the area were looking for new pastures and places to cut wood; in the late thirteenth century even the hillsides were partly occupied, and the medieval expansion had reached its limits (see Map 5).[9]

The very considerable expansion in the number and size of cities and towns in the eleventh and twelfth centuries is also an indicator of the rise in population. The fact that clearance of new lands and the expansion of settlement in the countryside coincides chronologically with a rise in urbanization and urban population makes it certain that there was no net transfer of population from countryside to town but, rather, an overall population increase.

It is virtually impossible to aggregate from the scattered data and give a firm number to the overall population. Wildly different estimates have been offered by different scholars. My own estimate, which is also speculative, and is based on the generalization of sporadic information regarding the density of settlement, is for about 19 million in *c.*1025, and also for the late twelfth century, despite territorial contraction.[10]

In pre-industrial societies, the population tends to increase unless there are catastrophic interventions (epidemics, war), or a rise in the death rate due to a decline in the standard of living, or a conscious limitation of the birth rate, which is a socially determined decision. In other words, the population will rise in the absence of factors affecting it negatively. We have discussed in the previous chapter the beneficial effects of the cessation of the post-Justinianic outbreaks of the plague in the second half of the eighth century.

---

[8] A. E. Laiou, "The Byzantine Village (5th–14th century)," in J. Lefort et al., *Villages*, pp. 31–54. For the interpretation of the evidence in the land register, see A. Harvey, *Economic Expansion in the Byzantine Empire 900–1200* (Cambridge, 1989), pp. 63–4. For Bulgaria, see R. Rašev, V. Dinčev and B. Borissov, "Le village byzantin sur le territoire de la Bulgarie contemporaine," in Lefort et al., *Villages*, pp. 351–62.

[9] According to fragmentary evidence the population of Macedonia would have increased by 82 per cent between the twelfth and fourteenth centuries. Lefort, "The Rural Economy," *EHB* I, p. 274.

[10] For this estimate, and that of other scholars, see A. E. Laiou, "The Human Resources," *EHB* I, pp. 47–51.

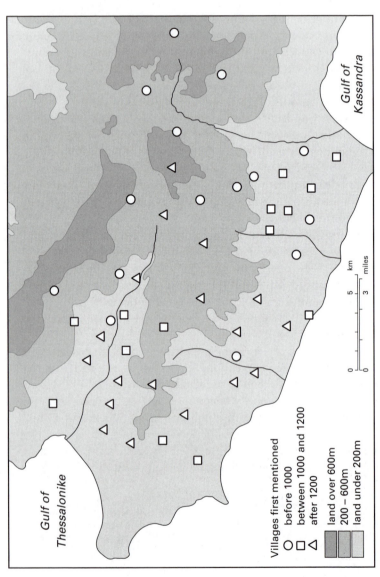

Map 5. Settlement (villages in Macedonia, tenth–thirteenth centuries)
(After J. Lefort, *Villages de Macédoine*, 1: *La Chalcidique ocidentale*, Paris, 1982)

Villages first mentioned
○ before 1000
□ between 1000 and 1200
△ after 1200

land over 600m
200 – 600m
land under 200m

Gulf of Thessalonike

Gulf of Kassandra

km
miles

In terms of security, the eleventh and twelfth centuries present a complex aspect. The restructuring of the countryside through measures that enhanced security had already gone a long way, and the positive effects of increased security were well established, especially in the Balkans. After the late eleventh century, some of the security function of the state was taken over by estate owners, who occasionally erected towers or undertook other security-enhancing measures on their estates; a phenomenon which increased in the fourteenth century.[11] Certainly, there were still invasions and insecure conditions in a number of areas, in some of which the effects were long-lasting. Thus, central Anatolia was lost to the Seljuks in the later part of the century, in the disintegration that followed the battle of Mantzikert, in 1071. In the twelfth century, the Byzantines continued to control the coastal areas. But along the mountainous areas of the southern frontier there were deserted areas, as near-anarchy prevailed.[12] In the Balkans, the incorporation of Bulgaria into the Byzantine state by Basil II (976–1025) removed for a time a factor of insecurity; but nomadic peoples (Ouzes, Petchenegs) made sporadic invasions, and the late eleventh century saw a period of instability, particularly because of the Petcheneg invasions which, however, were stemmed by Alexios I in 1092 and later on by his son, John II.[13] Real insecurity, or the fear of it, still governed the siting of certain settlements: in the part of Messenia covered by the Nichoria survey, even the twelfth-century settlements were sited away from the sea; in the southern Argolid, the new settlements of the early eleventh century were situated inland, in the upper reaches of the fertile valleys – perhaps for fear of pirates.[14] On the other hand, there was an influx of population into Byzantine areas from places now under foreign rule. Some

---

[11] See Laiou, "The Byzantine Village," p. 42.

[12] See especially the sources on the passage of the Third Crusade: *Gesta Friderici I imperatoris in Lombardia*, O. Holder-Egger (ed.), *MGH Script. Rer. Germ.* (Hannover, 1892), pp. 86 ff., 94; *Historia peregrinorum* in A. Chroust (ed.), *Quellen zur Geschichte des Kreuzzuges Kaiser Friedrichs I* (Berlin, 1928), p. 153; Ansbert, in *ibid.*, pp. 76 ff.

[13] See the list of invasions and troubles in Svoronos, "Société," p. 13; S. Vryonis, Jr., *The Decline of Medieval Hellenism in Asia Minor and the Process of Islamization from the Eleventh through the Fifteenth Century* (Berkeley, 1971), pp. 184 ff.

[14] W. A. McDonald, W. E. Coulson and J. Rosser, *Excavations at Nichoria in Southern Greece* (Minneapolis, 1983), p. 423; M. H. Jameson, C. M. Runnels and T. H. van Andel, *A Greek Countryside: The Southern Argolid from Prehistory to the Present Day* (Stanford, 1994), pp. 405–6.

Petchenegs were settled in the southern part of Serbia in the middle
of the eleventh century.[15] In the East, ever since the Byzantine reconquest of Cilicia (962) and until 1071, there was an influx of Syrian
Jacobites into northern Syria, Cilicia, Byzantine Mesopotamia and
the interior of Asia Minor. Armenian immigration, continuous since
the early tenth century, increased in the later part of the century and
became massive after 1071; Cappadocia was particularly affected. Jews
also migrated into Byzantine territory from Muslim lands in the late
tenth and eleventh centuries.[16] Thus, despite the ups and downs, the
demographic balance in the Byzantine possessions is certain to have
been positive, with some major local exceptions.

Finally, the upward demographic curve is doubtless linked to the
more general economic growth in a virtuous cycle, whereby a greater
population encourages production, specialization and exchange and
is in turn favorably impacted by them.

PRIMARY PRODUCTION

Agricultural activity and mechanisms

Agricultural activity took place in an economic environment marked
by greater urbanization and increased exchange activity. It must be
examined in terms of a number of important parameters, affecting
both the level of production and the impact of demand, in their
dialectical relationship. We will examine first the specificities of agricultural production during this period: the crops produced, the technological improvements and the institutional framework.[17] Intimately
connected with this is the level and structure of both domestic and

---

[15] E. Oberländer-Târnoveanu, "Les échanges dans le monde rural byzantin de l'est
des Balkans (VIe–XIe siècle)," in Lefort et al., *Villages*, pp. 381–401.

[16] G. Dagron, "Minorités ethniques et religieuses dans l'Orient byzantin à
la fin du Xe et au XIe siècle: l'immigration syrienne," *TM* 6 (1976),
pp. 176–216; D. Jacoby, "What do We Learn about Byzantine Asia Minor from
the Documents of the Cairo Geniza?," in *E Vyzantine Mikra Asia* (Athens, 1998),
pp. 87–9.

[17] Documentation becomes much more extensive in the thirteenth and fourteenth
centuries. In our discussion of certain aspects of production where conditions did
not significantly change in the intervening period, or where eleventh–twelfth-
century developments constitute trends that may be illuminated by the later
documentation, this documentation is used.

foreign demand for agricultural products. For, once the basic subsistence needs have been met, as well as the more extensive foodstuff needs of the elite, or of the non-producing but land-owning parts of the population (the state, the army in part, the great landlords, the Church hierarchy), there would be no need to increase production except in order to meet heightened commercial demand. Moreover, part of the production of the countryside (overwhelmingly, the products of woodlands and scrubland) always constituted objects of exchange.[18] Trade in agricultural products, therefore, is an essential component in the growth of agricultural production.

Specific to the period is the territorial contraction of the Byzantine state in Asia Minor and southern Italy. What was lost to the Seljuks was the plateau, which was primarily pastoral. In the earlier periods it had been an important source of cattle for the capital, and also of horses.[19] Southern Italy also was a stock-raising area. The loss of these provinces meant increased reliance on Thrace, Bulgaria and Macedonia, and, to a lesser degree, Serbia, as sources of meat and horseflesh.[20] Large-scale animal raising and horse breeding was practiced on large estates, and also by "specialized" transhumant populations, the Vlachs of both Byzantium and Serbia.

The remaining Byzantine territories included areas of heavy cereal production (Bulgaria, Thessaly, Thrace, Macedonia, Bithynia), as well as a long Aegean and Mediterranean coastland, and also islands, with high production of olive oil and wine.[21] All regions produced grain and some sort of fat; most produced wine; in all legumes were cultivated; all raised some animals, most had beekeeping. In the period under discussion, some significant amount of crop specialization is evident, quite apart from that encouraged by geographic and climatic conditions. Literary sources of the twelfth century,

---

[18] A. Dunn, "The Exploitation and Control of Woodland and Scrubland in the Byzantine World," *BMGS* 16 (1992), pp. 235–7 and *passim*.

[19] Koder, *EB*, Chapter 15.

[20] Hendy, *Studies*, pp. 53–6; Lefort, "The Rural Economy," *EHB* 1, pp. 263–7. Cf. L. Maksimović, "Le village en Serbie médiévale," in Lefort et al., *Villages*, p. 332; Harvey, *Expansion*, pp. 151 ff.; M. Kaplan, *Les hommes et la terre à Byzance du VIe au XIe siècle: propriété et exploitation du sol* (Paris, 1992), pp. 74–9. Large herds are also mentioned on islands such as Patmos, Rhodes and Cyprus. The number of cattle in Byzantine territories is considered remarkable by travelers of the twelfth century: A. P. Kazhdan and Ann Wharton Epstein, *Change in Byzantine Culture in the Eleventh and Twelfth Centuries* (Berkeley–Los Angeles–London, 1985), p. 29.

[21] Hendy, *Studies*, pp. 44–54.

including the poems of Ptochoprodromos, which mention varieties of cheeses and wines available in Constantinople,[22] make the case. In a well-known passage, the archbishop of Athens, Michael Akominatos (1175–1204), complained to the emperor about the burden imposed on the provinces by the demands of the capital city, inadvertently confirming the product specialization of various regions: "What do you [in Constantinople] lack? Are not the wheat-bearing plains of Macedonia, Thrace and Thessaly farmed for your sake? Are not the grapes of Euboia, Ptelion, Chios and Rhodes pressed for you? Are not your garments woven by our Theban and Corinthian fingers? Do not all the rivers of goods run toward the imperial city as if to the sea?"[23]

Cereal cultivation was, and remained, essential, even if in terms of market value cash crops were more profitable. In the eleventh and twelfth centuries, wheat and barley were the most important crops. Sporadic information does not permit us to establish with any certainty the proportion of the two grains; geography, and the fertility of the soil, must have played an important role – barley is a hardier grain than wheat.[24] Spring wheat, sown in February or March, was an important part of the crop rotation, and is mentioned both in the eleventh and the twelfth centuries. Innovations in cereal crops may well belong to our period. Rye appears for the first time in a late thirteenth-century document. Oats, presumably as fodder for horses, appear in the twelfth- and thirteenth-century sources. Millet was also cultivated, apparently in small quantities.[25]

It has been said that Byzantine agriculture suffered, especially in comparison to Western medieval agriculture, from a lack of technological innovation.[26] However, this negative assessment is in part misdirected and in part inaccurate. Technological "stagnation" is argued

---

[22] H. Eideneier (ed.), *Ptochoprodromos* (Cologne, 1991), Poem IV.

[23] S. Lampros (ed.), *Michael Akominatou tou Choniatou ta sozomena* (Athens, 1879/80) (repr. Groningen, 1968), II, p. 83.

[24] On various grains, see J. Teall, "The Grain Supply of the Byzantine Empire, 330–1025," *DOP* 13 (1959), pp. 87–139, especially pp. 99–100.

[25] Lefort, "The Rural Economy," *EHB* 1, pp. 250–1.

[26] Kaplan, *Les hommes et la terre*, pp. 46 ff., 68–9, 85–7; A. Harvey, "The Middle Byzantine Economy: Growth or Stagnation?" *BMGS* 19 (1995), pp. 244–5. John L. Teall was the first to realize that the agricultural tradition inherited by the Byzantines "embodied centuries of experiment by societies that had grown into . . . the Mediterranean environment": "The Byzantine Agricultural Tradition," *DOP* 25 (1971), pp. 35–59, here at p. 36; cf. his "The Grain Supply," pp. 129–30.

primarily on two grounds: the non-adoption of the heavy plough, as in Western Europe, and the absence of large-scale irrigation projects as in the Islamic world during the Abbasid period. To the first point, it has been objected convincingly that the traditional sole-ard is more appropriate than the heavy plough to the light, dry soils of the eastern Mediterranean regions, where a heavy plough might be disastrous.[27] As to irrigation, while there are no immense, state-funded projects in the Byzantine Empire, some large proprietors, such as the monastery of Lavra, did indeed carry out significant irrigation projects, as did, to a lesser extent, other estate owners; while the peasants also dug canals, for the construction of mills and possibly also for irrigation. Thus, the emphasis in recent literature is not on why the Byzantines did not adopt techniques used in Western European or Islamic countries, but rather on the fact that the tools and techniques they did use were well adapted to their environment.[28]

Backwardness or stagnation has also been argued with regard to an important capital investment, mills.[29] Hand mills, animal-drawn mills, water mills and windmills were all used in Byzantium. Water mills and windmills require an initial outlay of capital, but after that the only running cost is labor. In the *Farmer's Law*, water mills are erected by peasants.[30] In the eleventh–twelfth centuries, references to mills proliferate. While this may be due in part to the accidental nature of our sources, it may also indicate the spread of this labor-saving and profitable capital good in the period under discussion. This puts to rest yet another myth about the technological stagnation of Byzantine agriculture as opposed to the supposed technological revolution in Western Europe.[31] While most of the mills mentioned

[27] See also above, p. 31.
[28] Harvey, *Expansion*, pp. 122 ff. In any case, the great state-sponsored Islamic irrigation projects belong mostly to the early period and, besides, the agricultural system they served and promoted, with its excessive specialization, has been judged extremely fragile; the decline of agriculture began already in the tenth century: E. Ashtor, *A Social and Economic History of the Near East in the Middle Ages* (London, 1976), pp. 45 ff.; A. M. Watson, *Agricultural Innovation in the Early Islamic World: The Diffusion of Crops and Farming Techniques, 700–1100* (Cambridge, 1983), pp. 103–11, 139 ff.
[29] On mills in Western Europe, see J. Langdon, *Mills in the Medieval Economy* (Oxford, 2004).
[30] See also above, p. 31, on Late Antiquity.
[31] P. Toubert, "Byzantium and the Mediterranean Agrarian Civilization," *EHB* 1, p. 382.

in the sources belong to estate owners, peasants, too, continued to construct mills, since there was not, in the Byzantine countryside, a domanial structure that would force peasants to use the landlord's milling facilities, thus guaranteeing him a monopoly.[32] Windmills are attested more rarely. It is, however, certain that they were known and used in the Byzantine Empire. Documentary evidence attests their existence in Macedonia and Lemnos in the fourteenth and fifteenth centuries and in Rhodes in the mid-thirteenth century, before its conquest by the Hospitallers.[33]

There was, therefore, some innovation in Byzantine agriculture in the eleventh and twelfth centuries, but it was certainly not in the nature of anything resembling an agricultural revolution, a term which, in any case, is now not applied to Western Europe either. If there were no major technological innovations, what can account for increased agricultural production and productivity? It might be argued that increased production was a simple factor of the population increase. But there must have been increased productivity as well. The number of people who were not involved in agricultural labor but had to be fed had increased owing to urbanization. Not only are no famines attested in the twelfth century, there was even some export of agricultural commodities.[34] The rise in productivity is attributable to two factors, one social, but with economic causes and consequences among which the increased exploitation of the peasantry must be entertained, and one economic with social impact: institutional changes and the impact of the market. The two are closely connected.

---

[32] On mills, see *EHB* 1, pp. 110–12, 235–6, 280, 359–60, 381–2; Harvey, *Expansion*, pp. 128–33. The last point is made *ibid.*, p. 133; the same lack of domanial structure explains, according to Harvey, the fact that the Byzantines did not adopt the more expensive and complicated, but also more efficient, vertical water mill used in Western Europe. As for peasant investment in mills, that is clearly attested in the early fourteenth century: for documentation and analysis see A. Laiou and D. Simon, "Eine Geschichte von Mühlen und Mönchen: Der Fall der Mühlen von Chantax," *Bulletino dell'Istituto di Diritto Romano*, 3rd series, 30 (1992), pp. 619–76, esp. pp. 645 ff.; cf. Chapter V, pp. 176–77.

[33] G. Ntellas, "Oi mesaionikoi anemomyloi tes Rodou," *Archaiologika tekmeria viotechnikon engatastaseon kata te Vyzantine epoche, 5os–15os aionas* (Athens, 2004), pp. 279–301. Thus, the statement that "windmills may be associated with western innovation" (A. Bryer, "The Means of Agricultural Production: Muscle and Tools," *EHB* 1, pp. 111–12) must be modified.

[34] See pp. 135–38.

Landlords and peasants, production and investment

The major institutional change that took place over a period that extends from the tenth to the twelfth century is the shift from the village community of landowning, tax-paying peasants, prevalent in the earlier period, to the estate, cultivated by rent-paying peasants, that progressively dominated the countryside. Free landowning peasants who paid taxes to the state continued to exist until the end of the Byzantine Empire; but they were no longer dominant. This is a major shift, that implicates the relations of the state, the peasants and the great landlords; and it changed the nature of the state as well as of the economy, after the tenth century.

By the late eleventh century the estate had become an important institutional form in the organization of the countryside.[35] The estate, more or less large, cultivated by tenant farmers (*paroikoi*), became the structuring feature of the countryside. Estates belonged in the first instance to the state and the Church (the state remained the largest landowner throughout the period under discussion) and to individual large or medium-large landowners. The village retained a certain cohesion; in economic terms, there was probably cooperation among peasants who shared oxen or agricultural implements, or who cleared land together or constructed mills. There was also a degree of social cohesion manifested in the presence of the "first men of the village," the village elders, the *proestoi, kreittones, protogeroi* who mediated disputes and represented the village in its relations with outsiders.[36]

[35] N. Oikonomides, "The Social Structure of the Byzantine Countryside in the First Half of the Tenth Century," *Symmeikta* 10 (1996), p. 125 (reprinted in his *Social and Economic Life*, art. XVI), argues that already in the tenth century the free independent smallholder was on the way to becoming – if he had not already become – a minority, indeed, that in the mid-tenth century Peloponnese *paroikoi* were much more numerous than free landowning peasants. Cf. N. Oikonomidès, "La fiscalité byzantine et la communauté villageoise au XIe s.," *Septième Congrès international d'études du sud-est Européen, rapports* (Athens, 1994), pp. 89–102. Oikonomides' arguments are powerfully presented. It remains true that we cannot know the proportion of landowning peasants and *paroikoi*, and that some of the former survived deep into the thirteenth century and probably beyond. Also, regional differences must surely be taken into account.

[36] Laiou, "The Byzantine Village," p. 47. Cf. D. Kyritses and C. Smyrlis, "Les villages du littoral égéen de l'Asie mineure au Moyen Âge," in Lefort et al., *Villages*, pp. 437–51.

The process of the growth of the large estate must be sought in the land hunger of the *dynatoi*, the "powerful" civil, ecclesiastical and military officials who, by virtue of their office as well as the economic benefits conferred by it, were in a position to exploit weaker members of society, the *penetes*, that is, primarily the peasants.[37] The land hunger became evident in the tenth century, when the process was already under way. If there was a sustained population rise, as we have argued here, then necessarily the value of land relative to the other factors of production (labor and capital) would increase, explaining in economic terms (for there were also socio-political ones, given the high prestige of land in pre-industrial societies) the desire of powerful people to expand their landed holdings. This they achieved first by the purchase of the lands of smallholders and then, in the eleventh century and after, by the acquisition of lands through donation by the state itself, whether in full or in conditional tenure.

It is quite clear that landlords, starting with the state, were well aware of the increased profitability of land. Basil II, the emperor best known, in terms of agrarian policy, for his extraordinary measures aimed at stemming the increase of private estates, is also the emperor who, more than anyone else, promoted the creation of vast imperial estates, cultivated by tenant farmers and sometimes, until the early eleventh century, exploited directly through the use of slaves.[38] Among other measures, he took over the exploitation of lands left vacant for a period of 30 years (the *klasmata*), instead of ceding them on favorable terms to the neighbors of the original owners, as had been the practice in the tenth century. He furthermore tried to limit the potential rights of long-term (over thirty years) tenants to the usufruct of the land they leased, by moving them frequently. The Byzantine state continued such practices in the eleventh century, at the same time setting up its own units for agricultural production (*episkepseis, kouratoreiai*) in conquered territories. It did not hurt that these imperial estates had a huge turnover.[39] State and crown lands,

[37] The word *penes* (*penetes* plural) means "poor." However, in the present context the category is primarily social, not economic.

[38] References to slave labor in agriculture peter out later in the eleventh century; one might quote the telling statement from the *praktikon* of Miletos, in 1073: "No [income from] slaves, because they have died": M. Nystazopoulou-Pelekidou, *Eggrafa Patmou, 2: Demosion Leitourgon* (Athens, 1980), no. 50, pp. 122–3.

[39] N. Oikonomides, "The Role of the Byzantine State in the Economy," *EHB* 3, p. 1023.

however, decreased in the course of the eleventh–twelfth centuries, as a result of donations to individuals or institutions.[40]

While earlier generations of scholars saw nothing but gloom and decline, social, political and economic, in the rise of the estate,[41] over the last decades historians have started to look more closely at the economic benefits of this development.[42] These may be summarized as follows.

First, what the large estate did not do. It did not generate impressive economies of scale. To the extent that this was possible in the medieval context, the possibility was much reduced by the realities of land exploitation and the organization of production. Small-scale exploitation, that is, cultivation of the soil by peasant households cultivating small plots, rather than large-scale domanial exploitation, is typical of the Byzantine agricultural system in all periods, with the exception of imperial domains.[43] Exploitation is quite separate from land ownership, and must be differentiated from it. Whether land was owned by individual peasants or by estate owners, cultivation was primarily effected through and by the peasant smallholder, landowning cultivator or tenant farmer. There are, to be sure, some exceptions. At the time of Basil II, possibly, some state domains were, indeed, cultivated as large-scale enterprises; and there are some well-documented cases from a later period where domanial land, cultivated with labor services, formed a considerable part of an estate.[44] Furthermore, parts of the uncultivated territory, given out to pasture or exploited for the products of wood and forest, were exploited directly.

---

[40] See pp. 157–58.

[41] See, primarily, G. Ostrogorskij, *Pour l'histoire de la féodalité byzantine* (Brussels, 1956), p. 16; idem, *Quelques problèmes d'histoire de la paysannerie byzantine* (Brussels, 1956), p. 22.

[42] Harvey, *Expansion*, p. 161, Lefort, in various publications, and "The Rural Economy," *EHB* 1, pp. 284–99, are the salient examples. Western medievalists have revised earlier negative views: see P. Toubert, "La part du grand domaine dans le décollage économique de l'Occident (VIIIe–Xe siècles)," first published in *La croissance agricole du haut Moyen Âge, Flaran 10, 1988* (Auch, 1990), republished in his *L'Europe dans sa première croissance* (Paris, 2004), pp. 73–115.

[43] N. Svoronos, "Petite et grande exploitation à Byzance," *Annales* 11 (1956), pp. 325–35 (= N. Svoronos, *Études sur l'organisation intérieure, la société et l'économie de l'Empire byzantin* [London, 1973], art. II). Cf. M. Kaplan, "Remarques sur la place de l'exploitation paysanne dans l' économie rurale Byzantine," *JÖB* 32/2 (1982), pp. 105–14.

[44] The best-known such case is that of the village Mamitzon: see Chapter VI.

Nevertheless, the predominant form of land exploitation remained the peasant household.[45]

Whereas large economies of scale were thus not possible, more modest ones were. The landlords – or their stewards – had the means to organize production more efficiently. They had teams of oxen which they made available to peasants whose own animal power was insufficient. They owned agricultural implements as well as threshing grounds and mills which served to reduce the cost of doing agricultural business. Estate owners rationalized production in other ways as well. The estate steward (*epitropos*), a figure prominent in the eleventh century and after, represented the owner in the countryside, and oversaw projects of land improvement as well as the more humdrum aspects of production. Estate accounting, quite sophisticated in the eleventh century, gave the landlords an accurate and detailed view of their affairs, and would be helpful in guiding their decisions. Landlords, many of them educated men, took both a learned and a practical interest in agronomy and in the good management of their estates.[46]

The most important contribution of the estate owners may well lie in the fact that they were one of the two principal agents who carried out the land clearance and land improvement that made it possible for Byzantine agriculture to expand its production and improve its productivity in this period. A few examples will make the point. The eleventh-century Eustathios Boilas, exiled to eastern Anatolia for some political misdemeanor, cleared a considerable area previously uncultivated and uninhabited with the help of slaves, whom he subsequently freed and settled on plots as tenant farmers.[47] Later in the same century, Gregory Pakourianos, a Georgian aristocrat of a great family, and faithful general of Alexios I, effected improvements on the estates of the monastery he founded in Petritzos (Bachkovo). In the late tenth century, Athanasios, the *hegoumenos* of the monastery

---

[45] As, also, in parts of Western Europe: Toubert, "La part du grand domaine," *passim*.
[46] On this general topic, see Lefort, "The Rural Economy," *EHB* I, pp. 293–9. On the development of domanial accounting, which shows the existence of an economic concept of the profitability of land, see Lefort, "The Rural Economy," p. 296, with reference to Teall, "Byzantine Agricultural Tradition," p. 56. On the administration of imperial domains, see J.-C. Cheynet, "Episkeptitai et autres gestionnaires des biens publics (d'après les sceaux de l' IFEB)," *Studies in Byzantine Sigillography* 7 (Washington, D.C., 2002), pp. 87–117.
[47] P. Lemerle, *Cinq études sur le XIe siècle byzantin* (Paris, 1977), pp. 15–63.

of Lavra on Mt Athos, organized great land improvements, including an irrigation project. The state encouraged such activities by waving its right to tax the increased value of the land that resulted from them.[48] The other agent of land improvement is the peasantry.

What of the peasantry? It provided the labor for this agricultural expansion, to be sure. But did it profit from the increased production of wealth, or did expansion take place at the expense of the peasantry? It will be argued here that expansion took place in the context of greater exploitation of the peasantry, but also that the per capita income of the peasantry increased or, to put it in terms that will not raise philosophical hackles, that the peasantry was better off than in earlier periods. This is certainly not a contradiction; the argument hinges on the difference between a general rise in the standard of living, which trickles down to the poorer members of society and, at the same time, an increase in inequality that is concomitant with the accumulation of resources (land, primarily, in this period) in the hands of relatively few individuals or institutions. In the short and medium term, the two processes can coincide; in the long term, the standard of living of the poorer people will suffer when the expansion reaches its limits.

The accumulation of land meant that a large proportion of landowning smallholders became tenants on the estates. They became *paroikoi*, a designation usually rendered as "dependent peasant," although the terms of the dependence must be clarified.

This transformation is one of the social and economic developments most studied by scholars, though often in the somewhat unproductive context of a debate regarding Byzantine "feudalism."[49] The great historian George Ostrogorsky is the most eminent proponent of the view that the "feudalization" of the Byzantine Empire reduced the peasants to the level of serfs, impoverished them, and brought about the decline of both the economy and the state.[50] It was a powerfully argued and very influential view and, although the concept of "feudalism" in the Byzantine Empire has been vigorously debated, the idea that the transformation of the peasantry (or, to be precise, a

---

[48] Kaplan, *Les hommes et la terre*, p. 303; Lefort, "The Rural Economy", *EHB* 1, p. 298; Harvey, *Expansion*, pp. 160–1.

[49] See Harvey, *Expansion*, pp. 5–12.

[50] In the two major works already mentioned, *Pour l'histoire de la féodalité byzantine* and *Quelques problèmes* (above n. 41). On the debate see also J. Haldon, *The State and the Tributary Mode of Production* (London, 1993), pp. 71–5.

large proportion of the peasantry) into tenant farmers was the result of and itself resulted in impoverishment underlies a good deal of subsequent scholarship. More recent scholarship has corrected earlier views on the status of the *paroikoi*: they were not tied to the soil, although the head of household and his/her heir was, indeed, obligated to cultivate the land he held. From the eleventh century, they had the right to remain on the land they cultivated after thirty years had elapsed: the learned jurist who pronounced that decision said that long possession gave them quasi-proprietary rights, even though they were paying rent.[51] Eventually, the rights to the land became hereditary. Unlike the serfs of Western Europe, the *paroikoi* were not subject to (non-existent) manorial courts. Furthermore, a *paroikos* was not necessarily worse off than an independent farmer; much depended on individual circumstances. Finally, a fact of great significance is that, although there is, in Byzantium, legal literature that insists that *paroikoi* could not own and alienate landed property, in fact they did own land, vineyards and other assets, in the eleventh century to some extent, and increasingly later on.

In sum, recent scholarship has tended to evaluate the economic and even the social condition of the *paroikos* much more favorably than in the past. The decision of peasants to sell their land and become *paroikoi* is seen as a rational one since the landlords could protect them better from both the risks of bad crops or famine, and the exactions of the tax-collector, a serious risk in the eleventh century, when extraordinary taxes and corvées kept increasing. At the same time, many estate owners were acquiring privileges and immunities (*exkousseia*) which freed them from the obligation to pay the land tax; and their tenant farmers benefited from this exemption. As a result, it has been argued, the estate owners could essentially share with their *paroikoi* the benefits of tax exemption, and offer landowning peasants economic incentives to sell their lands and become tenant farmers.[52]

While these are important correctives to traditional ideas, the perceived benefits of the position of tenant farmer merit further discussion. The changes of the eleventh century, regarding security of tenure and ownership of property, were doubtless improvements for the rather limited number of people who, in the ninth century,

---

[51] *Peira* XV.2. Cf. *Peira* XV.3, and see, on this, N. Oikonomides, "E Peira peri paroikon," *Afieroma ston Niko Svorono*, I (Rethymno, 1986), pp. 238 ff.

[52] Oikonomidès, *Fiscalité*, pp. 211 ff.; Oikonomides, "The Role of the Byzantine State," pp. 1023–5; Lefort, "The Rural Economy," *EHB* I, pp. 237–9.

for example, had been *paroikoi* under an older legal regime. They were certainly no improvement for those who had been landowning smallholders with full property rights and full hereditary ownership; indeed, the positive changes surely came about because of the increasing presence of such people among the *paroikoi*. As for the economic results of the change of status, those seem to point to greater exploitation of the labor force, and the appropriation of a larger part of its surplus: the distribution of the value added of agricultural production changes to the peasant's detriment.

The basic land tax in Byzantium was still calculated as 1/24 of the value of the land. The peasants also paid a personal tax, and there were incidental taxes which became very heavy indeed after the 1030s. The rent owed by *paroikoi*, when paid in cash (*pakton*), amounted to double the base (land) tax the cultivator would have paid to the state if he had been a landowning peasant.[53] When the tenants worked in a share-cropping arrangement, they paid their rent in kind (one third of the harvest, most probably, a contract that appears in the eleventh century), but the *pakton* is better for purposes of comparison, since the tenant assumed the risks of cultivation as he would have done had he owned the land. J. Lefort has drawn up a theoretical model of the expenses and revenues of a farmer with a team of oxen (*zeugaratos*) in two different configurations: when he owned the land he cultivated, and when he was a tenant farmer. The landowning farmer would end up paying 23 per cent of his *income* in taxes; the tenant farmer would pay 33 per cent in rent. The budgetary surplus remaining in the hands of the *zeugaratos* (the richest category of peasant, with the exception of some few cases with two teams of oxen) would, in the first case, be 23 per cent of his total income; in the case of tenancy, the peasant would retain 14 per cent of his income.[54]

Caeteris paribus, what holds for fixed rent also holds for tax in coin when the tax burden is equal to or higher than the rent. But when it is lower than rent, as in Byzantium, then it would be in the economic interest of the peasant to own land. Therefore, in

---

[53] The calculation is made on the basis of the Miletos *praktikon* of 1073. Oikonomides, "The Role of the Byzantine State," pp. 1001 ff. *Praktika* are inventories of the possessions of laymen or ecclesiastics. In the thirteenth–fourteenth centuries, they include valuable information about the peasant household: the name of the head of household and all its members, their possessions, the tax and other dues owed by the household (but not the rent).

[54] Lefort, "The Rural Economy," *EHB* 1, pp. 302–3; Table I shows the budget of the peasant, and Table II that of the great landlord.

purely economic terms, the cereal-cultivating peasant would be better off owning arable land than renting it, whether in a share-cropping
arrangement or, *a fortiori*, in a fixed-rent agreement.

Some *paroikoi* cultivated their land with share-cropping contracts,
although we do not know how widespread this was during the period
under discussion. Modern studies have modified an older perception
that share-cropping is an inefficient form of cultivation because it dis-
courages investment on the part of both landlord and tenant. To the
contrary, it is arguable, and it has been argued, that share-cropping
serves *optimally* the interests of the tenant and the landlord taken
together (Pareto-efficiency); and that it is better than a fixed rent
for the peasant, since share-cropping implies risk-sharing.[55] Unfortunately, we do not know how widespread share-cropping was in this
period.

All in all, it seems accurate to say that there was increased exploitation of the peasantry, a greater part of whose production was divided
between the state and the landlords (including, in the latter category,
the state *qua* landlord, the Church, and private individuals). It does
not follow either that peasants were living at subsistence, let alone
near-starvation, levels or that tenant farmers were worse off in the
eleventh century than landowning peasants were in the ninth. Lefort's
calculations show that the peasant with a team of oxen had a budgetary surplus after the seed for the following year and the nutritional
needs of the household had been met: more of a surplus if he were
a landowner, less if he were a tenant, but nevertheless a surplus. He
was, thus, in a position to invest capital in land improvement.[56]

---

[55] Laiou, "The Agrarian Economy," pp. 345–6. Dennis Kehoe has argued, for
Roman agriculture, that share-cropping leads to less intensive cultivation and
to the expansion of the size of the holding until the marginal product of each unit
reaches zero. As he says, however, a necessary condition for this development is
that the shareholder have unrestricted access to open land, which was not the case
in Byzantium: D. P. Kehoe, *The Economics of Agriculture on Roman Imperial Estates
in North Africa* (Goettingen, 1988), pp. 177 ff. We may note, nevertheless, that
a real drawback for the peasant exists in all periods: if he cultivates land of low
productivity, what remains as his share may be insufficient for his survival.

[56] Kaplan's different, and much less optimistic, conclusions are to some degree due
to different assumptions about yield ratios in cereals: Kaplan (*Les hommes et la terre*,
pp. 81–2, 499) posits a ratio of 3.5:1, as opposed to Lefort's average of 4.8:1 for
first- and second-quality land: Lefort, The "Rural Economy," *EHB* 1, pp. 301,
259–60. Lefort also thinks the plots were smaller, therefore arguing for greater
efficiency: *ibid.*, pp. 247–8.

The evidence for investments by peasants (in the eleventh–twelfth centuries and later as well) is less abundant than that for landlords, in part because the main investment of the peasant was his labor (and that of his family, including the female members), and that did not enter any sort of calculation in the pre-modern period. It must, however, be admitted and evaluated by the historian. It was the peasant who created "invisible" agricultural capital, by keeping up wells and irrigation troughs, or, where necessary, building the stone ledges that kept the soil in place and permitted the cultivation of tiny strips of land. He also made more visible investments in high-yield assets. The most salient examples are investments in viticulture, sericulture, and mills. Investments in vineyards and olive trees were considered land improvement. The planting and cultivation of vineyards requires little capital; it does require labor. The vine was cultivated in most parts of the Byzantine Empire, therefore, and its fruits were potentially available to a large proportion of peasants as income supplement. The cultivation of the olive tree, which is limited to areas with a temperate "Mediterranean" climate, generally speaking not far from the sea-coast,[57] requires intensive labor during certain seasons, but little capital expenditure. Independent landholding peasants owned vineyards, and so did tenant farmers of the thirteenth–fourteenth centuries. The sources are very limited for the eleventh–twelfth centuries, but it is clear that tenant farmers owned vineyards at that time, as they did both earlier and later.[58] Putting land under vine

---

[57] P. Birot, *La Méditerranée et le Moyen Orient*, 2nd edn. (Paris, 1964), I, pp. 68–71, 78–9 (see Map 2); cf. Hendy, *Studies*, pp. 139–41.

[58] The information from the documents of the monastery of Iviron in the early twelfth century suggests that *paroikoi* owned vineyards. In the registry of 1104 (no. 54), where the possessions of the *paroikoi* are detailed, only arable land is registered. However, in line 394 we find the description of a parcel of (arable) land "near the vineyards of Komes." As it happens, we know two *paroikoi* of the same name in the same year or the same decade: a George "tou Kometos" (52.276, 51.61, and Appendix II), and a Kosmas, in-law of Komes, who was by far the richest *paroikos* registered in the account book of the steward of the monastery (53.300, and Appendix II). In many other instances, plots are said to lie near vineyards. It is logical to conclude that *paroikoi* did, indeed, own vineyards in this wine-producing area, although these were not registered presumably because the registers marked the rent-producing, not the tax-producing resources, something no longer the case in the thirteenth–fifteenth centuries. On the other hand, the purported ownership of 30 *modioi* of vineyard/garden held by a *paroikos* of Andronikos Doukas in 1073 (A. Harvey, "Risk Aversion in the Eleventh-Century Peasant Economy," *E Vyzantine Mikra Asia*, p. 80), is not relevant: the parcel seems to have belonged

cultivation is an investment in the sense that wine, quite apart from filling some of the caloric needs of the peasant household, was also a cash crop *par excellence*. Once peasants have access to the market, a situation that, with the proliferation of urban centers, large and small, was increasingly real in the period under discussion, the cultivation of vineyards becomes a profitable activity. A necessary condition for this development would be the legal right of peasants to own land, otherwise the incentive to invest would be lost. It has already been seen that the usual hysteresis of institutions in legitimizing real-life developments existed; but it is equally clear that tacitly that right was accepted.[59] This institutional flexibility is important to keep in mind.

Other revenue-producing agricultural activities were undertaken by the peasants. Apiculture produced wax and honey, both marketable. Fishing, the products of animal raising, and woodcutting must have provided some revenue.[60]

As for sericulture, in the eleventh and twelfth centuries, the cultivation of the mulberry trees and the production of raw silk became very active, responding to the increased demand of the silk industry.[61] The main areas of intensive silk cultivation and silk production were northern Syria, until it was lost in the wake of the battle of Mantzikert; the Byzantine possessions in southern Italy (the "theme" of Longobardia and especially Calabria; lost with the Norman conquests of the 1060s);[62] the Greek provinces – Boeotia, the Peloponnese; Asia

---

to the estate, and the *paroikos* was simply settled on it (as a part-time guard?). See M. Nystazopoulou-Pelekidou, *Vyzantina eggrafa tes Mones Patmou*, 2, *Demosion Leitourgon* (Athens, 1980), no. 50, pp. 274–6. For vineyards being the most profitable activity in cash terms, see Lefort, "The Rural Economy," *EHB* 1, p. 249; Harvey, *Expansion*, p. 148. On the importance of vineyards, see Kaplan, *Les hommes et la terre*, pp. 69 ff.

[59] See Chapter V for the later period, for which sources are abundant.

[60] Lefort, "The Rural Economy," *EHB* 1, p. 246. Horse-breeding was not a peasant activity but an estate one. In the eleventh century, there were two huge horse-breeding imperial estates in Asia Minor: Oikonomides, "The Role of the Byzantine State," p. 994.

[61] Much of what follows is indebted to D. Jacoby, "Silk in Western Byzantium Before the Fourth Crusade," *BZ* 84/5 (1991/2), pp. 452–500 (reprinted in his *Travel, Commodities and Shipping in the Medieval Mediterranean* (Aldershot, 1997), art. VII); also useful is G. C. Maniatis, "Organisation, Market Structure, and Modus Operandi of the Private Silk Industry in Tenth-Century Byzantium," *DOP* 53 (1999), although it refers to an earlier period.

[62] A. Guillou, "Production and Profits in the Byzantine Province of Italy (Tenth to Eleventh Centuries): An Expanding Society," *DOP* 28 (1974), pp. 91–109 and his

Minor; perhaps Macedonia; and the islands, primarily Andros. It was a very lucrative rural business, in which the peasant household held an important position.[63]

Peasants cultivated the mulberry tree and collected the cocoons, both activities that require much labor and attention. Smothering the larvae is a little more complicated. The subsequent stages of silk production need specialized care, and were most probably not carried out in the countryside. But peasants profited from the first stage of production, despite the fact that the purchase of cocoons took place in quasi-monopsonistic conditions that normally place the seller in a disdvantageous position.[64]

Finally, peasants also engaged in artisanal activities, which increased in this period and continued to increase in the thirteenth and fourteenth centuries. Rough pottery and metal objects of local manufacture have been found in the Peloponnese, where a forge was also found in Nichoria, in Djadovo and Kovachevo in Bulgaria, in the village of Paterma in Thrace, in Boeotia and in southern Italy.[65] The metal objects of local manufacture were made of iron, whereas copper and bronze are thought to have been imported from nearby towns. There is evidence, too, of the production of domestic textiles. These objects may have been marketed, but we know nothing on the subject in this period.

If one takes into account the market-oriented activities of the Byzantine peasant, the following conclusions emerge. Strictly in terms of his payments in taxes and/or rent, the peasant lost from the expansion of the large estate; i.e., *the level of exploitation rose*. But *in terms of per capita income*, the eleventh–twelfth-century peasant was better off than his ninth-century counterpart, because of the fact that his cash-crop producing assets were made more valuable through the impact of market enlargement. The benefits of growth would have

"La soie du Katépanat d'Italie," *TM* 6 (1976), pp. 69–84 (= A. Guillou, *Culture et société en Italie byzantine (VIe–XIe s.)* (London, Variorum Reprints, 1978), arts. XII and XIII respectively).

[63] Guillou, "Soie," pp. 83–4.   [64] Maniatis, "Organisation."

[65] C. Bakirtzis and N. Zekos, "Anaskafe sta Paterma Rodopes," *Thrakike Epeterida* 2, 1981, pp. 23–37; and the articles by Martin and Noyé, "Italie méridionale," B. Pitarakis, "Témoignage des objets métalliques dans le village médiéval (Xe–XIVe siècle)," A. Avraméa, "Thessalie," and R. Rašev, V. Dinčev and B. Borissov, "Le village byzantin sur le territoire de la Bulgarie contemporaine," in Lefort et al., *Villages* , pp. 160, 247–65, 219, 351–62 respectively.

been felt by great landlords (increasingly), by the state (in competition with private landlords), and by the peasantry to the degree that it had market access and that it increased the production of marketable goods; this would have counteracted the increased exploitation through the traditional means of tax and rent. By the same token, the economic power of the landlords never reached its full potential, since the accumulation of resources into their hands was partial. These conclusions run counter to ideas of peasant impoverishment as well as to the idea of a net benefit accruing to the peasant from the expansion of estates, but it appears justified by the evidence and is consistent with certain theories of pre-industrial economic growth and development, which place the emphasis on the beneficial role of the market.

A few words must be said about the role of self-sufficiency, especially as it affects the peasant economy. Self-sufficiency (*autarkeia*) was an ideological constant in the Byzantine Empire, as it was in other pre-industrial societies.[66] The ideological construct has been taken as an expression of reality by too many scholars. Its role in the peasant economy has been misinterpreted as the most serious restriction on economic growth.[67] The "self-sufficiency" of the Byzantine peasant is tied to the fact that he engaged in polyculture and polyactivity. These characteristics of Mediterranean agriculture, which last in some regions to our day, in fact allow the peasant a good deal of flexibility. Depending on circumstances, the peasant can oscillate between the bare minimum, which is survival, and the maximum, which is investment and the accumulation of wealth.

Alan Harvey has stressed certain benefits of polyculture, primarily those that reduce the cultivator's risk and lead him to self-sufficiency. Polyculture reduces the risk inherent in the uncertainty of harvests from one year to the next – or, rather, the certainty that some years would be bad, for reasons of climate, locusts, plant disease or human interference. It is efficient in terms of the use of labor, since work is spread out throughout much of the year.[68] Legumes fertilize the soil,

---

[66] See the interesting defense of self-sufficiency on the part of the "literati," in a Chinese text of the first century BC: E. M. Gale transl., *Discourses on Salt and Iron* (Taipei, 1967), passim.

[67] Harvey, *Expansion*, p. 120. The author later modified his position: Harvey, "Risk Aversion," pp. 80–1.

[68] For an agricultural calendar, see A. E. Laiou, "War, Peace and Economic Development in the Medieval Balkans," in *South-Eastern Europe in History: The Past, the Present and the Problems of Balkanology* (Ankara, 1999), pp. 76–7: it shows a peak

and animals are, in a sense, a store of value and proteins: they can be slaughtered and consumed or sold in bad years.[69]

Polyculture and polyactivity as practiced in the Byzantine Empire should not be taken as markers of production that is limited to self-sufficiency and autoconsumption. They very much allow for exchange, either through the surplus production of staples or through greater investment in marketable crops. Whether they do in fact lead to exchange depends on more general economic conditions. Where market conditions exist, and except in times of appalling dearth, the peasant can always sell or exchange the surplus of his differentiated production.[70] The sources make it absolutely clear that peasants did market part of their production, whether in local fairs or in other ways.[71] Polyactivity has a similar role, since the products of woodcutting, beekeeping and fishing can also lead to market. Any idea that polyculture led to a stunting of growth can only survive as part of the following chain of reasoning: the peasant, flexible in terms of cultivation and activity, and frequenting the market, hindered, by these activities, the accumulation of ever-greater wealth into the hands of the estate owners; if agricultural surplus is a necessary precondition of economic growth, then the rate of growth may be reduced; however, it is not self-evident that ever-greater accumulation of agricultural capital and surplus in a few hands is by itself the major factor in economic growth.

The active economy of exchange in this period underlies much of the development of the rural sector. High elite demand would have stimulated the production of quality wines, quality cheeses, good smoked fish, and, above all, silks. It might have stimulated such

---

for cereal cultivation in October–November and again in July–August; the peak for activities related to vineyards is in October–November or March (planting), and again in September.

[69] Harvey, "Risk Aversion," pp. 76–80, emphasizes these beneficial aspects of polyculture. There is no evidence that legumes were used as part of crop rotation; they acted as fertilizer only in the gardens where they were, presumably, sown: Harvey, *Expansion*, pp. 126–7.

[70] For the modern period, see G. B. Dertilis, *Istoria tou Ellenikou Kratous, 1830–1920* (Athens, 2nd edn., 2005), I, pp. 216–18; on self-sufficiency and the market see also M. Aymard, "Autoconsommation et marchés: Chayanov, Labrousse ou Le Roy Ladurie?" *Annales ESC* 38 (1983), pp. 1392 ff.; cf. A. Laiou, "Methodological Questions Regarding the Economic History of Byzantium," *ZRVI* 39 (2001/2), pp. 12–15.

[71] For the role of fairs, see p. 137.

production even if the products circulated outside the marketplace; but this theoretical possibility, beloved by a certain school of thought, does not account for much of the circulation of goods, as will be shown below.[72] Elite demand, though, when sufficiently active, reduces the costs of doing business for all levels of transactions, and thus affects the peasant economy as well. The high level of demand, both domestic and foreign, created a considerable market for agricultural goods. This will be discussed in more detail in connection with trade. It might be useful, however, simply to list here some of the products of the countryside that circulated in significant quantities: grain, obviously, wines, raisins and nuts of various kinds, olive oil, cheeses, timber, wax, honey, raw silk, horses and cattle traveled along the routes of inter-regional trade. Timber, cheese, medicinal plants from Crete and Asia Minor found their way to Egypt; in the twelfth century, Venetian merchants sold olive oil, grain and other commodities both inside the Byzantine Empire and outside it. Obviously, it was not the peasants but the great landlords, with better access to the market and much more concentrated commodities to sell, who most profited from the active economy of exchange; but the peasants, too, went to market.

There were three agents in the agricultural economy: the peasants, the landlords/estate owners and the state. The Byzantine state had traditionally impacted on the agricultural economy not only *qua* landlord but also, and especially and particularly *qua* state: through its fiscal role, and the encouragement or discouragement of trade. In this period, it contributed in a number of ways to the fuller exploitation of land. In the eleventh century, klasmatic lands were granted to monasteries and also to private individuals, such as a man named Leon Kephalas (who has become famous because by mere chance the dossier of land grants given to him has survived), so that they might be placed under cultivation. The improvements effected on these lands were often exempted from taxes, and landlords did not pay taxes when they established on their estates *paroikoi* who previously had not paid taxes to the state.[73] It has already been mentioned that *paroikoi* who "improved" land paid no taxes, or low taxes on it.

Fiscal developments will be discussed in connection with the more general role of the state in the economy.[74] For agriculture, the primary effect of fiscal measures was that part of the added value that had been collected as tax passed into the hands of individuals or

---

[72] See pp. 134–35.   [73] Oikonomidès, *Fiscalité*, pp. 216–18.   [74] See pp. 158–59.

non-state institutions either through tax exemptions or through the grant of lands and privileges. Indeed, after the reign of Basil II, state actions facilitated the shift to an estate-based agrarian economy, with all the results which have already been discussed, including greater productivity and greater access to the market.

In our discussion, we have emphasized the market as a structuring mechanism of the agricultural economy. This may raise some eyebrows, but it should not. A number of scholars have acknowledged the existence of a market in agricultural products in this period.[75] Here we have simply put in relief the various ways in which the existence of an active exchange economy influenced the behavior of the state, the landlords and the peasants, orienting their economic activities.

SECONDARY PRODUCTION

In this period, manufacturing and artisanal production is closely linked to the urban economy. As in the previous chapter, we will discuss specifically the production of pottery, glass and textiles. We will then turn to the economic role of the cities, as centers of effective demand, production, distribution and consumption, and pose again the question whether the Byzantine city was primarily "parasitic," i.e. a center of consumption based on the agricultural economy, or whether production and distribution were also important activities. The link with the section on commerce is evident.

Pottery

Pottery is not only an important item of production in the medieval economy; it also constitutes, along with coins, the most plentiful archeological evidence, with multiple significance.[76] Certainly, the typology of Byzantine pottery is not as far advanced as that of ancient

---

[75] See Harvey, "Risk Aversion,"; Kaplan, *Les hommes et la terre*, pp. 515 ff. The authors of the two most pertinent chapters in the *EHB*, Jacques Lefort and Nicholas Oikonomides, develop the interpretation given here which, indeed, is partly based on their analysis and conclusions.

[76] We wish to thank Demetra Papanikola-Bakirtzi who kindly read the pottery segments and gave us the benefit of her considerable expertise. She is in no way responsible either for the remaining errors of fact or for divergent interpretations. Angeliki Laiou is. On the production of pottery, glass and textiles, see now A. E. Laiou "Metaxy paragoges kai katanaloses: Eichan oikonomia oi Vyzantines poleis?" in *Praktika tes Akademias Athenon*, vol. 81 (2006), pp. 85–126.

pottery, and the evidence it provides for production and diffusion is still limited. However, analysis has been proceeding apace in recent years, and new evidence comes to light constantly.[77] In what follows, we will discuss glazed ceramics almost exclusively. Since these were used by a very large proportion of the population, including, probably, well-off peasants, globally they had an extensive, perhaps mass, market.[78]

A technological change as well as a change in decoration technique took place in the period under discussion. The first consists of the use of stilts, tiny tripods with sharp ends on which layers of pottery rest in the kiln; the innovation first appears in the Byzantine Empire around the year 1200, so, at the very end of the period examined here, and was commonly used subsequently. It reduces wastage, and probably facilitates the production of large numbers of pieces of pottery at one time; it may to some degree explain the greatly increased production of pottery in the first part of the thirteenth century.[79] The innovation in technique consists of the use of white slip, which permits more elaborate decoration of the ceramics.[80]

The area of Constantinople remains among the major centers of production throughout the period. The production of various types of glazed white ware pottery is attested through the twelfth century, although apparently the production begins to decline in the latter part of the period, and stops in the middle of the thirteenth century.[81]

---

[77] The bibliography on ceramics is very extensive, and some of it is included in excavation reports. It is not possible to give all of it here. We simply include some of the most recent publications which include the earlier bibliography. See V. François and J.-M. Spieser, "Pottery and Glass in Byzantium," *EHB* 2, pp. 593–609; V. Déroche and J.-M. Spieser, *Recherches sur la céramique byzantine, BCH Suppl.*, 1989; *VIIe Congrès international sur la céramique médiévale en Méditerranée* (Athens, 2003), especially the article by D. Papanikola–Bakirtzi ("Ergasteria efyalomenes keramikes sto Vyzantino kosmo," pp. 45–66) with the recent bibliography; H. Maguire (ed.), *Materials Analysis of Byzantine Pottery* (Washington, D.C., 1997); D. Papanikola-Bakirtzi (ed.), *Byzantine Glazed Ceramics: The Art of Sgraffito* (Athens, 1999); S. Gelichi (ed.), *La ceramica nel mondo bizantino tra XI e XV secolo e I suoi rapporti con l'Italia* (Florence, 1993).

[78] Spieser and François, "Pottery and Glass," p. 599; V. François, "La céramique byzantine et ottomane," in B. Geyer and J. Lefort (eds.), *La Bithynie au Moyen Âge* (Paris, 2003), p. 293.

[79] Spieser and François, "Pottery and Glass," p. 606.

[80] Papanikola–Bakirtzi, "Ergasteria," pp. 50–1: attested in Corinth in the late eleventh century.

[81] Papanikola-Bakirtzi, "Ergasteria," pp. 47–50. The production of white ware has also been identified in Nicaea: *ibid*. On White Ware see J. W. Hayes, *Excavations in Sarachane in Istanbul*, II (Princeton, 1992).

The increased imports of ceramics in the same period may signal a substitution of the objects of (relatively) elite demand in ceramics. Polychrome ceramics continue until the middle of the twelfth century; the highest concentration is around the year 1000.[82]

The second major center of production was Corinth. Glazed pottery was made here from at least the late seventh century. Production is attested, among other things, by the archeological evidence for kilns and the existence of wasters. Corinth produced large amounts of glazed pottery in the eleventh and twelfth centuries. Corinthian production is characterized by considerable variety of shapes as well as various types of decoration: Slip Painted, Sgraffito Ware and Measles Ware. The pottery of the eleventh century and after becomes more expensive, giving evidence of large and relatively discriminating demand. Potters created objects of high aesthetic quality, presumably responding to the needs of a clientele with the time and money to appreciate fine furnishings.[83]

Constantinople and Corinth are the two centers which may with certainty be associated with the production of glazed ceramics for large markets, catering to regional and inter-regional, indeed international trade. The pottery was widely disseminated in the Byzantine Empire, Venice, Italy, and, in the early thirteenth century, the Middle East.[84] However, given the state of the archeological evidence, it cannot be excluded that there were other such centers. The evidence of the shipwreck of Alonnesos/Pelagonnesi, of the mid-twelfth century, is tantalizing. It contained a large cargo of Fine Sgraffito Ware (1,500 pieces have been recovered), of very fine quality and high aesthetic value, which seem closely related to Corinthian production.[85] While

---

[82] On this, see above, Chapter III.

[83] G. D. R. Sanders, "Corinth," *EHB* 2, p. 651. See also G. D. R. Sanders, "An Overview of the Chronology for 9th to 13th century Pottery at Corinth," *VIIe Congrès International*, pp. 35–44, with the earlier bibliography; J. Vroom, *After Antiquity: Ceramics and Society in the Aegean from the 7th to the 20th Century AC. A Case Study from Boeotia, Central Greece* (Leiden, 2003), pp. 231–2.

[84] V. François, "Sur la circulation des céramiques byzantines en Méditerranée orientale et occidentale," in *VIe Congrès International sur la céramique médiévale en Méditerranée* (Aix en Provence, 1997), pp. 231–6; *La ceramica*, passim.

[85] On this, see Ch. Kritzas, "To Vyzantinon nauagion Pelagonnesou Halonnesou," *Archaiologika analekta ex Athinon* IV (1971), pp. 176–82; E. Ioannidaki-Dostoglu, "Les vases de l'épave byzantine de Pélagonnèse-Halonnèse," in V. Déroche and J.-M. Spieser, *Recherches sur la céramique*, pp. 157–71. The similarly enigmatic shipwreck off Kastellorizo carried a large cargo of Aegean Ware, of the early thirteenth century; it will be discussed in Chapter V.

it is not known with certainty where the wares were produced or where they were going, the material points to highly organized and specialized production. Indeed, this is true of all the up-scale ceramics of this period. The decoration is carefully done, with original themes, suggesting the existence of large and well-organised workshops, in places such as Corinth and Constantinople and perhaps others, with artisans who specialized in decorative techniques.[86]

Of great interest to the economic historian is the investigation of production in other cities and towns. As archeological evidence mounts, so does the number of urban sites where kilns, wasters or ceramics finds suggest small- or not so small-scale production of glazed pottery. Such places include, in this period, Athens, Sparta in the Peloponnese, with diffusion to Apulia, and Larissa in Thessaly. Less secure archeologically, but probable on other grounds, is production in Chandax (Crete), Thessalonike, Verroia, Kitros (ancient Pydnos) in Macedonia, Amorion, Nicaea, Phocaea and Sardis in Asia Minor, and Ganos (on the European coast of the Sea of Marmara: it is not, however, a city;[87] see Map 6).

Was this production meant only for local use, including the marketing to the immediate vicinity of the cities or towns? Probably this was the case for a number of sites. However, it was clearly not all. First, one is struck by the existence, anecdotal in the eleventh century, but more generalized in the twelfth and thirteenth, of Byzantine pottery (an amphora of the tenth–eleventh century) and glazed pottery in Apulia and the south of France (Languedoc, Provence and Corsica). Of these, some seem to have been manufactured in Attica in the eleventh and late twelfth centuries.[88] Indeed, Athens or Attica exported ceramics to Genoa in the twelfth and early thirteenth centuries.[89] Athens is a good candidate to emerge as a major center of production and export when more archeological evidence is studied. Secondly, production probably continued in the city of Amorion in

---

[86] Papanikola-Bakirtzi, "Ergasteria," pp. 63–4.

[87] See the articles by D. Papanikola-Bakirtzi, I. Kanonidis, N. Poulou-Papademetriou, L. Starida, Ai. Bakourou et al., N. Gunsenin, all in *VIIe Congrès International*; and the chapters by C. Foss and J. A. Scott (Sardis) and M. Kazanaki (Athens), both in the *EHB* 2. Map 6 shows the places where production is most securely attested by archeological finds.

[88] L. Vallauri et al., "La Circulation des céramiques byzantines, chypriotes et du Levant chrétien en Provence, Languedoc et Corse du Xe au XIVe siècle," *VIIe Congrès International*, pp. 137–52.

[89] *La ceramica*, p. 70. Glazed ceramics had been exported to Apulia since the late 9th century; *La ceramica*, pp. 104 ff.

this period.[90] Third, one is struck by the ceramics production of a city like Sardis, which was rather small at this time. In Sardis, considerable amounts of pottery have been found dating to the twelfth–fourteenth centuries, with the heaviest concentration in the thirteenth century. The use of local clay indicates local production. There were also local imitations of Chinese celadon and Syrian sgraffito.[91] The combination of elements would seem to suggest that Sardis produced and disseminated at least into its hinterland, possibly elsewhere as well, some quantities of ceramics. Finally, in the Dobrudja and in Cherson, there is imported Byzantine pottery, some from Constantinople but some also from Asia Minor, Greece, and other, unidentifiable places.[92]

The evaluation of the existing evidence from ceramics points to the following conclusions. The volume of production increased significantly from the tenth century onwards, not only in the major centers of production but also in smaller cities and towns. The production of unglazed ceramics is connected with the storage, transport and doubtless also the trade of agricultural products, as well as with increased demand for kitchenware. The production of glazed ceramics is connected with trade, local, regional and international. Unsurprisingly, there are hierarchies. One imagines that there were centers of production, perhaps in a household organization, where the producer might also be the seller, for local dissemination: the production of Chandax, in Crete, might well be of that kind. There are also intimations of regional dissemination: the case of Sardis, perhaps also Amorion, which was a trade center for Anatolia, as well as the nameless places which sent ceramics ino the Black Sea areas. The paucity of evidence in this respect is much to be regretted, since, as our colleagues who study the Western Middle Ages have pointed out, it is regional trade which, in many ways, forms the building blocks for larger commercial activity as well as, eventually, for international trade, at least in non-elite products. The production of Constantinople and Corinth, in well-organized workshops and with international diffusion, has already been discussed.

---

[90] Ch. Lightfoot, "The Public and Domestic Architecture of a Thematic Capital: the Archaeological Evidence from Amorium," *E Vyzantine Mikra Asia*, pp. 303–20.

[91] Foss and Scott, "Sardis," pp. 619–20 and J. A. Scott and D. C. Kamilli, "Late Byzantine Glazed Pottery from Sardis," *Actes du XVe Congrès international d'études byzantines, Athens, 1976*, vol. II.2 (Athens, 1981), pp. 679–96.

[92] I. Barnéa, "La céramique byzantine de Dobroudja, Xe–XIIe siècles," and V. N. Zalesskaya, "La céramique byzantine des XIIe–XIIIe siècles de Chersonèse," in Déroche and Spieser, *Recherches*, pp. 131–42 and 143–4 respectively.

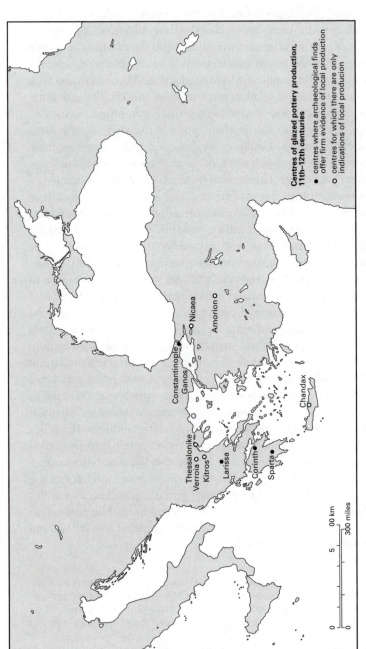

Map 6. Centers of glazed pottery production, eleventh–twelfth centuries
(Map by Demetra Papanikola-Bakirtzi)

● centres where archeological finds offer firm evidence of local production
○ centers for which there are only indications of local production

Centres of glazed pottery production, 11th–12th centuries

● centres where archaeological finds
offer firm evidence of local production

○ centres for which there are only
indications of local producion

We may also reach some conclusions about the structure of demand. The coexistence of local centers of production and the widespread diffusion of certain types of ceramics show the strength of domestic and foreign demand for these products; certainly an urban demand, possibly also a rural one.[93] The production of high-quality glazed ware points to a large market of relatively discriminating buyers: a relatively wealthy urban market that goes beyond the civil and military officials or the Church. The emerging differentiation of styles (between Constantinople and Corinth, for example) points to the same conclusion. A fact of great significance is the export of Byzantine ceramics to the Veneto and the rest of Italy in the eleventh–twelfth centuries, where they partly supplanted Sicilian and Egyptian ware. They were semi-luxury objects of sorts, and catered to a demand for "exotics." Techniques were also probably imported into Italy, helping to define the early production of Sgraffito Ware, especially in the Veneto.[94] This was a promising export market for Byzantine pottery.

Glass

This will be dealt with in rather a summary way.[95] More than in the case of ceramics, we have differentiated production of glass objects: luxury items for a small market; "architectural" glass, for window panes, tiles, and tesserae used for mosaics; and glass objects for everyday use, such as lamps, cups and other hollow vessels, small bottles, lamps or jewelry, especially beads and bracelets. There are, accordingly, three different markets and possibly three different types

---

[93] For examples of some glazed pottery of this period, see D. Papanikola-Bakirtzi (ed.), *Everyday Life in Byzantium* (Athens, 2002), pp. 325–69.

[94] G. Gelichi in *La ceramica*, pp. 9–46.

[95] The bibliography for glass is less extensive than for ceramics, except for particular cases, especially Corinth. See, in general, François and Spieser, "Pottery and Glass," pp. 592–8; J. Philippe, *Le monde byzantin dans l'histoire de la verrerie* (Bologna, 1970); articles in *First International Anatolian Glass Symposium, April 26th–27th 1988* (Istanbul, 1990); for glass as it appears in the written and visual sources, see A.-M. Talbot, "Evidence about Byzantine Glass in Medieval Greek Texts from the Eighth to the Fifteenth Century," *DOP* 59 (2006), and M. Parani, "Representations of Glass Objects as a Source on Byzantine Glass: How Useful are They?" *ibid*. I thank the authors for allowing me to see these articles before publication.

of production: the one-of-a-kind luxury objects which today grace the museums of Western Europe[96] were the work of highly specialized craftsmen and were produced for a small market: the emperor, the court, high officials of all kinds. The glass panes, including stained glass, and the tesserae were made specifically for buildings, including churches, probably the more important ones. The objects of everyday use can be found on almost all archeological sites and had a mass market.

Little is securely known about the centers of production of glass. It is assumed that Constantinople remained a center of production of luxury objects. The concentration of elite demand in the capital and the presence of highly skilled artisans producing other luxury items suggest that luxury glass objects were, indeed, manufactured here, but other centers may not be excluded.

Archeological evidence shows that stained window glass was manufactured in Constantinople in the twelfth century: two groups of finds place the production in 1124–1136 (church of the Pantokrator – Zeyrek Çamii), and 1120 (monastery of Chora – Kariye Çamii). The date of this glass has been much debated. The argument has been presented that the stained glass was manufactured after the Fourth Crusade, under Western influence. Scientific analysis, however, suggests that it was made locally by Byzantine artists.[97]

Glass tesserae for mosaics were also produced in Constantinople according to narrative sources of the eleventh century, and possibly in various other parts of the Byzantine Empire.[98] The production of tesserae can be considered quasi-industrial, since very large numbers of the tiny glass cubes are needed for wall mosaics and for mosaic

[96] For example, at the Treasury of San Marco: *The Treasury of San Marco* (Milan, 1984), pp. 191–9.

[97] J. Henderson and M. Mundell Mango, "Glass at Medieval Constantinople; Preliminary Scientific Evidence," in G. Dagron and C. Mango (eds.), *Constantinople and its Hinterland* (Aldershot, 1995), pp. 346–56. At the very least, chemical analysis shows that the glass was made in the East, not imported from the West: R. H. Brill, "Chemical Analysis of the Zeyrek Çamii and Kariye Çamii Glass," *DOP* 59 (2006). There is no reason to suppose, as does F. dell'Acqua, that it was made by Western artists in the Komnenian period: "Enhancing Luxury through Stained Glass from Asia Minor to Italy," *ibid.* I thank both authors for allowing me to see their articles before publication.

[98] A. Cutler, "The Industries of Art," *EHB* 2, pp. 560–1, with reference to L. James, *Light and Colour in Byzantine Art* (Oxford, 1966), pp. 23–4.

icons. Loads of tesserae were the object of international trade, with Kiev, for example.[99]

Architectural glass (window panes) of local manufacture has been found in Sardis, Amorion and Corinth.[100] It is also mentioned in written sources that refer to the palace and a church in Constantinople.

Our knowledge of the centers of production of glass objects for everyday use is vague. Corinth is a prime candidate for the production of large quantities of such objects, of varying quality, including colored, decorated, and gold-painted ones. G. R. Davidson had identified two glass workshops in Corinth, dating them to the eleventh–twelfth centuries. Subsequently, D. Whitehouse found the dating insecure, and suggested, on equally insecure grounds, that one of the workshops dated from the Frankish period (thirteenth–fourteenth centuries), and that the artisans were Italian.[101] More recently, C. S. Lightfoot has found similarities between glass excavated in Amorion and some Corinthian production; since Amorion was abandoned in the late eleventh century, this would argue against Whitehouse's suggestion.[102]

Large quantities of glass for everyday use have been found in Corinth, Sardis (datable to the thirteenth–fourteenth centuries), Pergamon, and now Amorion (about 7,500 fragments have been published so far, but not all from the tenth–eleventh centuries).[103] There

---

[99] For the information in this paragraph, see Cutler, "The Industries of Art," pp. 557–61.

[100] Henderson and Mango, "Glass," p. 343.

[101] G. R. Davidson, "A Medieval Glass Factory at Corinth," *AJA* 44 (1940), pp. 297–327; D. Whitehouse, "Glassmaking at Corinth: A Reassessment," *Ateliers de verriers: de l'antiquité à la période pré-industrielle* (Rouen, 1991), pp. 73–82. The glass was published by G. R. Davidson, *Corinth*, XII, *The Minor Objects* (Princeton, 1952).

[102] C. S. Lightfoot, "Glass Finds at Amorium,"*DOP* 59 (2006), at note 33. I thank the author for allowing me to see this article before publication. We also thank Dr Lightfoot for helping us with the pottery and glass from Amorion. In a very recent paper, Lightfoot shows that findings of glass cullet, waste threads and so on posit the existence, in a period earlier than the 11th century, of glass workshops within the city. Henderson and Mango (pp. 343–4) also seem somewhat skeptical about Whitehouse's theory.

[103] M. A. V. Gill, *Amorium Reports, Finds I: The Glass (1987–1997)* (Oxford, 2002), esp. p. 58. Cf. E. Ivison and C. S. Lightfoot, "Concluding Remarks," in the same volume, 259–64.

are traces of glass manufacturing in Kherson and Preslav.[104] Glass vials of the twelfth century have been found in Paphos (Cyprus). Glass is poorly studied, and only recently have archeologists given it much importance, especially on the lesser sites. The case of Amorion, therefore, acquires some importance. The discovery of large amounts of glass for everyday use in this city, and the existence of glass cullet, shows that the use of glass was widespread, and that there was very considerable local production of glass. A large workshop with master craftsmen who painted glass and produced a good number of bracelets has been proposed.[105]

Finally, mention must be made of the Serçe Limani shipwreck. This was a Byzantine ship, perhaps built in or around Constantinople, with a mixed Greek–Bulgarian crew, which was sailing west from Syria, and sank off Rhodes, in the 1020s. It carried, among other things, three tons of glass cullet, as ballast. The destination must have been a Byzantine center of large-scale glass production – Corinth?[106]

Conclusions on the production of glass must be tentative, and may change as the archeological record grows and finds are analysed. Elite demand governed the production of luxury glass. It is also probably the case that the production of elite glass, including glass tesserae, predated the manufacturing of more mass-oriented products. If this is so, then elite demand may have spurred the demand for cheaper substitutes. The active urban construction business of the eleventh–twelfth centuries led to the local production of architectural glass. At the same time, there was very considerable production of glass for everyday use, both locally and, most probably, at large production centers still to be securely identified; Corinth is a very likely candidate. What we clearly have, given the quantity of glass finds, is large-scale production. It is noteworthy that even the production of some inexpensive glass items requires a high level of technical expertise. Byzantine artisans, active in the cities, produced glass objects for everyday use; and trade in the same items is an extremely strong

---

[104] A. Bortoli and M. Kazanski, "Kherson and its Region," *EHB* 2, p. 663; I. Jordanov, "Preslav," *EHB* 2, p. 669.

[105] C. S. Lightfoot, E. A. Ivison et al., "The Amorium Project: 1998 Excavation Season," *DOP* 55 (2001), pp. 394–6.

[106] F. Van Doorninck Jr., *EHB* 2, pp. 902–3; F. Van Doorninck Jr., "The Byzantine Ship at Serçe Limani," in R. Macrides (ed.), *Travel in the Byzantine World* (Aldershot, 2002), pp. 137–48. Another ship from Syria, with similar cargo, has been found very close by.

possibility. Byzantine glass of the eleventh and twelfth centuries, for example, has been found in Novgorod and the Dobrudja.[107] The domestic market was the urban population, possibly the rural one as well for the cheaper items that have been found on rural sites.

Textiles

Any discussion of textiles in Western Europe would be focused on woolen cloth as far back as the time of the Carolingians.[108] For the Byzantine Empire, we have exiguous information regarding the production and sale of woolen cloth in this period. Doubtless woolen garments were made not only at and for the home, but also in larger units. Asia Minor was known for its woolen cloth and carpets. But the details of the organization of production and the mode of distribution escape us.[109]

Silks are another matter. The production of silk textiles was an important part of the Byzantine economy. Silks were, originally, a high-status item, a status symbol as well as a store of value. However, the dissemination of silks ran the gamut between a "coupon system" of diffusion by imperial gift, and commercial marketing.[110] High-quality Byzantine silks, often given as gifts to foreign monarchs, survive in a number of European museums.[111] The story of second-quality silks or garments made of silk and other yarns, has to be reconstructed solely from documentary evidence.[112]

---

[107] Philippe, *Le monde byzantin*, pp. 176–8, 185.

[108] See A. Verhulst, *The Carolingian Economy* (Cambridge, 2002), pp. 73 ff.

[109] S. Vryonis, Jr., *The Decline of Medieval Hellenism*, (Berkeley, 1971), p. 23.

[110] I borrow the expression "coupon system," meaning a system in which access to status-conferring goods is restricted and is given as part of a political or diplomatic, not an economic, process, from K. Pomeranz, *The Great Divergence* (Princeton, 2000), pp. 128 ff. His description of the shift from a coupon system to a fashion system in China is pertinent to any discussion of the silk industry in the Byzantine Empire in the tenth–twelfth centuries.

[111] See, for example, the catalogue of the exhibition at the Louvre, *Byzance* (Paris, 1992), pp. 370 ff.

[112] A large bibliography exists on the silk industry. There is no question of reproducing it here. The reader is referred to the following studies, for the period under discussion: R. S. Lopez, "Silk Industry in the Byzantine Empire," *Speculum* 20 (1945), 1–42 (= R. S. Lopez, *Byzantium and the World around it* (London, 1978), art. III); the various studies of Anna Muthesius, some of which are reproduced in her *Studies in Byzantine and Islamic Silk Weaving* (London, 1995); A. Muthesius, "Essential Processes, Looms, and Technical Aspects of the Production of

As with the other major manufactured commodities, emphasis will be placed here on the patterns of demand and the markets to which production responded, as well as the centers of production. The marketing of silk cloth will be dealt with, for the most part, in the section on trade.

The demand for silk cloth was variegated, since a number of different types of silk existed. There was, that is, a very high elite demand for silks, which lasted through the twelfth century. Elite demand undoubtedly affected the rest of the industry: the acquisition of this item of great symbolic value was desired by members of the upper class, but also by others. It is no accident that dowry goods included silk kerchiefs or brocade bedcovers.[113] The existence of half-silks, silk mixed with other yarns, shows that demand trickled down to the level of people of very moderate wealth.[114]

Demand for silks of all qualities increased in the course of the eleventh and twelfth centuries.[115] The increased wealth of both the aristocracy and the urban population at large made it possible for more people to indulge in their desire to acquire pieces of this status commodity. There was also foreign demand, as Byzantine silks were marketed by the Venetians and Genoese in Western Europe, and by the Byzantines in Egypt. As the prohibition of the export of very high quality of silks appears to have lapsed, so the commercialization of production rose.[116] Indeed, the court demand for top-quality silks may have declined as a proportion of total demand, as is evidenced by the fact that diplomatic gifts of silk cloth were much reduced. The last big gift in silk robes to a western potentate was that to

---

Silk Textiles," *EHB* I, pp. 147–68; D. Jacoby, "Silk in Western Byzantium before the Fourth Crusade," *BZ* 84/5 (1991/2), pp. 452–500, a valuable work in terms of the information collected therein, even though I disagree with many of its assumptions. See also M. Kaplan, "Du cocon au vêtement de soie: concurrence et concentration dans l'artisanat de la soie à Constantinople aux Xe–XIe siècles," EYΨYXIA, *Mélanges offerts à Hélène Ahrweiler* (Paris, 1998), pp. 313–27: mostly on the tenth century, but with interesting forward projections.

[113] The information comes from the dowry of Jewish brides in the twelfth century: S. D. Goitein, *A Mediterranean Society*, vol. 4 (Berkeley and Los Angeles, 1983), pp. 299–303, 322–5.

[114] Jacoby, "Silk in Western Byzantium," pp. 474–5, with an imaginative and felicitous use of sources.

[115] *Ibid.*, pp. 472–3.

[116] A. E. Laiou, "Monopoly and Privileged Free Trade in the Eastern Mediterranean (8th–14th century)," *Chemins d'outre-mer: études d'histoire sur la Méditerranée médiévale offertes à Michel Balard* (Paris, 2004), pp. 515–17.

Robert Guiscard, in 1074 (one hundred pieces of silk cloth), although an annual gift of forty pieces of silk seems to have been promised to the Sultan of Iconium in the late twelfth century.[117]

There was increased and variegated demand, then, for top-quality, "imperial" silks, as well as for silks of lesser quality. Production responded very satisfactorily. There is plentiful evidence (relatively speaking) of the expansion of the manufacture of silk cloth outside Constantinople, especially in the cities of Greece and the Peloponnese, but probably in other provincial centers as well. The production of half-silks is notable. These were exported, but they were also, doubtless, marketed internally, and could have developed into an important branch of the trade if conditions had not changed in the thirteenth century.[118]

Constantinople remained a center of production of silk cloth, although not much is known about the details. One assumes that the private manufacture of silk, with its complex guild structure, continued until the end of the twelfth century. With the Fourth Crusade, the level of demand fell and the industry was disrupted; in its place, the empire of Nicaea began to produce silk cloth, presumably for the needs of the Byzantine court which had removed itself there. The silk industry was not restored in Constantinople after 1261, when the city became again the capital of a much reduced empire.[119]

The novelty is that provincial centers proliferated in this period, and sent some of their production to Constantinople. The major silk-producing city was Thebes, closely followed by Corinth. The silk production of Thebes is well attested. Indeed, we have here the only surviving archeological evidence of what seem to be dye shops for textiles. The city was situated in a fertile plain where the mulberry tree could grow; it also had excellent water, used in silk production. And it was relatively close to the major source of supply of *murex*, the city of Athens.[120] Both men and women worked at the Theban silk factories; this is one of the rare cases in which the labor of women is specifically mentioned. They produced red samite along with other kinds of cloth. So famous were the silk weavers of Thebes and Corinth, that

---

[117] See, in the last instance, Laiou, "Monopoly," p. 516.   [118] See pp. 189–92.

[119] D. Jacoby, "The Jews and the Silk Industry of Constantinople," in idem, *Byzantium, Latin Romania and the Mediterranean* (Ashgate, 2001), art. XI, 18–19.

[120] For the dye workshops, see C. Koilakou, "Viotechnikes egkatastaseis Vyzantines epoches ste Theva," *Arkhaiologika tekmeria*, pp. 221–41; water pipes have also been found in Thebes.

in 1147 the Norman king, Roger II, not only sacked these cities and took silks as loot, he also carried away to Sicily the silk workers and set them to work at the royal factories in Palermo, or so the story goes.[121] When Benjamin of Tudela went through Thebes in the early 1160s, he found Jewish silk workers among the two thousand Jews who lived there; he writes that they were the "best craftsmen in the land of the Greeks at making silk and purple garments."[122]

The importance of Thebes as a major center of production of silk textiles is doubtless the main reason why the Venetians had a strong presence there, while in 1171 the Genoese wanted to get permission to buy silk cloth in Thebes "as the Venetians habitually did." The city produced silks of very high quality, but also, one supposes, less valuable silk cloth; this would be natural once the initial investment in silk works had been made.

Other centers of silk manufacturing in Greece include Corinth, Thessalonike, Patras, Euboea and Andros. Silk cloth was also probably produced in Asia Minor. It must be stressed that the available information is fragmentary and fortuitous; there is no reason to believe that silk production was limited to these cities and areas.

The silks were disseminated in a couple of different ways. If Benjamin of Tudela is to be believed, some of the high-quality silks ("silk and purple garments") were sent to Constantinople as tribute or tax.[123] But it is absolutely certain that in large part the silks were sold on the open market. The *Timarion*, a satirical work written around 1110, mentions that at the great fair of St Demetrios (26 October) in Thessalonike, textiles and yarns from Boeotia and the Peloponnese were sold. Documentary evidence shows that in the course of the twelfth century Byzantine silks, both of good quality and cheaper stuffs, were sold in Western Europe as well as in Egypt.[124] Imitations of Byzantine silks were produced in Palermo and in Egypt, a

---

[121] Choniates, ed. van Dieten, pp. 73–6, esp. p. 74; Otto of Freising, Monumenta Germaniae historica, *Scriptores*, XX, 370; *Ioannis Cinnami Epitome rerum ab Ioanne et Alexio Comnenis gestarum*, ed. A. Meineke (Bonn, 1836), pp. 92, 118–19, 174–5.

[122] M. V. Adler (transl.), *The Itinerary of Benjamin of Tudela* (Malibu, 1983), p. 68. The translation quoted here is from Jacoby, "The Jews and the Silk Industry," p. 8, who considers the existing translations to be inexact.

[123] Jacoby, "The Jews and the Silk Industry," p. 9.

[124] R. Romano (ed.), *Timarione* (Naples, 1974), p. 54; Jacoby, "Silk in Western Byzantium," and see also his "Byzantine Trade with Egypt from the Mid-tenth Century to the Fourth Crusade," *Thesaurismata* 30 (2000), pp. 25–77.

clear indication of the demand for Byzantine silks, which led to the fabrication of imitations, the way modern seamstresses might copy Parisian styles.

The high demand for silks both inside the Empire and in foreign markets must be responsible for the increase in production. At about the same time, around the year 1000, a more advanced hand draw-loom was introduced which made the production of some silk cloth (lampas weave) less labor-intensive and cheaper.[125]

It has been suggested that the investors in the provincial silk pro-duction, specifically that of Thebes, must have been the local *archontes*, the landowners of the Boeotian plain, since no other group had the money to invest in the necessary infrastructure.[126] There is no rea-son why enterprising provincial landowners could not have invested in the silk industry; but it must be equally stressed that there is no direct evidence to that effect, and that the argument rests on conjec-ture. Another likely group of investors would be the merchants, who had the advantage of knowing the market, having easy access to it, and being able to buy cocoons and yarn both in the countryside and in foreign markets: Italian raw silk, at least, was used in this period. The organization of the silk industry of Constantinople in the tenth century is well known (even though there is much disagreement on details) from the *Book of the Prefect*. It may provide some clues for the twelfth-century provincial industry. The guild of the *metaxarioi*, who wove the silk, dyed it and cut it, occupied a pivotal position, but the guild structure in the tenth century did not allow for vertical or horizontal integration.[127] There is no evidence that strict controls or such a guild structure existed in the provincial industry.[128] If it did not, then there would be nothing to hinder the manufacturers from selling their cloth, and the functions of manufacturer and merchant could well have fused; merchant capital could have been invested in

---

[125] Muthesius, "Essential Processes," p. 158, with reference to her *Byzantine Silk Weaving*, Chapter 9.

[126] Jacoby, "Silk in Western Byzantium," pp. 477–80.   [127] See above, Chapter III.

[128] The information on provincial craft associations is exiguous. The existence, in Thessalonike, of a "protos ton kamelaukadon" has led N. Oikonomides to speak of "a free trade grouping the craftsmen fabricating the hats called *kame-laukia*," of which this man was the head: N. Oikonomides, "The Economic Region of Constantinople: From Directed Economy to Free Economy and the Role of the Italians," in G. Arnaldi and G. Cavallo (eds.), *Europa medievale e mondo bizantino* (Rome, 1997), pp. 221–38 (= N. Oikonomides, *Social and Economic Life in Byzantium* (Aldershot, 2004), art. XIII), 236, n. 48.

the production of silk textiles. While this, too, is conjecture, it is not an unlikely one.

As for the workers, all we know for certain is that the silk industry employed people with high technical skills. Because of Benjamin of Tudela's travel narrative, we know that Jews were among the silk workers, and that they were considered very skillful; but they were certainly only part of the labor force. We also know that both men and women worked in the silk industry, even in the most skilled aspect of it, which was weaving.[129]

In the eleventh and twelfth centuries the silk industry expanded. It was well organized, producing both very high-quality silks which responded to elite demand, and silks of lower value for a much larger market. It catered to both a domestic and a foreign market. The cities where silk was produced had a complex economy, and part of their population prospered whether from their investment in silk, or by working in the industry, or by marketing the final product.

THE URBAN ECONOMY

Urban expansion reached its apex in the eleventh and twelfth centuries. It is visible primarily in the Balkans, for Asia Minor, especially the interior, was disrupted by the Turkish advance in the late eleventh century. Earlier in that century, the important city of Amorion did expand and became an important commercial center. The urban expansion was physical, as many agglomerations which had contracted severely in the seventh and eighth centuries began to spread outside the early medieval nucleus. Constantinople seems to have covered the entire sixth-century site.[130] The increase of the urban

---

[129] In this connection, one must recall the existence, in eleventh-century Constantinople, of organized groups of female textile workers, wool and linen carders, spinners and weavers who may even have been members of guilds, and who certainly had their own annual festival: A. Laiou, "The Festival of 'Agathe'; Comments on the Life of Constantinopolitan Women," *Byzantium; Tribute to Andreas N. Stratos* (Athens, 1986), I, pp. 111–22.

[130] P. Magdalino, "Medieval Constantinople: Built Environment and Urban Development," *EHB* 2, 535. On cities, see G. Dagron, "The Urban Economy, Seventh–Twelfth Centuries," *EHB* 2, pp. 393–461; C. Bouras, "Aspects of the Byzantine City, Eighth–Fifteenth Centuries," *EHB* 2, pp. 539–54 and the various case studies in the same volume; Harvey, *Economic Expansion*, Chapter 6; M. Angold, "The Shaping of the Medieval City," *ByzForsch* 10 (1985), pp. 1–38, with which the present analysis disagrees on a number of points. For a list of Byzantine towns

population in some places was dramatic. Constantinople reached a population of 400,000. Thessalonike was certainly the second most important city of the Empire, but we have no real information about its demographics; by analogy, one might imagine a figure of about 150,000. Corinth has been estimated as having a population of 20–25,000 and Monemvasia one of 20,000. Other cities, like Thebes, must have reached similar figures. Much smaller agglomerations abounded. It is instructive that al-Idrisi, the Arab geographer from Sicily who wrote in 1154, mentions a very large number of cities in the Balkan provinces which he describes as well populated and with commercial activity. In the Peloponnese alone, he says that there were 50 cities, thirteen or sixteen of which were important and renowned. He mentions such cities along the sea coasts but also in the interior; he notes the existence of three major cities in Cyprus, and cities in Chios, Samos, Skiros and other Aegean islands.[131]

The cities of the seventh, eighth and ninth centuries had functioned primarily as administrative and military centers, refuges, and centers of ecclesiastical administration. It is clear, however, that they also acquired, soon enough, the usual role of an urban agglomeration, as places where both production and exchange of commodities took place. By the tenth century, and much more clearly in the eleventh and twelfth, a very large number of cities, not only coastal ones but also cities situated inland, such as Ochrid, Thebes and Ioannina in the Balkans, Euchaita and Amorion in Asia Minor, played an important commercial role.[132] The fragmentary record shows that almost all the cities for which we have any kind of archeological information were also centers of production, and that among them many more cities than we realized had large-scale production of some of these items, for the market. Furthermore, the very expansion of the urban space produced something of a building boom.

that were created in the medieval period, and those that expanded from an earlier nucleus see Bouras, "Aspects," pp. 501–3. See also T. Loungis, "E exelixe tes Vyzantines poles apo ton 4o sto 12o aiona," *Vyzantiaka* 16 (1996), pp. 32–67, esp. p. 67, based mostly on written sources; A. Dunn, "The Survey of Khrysoupolis and Byzantine Fortifications in the Lower Strymon Valley," *JÖB* 32/4 (1982), pp. 605–15. For Macedonian cities, see F. Karagianne, "Oi oikismoi ste Makedonia kata te Mese kai Ystere Vyzantine periodo mesa apo ta archaiologika dedomena," *Mnemeio kai perivallon*, 7 (2001), pp. 57–74.
[131] P. Jaubert (transl.), *La géographie d'Idrisi* (Paris, 1836), vol. II, pp. 121–32, 286–303.
[132] On commerce, see pp. 133 ff.

Effective demand for manufactured products was concentrated in the cities: for one thing, the Byzantine aristocracy was an urban one. Elite demand for expensive, high-status items increased in the eleventh–twelfth centuries. Rich aristocrats and urban elites manifested a new interest in luxuries. But the urban middle class was not far behind; its members, too, were interested in what the aristocracy enjoyed. And demand trickled down, even to less affluent people, and even to the countryside, with its modest need for inexpensive glass or metal jewelry.[133] As demand went down the social scale, semi-luxury items or goods of good quality but not of very high cost were produced to meet it. Evidence of greater wealth, this broad-based demand for manufactured products leads not only to greater production but also to specialized and even complementary production in certain cities: see the complementarity of Thebes with its silk industry and Athens with its red dye and soap. Constantinople still occupied a special place as a great center of consumption of alimentary products and raw materials, a city where the service sector was very active, and a center for the production of all sorts of manufactured items and buildings. It still set the fashion. But the decentralization of the state[134] was mirrored in the progressive decentralization of demand, leading to the creation of provincial networks that were less dependent than before on the pull of Constantinople.

The people who responded were the investors, about whom nothing will be added to what little has already been said, and the artisans. In terms of their participation in production, artisans may be distinguished into three groups: those who worked in the construction industry and shipbuilding; those who produced truly expensive and unique objects for the luxury trade; and those who produced objects that commanded a much larger market. Their activities were differentiated according to the imperatives of the production process and the markets they served. Some worked as individuals or in small workshops: the icon painters, those who made enamels, precious metal objects, ivories, that is, artists rather than artisans.[135] Others

---

[133] On the increase of demand for luxury items in the eleventh–twelfth centuries, and the trickling of demand down the social scale, see M. Gerolymatou, "Emporio, koinonia kai aistheseis, 110s–120s aionas," in Ch. G. Angelidi, *To Vyzantio orimo gia allages* (Athens, 2004), pp. 257–68.

[134] See pp. 156–60.

[135] For all references to the "industries of art," Cutler's felicitous term, see his "The Industries of Art."

were not artists at all but small-scale producers of pottery, metal objects and other goods, who marketed their own production. Others still worked in large workshops with organized production: the mosaicists and fresco painters, potters, silk workers and glass workers in the major centers of production – quasi-industrial organization in all cases. One important general trait is high technical expertise, which is also manifested in technology transfers through the export of artisans and objects, pottery and perhaps glass to Italy, mosaicists to Kiev.[136]

Their production was geared primarily to the domestic market. In the foreign markets, they seem to have held a comparative advantage in luxury and semi-luxury items: silks, half-silks, glazed pottery, perhaps glass; a promising niche, where good profits could be made. But the Western markets for such products were just expanding in the eleventh century, much more so in the twelfth, and much depended on access to them. The Near Eastern markets were, it would seem, more active for the moment.

The traditional view of the Byzantine city as a parasitic one, a center of consumption producing only for the needs of its population which spent there the surplus of the countryside, is manifestly wrong as far as this period is concerned.[137] Archeology and closer study of the texts has established that they were, among other things to be sure, the domicile of *homo faber* – active centers of production.

EXCHANGE

Demand and distribution

The economy of exchange had been expanding since the tenth century. In the period under discussion, it became very active. Both the

---

[136] For Kiev see, in the last instance, T. Noonan, R. Kovalev and H. Sherman, "The Development and Diffusion of Glassmaking in pre-Mongol Russia," in P. McKray (ed.), *The Prehistory and History of Glassmaking Technology* (Westerville, Ohio, 1998), pp. 293–314.

[137] There is widespread belief in rural dominance over Byzantine cities, with the obvious exception of Constantinople: see Angold, "The Shaping," passim. See also M. Angold, "Archons and Dynasts: Local Aristocracies and the Cities of the Later Byzantine Empire," in M. Angold (ed.), *The Byzantine Aristocracy, IX–XIII Centuries* (Oxford, 1984), pp. 236–53, on the power wielded by the important men in a city. Harvey has already undermined this idea.

commerce of bulk items, showing a deepening of economic growth, and international trade based on luxuries were on an upward trend. The increased activity resulted from the conjunction of two factors: the internal Byzantine developments which have already been discussed, and the opening up of Western European markets with a rising demand for eastern products, especially, in this period, luxury products, which led to institutional changes adopted by the states of the eastern Mediterranean, as will be seen below.

Non-economic exchange in the form of gifts was not significant in this period. Gifts to foreign rulers, despite the reported two tons of gold sent by Constantine IX to the caliph in Baghdad, and other large sums of money (and silk cloth, but not in large quantities) were not very extensive in comparison to the overall economy. Besides, the liberalization of the silk trade led to commercialization of this important commodity whose symbolic value now became market value.[138]

Scholars have sometimes argued that agricultural products followed a pattern of non-market exchange, given the existence, in the cities, of great aristocratic or ecclesiastical households, the *oikoi*, economic complexes of some weight. To what extent did the urban *oikoi* simply import the production of their own estates, thus taking a significant part of the grain trade, for instance, out of the market? In other words, how significant was "tied trade" in this period?[139]

Grain provides the best test case. There were doubtless still state granaries, and the Church distributed grain in times of crisis.[140] This, however, does not simply have the effect of taking grain out of the marketplace. Indeed, it may have beneficial long-term effects on trade, since it provides an umbrella against seasonal price fluctuations and price increases in times of crisis, and thus makes it possible

---

[138] On gift exchange with the Arab lands, see A. Cutler, "Gifts and Gift Exchange as Aspects of the Byzantine, Arab, and Related Economies," *DOP* 55 (2001), pp. 247–78. For a more general discussion, see A. E. Laiou, "Economic and Noneconomic Exchange," *EHB* 2, pp. 681–96.

[139] For the concept of tied trade, see C. R. Whittaker, "Late Roman Trade and Traders," in P. Garnsey, K. Hopkins and C. R. Whittaker (eds.), *Trade in the Ancient Economy* (London, 1983), pp. 163–80. On aristocratic households, see P. Magdalino, "The Byzantine Aristocratic *Oikos*," in Angold, *The Byzantine Aristocracy*, pp. 92–111.

[140] On granaries, see J.-Cl. Cheynet, "Un aspect du ravitaillement de Constantinople aux Xe–XIe siècles d'après quelques sceaux d'hôrreiarioi," *Studies in Byzantine Sigillography* 6 (Washington, D.C.,1999), pp. 1–26.

for people to diversify into other than grain-producing activities.[141] Doubtless, there was some transfer from country to urban estate, but this affected only part of the grain reaching Constantinople in the twelfth century, while the rest went through the normal commercial process.[142] Furthermore, considerable evidence exists to show that monasteries sold their production of foodstuffs, but also purchased what they did not produce, in other words that they were actively involved in market activities. Other landlords, such as the *archontes* of Sparta, sold their olive oil to Venetian merchants.[143]

The demand of the *megalopolis* of Constantinople drew to it agricultural commodities not only from the areas adjacent to it but also from the Black Sea areas and Greece proper. There was no visible state interference in the distribution of grain in this period. An incident that took place in the late eleventh century provides insights into the marketing of grain and the process of price formation. Not far from Constantinople, in the grain-rich fields of Thrace, was the city of Raidestos, then and later a major outlet for the wheat of the region. Much of this went to Constantinople by the following process: the peasants and small or medium landowners of the area sold their grain in conditions of perfect competition: numerous sellers traded with numerous buyers, both the consumers themselves and merchants who imported it to Constantinople. The price was formed by the market. The Church and the urban real-estate owners of Raidestos made some money on rents from the stalls; no transactions tax (*kommerkion*) was collected by the state. In the 1070s, the finance minister, Nikephoritzes, tried to introduce reforms. He forbade the direct and decentralized sale of grain; instead, he organized a central marketplace (a *phoundax*) outside the city; all transactions were to take place there, and the state collected both rent and a transactions tax. This developed into an oligopsonistic situation, since the buyers now were a few big merchants. The results were utterly predictable: the wholesale merchants bought at low prices, and resold in Constantinople (in oligopolistic conditions) at very high prices. The price of grain, says the Byzantine historian Attaleiates, directly affects other prices and particularly the price of labor, forcing people to seek higher wages.

---

[141] Pomeranz, *The Great Divergence*, pp. 249–50.

[142] P. Magdalino, "The Grain Supply of Constantinople, Ninth–Twelfth Centuries," in Mango and Dagron, *Constantinople and its Hinterland*, p. 43.

[143] On this and what immediately follows, see A. E. Laiou, "Exchange and Trade, Seventh–Twelfth Centuries," *EHB* 2, pp. 740 ff.

Everyone suffered, except for the few merchants buying in bulk and
the state that collected the *kommerkion*. It was a most unpopular measure, and was discontinued soon thereafter. The incident has been
much commented upon, and often misinterpreted.[144] It was not an
effort by the state either to establish a monopoly of the grain trade or
to control the price of grain but, rather, a measure with a fiscal intent
which certainly had important economic consequences. Apart from
this case, there is no evidence of any kind of interference in the grain
trade in this period. Raidestos itself was, and remained, a free market
in grain[145]

Trade and commerce certainly did not produce most of the GNP:
we have suggested elsewhere that in the twelfth century 25 per cent
of GNP, and perhaps 40 per cent of monetized GNP, came from
trade and manufacturing. From the eleventh century on, commerce
was the dynamic sector, which lent the economy complexity and
which became the motor of the Byzantine economy. It integrated
the domestic market at exactly the same time that the international
markets acquired greater importance. How trade related to the agricultural and urban economies has already been discussed.

There were numerous centers of regional trade, primarily in agricultural products. Some of them served also as outlets for a larger,
inter-regional and international trade. Such centers in Greece were,
for example, the city of Halmyros, in Thessaly, where the production
of the area was concentrated, and was then picked up by Byzantine
and Italian traders for further distribution. The city of Ochrid, in
Epiros, seems to have had a similar role; Dyrrachion, Sparta, Patras,
Corinth, were all regional trade centers with connections to inter-
regional trade. Some of the very numerous coastal cities mentioned
by Idrisi as having markets catered both to local trade (such is the case
in Cyprus, probably), while others, including some of the ones just
mentioned, were involved in regional trade, as may be surmised by

---

[144] The sources are: Attaleiates: I. Bekker (ed.), *Michaelis Attlaeiote Historia* (Bonn,
1853), pp. 201–4, and Skylitzes Continuatus: E. T. Tsolakes (ed.), *He Synecheia
tes Chronographias tou Ioannou Skylitse* (Thessalonike, 1968), p. 162. For various
interpretations see Harvey, *Expansion*, pp. 236–8; Kaplan, *Les hommes et la terre*,
pp. 468–70; Magdalino, "Grain Supply," pp. 40–1; G. I. Bratianu, "Une
expérience d'économie dirigée: le monopole du blé à Byzance au XIe siècle,"
Byzantion 9 (1934), pp. 643–62; Angold, "Cities," p. 31, thinks the state tried to
fix the price of grain; for the interpretation adopted here, see Laiou, "Exchange
and Trade," pp. 741–2.

[145] Oikonomides, "The Economic Region of Constantinople," p. 229: he calls
Raidestos a "satellite" market of Constantinople.

their presence on the list of cities in which the Venetians requested and received specific mention of the right to free access, in the privileges granted them in 1082 and 1198.[146] Asia Minor is less well documented, although the cities of the western coast and Attaleia in southern Asia Minor seem to have been involved in trade in agricultural products with the interior.[147] Euchaita and Amorion were centers of regional trade, perhaps inter-regional in the case of the latter.

As for inter-regional/international trade, before the catastrophes of the late eleventh century the great spice routes passed through Asia Minor. Centers of this trade were Artze and Trebizond, a traditional outlet for the trade of Persia and the Indian Ocean. But in the late tenth century, the instability of the Persian Gulf area diverted the "spice" trade to Egypt, a trend encouraged by the Fatimids.[148] As Alexandria became the main Mediterranean outlet, Trebizond declined in importance and was supplanted by Rhodes, Chios, Crete and other islands, as well as by the ports of the southern coast of Asia Minor, primarily Attaleia. In the tenth and eleventh centuries this city was one of the most important Byzantine commercial centers, with an active trade with Syria, Palestine and Egypt.[149]

Thessalonike, the second most important city of the Byzantine Empire, with an excellent port and the natural outlet for the products of the southern Balkans, functioned as a center of regional, inter-regional and international trade. The great annual fair of St Demetrios brought to the city merchants from "Boeotia and the Peloponnese" as well as Italy, all carrying textiles; merchants also came from Egypt, Syria, and Spain; from the Black Sea area merchandise came by land through Constantinople. This was both a fair for textiles and a cattle fair; other items of trade, agricultural produce and yarns, for example, are not mentioned but were doubtless sold there.[150]

[146] Published in M. Pozza and G. Ravegnani (eds.), *I trattati con Bisanzio 992–1198* (Venice, 1993), pp. 40 and 131 respectively.

[147] M. Gerolymatou, "Paratereseis gia to Mikrasiatiko emporio ton 11° aiona," *E autokratoria se krise(?); to Vyzantio ton endekato aiona (1025–1081)* (Athens, 2003), pp. 191–200.

[148] E. Ashtor, *A Social and Economic History of the Near East in the Middle Ages* (London, 1976), pp. 119 ff.; Jacoby, "Byzantine Trade with Egypt," pp. 30 ff.

[149] On Attaleia in the late tenth–eleventh centuries, see C. Foss, "The Cities of Pamphylia in the Byzantine Age," in his *Cities, Fortresses and Villages of Byzantine Asia Minor* (Aldershot, 1996), art. IV.

[150] Romano, *Timarione*, pp. 54–5.

Constantinople was still, as before, a case apart. It exercised high demand for alimentary products and raw materials for its industries. It was, also, still, a great entrepot for international trade. Benjamin of Tudela could compare it only to Baghdad. He mentions the presence of merchants from most of the world known to him: Egypt, Persia, Syria/Palestine, Russia, Hungary, the northern shores of the Black Sea, Lombardy and Spain.[151] Great changes, however, had already taken place in Constantinople at the time of his writing. The distinctiveness of the city as a closed and protected market, where foreign merchants were housed in special buildings, with a limited period of residence, where all merchants paid an entry duty and whose exports were controlled had been eroded by the grant of privileges to Venetian and Pisan merchants. Constantinople was on the way out as a port of trade, acquiring instead the characteristics of a vast international market where freedom of trade was becoming much greater.[152]

Byzantine merchants extended their activities to the international markets. Benjamin of Tudela mentions Byzantine traders in Barcelona and Montpellier. What they brought there is a matter of conjecture: silk stuffs and pottery come to mind. They also traveled to Russia, as far as Novgorod; one assumes they exported silks and spices. Very important was Byzantine trade with Arab countries. It has now been firmly established that there was considerable trade between Byzantium and Egypt, as well as Palestine, since the middle of the tenth century, and very active trade in the eleventh and twelfth. Merchants went there from Crete, southern Asia Minor, Constantinople and possibly other parts of the Empire. Byzantine exports included agricultural products: cheese primarily from Crete but also from Asia Minor; medicinal plants from Asia Minor, a special kind of incense from Crete; timber from Asia Minor. The products of Byzantine manufacture, silk cloth, expensive brocade bedcovers, wooden furniture, were also exported. The marketing of both bulk products and luxury products is a remarkable indicator of the productivity of the Byzantine economy. Noteworthy also is the fact that the factories of mid-eleventh-century Tinnis produced imitations of

---

[151] *Itinerary of Benjamin of Tudela*, pp. 70–1.

[152] For the location of business and commercial quarters in Constantinople during this period, see M. Mundell Mango, "The Commercial Map of Constantinople," *DOP* 54 (2000), pp. 198–205; cf. P. Magdalino, "The Maritime Neighborhoods of Constantinople: Commercial and Residential Functions, Sixth to Twelfth Centuries," *DOP* 54 (2000), pp. 209–26.

luxury Byzantine silks, surely an indicator both of significant trade and of the value in which Byzantine textiles were held.[153] What the Byzantines imported from Syria and Palestine included spices and glass cullet as well as some glass objects, as indicated by the Serce Limani shipwreck. Other commodities were doubtless exchanged, but we lack any evidence as to what they were. From Egypt Byzantine merchants imported the usual luxury products of the eastern trade: spices, expensive goods, indigo – the very stuff on which the wealth of Venice was to be built.[154] Their purchasing power was such that it could influence the price of spices on the marketplaces of Cairo and Alexandria. The Constantinopolitan merchants who frequented Cairo in the early twelfth century and brought there many kinds of merchandise, are reported to have been very rich, and well acquainted with the conditions of trade in that city.

Byzantine merchants on Byzantine bottoms, marketing Byzantine agricultural products and luxury items, importing the high-value, high-profit merchandise of the East: we have the makings of a very healthy exchange system. Yet increasingly in the course of the twelfth century Venetian and Genoese traders participated in this trade, carrying Byzantine agricultural products and perhaps silk to Egypt. By the thirteenth century, the Venetians were on the way to dominating this trade, because of three important factors: their sea power, the extensive privileges they acquired in the Byzantine Empire, and the privileges they were to acquire in Egypt:[155] the last two being directly related to the first, and to the fact that the Italian merchants were dominant in the economy of Syria and Palestine, complementary in terms of trade to the Egyptian markets.

Merchants, bankers and investment

Recent research has eroded the traditional idea that the economic behavior of the Byzantine merchant was that of a not very enterprising man, who stayed at home and benefited from government protection, growing fat on passive trade with the foreign merchants who came to him. This image has been subverted. First the provincial merchants and then the merchants of Constantinople have been

[153] Jacoby, "Byzantine Trade with Egypt," pp. 39–40.
[154] On this see Jacoby, "Byzantine Trade with Egypt," passim; Laiou, "Exchange and Trade," pp. 749–50.
[155] Jacoby, "Byzantine Trade with Egypt," passim, and see Chapter V.

shown to have been mobile. They certainly took advantage of and profited from the conditions that encouraged a more active exchange of commodities, and they traveled all over the Mediterranean.[156] The merchants of Constantinople became a large, rich and influential group, which could pose a threat to emperors, as they did in the mid-eleventh century, and again in the late twelfth. By that time, they had long been in contact with Italian merchants, had cooperated with them, had clashed with them, and had become versed in international money transactions.

An essential prerequisite for both commercial and industrial expansion is the availability of credit; it multiplies the available funds and increases the efficacy of the money supply. The funding mechanisms which the Byzantine merchants had at their disposal were mostly traditional, but with some significant changes that responded to the increased need for capital and credit. Merchants continued to invest funds in contracts of *chreokoinonia*, the equivalent and perhaps the ancestor of the Italian *commenda*. By the twelfth century, we also find business associations in which the investor shared only the profits and not the losses, thus minimizing the risk to capital. The terms of borrowing money also changed. Official interest rates had remained virtually unchanged since the sixth century (6 per cent for normal loans, 8 per cent for loans given by merchants and bankers, 12 per cent for maritime loans, while aristocrats could only charge 4 per cent), reflecting both a stability in profit rates and possibly the fact that interest rates had acquired a certain non-economic aspect, in an economy where there was redistribution rather than augmentation of resources. Sometime in the late tenth or early eleventh century, interest rates

---

[156] N. Oikonomidès, "Le marchand byzantin des provinces (IXe–XIe s.)," in *Mercati e mercanti nell'alto medioevo: l'area euroasiatica e l'area mediterranea* (Spoleto, 1993), pp. 633–5 (reprinted in *Social and Economic Life*, art. XII); A. E. Laiou, "Byzantine Traders and Seafarers," in S. Vryonis (ed.), *The Greeks and the Sea* (New Rochelle, 1993), pp. 79–96; A. E. Laiou, "Byzantine Trade with Christians and Muslims and the Crusades," in A. E. Laiou and R. P. Mottahedeh (eds.), *The Crusades from the Perspective of Byzantium and the Muslim World* (Washington, D.C., 2001), pp. 157 ff.; Jacoby, "Byzantine Trade with Egypt," pp. 25–77; R. S. Lopez suggested that the government stifled the initiative of merchants: "Beati monoculi: The Byzantine Economy in the Early Middle Ages," in *Cultus et cognitio; Festschrift Alexander Gieysztor* (Warsaw, 1976), pp. 347–52 reprinted in his *Byzantium and the World Around it*, art. I.; M. Hendy, *Studies*, 564 ff., argues that trade itself was not important in the Byzantine Empire before the Fourth Crusade, a position subsequently shown to be wrong.

rose unofficially, but in a way that made them enforceable in court, to 8.33 per cent for all loans except maritime loans which rose to 16.67 per cent, and loans given by aristocrats which rose to 5.55 per cent. A real average rate of 8.33 per cent seems to have been prevalent in the marketplace.[157] It was now profitable even for aristocrats to invest in trade, since they could make as much from straight loans as from rents, and much more if they invested in maritime loans, while the system by which one could invest funds in the purchase of a court title and receive an annual revenue (between the ranges 2.5–3.5 per cent and 5.55–8.33 per cent of the capital in the tenth century), albeit forfeiting the capital, came to an end in the late eleventh century.[158] The combination of these developments meant that captive capital was potentially liberated; it is certain that both clerics and monks took advantage of this opportunity, and there are indications that some aristocrats did so as well, although their investments were primarily in land.

Byzantine society was in a state of transition in the eleventh century; it seemed for a moment that the wealthier merchants might acquire formal political power, which would have changed the entire aspect of the Byzantine social and political system. Indeed, successive emperors gave merchants the right to become members of the Senate, that is, to participate in the ruling elite, in the second half of the eleventh century. This was stopped when the landholding aristocracy secured the throne for a hundred years and more, with the accession of Alexios I, in 1081. The "aristocratic" view of society, held also by those who aspired to aristocratic status, like the learned Michael Psellos, became part of imperial ideology in the court of the Komnenian emperors. The economic power and wealth of the Constantinopolitan merchants and bankers, however, seems to have continued and even increased, if we are to judge by one of the few merchants known to us by name, Kalomodios who, in the late twelfth century, was both a banker and a merchant investing in

---

[157] A. E. Laiou, "Byzantium and the Commercial Revolution," in Arnaldi and Cavallo, *Europa medievale e mondo bizantino*, pp. 239–53; A. E. Laiou, "God and Mammon: Credit, Trade, Profit and the Canonists," in N. Oikonomides (ed.), *Byzantium in the Twelfth Century* (Athens 1991), pp. 261–99, and A. E. Laiou, "*Nummus parit nummos*: l'usurier, le juriste et le philosophe à Byzance," in AIBL, *Comptes rendus* (Paris, 1999), pp. 583–604.

[158] N. Oikonomides, "The Role of the Byzantine State," *EHB* 3, pp. 1008–10, 1020–1.

long-distance trade.[159] At times of crisis, during the Third Crusade and again in the reign of Alexios III (1195–1203) this group emerges as one of recognized political clout, honored, once again, with court titles.[160]

The Byzantine merchant of this period took intelligent advantage of the opportunities offered by new conditions. Why, then, does he not emerge as a figure of importance, and why did Venetian and Genoese merchants dominate maritime trade by the thirteenth century? In part the problem is simply historiographical: the officials and intellectuals who wrote the history of their times served the aristocratic state and drew their sustenance from it; they embraced and perpetuated the aristocratic ideal which downplayed the importance of trade and considered inferior the activities of craftsmen and merchants. There were, however, other reasons, which have nothing to do with the state of the sources. Quite simply, the non-privileged Byzantine merchant had to compete with Italian merchants who had institutional advantages guaranteed by privileges, and who also were creating an extensive commercial network in the eastern Mediterranean, from Italy to Constantinople to Syria-Palestine to Egypt, secure from their bases in the Latin Crusader states. They also had, not yet a dominance, but a firm upper hand in the exercise of maritime violence, guaranteeing them an increasingly powerful position in maritime commerce. The capture of Constantinople in 1204 was an important step in this development. The Byzantine merchant, helped by his knowledge of local conditions, would subsequently become auxiliary to the activities of Italian merchants.[161]

Byzantium and the opening markets

Trade and manufacturing grew because of internal factors. However, the Byzantine Empire inhabited a larger space where world-altering developments were taking place. For one thing, the Western European economy was quickening; demand for luxury and semi-luxury products was rising, and such products were still to be found in

---

[159] Choniates, 172; Jacoby, "Byzantine Trade with Egypt," thinks that his investments were in trade with Egypt.

[160] On the eleventh century, see Lemerle, *Cinq études* (Paris, 1977), pp. 287 ff.; on the late twelfth century, see Laiou, "Byzantine Trade with Christians," pp. 176–8.

[161] See Chapter V.

the eastern Mediterranean and the Middle East. Venice and Amalfi, whose merchants were already in Constantinople in 944,[162] had long ties with the Christian and Muslim East, areas which were becoming increasingly profitable. Eventually, in the course of the twelfth century, the presence especially of the Venetians and eventually of the Pisans and the Genoese, would become weighty in the ports and marketplaces of the eastern Mediterranean. By the mid-thirteenth century they were dominant. This development had considerable effects on the economies of the states of the eastern Mediterranean, in the first place Byzantium, which was peculiarly vulnerable, but also on the Muslim states. The sea lanes of the eastern Mediterranean were very busy in the eleventh–twelfth centuries, and this necessitated new international arrangements: access to markets and ports, and institutional mechanisms that would reduce the cost of doing business. The Byzantine state played a pivotal role.

Two events of the late eleventh century set the stage. The first is the grant, by the Emperor Alexios I, of extensive commercial privileges to the Venetians; the privileges were granted in exchange for the naval help given by the Venetians at the time of the attack on Byzantium of the Norman leader Robert Guiscard. The second is the crusading movement, which began officially in 1095 and resulted in the creation of the Kingdom of Jerusalem after the conquest of that city in 1099. Italian merchants soon established themselves in the crusader states, where they found regimes uniquely favorable to them and their activities. Syria and Palestine occupied an important place in the commercial networks created by the Italians and linking Italy, Egypt and the Byzantine Empire. In both cases, the crusades and the grant of privileges, there is a striking combination of commercial activity and naval power: the Italian maritime cities leveraged their sea power against the acquisition of privileges which gave them a powerful competitive edge in what had been protected environments. Especially in the Byzantine Empire, the twelfth century is punctuated with acts of violence on the part of the Italian maritime cities, whenever they wanted new or renewed commercial privileges. The result was the creation of increasingly favorable conditions for the merchants of these cities, in the Byzantine Empire, in Syria and Palestine and eventually in Egypt. By the end of the twelfth century,

---

[162] On Amalfi, see M. Balard, "Amalfi et Byzance (Xe–XIIe siècles)," *TM* 6 (1976), 85–96.

the Byzantine merchant was being edged out of areas and activities which had been his own.

The first commercial privilege, granted by Alexios I in 1082 (the Venetians had received an earlier privilege, in 992, but its effects were limited) set the stage for subsequent developments. The emperor granted the Venetians, who were still nominally Byzantine subjects, the right and freedom to trade in the Empire without paying either the *kommerkion* of 10 per cent or a number of other charges. Furthermore, they had the right to establish themselves in Constantinople and other cities, without limit as to the time they spent there or as to the place where their activities would be carried out. In Durrazzo and Constantinople, they acquired their own quarters, but were not limited to them. Thus Constantinople, where foreign merchants had traditionally been housed in *mitata* (the equivalent of the Muslim *funduq*), was to acquire Italian colonies, whose population became stable in the course of time.[163] When these privileges were extended, in 1126, there was a very significant addition: all Byzantines who bought or sold anything from or to the Venetians would not pay the transactions tax that was otherwise required. Similar, although far less extensive privileges were granted to relative newcomers who had, however, already established themselves in the crusader states: the Pisans in 1111 and the Genoese in 1155.

The privileges were important enough by themselves. Furthermore, they were attended by, or carried in their wake, an unspoken liberalization of trade. The free trade promised in the privileges appears to have extended to the *kekolymena*, the items whose export had long been prohibited: gold and silver, highest-quality silks, foodstuffs, salt, iron and war materials. Indeed, we know that Venetian merchants (the extant documentation is heavily biased in favor of Venice) but others as well exported both silks and agricultural products to Western Europe and Egypt. Salt and war materials, except timber, apparently were not exported in this period. Of course, once the prohibitions had been lifted, they could no longer be fully

---

[163] R.-J. Lilie, *Handel und Politik: zwischen dem byzantinischen Reich und den italienischen Kommunen Venedig, Pisa und Genua in der Epoche der Komnenen und der Angeloi, 1081–1204* (Amsterdam, 1984), passim; D. Jacoby, "Italian Privileges and Trade in Byzantium Before the Fourth Crusade: A Reconsideration," *Annuario de Estudios Medievales* 24 (1994), pp. 349–68 (= his *Trade, Commodities and Shipping in the Medieval Mediterranean* (Aldershot, 1997), art. II); Laiou, "Byzantine Traders and Seafarers," pp. 79–96.

implemented with regard to Byzantine merchants either. The liberalization of trade, in the terms outlined here, took place, on the one hand, under the pressure of Italian (and possibly also Byzantine) merchants, who in any case had been smuggling silks out of the Empire since the tenth century, and, on the other hand, as a result of the action of the state which gave institutional force to what the marketplace demanded.[164] The early privileges became the model for what Italian merchants sought and to a large extent received, despite periodic setbacks in their relations with the Byzantine state.

Merchants need security, and businessmen need to lower the costs of their transactions. In the Middle Ages, foreign merchants carrying out international trade had to deal, among other things, with a multiplicity of laws concerning piracy and reprisal, the fate of shipwrecked goods, the fate of the property of merchants dying in a foreign land, intestate or not. The states of the eastern Mediterranean had, *grosso modo*, safeguarded the interests of their own fisc rather than those of the merchant. This changed in the course of the twelfth century, as rules were adopted which generally speaking were of similar tenor, indeed formed a common law of the sea that gave greater protection to the foreign merchant and his property. The states, then, gave up some of their prerogatives and made it possible for men and merchandise to move more freely. Byzantium and the crusader states played an important, indeed pivotal role in this development, elaborating rules that then were adopted, in more or less the same form, by the Empire of Nicaea, Egypt, Cyprus, Rhodes, and the Sultanate of Konya.[165] The creation of virtually international mechanisms that improved the terms of trade profited Italian merchants, but it lowered the transactions costs for native merchants too, to the degree that arrangements were reciprocal.

The question has long been discussed whether the presence of Italian merchants in the Byzantine Empire in the eleventh and twelfth centuries was detrimental or beneficial to the Byzantine economy. An earlier orthodoxy posited that the Byzantine merchant, who had basked in the protective warmth of the government, was destroyed by free trade, and so was the Byzantine economy. The new orthodoxy is based on the idea that the opening up of markets and the

---

[164] On this and what follows, see Laiou, "Byzantine Traders" and "Monopoly," pp. 511–26.
[165] Laiou, "Byzantine Trade with Christians," pp. 183–7.

quickening of trade generally, which was spearheaded by Italian merchants, profited the Byzantine economy; indeed, we have gone too far in attributing most positive economic developments in this period to the Italian merchants who, moreover, it is also argued, were too few to do much harm.[166] Neither of these positions takes account of all the facts, and both fail to distinguish between trade and merchants. In the first instance, it is quite clear that the Byzantine economy was on an upward swing long before the first grant of privileges to the Venetians. Secondly, the argument may indeed be made that the presence of Italian merchants, stimulating as it did both exchange and the mechanisms that favored it, influenced positively the development of trade. But its effects on Byzantine merchants are another matter.

Venetian and other Italian merchants became involved not only in international trade, not only in the export of Byzantine commodities, but also in the internal trade of the Byzantine Empire in the course of the twelfth century. This was inevitable once trade restrictions had been lifted and privileges had been granted. Olive oil, other alimentary products and cloth were bought and sold on Byzantine territory. It makes perfect sense that the Venetians, profiting from the fact that they were not paying the 10 per cent duty, were in a privileged position to buy, since they could split their profit by offering slightly higher prices. The same, *mutatis mutandis*, holds for their dealings with Byzantine merchants: if they split between them, however unequally, the profits from the tax exemption, it would be more advantageous for Byzantines to trade with Venetians than with each other. Initially and for a while, Byzantine merchants may have profited from such arrangements. But in the long run, the logic of the situation gave the Italians a larger share of domestic trade, thus creating a situation where profit-sharing with the native merchant was no longer necessary. While it is not clear that this point had been reached in the late twelfth century, the negative attitude of the Byzantine state, as well as the urban population, especially that of Constantinople, toward the Venetians and other westerners at that time certainly has much to do with the worsening of the conditions of trade for the Byzantines.

---

[166] The new orthodoxy is best argued by M. Hendy in his "Byzantium, 1081–1204: An Economic Reappraisal" and "'Byzantium, 1081–1204': The Economy Revisited," in M. Hendy, *The Economy, Fiscal Administration and Coinage of Byzantium* (Northampton, 1989), arts. II and III. It has been adopted, with variations, by R.-J. Lilie, D. Jacoby, A. Harvey and others.

By the end of the twelfth century, the stage was set: those Byzantine merchants who had no trading privilege, and they were the great majority, were placed by their own government in a highly disadvantageous position with regard to their Italian colleagues. However, what eventually happened, which was the relegation of the Byzantine merchant to a subordinate position, was not the natural result of these twelfth-century developments. The conquest of Constantinople by the crusaders and the Venetians, in 1204, played a determining role.

MONETARY DEVELOPMENTS[167]

The main feature of the period is the accelerated expansion of monetization whose first signs were outlined in Chapter III. The increasing share of the monetized sector in the public and private spheres explains the impact of the momentous debasement of the late eleventh century. The recovery in the Komnenian period and the triumph of the Byzantine gold coin, the *besant*, pay tribute to the dynamism of the economy, which still supported the status of Byzantium as a great medieval power at the time of the Crusades, as well as the Mediterranean ambitions of Manuel I (1143–80).

The eleventh-century Byzantine coinage was an articulated one: in the 1030s, the *miliaresion* was provided with divisions of $\frac{1}{3}$ and $\frac{2}{3}$ to facilitate smaller transactions. The lightweight gold coin (the *nomisma tetarteron*) continued to be struck by every successor of Nikephoros II till 1092. Until *c.*1005 it remained outwardly undistinguishable from the full-weight *nomisma* (called *nomisma histamenon* i.e. "standard"); afterwards it was clearly recognizable through its smaller diameter and thicker flan and its different typology. Neither the conditions of its circulation, nor its market value are known; they have raised much speculation. Although most specimens have been found beyond the frontiers of the Empire, it certainly circulated within, as several documents or preserved coin weights inscribed with its name demonstrate.[168] One may assume that the state was paying at least part of its expenses in this lighter coin.

---

[167] For the general bibliography on the subject, see Chapter III, p. 85, n. 131.
[168] See Chapter III, p. 60, n. 37, for references to Ahrweiler's and Hendy's relevant studies. See also M. Hendy, "Lightweight Solidi, Tetartera, and the Book of the Prefect," *Byzantinische Zeitschrift* 65 (1972), pp. 57–80 (= idem, *The Economy, Fiscal Administration and Coinage of Byzantium* (Northampton, 1989), art. IX).

The "creeping" debasement of the gold coinage, which had started in the 950s, continued at the same slow pace of −0.04 per cent a year till the reign of Michael IV (1034–41).[169] The fineness had now fallen into a 94–90 per cent bracket (*c.*22$\frac{1}{2}$–21$\frac{1}{2}$ carats).[170] During that phase, the increase in the silver content of the alloy led the moneyers to enlarge the diameter of the coin in order to maintain the full weight of the *nomisma* (the density of silver is half that of gold). At the same time, to save on energy and keep the striking to two hammer blows, they decreased the diameter of the figures' imprint (the dies) on the blank. This gave birth to the characteristic fabric of the eleventh-century *nomismata* with their broad, thin blank, called *nummi scifati* in south Italian documents because of their triple conspicuous border (Arabic *shiffi*).[171] Mechanically, this striking of a partial area rendered the *histamena* concave, a peculiar and rare shape for coins, most conspicuous from the 1050s onward. The moneyers managed to master it by technical improvements[172] which testify to their elaborate metallurgical skills – which is why we draw attention to this complex development here. At that time, even the Islamic world did not know such refinements.

---

[169] The fact that he had been a moneychanger is considered a proof of his responsibility in the *start* of the debasement (P. Grierson, "The Debasement of the Bezant in the Eleventh Century," *Byzantinische Zeitschrift* 47 (1954), pp. 379–94) but analytical data do not support this judgement. Scholars who repeat this statement (Hendy, *Studies*, Harvey, *Expansion*, C. Kaplanis, "The Debasement of the 'Dollar of the Middle Ages,'" *The Journal of Economic History* 63.3 (2003), pp. 768–801) ignore the evidence for the first phase of the debasement.

[170] The carat (*keration*) is an ancient weight based on the carob seed, equivalent to 1/1728 of the Roman pound (± 0.189g). Constantine I fixed the *solidus* weight at 24 carats of pure gold. This is the origin of its past – and present – use as a measure of the fineness of gold (24 = 100 %, 18 = 75 %, 12 = 50 % and so on). Of course, Byzantine calculations were not decimalized (!) but in fractions, with a preference for the duodecimal pattern.

[171] P. Grierson ("*Nummi scyfati*: The Story of a Misunderstanding," *Numismatic Chronicle* 11 (1971), pp. 253–260) discovered the true etymology and showed that seventeenth-century scholars were wrong in calling 'scyphates' Byzantine coins in the shape of cup (*skyphos*), an error which persists to our time.

[172] See F. Delamare, P. Montmitonnet and C. Morrisson, "L'apparition de la concavité des monnaies d'or frappées à Constantinople au XIe siècle," *Revue Belge de Numismatique* 145 (1999), pp. 249–59 with references to earlier studies, among which, C. Morrisson *et al.*, "A Mechanical Approach to Coin Striking and its Application to Studying the Evolution of the Fabric of Byzantine Gold Solidi," in W. A. Oddy et al. (eds.), *Metallurgy in Numismatics* 2 (London, 1988), pp. 41–53 (= C. Morrisson, *Monnaie et finances*, art. XIII).

In a second phase, from Constantine IX Monomachos (1041–55) to Romanos IV Diogenes (1068–71), the rate of debasement was around −0.4 per cent a year, a tenfold increase compared to the preceding period, and the purity of the *nomisma* fell from *c.*90 per cent to 70 per cent (21$^1/_2$ to 17 carats). No contemporary text alludes directly to the phenomenon. However, the special designations for gold coins which appear in monastic and other documents, referring either to the name of the emperor (*romanatus* for Roman III, *mikhaelaton*, for Michael VII) or the iconography (*helioselenaton, stellatus, skeptraton*) or to a combination of both (*stauromikhaelaton*), were intended to rate their fineness and value them, as was done later with the lists of coins in merchants' handbooks, as we will see.

Eleventh-century writers, without citing this second phase of debasement, blame Zoe and Constantine IX for having depleted the treasury and for having started with lavish expenditures "the decline of public affairs and their collapse."[173] But luxury constructions were not the only reason for tampering with money, a process which, in an era of limited credit, was the only way to increase public income. The measure may well have been prompted also by the need to finance the protracted war against the Pechenegs in the second half of Constantine IX's reign.[174] Whatever the immediate causes for the earlier alteration and this one, they do not seem to have had a negative impact on the economy. The increase which they permitted in the number of gold coins struck was matched more or less in the long run, from the 950s to the 1060s, by a corresponding increase in the number of monetized transactions. There is some evidence, though slight, which points to price stability in the same period. This would not have been the case if the deficit of the Treasury had been the only reason for the debasement.[175]

After 1068, debasement followed a much more dramatic pattern. Chronicles refer to the dire straits of imperial finances and to the expertise of the emperor Michael VII (1071–8) in monetary matters:

[173] Michael Psellos, *Chronographie*, ed. E. Renauld, 2 vols. (Paris, 1926–8), I, p. 119. For this and other references, see P. Grierson, "The Debasement of the Bezant in the Eleventh Century," *Byzantinische Zeitschrift* 47 (1954), pp. 379–94, a pioneering article in which the debasement of the 1040s–1060s was first identified through specific gravity measurements.

[174] C. Kaplanis, "The Debasement of the 'Dollar of the Middle Ages,'" pp. 1–34.

[175] For the details of the argument, relying on Fisher's equation, see C. Morrisson, "La dévaluation de la monnaie byzantine au XIe siècle: essai d'interprétation," *Travaux et mémoires* 6 (1976), pp. 3–47 (= C. Morrisson, *Monnaie et finances*, art. IX).

He understood every detail of finance exactly: its organization and management; how much the treasury paid to each person and how much each paid back to the treasury, the production of coins and the equilibrium of a balance; excesses and deficiencies of weight, how the touchstone worked; and how many measures of pure material each of the pieces of stamped gold contained.[176]

They now mention debasement and its severe economic consequences including the rise in prices, aggravated by insecurity and the attempt to establish imperial control on the cereal trade in the Thracian port of Rhaidestos. Michael VII was nicknamed Parapinakes, because in his reign a *nomisma* bought only a *modios* of wheat less a *pinakion* (1/4 *modios*) instead a full *modios* as before.[177] In this dramatic phase, the gold content fell from 70 per cent to a mere 10 per cent. The process now implied adding silver – and no longer non-refined gold – to the alloy. For that reason it allowed for a much smaller increase in the number of coins struck. It also entailed an alteration of the silver coinage since access to eastern mines had been lost. Existing *miliaresia* had to be melted and minted into white gold coins, in turn new silver coins were alloyed with copper, and the subsequent reminting of these debased *miliaresia* into *nomismata* resulted in the whitish 'gold' coins of the 1080s containing as much as 18 per cent copper and 71 per cent silver against only 10 per cent gold.[178] Nikephoros Bryennios clearly describes the situation in the reign of Nikephoros Botaneiates (1078–81):

He did not grant the highest honors to the most notable . . ., the military, . . . but to all those who asked for them. He did the same with what the Romans [i.e. the Byzantines] called *offikia* so that as a consequence, expenditure exceeded revenue by several times. And so, for this reason . . . money was lacking, *the nomisma was debased* and the gifts of money attached . . . to offices were brought to an end. For the influx of money which derived from Asia and which went to supply the treasury ceased because the whole of Asia fell into the possession of the Turks, and since that deriving from Europe also decreased drastically, because of its ill-use by earlier emperors, the imperial treasury found itself in the greatest want of money.[179]

[176] Psellos, *Chronographie*, vol. II, p. 173, translated by Hendy, *Studies*, p. 241.

[177] Skylitzes Continuatus, p. 162; Zonaras, ed. Bekker, III, p. 712. On prices in this period, see Cheynet et al., "Prix et salaires à Byzance (Xe –XVe siècle)," in *Hommes et richesses* 2, pp. 361–3.

[178] C. Morrisson et al., *L'or monnayé* (Paris, 1985), pp. 127–53.

[179] Nikephoros Bryennios, *Historiae* IV.1, translated by Hendy, *Studies*, p. 235.

The monetary situation in the first decade of the reign of Alexios I Komnenos (1081–1118) was chaotic and very detrimental to tax collection in the areas over which the emperor was slowly regaining control in the Balkans and some parts of coastal Asia Minor.[180] As soon as he could, after defeating the Petchenegs in 1091 and recovering the islands of Chios, Samos and Rhodes, he staged a major reordering of the monetary system, which coincided with the coronation of his son John in 1092. First elucidated by M. Hendy in 1969,[181] the monetary reform consisted in the reordering summed up in Table 4.1 below. Metallurgical constraints and the paucity of new metal explains the standards chosen by the mint authorities: the restored gold coin (*hyperpyron*, i.e. "fire-refined") was not "hyperpure" but corresponded to the 20$\frac{1}{2}$ carats average of debased coins in 1028–56. Its division of a $\frac{1}{3}$, the new *trachy aspron*, with 30 per cent gold, 60 per cent silver and 10 per cent copper, stemmed from the reminting of the "gold" coins of the period 1070–91. There were no more silver coins but a copper-silver (billon) alloyed one, also called *aspron trachy* in official texts, but *stamenon* in common usage. *Folles* were replaced by smaller coins (the copper *tetarteron* and its half). This was the most elaborate monetary system of the period compared to the Western ones, which generally knew only the silver denier and its half, and even to the Islamic ones, which, though trimetallic, did not include such a wide range of denominations. It was, together with the Justinianic system, the most articulated pattern of coins Byzantium had ever had. This indicates, in our opinion, that the state wanted to provide a means adapted to a variegated scale of exchanges and not only to the simple needs of tax collection.[182]

---

[180] This is described by Zonaras (ed. Büttner-Wobst, III, p. 738, translation and commentary by Hendy, *Studies*, p. 516 and Hendy, *Catalogue of the Byzantine Coins in the Dumbarton Oaks Collection and in the Whittemore Collection* (hereafter *DOC*), vol. 4, p. 184. This passage comes after the narration of events dating to the early 1090s. I am still of the opinion that it describes the situation prevailing before, not after, Alexios' reform.

[181] M. F. Hendy, *Coinage and Money in the Byzantine Empire (1081–1261)* (Washington, 1969), pp. 14–49; idem, *Studies*, pp. 513–17; idem, *DOC* 4.1, pp. 181 f.

[182] On the problems of tax-collection before and after the reform of Alexios I, see Hendy, *Coinage*, pp. 50–64, idem, *DOC* 4.1, pp. 40–1, and the slightly different interpretation of the *Palaia kai nea logarike*, a fundamental fiscal document, with translation, by C. Morrisson, "La Logarikè: réforme fiscale et réforme monétaire sous Alexis Ier Comnène" (= C. Morrisson, *Monnaies et finances*, art. VI).

Table 4.1 *The Byzantine monetary system in the eleventh and twelfth centuries*

The eleventh-century coinage

GOLD		SILVER				COPPER
Nomisma histamenon (24 carats-wt)	Nomisma tetarteron (22 carats-wt)	Miliaresion	2/3 mil.	1/3 mil.	Carat/keration (money of account)	Follis
(~4.5g 98 % to 10 % Au)*	(≈4.13g 98 % to 10 % Au)*	(3g to 2g 98 % 65 % Ag)*	(2g to 1.4g 98 % to 61 % Ag)*	(0.9g to 0.6 g)		(≈14g to 3g)
1	1 (?)	12	16	36	(24)	288

* Extreme values in the debasement process.

The Komnenian reformed system (1092–1204)

GOLD Hyperpyron nomisma	ELECTRUM Nomisma trachy aspron (trikephalon)	BILLON Aspron trachy (stamenon)	Carat/keration (money of account)	Follis (money of account)	COPPER Tetarteron	Half-tetarteron
(~4.3g ~87 % Au)	(~4.3g; 30 % to 10 % Au and 60 % to 70% Cu)	(~4.3g; Cu + 6 % to 2 % Ag)			(~4g)	(~2g)
1	3	48	(24)	(288)	864(?)	1728(?)

The *hyperpyron* remained relatively stable during the twelfth century; it drifted only in the 1180s from the initial 87 to 82 per cent in 1204. But the electrum coin was debased and its value fell to 1/4, then to 1/6 *hyperpyron*, while the *stamenon* decreased from 1/48 in 1136 to 1/120 in 1190 and 1/184 in 1199. This multiplicity of specie certainly caused surprise to crusading armies crossing the Empire in the twelfth century and conflicts over exchange rates had to be solved by special arrangements, even treaties, which are a welcome source of information for the modern historian.[183]

Over the entire period (1000–1204), the increase in the level of monetization, which we stressed in Chapter III, accelerated. The phenomenon has been well studied and is well known for many urban sites.[184] For instance, the annual index of the number of coins found increases in Corinth by some 100 per cent between 1034 and 1081, by 30 per cent in 1081–1143, and by 10 per cent more from 1143 to 1204. It is true that the use of coin was not universal, as we have already mentioned with regard to Bulgaria, where it progressed only slowly in the course of the eleventh century and was impeded in the 1030s and 1080s by troubles and incursions. But recent studies have shown that it increased remarkably in the rural areas of many regions.[185] Byzantine coins spread even across the frontier as happened in northern Syria where the gold *mikhaelaton* and the bronze *folles* circulated in the late eleventh and twelfth centuries, compensating for the local shortages.[186] In the twelfth century, finds of *stamena* predominate in Asia Minor and in Thrace, and the lighter *tetartera* and half-*tetartera* in Greece. This contrasted distribution may have

---

[183] Laiou, "Byzantine Trade with Christians and Muslims and the Crusades" (above, n. 156), pp. 158–96.

[184] D. M. Metcalf, *Coinage in South-Eastern Europe 820–1396* (London, 1979); V. Penna, "Life in Byzantine Peloponnese: The numismatic evidence (8th–12th)," *Mneme Martin Jessop Price* (Athens, 1996), pp. 265–88.

[185] For South Danubian regions see E. Oberländer-Târnoveanu, "Les échanges" (Chapter III, n. 137); for northern Syria, T. Vorderstrasse, "Coin Circulation in Some Syrian Villages (5th–11th Centuries)," in *Villages*, pp. 495–508. Evidence from Amorion and some Turkish museums in Phrygia (Bolvadin) or the Pontus (Amasra/Amastris and Amasya/Amaseia) also illustrates the rise in the number of eleventh-century bronze coins (C. Lightfoot, "Byzantine Anatolia: Reassessing the Numismatic Evidence," *Revue numismatique* 158 (2002), pp. 229–39).

[186] S. Heidemann, *Die Renaissance der Städte in Nordsyrien und Nordmesopotamien: Städtische Entwicklung und wirtschafliche Bedingungen in ar-Raqqa und Harrān von der Zeit der beduinischen Vorherrschaft bis zu den Seldschuken* (Leiden, 2002).

(a)

% of fine metal (Au or Ag)

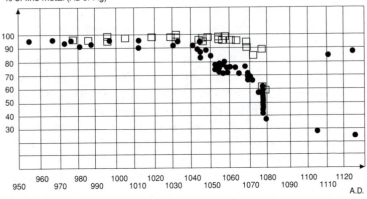

☐ Silver coins

● Gold coins

(b)

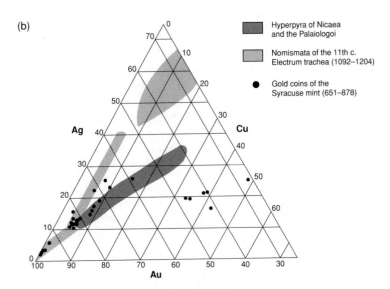

Figure 1.   Gold fineness
a. The debasement of the Byzantine gold and silver coinages
(after C. Morrisson, *Monnaie et finances à Byzance: Analyses, techniques* [Aldershot,
1994], art. IV, p. 300)
b. The different processes of debasement of gold coinage in Byzantium
(C. Morrisson, *EHB* 2, Ch. 42, figs. 2 and 3)

reflected a difference in the level of prices and more active small-scale exchanges in the western part of the Empire.

Byzantine money, in the form of the gold *nomisma*, played a major role in the eastern Mediterranean trade in the eleventh–twelfth centuries. The debasement of 1050–91 was a brief episode that apparently did not impair its reputation. In the West, *besantius, bisantius, besant* from the tenth century onward designated the Byzantine coin and even became a common word for any gold coin of the time. The Komnenian *hyperpyron* enjoyed a wide circulation in Mediterranean trade as evidenced, for example, in Venetian documents of the period.[187] With the Fatimid *dinar* in the East and the Almoravid (*morabitino*) in the West, it was one of the "dollars of the Middle Ages," an international currency with high intrinsic value and purchasing power,[188] with a stable quality (except in the second half of the eleventh century), supported by a powerful economy. As Carlo Cipolla wrote: "the triumph of the nomisma would have been completely inconceivable without the industrial and commercial power of the Byzantine Empire in the first part of the Middle Ages."[189]

THE STATE RECEDES

Policies

The role of the state in the economic process underwent significant changes in the course of the eleventh and twelfth centuries. However, there are important chronological distinctions. Basil II (976–1025), despite the fact that some of his policies were harbingers of the future,[190] was also the last Byzantine emperor to rule an expanding state with a large and centralized administration, and also the last to pursue the policies of successive tenth-century emperors which aimed at inhibiting the accumulation of wealth in the hands of individuals and also at protecting the citizen and the consumer.[191]

---

[187] Laiou, "Byzantine Trade with Christians and Muslims," pp. 156–96.

[188] A *nomisma* could buy some ten lambs or six sheep, 3 *modioi* of land (*c.* 3,000m²) or 3 *modioi* of wheat (38 kilos). In Venice, a *nomisma* was worth 120 *denarii* in 1000 AD, 496 *denarii* in 1196.

[189] C. Cipolla, *Money, Prices and Civilization in the Mediterranean World* (New York, 1967), pp. 13–26, at p. 24.

[190] Particularly so in the rural economy, see above, pp. 102–3.

[191] He also left a vast amount of money in the treasury: see Chapter III.

Basil II's successors, until 1081, followed different and sometimes conflicting policies: the granting of privileges became more extensive, some state lands were alienated, the power and wealth of the Constantinopolitan merchant and manufacturer were recognized. In the 1070s, the large state Basil II had ruled suffered considerable territorial diminution. The grave difficulties of the late eleventh century were to some extent reversed by the policies of Alexios I (1081–1118), who, however, ushered in a new era, which I have called "feudal authoritarianism." In politics, this is characterized by the diffusion of imperial power into the hands of a small group of aristocrats who were allied to the imperial family; in the economic sphere, there is diffusion of economic power. These transformations found expression as well in the ideological concepts regarding the economy, and in the broader economic policies of the government.[192]

The major development in this period is the progressive abandonment by the state of its traditional fiscal policy, which had been based on the collection of the land tax from all landowners which, until the eleventh century, had meant primarily from landowning peasants organized in village communities. In the course of the eleventh and twelfth centuries, the state abandoned the efforts of the tenth-century emperors to stop or reduce the acquisition of peasant lands by the *dynatoi* and their absorption into estates. At the same time it more and more frequently granted privileges (*exkousseiai*) to individual landowners and monasteries; the privileges consisted of the exemption of the beneficiary from secondary taxes or even, occasionally, from the base tax. If the estate owner was not exempted from taxation, he paid his base land tax to the state; but exemptions proliferated, until, after the late eleventh century, they became systematic.

Confusion and uncertainty remain in the literature regarding the monetization or otherwise of taxes and dues, and of the state economy itself. It has been argued by the same scholar both that secondary taxes and corvées, which had been paid in kind or services, were collected in cash in the eleventh century, and that the tax system

---

[192] Important references for this chapter include: Oikonomides, *Fiscalité*, and his "The Role of the Byzantine State," pp. 1019 ff.; A. E. Laiou, "Koinonike dikaiosyne: to synallattesthai kai to euemerein sto Vyzantio," *Praktika tes Akademias Athenon* (1999), pp. 103–30, and her "Economic Thought and Ideology," *EHB* 3, pp. 1123–44. Other references will be given as needed.

was less monetized in the eleventh–twelfth centuries than before. The conclusions of other scholars are not more secure.[193] In fact, the sources are confusing, which may be due to two conflicting processes: the state was trying to increase its revenues by increasing taxes and services and monetizing some of them (the monetization, in the eleventh century, of the *strateia*, the obligation to serve in the army, is a good example), while at the same time granting privileges that reduced its ability to collect the taxes it had always collected in cash in the past.

The state also granted to private individuals state lands in hereditary succession, although it continued to own large crown estates deep into the twelfth century. Starting with the late eleventh century, some grants were given in *pronoia*, that much-discussed Byzantine institution. A *pronoia* is a grant of fiscal revenues to an individual in return for services, military most often, but also civil. It was, until the reforms of the late thirteenth century, a grant limited to the lifetime of the beneficiary. The *pronoia* has been much discussed because in some ways it is reminiscent of the Western fief, and as an institution it has been at the basis of discussions regarding the presence or absence of "feudalism" in the Byzantine Empire; however, these discussions are not in themselves pertinent here.[194] More pertinent is the fact that in recent years the economic rather than institutional role of the *pronoia* has entered the discussion. But its economic function depends, to a large extent, on one's estimation of how widespread it was in the

[193] N. Oikonomides, "Se poio vathmo etan ekchrematismene e mesovyzantine oikonomia?," *Rodonia, Time ston M. I. Manousaka* (Rethymnon, 1994), p. 365 and n. 5 (reprinted in *Social and Economic Life*, art XIV); Oikonomidès, *Fiscalité*, pp. 218–19; P. Magdalino too states that taxes and dues in cash increased in the twelfth century: "The Grain Supply of Constantinople, Ninth–Twelfth Centuries," in Mango and Dagron, *Constantinople and its Hinterland*, p. 39; Harvey, *Expansion*, pp. 89–90, stresses that state action in the countryside (in the form of compulsory purchases) increased monetization; he documents the increase of the commutation (into cash) of obligations and services in kind, and the greater circulation, therefore, of money in the countryside (cf. pp. 102, 105–15).

[194] The most influential work has been that of Ostrogorskij, *Pour l'histoire de la féodalité byzantine* (Brussels, 1954), which generated a good deal of discussion. In his earlier works, A. P. Kazhdan adopted the concept of Byzantine feudalism, but his position became more nuanced later. Paul Lemerle was among the first to reject its usefulness or appropriateness for Byzantium: *The Agrarian History of Byzantium* (Galway, 1979), p. 89 and n. 1, 201–2; cf. Harvey, *Expansion*, pp. 5–12, and 72, with the earlier bibliography.

twelfth century, on which issue scholarly opinions differ widely.[195] All that can be said here is that, since in practice the grant of *pronoia* meant the cession of land with tenant farmers who paid all their taxes (as well as rent) to the *pronoia*-holder, the end result was that the treasury lost a good deal of its revenues, proportionate to the presumed extent of the *pronoia* system.

In the absence of any possibility of numerical estimates, it is best to insist on the *process* of alienation of state and crown lands and revenues, the accumulation of land (whether in hereditary or in temporary possession) into the hands of individuals, the grant of fiscal privileges and exemptions, all processes which, with the brief interlude of the years of imperial exile in Nicaea (1204–61) were to continue into the thirteenth, fourteenth and fifteenth centuries.

Thus, gradually, in the course of the eleventh century, the fiscal role of government started to weaken through the very actions of the state, which responded to the interests of the wealthy and powerful people, whether their wealth came from the government itself or from landed possessions. The grant of privileges, while it may have played a positive role in the rural economy, had a detrimental effect as far as the fiscal system was concerned, since it took some land revenues out of the hands of the state. At the same time, the collection of taxes became decentralized. Instead of imperial officials collecting taxes that went directly into the state coffers, and receiving a salary for their services, the state began to farm out taxes, a system which almost privatizes a state business and squeezes the taxpayer. Of course, the state still, and always, retained the monopoly of calculating the tax people owed, but its collection changed significantly. Furthermore, powerful individuals, whether members of the imperial family or others, received, from time to time, the right to collect the taxes of entire provinces. Finally, the grant of lands and land exemptions meant that a much larger proportion of the surplus went into the hands of individuals who then channeled much of it into the marketplace. The circulation of money was now more rapid; but it was not, even as far

[195] See the contrasting views of, on the one hand, Harvey, *Expansion*, p. 7; A. Hohlweg, "Zur Frage der Pronoia in Byzanz," *BZ* 60 (1967), pp. 288–308; D. Jacoby, "Les archontes grecs et la féodalité en Morée franque," *TM* 2 (1967), pp. 421–81, esp. 445, 465, 479–81, and, on the other, Oikonomidès, *Fiscalité*, esp. pp. 222–3, and "The Role of the Byzantine State," pp. 1042–8. Cf. also P. Magdalino, *The Empire of Manuel I Komnenos* (Cambridge, New York, 1993), pp. 175–7, 231–2.

as the fiscal system was concerned, set in motion by the state to the same degree as earlier.

The eleventh century system collapsed in the wake of the monetary and military crises of the 1070s. The payment of taxes was reformed by Alexios I Komnenos in a way that ensured the collection of higher taxes, paid in the debased gold coin (*aspron trachy*) as well as in silver and copper. The grant of land and privileges, however, and tax-farming as well, continued and increased in the twelfth century. The on-going decentralization and privatization of fiscal services is evident in the fact that the government greatly reduced the payment of salaries in cash: some military men and civil officials were receiving the reward of their services through the grant of lands and revenues, a situation which to some extent bypassed the central administration.

In the Komnenian period, state lands were reduced through grants, the collection of taxes by the state suffered a proportional diminution, and so did the expenditures of the state. The fiscal services became simplified. The qualifications with which all of the above statements must be made ("some," "proportionately," "to some extent") is an important part of the story. Some emperors tried to stop the process: Isaak I Komnenos (1057–59), looking at state expenses and the need for military campaigns, instituted savings, increased taxes, reduced the salaries of officials, and, most importantly, took back state lands granted in a perfectly binding way by his predecessors (as well as the excess lands appropriated by some monasteries). In this way, "the fisc, which was pressured from many sides to give up its own, saw its resources increase considerably . . ."[196] Neither he nor his measures lasted long. Furthermore, there is some evidence that the Komnenian state enforced regalian rights which had lapsed: the confiscation of the property of a murderer (*phonikon*), and perhaps the rights of treasure trove (*heuresis thesaurou*), a fine for rape (*parthenophthoria*), and the confiscation of the property of those dying intestate or without heirs (*abiotikion*).[197]

In the mid-twelfth century, the Byzantine government was still very wealthy, not only from the revenues of customs duties and

---

[196] Attaleiates, ed. Bekker, pp. 60–1.

[197] A. E. Laiou, "Le débat sur les droits du fisc et les droits régaliens au début du 14e siècle," *REB* 58 (2000), pp. 97–122. The first explicit mention of the state exercising these rights dates from the beginning of the thirteenth century (in the case of the *phonikon*), and the mid-thirteenth century for the others. But the development began earlier.

commercial taxes but also from the production of state lands and the proceeds of land and personal taxes. Only a portion, not a large one, of state lands was granted to individuals; and not all grants carried tax exemption. The wealth and luxury of the court of Manuel I Komnenos (1143–80) was immense; the cost of his military campaigns also. A single, and unsuccessful, campaign in Italy cost 2,160,000 gold coins, the equivalent of 15 per cent of the huge gold reserves left by Basil II.[198] The decentralization of taxes and the diminution of the fiscal role of the state were on-going processes, very far from completed in the late twelfth century; they would become more acute after the recovery of Constantinople in 1261. What did happen, however, was that heavy and inequitable taxation, which fell disproportionately on the poorer people in the countryside, the extension of the non-state sector, and the great cost of Manuel's military and diplomatic campaigns, coupled with the lackadaisical attitude of his successors, led to a major fiscal crisis in the late twelfth century, from which the state did not emerge.

Ideology

The Byzantine state had, in the past, also played an economic role that transcended both fiscality and the special weight of the state as the greatest landlord. Some of the changes that occurred in the eleventh–twelfth centuries have already been mentioned: for example, the shift in elite demand, which in the past had been primarily state demand, but which now was diffused among the rich landowners, the members of the bureaucracy and the wealthier merchants. Economic relations between the state and the citizen/consumer also changed, in a process that began in the early eleventh century. For one thing, the redistributive and equalizing role of the state was greatly attenuated. The idea that justice is an important function of the emperor remained, but whereas in the past that meant impartiality and the privileged treatment of the weak, now the concept of impartiality retreated as "leniency" raised its head; and the cases of leniency reported by the historians of the eleventh century affect privileged members of society. An abortive effort to institutionalize justice by placing additional importance on law and lawgiving, during the reign of Nikephoros III Votaneiates (1078–81), is inscribed

[198] Choniates, ed. Van Dieten, p. 97.

among the progressive elements of eleventh century; but it did not continue.[199]

Among other things, in this period the state promoted rather than inhibited the accumulation of wealth in the hands of individuals. We find reflections of this in the law that governs economic transactions, and in philosophical and legal statements. The protection that had been granted to individuals who were perceived to have been excessively harmed by a transaction was under attack in the eleventh century. It was still applied selectively. Some people, however, conceived the "just price" as a spectrum of prices, where the lowest point is 50 per cent of the "just" price (whether that is the market price or an administered price), but anything over that is legitimate. From this point of view, the price is regulated by the market, with the proviso (and the only legal prerequisite) that a minimum be met. Market forces seek to gain the upper hand.[200]

Justice in exchange survived as an ideal. At the same time, there is a proliferation of positive comments about profit, a concept which was traditionally suspect and which, it had been thought, had to be kept within bounds. The great Symeon the New Theologian composed, sometime between 1000 and 1009 a treatise on Eph. 5:16, "redeeming the time because the days are evil." In it, he uses as a parable the practices of good and less good merchants. The example to be followed, according to this text, is the actions of the diligent merchant who, in the pursuit of profit, runs risks, pays attention to his business, judges market conditions and returns home with great profits. Not a single word is breathed about just and unjust profits; the behavior that is described and lauded is a profit-maximizing, economic behavior. Other texts from a similarly religious milieu speak of the pursuit of profit and of the obligation of merchants to turn capital to productive uses.[201]

A number of jurists, judges, canonists and philosophers of the eleventh and twelfth centuries exhibit a very good understanding of

---

[199] A. E. Laiou, "Law, Justice and the Byzantine Historians: Ninth–Twelfth Centuries," in A. E. Laiou and D. Simon (eds.), *Law and Society in Byzantium, Ninth–Twelfth Centuries* (Washington, D.C., 1994), pp. 173–85.

[200] *Peira* 38.5. A. E. Laiou, "Oikonomika zetemata sten 'Peira' tou Eustathiou Romaiou," in *E autokratoria se krise*, 183–4; Laiou, "Koinonike dikaiosyne," p. 116.

[201] A. E. Laiou, "Händler und Kaufleute auf dem Jahrmarkt," in G. Prinzing and D. Simon (eds.), *Fest und Alltag in Byzanz* (Munich, 1990), pp. 53–70.

the market, and an advanced concept of money and its uses. Among the canonists, Valsamon and Zonaras describe the use of unconventional types of association created by clerics who wanted to bypass the interest legislation.[202] Michael Psellos, the most erudite man of the eleventh century, and a perfect snob, understood well the depressing effects of sudden price rises. More impressive is the example of Michael Attaleiates, who was a judge as well as a landowner of middle rank, with urban and rural real estate in Raidestos and commercial real estate in Constantinople. He was also a historian, who wrote on the affairs of the late eleventh century. His description of the affair of the *phoundax* of Raidestos, although economical of expression, betrays a deep understanding of economic phenomena. He gives a perfect description of the effects of oligopsony (low prices for the grain producer) and oligopoly (a great increase in consumer prices). He also makes a more sophisticated point of economic analysis: that a price rise in inelastic commodities, grain in the case in point, exercises an upward pull on all prices as well as demand for higher wages and salaries.[203]

Other intellectuals of the eleventh and twelfth centuries were concerned with the formation of prices and wages as a function of supply and demand, and with understanding the role and function of money in the economy. In the twelfth century, Michael of Ephesos wrote a commentary on the fifth chapter of Aristotle's *Nicomachean Ethics* that subsequently was much read by Western medieval theorists on money. While he followed faithfully Aristotle's text regarding justice in exchange, commensurability and the common measure of value, and while he regarded money primarily as a medium of exchange, he made some important departures from the Aristotelian text, in particular on money as a measure of value. Basically, he tried to understand the economic processes that lead to price formation, and saw them as interconnected parts of a whole that is subject to change. For Aristotle, the common measure of value was *chreia* (use, need, lack of something) and money was, in some way, a substitute for it. For Michael of Ephesos, *chreia* is not stable but changes; money measures

---

[202] A. E. Laiou, "God and Mammon: Credit, Trade, Profit and the Canonists," in N. Oikonomides, ed., *To Vyzantio kata ton 120 aiona* (Athens, 1991), pp. 261–300; cf. above, p. 141.

[203] Attaleiates 202–4, and cf. above, pp. 135–36. G. I. Bratianu is one of the few scholars who has noticed the sophistication of these statements: "Une expérience d'économie dirigée" (see n. 144), pp. 643–62, especially pp. 651–2.

it and its changes. In context, this must be taken to mean that the just price is the market price. He also, impressively for a medieval society, understood the value of money not as something intrinsic, which would have been natural in an economy with coins capable of being devalued, but on the one hand as established by human convention and, on the other, as a commodity, whose value changes according to the supply and demand for commodities. Equally interestingly, he finds a new role for Aristotle's corrective justice: it is to guarantee the contracts which have been concluded with the free will of the parties, a truly original approach.[204] Thus the Byzantine state, formerly conceived as the "judge" who guarantees just exchange, becomes the legal authority that safeguards the sanctity of private contracts. An anonymous jurist who wrote, *c.*1140, a commentary on the first ten books of the *Basilics*, also insisted on the role of contracts. He further argued that interest on loans is the profit of the money lent. Thus, he conceived of money as capital in some sense.[205] The possibility of creating value through the investment of capital appears here in advance of similar developments in Western Europe.

There is thus a confluence of new ideas: money is seen in its various roles as medium of exchange, as conventional measure of value, as commodity and as capital; freely negotiated economic agreements have not only legal but almost moral force. The state functions as the guarantor of economic agreements. Profit acquires positive connotations in unexpected texts. There was no full-blown social theory based on the acceptance of the pursuit of profit, and traditional ideas that saw spiritual and moral danger in mercantile activity and in the pursuit of profit existed at the same time. In a medieval Christian society, the traditional ideas had long-lived resonance. But that ideological innovations appear in this period shows the shifts that were taking place in the Byzantine economy.

The role of the state in the economy receded not only because the state gave away part of its fiscal prerogatives but also because market operations had become important in structuring the economy and even, to some extent, economic ideology. Economic power was no longer heavily in the hands of the state. The motor of the economy was no longer the centralized state; it probably was the economy of exchange. The phenomenon is particularly clear in the twelfth

[204] On the above, see Laiou, "Koinonike dikaiosyne," pp. 118–24.
[205] Laiou, "*Nummus parit nummos*," pp. 590–2.

century and has parallels in the transformed character of the state. The Komnenian state lost the absolute character which in the past had been embodied by the emperor and his functionaries. Its imperial power became diffused, as parts of it were embodied in the various dignitaries who drew their power from their biological proximity to the Emperor.[206] Therein lay a grave danger for the economy, for the people who shared in the imperial power were, as a group, grasping and self-serving; the political failure of the Komnenian system undermined the evolving economic system.

CONCLUSION

Byzantium in the eleventh and twelfth centuries exhibits some aspects of pre-industrial intensive growth. It has been seen that there was increased production in the countryside, and intensification of activity in secondary production. Our limited evidence indicates that there was probably a secular increase in the per capita income, clear both in the accumulation of wealth and in the notable well-being of merchants and the richer artisans. The growth of trade, fostering division of labor, was an important engine of this development. Parts of the economy continued to grow in the thirteenth century, notably the agrarian economy; but one can no longer speak of systemic or intensive growth after the first dissolution of the Byzantine Empire in 1204.

The interruption in the development of the Byzantine economy came about both because of internal disabilities and because of political failure. As far as the first factor is concerned, there was, as yet, no Malthusian bind. Rather, there were limiting factors. One was the usual pre-industrial phenomenon that the effective demand exercised by the bulk of the population was, still, low. Another was the fact that access to international markets, which might have absorbed the manufactured products and further stimulated production, was becoming first facilitated and then blocked by Italian traders who acted from a privileged position. The political failure was multiple. Most of the successful adjustments of the Byzantine state to the new economic conditions had taken place in the course of the eleventh

---

[206] It became 'royalized,' in the words of G. Dagron, "Empires royaux, royautés impériales: lectures croisées sur Byzance et la France médiévale," in *Summa: Dieter Simon zum 70. Geburtstag* (Frankfurt, 2005), pp. 81–97, esp. p. 94.

century, including the early years of Alexios I. The only major adjustments of the twelfth century concern the development of maritime and merchant law. For the rest, the ruling Komnenian clan exhibited an extractive behavior that alienated its subjects, especially in the provinces. Furthermore, the political elite undermined the progress of the dynamic commercial sector in two major ways: first, by cutting off the participation of men of affairs in government, and secondly by placing them in an unfavorable situation compared to privileged individuals and groups. The third failure of this extractive ruling class was fatal: by alienating both Western merchants (whose privileges were extensive but never secure) and other Western powers, in the late twelfth century, they made possible the conquest of Constantinople and the dissolution, for nearly sixty years, of the Byzantine Empire with Constantinople as its capital.

V

SMALL-STATE ECONOMICS (FROM SOMETIME IN THE THIRTEENTH CENTURY TO THE FIFTEENTH CENTURY)

———— • ————

Problems of periodization challenge the historian of this broad period even more than of the ones preceding it. Because the Byzantine Empire had been an organized political unit that played a powerful role in the economy, economic developments were strongly affected by political ones. And they are dramatic: Constantinople fell to the members of the Fourth Crusade in 1204. This constitutes the first framing event of the thirteenth century. It resulted in the dissolution of the political space, never again reunited until the establishment of the Ottomans in Constantinople/Istanbul. There are, thus, powerful elements of discontinuity. Yet economic factors develop over the long term, and it takes a while for them to be affected by political events. So certain sectors of the economy (notably agriculture, but also pottery manufacturing) exhibit patterns of production and distribution similar to those of the earlier period, through the early part of the thirteenth century in the case of pottery production, until the late part of the century in the case of agriculture; others, like silk cloth manufacturing, declined early. Therefore, the dividing line between this period and the previous one depends on what aspect of the economy one examines. Some scholars have written of a "long thirteenth century" in Western Europe, hard to date because it is notional: it refers to "the temporal duration of a unique set of forces," the forces of expansion.[1] In Byzantium, the equivalent might

---

[1] D. C. North and R. P. Thomas, *The Rise of the Western World: A New Economic History* (Cambridge, 1973), pp. 46 ff. For the term "the lost thirteenth century," see A. E. Laiou, "The Byzantine Economy: An Overview," *EHB* 3, p. 1158.

be the "long twelfth century." At some point, there began the "lost thirteenth century," a period in which the economy of the Byzantine or formerly Byzantine territories was unable to profit from the positive effects of Western markets and, instead, eventually relinquished control of commerce and manufacturing to the Western Europeans, most particularly to the merchants of the Italian maritime cities. The dominance of Italian merchants in the eastern Mediterranean is the second important framing factor.

The role and importance of scale

After 1204, the Empire was succeeded by a number of small states. Westerners created states or enclaves in parts of imperial territory (the Latin Empire of Constantinople, until 1261, the Principality of Achaia, Venetian-held Crete after 1211, other Venetian-held islands of the Aegean and eventually the Ionian Sea, the trading stations of Modon and Coron). The Greek successor states were the Empire of Nicaea until 1261, the Empire of Trebizond (both, originally, in Asia Minor), and the so-called Despotate of Epiros. The Slavic lands, Bulgaria and Serbia, once parts of the Byzantine Empire, became independent shortly before the Fourth Crusade and remained independent until the Ottoman conquest, fragmenting into smaller units. We thus have small-scale states in a fragile, unstable system whose logic was toward warfare. The emergence of small successor states resulted in multipolarity tending toward fragmentation and then pulverization of political power: everything was small-scale, starting with the size of the state and the impact of elite demand. Small states followed small-state economics. The global cost of government was high: royal or "imperial" courts multiplied, even though each one was much poorer than the Komnenian palace; there was competitive spending on buildings, and the competition for income or resources necessitated expenses for military action. Meanwhile, the resources of the various states dwindled and their role in the upkeep of infrastructures declined or disappeared.[2] There was a proliferation of weights

---

[2] For this, and much of what follows, see A. E. Laiou, "Byzantium and the Neighboring Powers: Small-state Policies and Complexities," in *Faith and Power (1261–1557): Perspectives on Late Byzantine Art and Culture* (New York, 2006), 42–53; for theoretical discussions of the chaos theory that underlies this article see A. M. Saperstein, "The Prediction of Unpredictability: Applications of the New Paradigm of Chaos in Dynamical Systems to the Old Problem of the Stability of a System in Hostile

and measures, eventually of coins, and of legislation, all of which raised the costs of doing business compared to the earlier period of a "national" market.[3] In terms of production, agriculture eventually (in the fourteenth century) suffered from constant insecurity and warfare, some due to competition among the various states, some to incursions from outsiders, Tatars in the Balkans, Turks in Asia Minor and eventually also in the Balkans. Resources, land, cattle and liquid capital were transferred from one group of people to the other in the course of wars or raids, while much capital was destroyed in the process. Nevertheless, agriculture was the last to be affected in terms of structures, with the rather important exception of the fact that, after 1261, the properties of the state became progressively much reduced. Manufacturing became small-scale. The participation of Byzantines in inter-regional and international trade diminished, although in local and regional trade it may have increased.

Differential regional development, already under way in the previous period, was reinforced, as particular states followed different policies in agriculture or trade. Furthermore, as various regions became inscribed in subsections of the Mediterranean trade system, their agriculture and industry were affected: Latin Peloponnese and Cyprus had a distinct development from Byzantine Macedonia.

The Byzantine economy suffered from all of these developments, as well as from the permanent loss of resources. The independence of Bulgaria and Serbia meant that cereal-producing and cattle-producing areas were no longer a part of the Byzantine economy, while some of Byzantine Macedonia came under Serbian control after 1282; the loss of Cyprus and Serbia meant the loss of copper and silver mines. After the early fourteenth century, the grain of the Bulgarian coast was no longer part of a domestic, Byzantine exchange system, even as it entered the international market. Furthermore, the Byzantine economy, such as we have seen it in the period down to the end of the twelfth century, was disaggregated during the period of Latin occupation of Constantinople. After the re-establishment of Byzantine sovereignty in that city, it became partially articulated once more through the diminished, but nonetheless present role of

Nations," in L. Douglas Kiel and E. Elliott (eds.), *Chaos Theory in the Social Sciences: Foundations and Applications* (Ann Arbor, 1996), pp. 139–55. See also A. Alesina and E. Spolaore, *The Size of Nations* (Cambridge, Mass. and London, 2003), pp. 95 ff.

[3] On coins, see pp. 215 ff.

the state, as well as through the existence of a rational integration of agricultural production, industrial production and marketing activities. However, all of that unraveled in the last hundred years of the formal existence of the Byzantine state.

In these circumstances, the question arises whether one may any longer speak of a Byzantine economy, and to what areas such a description might apply. The answer has to be hedged in so many ways that perforce it becomes conventional in the primary meaning of the word, that is, based on agreement. As "Byzantine" economy we will understand the economy of areas which were Byzantine before the Fourth Crusade and eventually became reintegrated into the Byzantine state after it had been reconstituted with its capital in Constantinople after 1261: broadly speaking, the coastal areas of Asia Minor (except the Empire of Trebizond) until they fell to the Turks, Constantinople itself with its Thracian hinterland, Macedonia, the lands of Epiros and Thessaly, the islands of the eastern Aegean, and the Despotate of the Morea. Diverse regional development is evident here too, and will be treated to the degree allowed by the length of this book. To what extent this was a "national" economy will be discussed in the section regarding the state. As for chronology, the major points to be taken into consideration are: the conquest of Constantinople in 1204, the period of the Empire of Nicaea (1204–61), the period from 1261 until the middle of the fourteenth century, and the period from *c.*1348 to the final capture of Constantinople by the Ottomans, in 1453. Discussion of developments in Latin-held parts of the old Byzantine Empire will be kept to a minimum, and used for comparison only. Otherwise, this chapter would become too long and diffuse.

DEMOGRAPHY

The secular demographic trend seems to have continued for a time. On the other hand, the virtually constant hostilities and wars took a toll. In the late thirteenth century, we find both evidence of new settlements and, on the contrary, the signs of abandonment of settlements. The demographic information one may glean from sources that admit statistical analysis (that is, from the *praktika*, the census of various large properties, mostly ecclesiastical, that now register the peasant household with, generally speaking, all its members) is also mixed. A Malthusian impasse seems to have been reached in the late thirteenth century: new settlements were then mostly in marginal lands. In Macedonia, where population movements may be traced with some certainty, the population maximum was reached either in the early fourteenth century or a little later. Certainly, the population was already declining by the 1340s, before the plague. In the second half of that century, the population suffered a precipitous and catastrophic decline because of the combined effects of recurrent outbreaks of the plague, invasions, wars, and civil wars on an already weakened population.[4] The overall effects of the plague were of the classic variety, but exacerbated by political instability and warfare.

The prosperity of the majority of the population, the peasants, followed a curve whose slope might be expected from what has been said about population movements. The first half of the thirteenth century was relatively prosperous for the peasantry of Asia Minor,[5] while in Macedonia and the Peloponnese signs of a modest prosperity continue into the latter part of the century. Then, in the first half of the fourteenth century, the visible wealth of peasant households begins to decline, although the agrarian economy was still well articulated. After the middle of the fourteenth century, some peasants become rich in land, some even in cattle, but one may not speak of prosperity in such difficult circumstances, whatever the equations beloved of the "dismal" science.

PRIMARY PRODUCTION

Agricultural resources and production

Polyculture and polyactivity still prevailed.[6] Nevertheless, there are regional differences and a certain amount of specialization, due in part to endowments in natural resources and in part to the demand

---

[4] For population movements, see A. E. Laiou, "The Agrarian Economy, Thirteenth–Fifteenth Centuries," *EHB* 1, pp. 312 ff., based on A. E. Laiou-Thomadakis, *Peasant Society in the Late Byzantine Empire: A Social and Economic Study* (Princeton, 1977) Chapter 6, and the somewhat different views of J. Lefort, "Population et peuplement en Macédoine orientale, IXe–XVe siècles," in *Hommes et richesses dans l'empire byzantin*, II (Paris, 1991), p. 75.

[5] See, in the last instance, D. Kyritsès and K. Smyrlis, "Les villages du littoral égéen de l'Asie Mineure au Moyen Âge," in J. Lefort, C. Morrisson and J.-P. Sodini (eds.), *Les Villages dans l'empire byzantin (IVe–XVe siècle)* (Paris, 2005), pp. 437–51.

[6] On this topic see above, Chapter IV.

exercised by the Western European markets to which part of the production of the region was increasingly exported. Byzantine Asia Minor had its heyday during the Laskarid period, partly because the efforts of the emperor John III Vatatzes made the area self-sufficient in grain, olive oil and animal products. Nicaea was even able to export grain to the Seljuks in times of crisis. Cash crop-producing assets, mainly olive trees and vineyards, were important, and were partly owned by peasants.

Production in the Morea, both the part held by the Byzantines and that held by the Angevins until 1377, was geared around olive oil, for which it was famous in Europe, wine, and silk, which was exported to Italy. Interestingly, raw silk production appears to have ceased in the area around Corinth. The Morea also produced wool, cotton and linen, and exported dyestuffs, mainly kermes, and acorns, for the use of tanners. By the 1420s, however, the production of the peninsula had fallen off grievously.[7] Thessaly was primarily grain-producing, but also raised cattle and horses, while the area around Volos produced wine. Epiros, a mountainous area, had a well-developed animal husbandry sector; its population raised cattle, horses and a great number of sheep.[8]

Macedonia and Thrace are the paradise of polyculture: they produced grain, some of it still exported to the West even in the fifteenth century, less than ten years before the capture of Constantinople; imperial agents and imperial officials were involved in this trade, which may have been the commercialized grain production of lands belonging to the imperial family.[9] Around the middle of the fourteenth century, Francesco Balducci Pegolotti praised the wheat of Rodosto as being the best in the East. But the landowners and peasants of Macedonia also raised sheep and cattle and horses. Animal husbandry was a profitable activity, and a necessary one: not only were the beasts marketable (and oxen necessary for cultivating the

[7] D. Jacoby, "Silk Production in the Frankish Peloponnese," in his *Trade, Commodities and Shipping in the Medieval Mediterranean* (Aldershot, 1997), art. VIII, p. 48; D. Jacoby, "Silk Crosses the Mediterranean," and "From Byzantium to Latin Romania: Continuity and Change," in his *Byzantium, Latin Romania and the Mediterranean* (Aldershot, 2001), arts. X and VIII respectively; Laiou, "The Agrarian Economy," pp. 322–4.

[8] L. Schopen and B. G. Niebuhr (eds.), *Ioannis Cantacuzeni eximperatoris, historiarum libri quattuor*, 3 vols. (Bonn, 1828–32) (hereafter, Cantacuzenus), I, pp. 497–8.

[9] A. Laiou-Thomadakis, "The Byzantine Economy in the Mediterranean Trade System: Thirteenth–Fifteenth Centuries," *DOP* 34–35 (1980–81), pp. 218 ff.

fields), but animals, as has long been observed, functioned as protein reserves at a time when poor weather conditions could be expected to damage the crops with depressing regularity. The importance of animal husbandry is attested by the high value placed on meadow land that produced fodder for the winter: it was considered more valuable than first-quality arable land.[10] Fruit trees, including mulberries, grew in Macedonia, as did vines that produced good and marketable wine. The Chalkidike had olive trees, although Macedonia was not a heavy olive oil producer. Fishing and beekeeping supplemented the caloric needs and the peasant budget. Linen, cotton and flax were industrial crops. The products of wood and forest were marketed, as they had been for a long time, and salt was produced in both Macedonia and Thrace.

Salt was also produced in Naupaktos, in western Greece, on the Black Sea coast, in Crete, the Peloponnese and Cyprus. The Byzantine official Alexios Apokaukos, in the first half of the fourteenth century, made a fortune from the management of the state-owned salines.

Mining activity might be mentioned in the context of primary production. The Byzantine state lost, in this period, the precious metal mines of Asia Minor, as well as the copper mines of Cyprus. The great new development in the general area was the exploitation of silver and gold mines in Serbia, centered around the area of Novo Brdo and manned by German miners. The expansionist policy of successive Serbian kings in the fourteenth century was underwritten by the production of these silver mines. The area of Siderokauseia, in Chalkidike, produced iron in this period, and iron mining and smelting furnaces are found in other parts of the Empire.[11] The Byzantines, however, lost out on the most profitable development in mining. In the course of the late thirteenth and fourteenth centuries, indeed, until the 1460s, fortunes could be and were made in alum, a general

---

[10] Laiou, "The Agrarian Economy," Table 2A, p. 333. For the price of livestock, see C. Morrisson and J.-C. Cheynet, "Prices and Wages in the Byzantine World," *EHB* 2, pp. 839–44.

[11] On this, see K.-P. Matschke, "Zum Anteil der Byzantiner an der Bergbauentwicklung und an den Bergbauerträgen Südosteuropas im 14. und 15. Jahrhundert," *BZ* 84/5 (1991/2), pp. 49–71. Cf. B. Pitarakis, "Mines anatoliennes exploitées par les byzantins: recherches récentes," *RN* 153 (1989), pp. 141–85. The Empire of Trebizond did extract silver in the thirteenth century: A. Bryer, "The question of Byzantine Mines in the Pontos: Chalybian Iron, Chaldian Silver, Koloneian Alum and the Mummy of Cheriana," *Anatolian Studies* 32 (1982), pp. 133–50.

name for a number of white astringent mineral substances. Alum fixes the dyes in cloth and lends brilliance to the colors. It was therefore essential to the rapidly developing textile industry of Western Europe, especially in this period when brilliant colors were in fashion. Alum was produced in Egypt, but the best quality was mined in Asia Minor: Koloneia and other parts of the Pontic coast, Phocaea, and Kutahiya, as well as in Thrace and the islands of the Aegean (Map 4). In 1275, the emperor Michael VIII granted to two Genoese brothers, Manuele and Benedetto Zaccaria, the alum mines of Phocaea. The Zaccaria made a vast fortune based on, but not limited to, alum, and the Genoese virtually monopolized the extraction and commercialization of the mineral. Thus, a major potential source of income was turned over to the Genoese. The alum mines of Phocaea lost their importance only with the Turkish conquest; providentially, alum was then (1460) discovered in Tolfa, on papal estates.

Landlords and peasants, production and investment

Most scholars argue that the large estate continued to spread in the thirteenth century and after, although, following the arguments of the same scholars, one would think that it did not have much further to go. The state no longer owned very extensive domains, but there were some very large estates, both lay and ecclesiastical, in this period. The property of someone like John Kantakouzenos, a great aristocrat who usurped the throne, was probably the largest held by an individual. Much of his property was located in the rich Strymon valley, in Macedonia. He claimed to have lost, in the course of the civil war of 1341–54, 1,000 pairs of oxen, 50,000 pigs and 70,000 sheep, which must have produced a prodigious quantity of wool. Three hundred mules, 500 donkeys, 2,500 mares and 200 camels completed the animal resources of his estates. He does not give the size of his properties, but does speak of an "incredible" quantity of crops, as indeed one would expect from estates cultivated with 1,000 pairs of oxen.[12] These statements paint a doubtless exaggerated but compelling picture of a very large estate. Such wealth was unusual among laymen. Collectively, it was the monasteries that were the largest landlord in this period. The monastery of Lavra, the richest monastery of Mt Athos, is a good example. In 1321, the monastery possessed 185,000

[12] Cantacuzenus II, p. 192.

modioi (*c*.18,500 hectares) of land in the "themes" of Thessalonike and Strymon and the island of Lemnos. Its annual fiscal revenues, consisting of the dues of the *paroikoi* and various tax exemptions (which are not real revenues but, rather, savings on expenses), amounted to 4,000 gold coins. Its economic revenues would be in the order of magnitude of 4,300–4,900 gold coins.[13]

There were also, however, a considerable number of proprietors, urban or rural, that is, living in cities or in the countryside, with much smaller properties. These were *pronoia*-holders, or landlords with limited lands but with fiscal privileges, or urban-dwellers who nevertheless owned land in the countryside; this last category includes merchants, such as Theodore Karavas, who redacted his testament in Thessalonike in 1314, and who owned 61 *modioi* of vineyard, but very little arable land.[14] Furthermore, there were peasants who both owned and farmed land, and who seem to have been in a condition of dependence on large proprietors, without being termed *paroikoi*: was this dependence political or economic?[15]

It is therefore best to qualify the statements about the expansion of the large estate, and to speak instead of a continuum. At the one end there would be the very large proprietors, exemplified here by Kantakouzenos and Lavra; the middle of the spectrum would be occupied by middle-size proprietors, for example Theodore Skaranos,[16] people who held lands either in full possession or in *pronoia*,[17]

---

[13] Laiou, "The Agrarian Economy," pp. 349–50.

[14] M. Živojinović, V. Kravari and C. Giros (eds.), *Actes de Chilandar*, I (Paris, 1998), pp. 208–19; cf. A. E. Laiou, "E Thessalonike, e endochora tes kai o oikonomikos tes choros sten epoche ton Palaiologon," in *Diethnes Symposio Vyzantine Makedonia 324–1430* (Thessalonike, 1995), p. 188; C. Morrisson, "Byzantine Money: Its Production and Circulation," *EHB* 3, pp. 939–40. Similar is the case of Basil Krasinos, who lived in the city of Verroia in western Macedonia in the early thirteenth century, exploited more than 64 *modioi* of vineyard, and also engaged in trade: G. Prinzing, *Demetrii Chomateni ponemata diaphora* (Berlin, 2002), no. 84; cf. A. E. Laiou, *Mariage, amour et parenté à Byzance aux XIe–XIIIe siècles* (Paris, 1992), pp. 157 ff.

[15] See, for example, the peasants of Dryanouvaina in Thessaly, in F. Miklosich and J. Mueller, *Acta et diplomata graeca medii aevi sacra et profana*, 6 vols. (Vienna, 1860 –90), IV, pp. 391–3, 396–9, 410–11.

[16] J. Lefort , "Une exploitation de taille moyenne au XIIIe siècle en Chalcidique," *Afieroma ston Niko Svorono* (Rethymnon, 1986), pp. 362–72.

[17] The average value of a middle-size *pronoia* (that is, the value of the guaranteed property of a *pronoia*-holder) in the 1320s would be 70–80 gold coins: N. Oikonomidès, "À propos des armées des premiers Paléologues et des compagnies de soldats," *TM* 8 (1981), p. 354, reprinted in *Society, Culture and Politics*, art. XVI.

with or without privileges; peasant cultivators who might own arable, and most often would own vineyards, formed the largest category in terms of numbers; and peasants with virtually no resources occupied the other end of the spectrum. It is to be noted that the peasants in the last two categories could be either *paroikoi* or small-scale free proprietors or people who owned only their labor. In terms of ownership and the process of production, then, there is considerable variety, and the Byzantine countryside presents a much more complex picture than is usually painted.

There are economic implications in this picture in terms of investment in the agrarian economy, in terms of the appropriation of the surplus and, as a result, in terms of the disposal of the products. What follows obtains primarily for the period until the disarticulation of the economy, which started in the 1340s.

In terms of investment, what was profitable to the great landlord was different from what was profitable to middle and small proprietors. Large landlords showed a marked tendency not only to enlarge but also to rationalize their holdings. We know this especially of large ecclesiastical landlords, for whom the accumulation of property through donations, by the state or individuals large and small, and through purchase, or the gifts of people who entered a monastery, was easier. They sought to buy or acquire through donations lands that were contiguous to their existent holdings. The economic benefits are obvious, since transportation costs between various parts of the domain are minimized, and the costs of management are reduced. A prime example of such rationalization of property ownership is the monastery of the Great Lavra, whose arable and vineyards increased considerably between 1300 and 1321, and which sought to acquire continuous parcels of land.[18] Similar was the case of the monastery of Iviron, and other monasteries.[19]

Large landlords or the state had exclusive rights over uncultivated areas. Insofar as activity in the cultivated areas is concerned, landlords invested both in cereal cultivation and in cash crops as well as in agricultural capital, such as mills, as they had done in the earlier period. Estimates have been made of the yield of investments in these various enterprises. It has been established that investment in cereal

---

[18] Svoronos, "Le domaine de Lavra," in P. Lemerle, A. Guillou, N. Svoronos and D. Papachryssanthou (eds.), *Actes de Lavra*, 4 vols. (Paris, Paris, 1970–82), IV, p. 170.
[19] Laiou, "The Agrarian Economy," p. 351.

cultivation, primarily in the form of land clearance or improvement, as well as investment in oxen, draft horses and equipment, was primarily profitable for large estate owners, since the marginal profit per unit was rather small and profitability was thus a function of size.[20] It is not surprising that the best-known example of investment in the organization of cereal production is that of the Emperor John III Vatatzes, or that, in his effort to increase the agricultural production of the empire of Nicaea, he granted estates to large proprietors, namely, the monasteries, thus enlarging the size of units.[21] To this should be added the fact that the profitability of cereal cultivation for large proprietors was enhanced when the state donated a captive labor force, and also extended fiscal privileges to the proprietor. This of course applies also to privileged landowners of middle size. It is not accidental that fertile plains which were given over to cereal cultivation were also the locus of large proprietors.

Investment in cash crops was both more profitable per unit and accessible to a greater variety of people.[22] Vineyards require land clearance, cultivation, and patience, since the vine would take about five years to bear fruit. Investment in vineyards was made by landlords, and for good reason. In the early fourteenth century, the price of vineyards was 5.5 to 10 times higher than that of arable land, while their fiscal value was eight to twelve times higher than that of the best-quality arable.[23]

This was also an area for peasant investment. Occasionally, the investment was very considerable indeed: sometime before 1300, the inhabitants of Avramiton, a village in the Chalkidike which was, then as now, a wine-producing area, cleared and planted 400 *modioi* (about 40ha) of vineyards.[24] In other cases, investments were more modest. Where the vine grows, the great majority of peasants owned vineyards, whether by inheritance, by purchase or through their own investment: in Macedonia, in the fourteenth century, more than three-quarters of households owned some plot planted with vines. In the first half of the fourteenth century, among the *paroikoi* of the

[20] *Ibid.*, pp. 353–5.

[21] L. Schopen and I. Bekker (eds.), *Nicephori Gregorae byzantina historia*, 3 vols. (Bonn, 1829 –55), I, pp. 41–2 (hereafter, Gregoras).

[22] As, also, was investment in mills: see Chapter IV and, for thirteenth-century Asia Minor, Kyritsès and Smyrlis, "Les villages du littoral égéen," pp. 444–5.

[23] Laiou, "The Agrarian Economy," pp. 360 ff.

[24] D. Papachryssanthou (ed.), *Actes de Xénophon* (Paris, 1986), no. 3.

village of Gomatou that has been studied as an example, the Gini Coefficient, which measures inequality, ranged between 0.406 and 0.545.[25] This is a far more equal distribution than that of any other resource, and shows the importance of the grape both as a source of calories for autoconsumption and as a cash crop. Most plots were small, but peasants with vineyards of 20 *modioi* or so are also attested.

It has been argued in the previous chapter that the possibility of the peasant investing in vineyards (or mills, or olive trees, or mulberry trees and sericulture) could not have come about unless changes were made to the traditional status of the *paroikos*. In the thirteenth and fourteenth centuries, further institutional/juridical developments took place on the ground, in the perennial process of negotiation which, in various forms, characterizes agrarian relations in the Byzantine Empire.

When a peasant created a vineyard on his own land, it was his property, on which he owed tax.[26] What was problematic was the status of vineyards cultivated (or mills built) on the land of someone else, whether the landowner whose *paroikos* the peasant was, or a third person. These were considered improvements of the land, and in such cases the law would require that the vineyard (or the mill) belong to the owner of the land. In practice, however, various arrangements were made, on the informal understanding that the investment of cash or labor on the part of the person effecting the improvement created a presumption of ownership. Most frequently, the resolution of the dispute gives the investor rights of exploitation and indeed of ownership, whether full or, more often, partial, in which latter case the profits would be shared with the master of the land.[27] Intentionally or not, these arrangements promoted investment in revenue-producing assets. Indeed, the state itself was interested in facilitating such investments, since it either did not tax or taxed at very low rates the new lands cleared with the labor of *paroikoi*.[28]

---

[25] Laiou-Thomadakis, *Peasant Society*, pp. 164 ff.

[26] The documentation is considerable. See, by way of example, L. Petit (ed.), *Actes de Chilandar*, VV 17 (1911; repr. Amsterdam, 1975), nos. 93, 99; J. Bompaire (ed.), *Actes de Xéropotamou* (Paris, 1964), no. 17; *MM* IV, 35–41.

[27] Cf. A. E. Laiou and D. Simon, "Eine Geschichte von Mühlen und Mönchen: Der Fall der Mühlen von Chandax," *Bollettino dell' Istituto di Diritto Romano*, 3rd ser., 30 (1992) esp. pp. 645 ff.

[28] N. Oikonomides, "The Role of the Byzantine State in the Economy," *EHB* 3, p. 1035 and n. 166, with reference to M. Bartusis, "Εξάλειμμα: Escheat in

The basic unit of land exploitation, as opposed to ownership, continued to be the peasant household, consisting, typically, of the householder and his/her immediate family, although, following the family cycle, there were vertically or horizontally extended households at various points, and also joint households of brothers or, at most, first cousins.[29] Statistical studies of the property of *paroikoi* have shown that the majority of households owned no oxen; rather few owned a full team. This necessarily implies that there was cooperation among the peasants; it is also known that landlords had their own teams of oxen, which they presumably made available to the peasants. Most households would own a piece of vineyard, presumably also a garden; some would own fruit trees and olive trees; sheep and goats were extremely unequally distributed, but no flock under four animals is registered, which suggests that a couple of sheep or goats were neither recorded nor taxed; neither were pigs or hens.[30]

The ownership of arable by *paroikoi* varies very considerably from domain to domain, and landlord to landlord. In some villages, the *paroikoi* seem to own no arable; in others, they might own an average of 25–50 *modioi*, land sufficient for survival. The question of land ownership is connected to questions of the form of land exploitation and the distribution of the surplus. When a *paroikos* owns land, he cultivates it in the way which is most advantageous to him: he pays tax on it – to the landlord, now, no longer to the state, and the tax is usually estimated at one *hyperpyron* (gold coin) per fifty *modioi* of land (regardless of quality), a somewhat, but not significantly, lower rate than that for first- and second-quality land in the eleventh century.[31] The budgetary surplus, after payment of the tax, belongs to him. Similarly, he keeps the surplus, after tax, of vineyards and all other property he holds. On the land he leases from the landlord he pays a rent, typically, in this period, as a share of the produce: one third on cereals on the threshing floor, one half of the new wine,

Byzantium," *DOP* 40 (1986), pp. 79–81; Oikonomides interprets the cases mentioned by Bartusis in a different way from the author, and this interpretation is followed here.

[29] On this important question of co-ownership and co-residence, see Laiou, *Mariage*, pp. 137–85.

[30] Laiou-Thomadakis, *Peasant Society*, p. 174. On rates of taxation, see J. Lefort, "Fiscalité médiévale et informatique: recherches sur les barèmes pour l'imposition des paysans byzantins du XIVe siècle," *RH* 512 (1974), pp. 315–56.

[31] Laiou, "The Agrarian Economy," p. 332 and Table 2A, to be read in conjunction with Oikonomides, "The Role of the State," p. 1033.

and he incurs all of the expenses of cultivation. This, as we have argued, is the optimal arrangement as far as the landlord-peasant unit is concerned.[32] Finally, almost all peasants owe corvée labor, although its extent varies widely, from 12 days a year, to 24 days, to a single instance of 52 days (all in Macedonia). Unless they were commuted to cash payments, as sometimes happened, corvée services were used for the cultivation of domain lands, the most profitable part of the enterprise for the landlord.

What emerges is a mixture of land tenures and modes of cultivation. As in previous centuries, so also now the Byzantine estate did not have a large domanial preserve cultivated by labor services. It has been estimated that if they owed 24 days of labor, the peasants could cultivate a maximum of 20–24 per cent of the lands of the monastery of Lavra, quite a generous estimate.[33] With twelve days of service, this would drop precipitously; indeed labor services would then be limited to periods of high activity, sowing or harvesting. The direct exploitation of the domain was a limited activity indeed.

The variability of modes of exploitation, division of the surplus, and sources of revenue may be seen in the example of the village of Mamitzon, which encompasses many of the possible permutations. The village had belonged to the state until, in 1322, the Emperor granted one third of it to the monastery of Chilandar and two-thirds to a hospice. The information comes from the third that belonged to Chilandar. We find here three clearly differentiated modes of land exploitation and surplus distribution. All of the peasant households own arable, mostly in sizeable plots. This they cultivate and pay tax on, as they do on their vineyards, gardens, mills, animals and other possessions. Exceptionally, the majority of households own oxen, almost half owning a full team. The landlord's portion, consisting of 2,100 *modioi* (210ha), is divided into two parts. Almost 30 per cent of it is under direct exploitation, cultivated by labor services; the surplus goes to the landlord in full. The rest is shared out in share-cropping arrangements, and therefore the surplus is shared between the land-lord and the peasants, the registered *paroikoi* or others. Clearly, this is a rich domain, and the peasants are well off. While the distribution of wealth is not typical, nevertheless the combination of arrangements, the fact that the *paroikoi* both owned property and owed labor ser-vices and rented land, and that they paid both fiscal dues and rent is a characteristic situation, and one that would have been very peculiar in Western Europe.[34]

How productive was the Byzantine agrarian economy in the thirteenth and fourteenth centuries? It may be said with some certainty that when extraneous factors did not intervene, it was quite productive. Monasteries and landlords grew rich from agriculture. The peasants less so, since they were the first to feel the negative effects of the balance between population and land in the late thirteenth century, and since the exploitation of the peasantry may have increased. Nevertheless, peasants sold their produce to merchants, both local and Western. If they paid their rent in kind, they profited less from the marketability of agricultural products than did the landlords, who in any case had easier access to the market; yet some peasants were able to supplement their income not only from cash crops but also from artisanal production. Those rich in sheep and goats must have marketed the raw wool or yarn, as they did woolen cloth. Small rural fairs, usually associated with a monastery, dotted the Byzantine countryside until the 1340s, and here too peasants marketed their production.[35] And, certainly, the landlords were able to sell a part of their surplus both in the urban markets and to foreign merchants: there seems to have been a relatively thriving commercial network in the Balkans, and Western merchants sought to buy Byzantine wheat and wine, although the first two Palaiologan emperors tried to impose restrictions on the purchase and export of grain by Westerners.[36] It is in this sense that we consider the Byzantine economy to have remained articulated through the first half of the fourteenth century.

However, extraneous factors did intervene. Byzantine Asia Minor fell prey to Ottoman incursions in the late thirteenth century, and within a few decades its territories had been rapidly reduced, some of the population had fled, agricultural activities were disrupted in

---

[34] The document may be found in Petit, *Chilandar*, no. 92, pp. 194–5. On this, see Laiou, "The Agrarian Economy," pp. 328 ff, and the comments by P. Toubert, "Byzantium and the Mediterranean Agrarian Civilisation," *EHB* 3, p. 390.

[35] K.-P. Matschke, "Commerce, Trade, Markets, and Money, Thirteenth-Fifteenth Centuries," *EHB* 2, pp. 802–3; Laiou, "The Agrarian Economy," pp. 347–8. Outside the Empire, Venetian-occupied Crete witnessed an increase in both population and agricultural production until 1348; it was helped by the commercialization of agriculture: Ch. Gasparis, "Il villaggio a Creta veneziana (XIII–XV sec.)," in Lefort et al., *Villages*, pp. 237–46.

[36] On the prohibition, Laiou-Thomadakis, "The Byzantine Economy," pp. 213–14, and below, p. 204.

the short term. In the European provinces, periods of insecurity were frequent. Starting with the late twelfth century, the Byzantine–Bulgarian frontier was the scene of incursions and wars; the economy on either side was disrupted, as may be seen by the interruption of coin circulation. Repopulation occurred after the Ottoman conquest.[37] Tatar incursions disrupted the agriculture of Thrace in the 1320s, the Catalans did the same for a brief but terrible period, and the civil wars that became endemic after 1321 brought both insecurity and destruction of resources. But these disruptions do not begin to compare with the catastrophes that struck in the late 1340s and continued unabated until the end of the Empire. As a result, the countryside was depopulated and the agrarian economy became disarticulated, as did the entire economy. Land became worthless, and was not even taxed in the fifteenth century. The loss of productive capacity affected the landowning aristocracy as well, large numbers of whom became impoverished. They had won, in the great civil war of 1341–54, a Pyrrhic victory that left them dispossessed and weak. The most secure productive units remained the monasteries, especially those of Mt Athos, which were able to receive privileges from successive conquerors. But even their production diminished for lack of manpower.[38]

An excavated village of this late period in a region in Latin hands, between Thebes and Athens, provides interesting information. The area was very unstable politically. The village of Panakton was created on a defensible hilltop, and had a stronghold with a large tower, part of which remains in place. The settlement lasted only for about a hundred years, from sometime in the fourteenth century to the middle of the fifteenth. Its economy clearly rested on agriculture. The pottery, metal, and glass finds show a modest economic differentiation among the peasantry. Most of the coarse pottery for household use was made locally, in the area of Thebes, whereas glazed pottery, mostly found in the church, is similar to mid-thirteenth-century Corinthian wares. There was also a little glass. The inhabitants lived very modestly, and the burial remains suggest that men also served as soldiers in the constant wars that afflicted the area.[39]

---

[37] R. Rašev, V. Dinčev and B. Borissov, "Le village byzantin sur le territoire de la Bulgarie contemporaine," in Lefort et al., *Villages*, p. 361.

[38] N. Oikonomidès, "Monastères et moines lors de la conquête ottomane," *SüdostF* 35 (1976), pp. 1–10.

[39] S. E. J. Gerstel, M. Munn et al., "A Late Medieval Settlement at Panakton," *Hesperia* 72 (2003), pp. 147–234, esp. pp. 218–21.

Only in the early fifteenth century did the Byzantine state take small and sporadic measures to address the problems. We know of imperial efforts in the Chalkidike and in Lemnos to restore lands to productive capacity, attract a labor force and entrust the subsequent management to large economic units, that is, monasteries. But it was much too little, and much too late. The Byzantine state had only a few decades to live, and its own resources were, by now, negligible.

SECONDARY PRODUCTION

The development of secondary production, that is, manufacturing, the production of objects of art, building and shipbuilding, was profoundly affected by the prevailing political and economic factors. The political vicissitudes that have already been adumbrated created an environment in which cities, where much of manufacturing was located, while relatively integrated in larger economic systems until the middle of the fourteenth century, became increasingly independent politically. This was a process long in the making, already developed before the crisis of the mid-fourteenth century, which made of most cities little more than isolated units, at best in intimate connection with their immediate hinterland. Secondly, and to some extent connected with this process, artisanal activities in the countryside increased. Thirdly, and powerfully, the products of Byzantine manufacturing had to compete, certainly in foreign markets but also in Byzantine ones, with the production of other centers, especially Western European ones, but also from Turkish-controlled Asia Minor. In a world increasingly unified by the activities of Italian merchants and the demand as well as the supply of the developing Western industries, the structure of Byzantine production and trade changed.

Shifts in demand and production

The structure of demand was quite different in this period from what it had been at the time of a unified "national" market and economic expansion. Both the Byzantine state and the aristocracy were poorer than before, so that elite demand declined, especially after the mid-fourteenth century. Urban demand is hard to gauge; urban populations may have been generally rather well off until about 1350; thereafter, the population declined and the concomitant concentration of capital into fewer hands probably did not profit Byzantine manufacturing, since by now there was Western competition in major sectors. Rural demand was served to some extent, although never fully, by local supply. By contrast, the international market created new pockets of demand. However, this increasingly implicated raw materials, while the rapidly expanding Western manufactures displaced Byzantine products. In the circumstances, Byzantine manufacturing and secondary production in general were characterized by a reduction in the scale of the objects produced as well as a retraction of the geographical areas of distribution. Production of some items ceased altogether.

As in the previous chapter, certain relatively well-documented sectors will be discussed in more detail here.

The manufacturing of art objects, as well as the building and decoration of churches, is characterized both by smallness of scale (with some exceptions, like the late-thirteenth-century church of the Paregoritissa, in Arta), and excellence of quality. The monumental decorative art par excellence, mosaic decoration of churches, is not attested after 1320, except for the restoration of part of Saint Sophia in the 1350s, with Russian money. Instead, in the Palaiologan period we see the multiplication of mosaic icons: works of great beauty, and fine examples of the mosaicist's art, they are nevertheless not comparable, in terms of scale, to the great programs of church decoration. The smallness of scale is encapsulated in these icons.

There was also a process of substitution of cheaper objects for more expensive ones. It was attended by a shift in the place of manufacturing from Byzantine territories to Western European ones. Byzantine cameos, with intaglios of the saints, were a luxury object in the twelfth century. In the thirteenth century, until around 1261, there is mass production of objects similar in shape and iconography, but manufactured of glass paste, and thus available to a much larger and diversified market. They were made in Venice, and their production must be closely tied to the access of Venetians to large markets in the eastern Mediterranean as well as in the West; the iconography was tailored to fit the tastes of various areas. The supply of such objects served as a stimulus to demand. Similarly, expensive Byzantine enamels, a luxury object, were replaced by Venetian-made miniatures under crystal, fashioned to imitate the more expensive enamels. They were made between the late thirteenth and the middle of the fourteenth century, and were marketed both in Western Europe and in Serbia, where King Stefan Urosh II Milyutin (1282–1321) ordered two such objects. Here we have the substitution of semi-luxury objects for the Byzantine luxury ones, again to cater to the needs of a market which in terms of taste was oriented toward Byzantine style, but could more easily afford the cheaper substitute.[40] The chronological limit of this production may define a transitional period in which the taste for Byzantine objects was not yet overwhelmed by the production of Western *cristallarii*.

Pottery

The production and distribution of pottery shows continuity with the twelfth century until the early thirteenth, and distinct differences thereafter. Of course, the dissemination of the use of stilts constitutes an important technical innovation that characterizes production after 1200. But the organization of production and distribution continued on twelfth-century patterns for a while.[41] As a continuation of earlier patterns we may count the production and distribution of Zeuxippus Ware and Aegean Ware, both dated to between the end of the twelfth century and the middle of the thirteenth. Both are high-quality pottery. Zeuxippus Ware is characterized by its meticulous decoration and brilliant glaze. Aegean Ware is considered less sophisticated in terms of technique of production, but has an original decorative style of high aesthetic value in its simplicity. For neither is the primary place(s) of production ascertained, but they are thought to have been produced in a single, or very few, centers, while Zeuxippus Ware derivatives are known in a number of centers, including Pergamon, and Aegean Ware appears in Sardis in the first part of the thirteenth century. Since Pergamon in this period was a relatively small city (a thirteenth-century maximum of 3,000 inhabitants), and undistinguished otherwise, it may be assumed that similar phenomena occurred in other areas of the Byzantine Empire.[42]

---

[40] On the above, see A. E. Laiou, "Venice as a Centre of Trade and of Artistic Production in the Thirteenth Century," *Atti del XXIV Congresso del Comitato Internazionale di Storia dell'Arte, sez. 2* (Bologna, 1982), pp. 11–26.

[41] D. Papanikola-Bakirtzi considers that Aegean Ware must be seen as the end of the Middle Byzantine tradition in glazed ceramics and Zeuxippus Ware as the beginning of Late Byzantine production.

[42] On this, and what follows for ceramics, see in the first instance D. Papanikola-Bakirtzi, "Ergasteria efyalomenes keramikes sto Vyzantino kosmo," *VIIe Congrès international sur la céramique médiévale en Méditerranée* (Athens, 2003), pp. 45–66.

Both Zeuxippus and Aegean Ware conform to the twelfth-century pattern of large and well-organized workshops. Both were widely disseminated, from Italy to the crusader states and even to Alexandria.[43] The most brilliant examples of Zeuxippus Ware pottery have been found in the Crimea. Zeuxippus and Aegean Ware, however, were only a part of a widespread production of pottery, including Islamic pottery, that has been found on the same sites, at least in Italy and the crusader states. Clearly, its production was closely linked to and benefited from the expansion of trade and the opening of markets all over the Mediterranean and the Black Sea. By the middle of the thirteenth century, all of this stops. The production of Glazed White Ware in Constantinople comes to an end.[44] Corinth no longer produces fine pottery in large workshops. Production of fine ware of a local type continued into the early thirteenth century, but later in the century large-scale imports of Italian and Egyptian ceramics brought local production to an end.[45] For in the meantime another process of substitution had taken place.

In the crusader states, including Cyprus, local pottery, like St Symeon Ware, supplants Byzantine pottery. Southern Italy, Liguria and the Veneto produce Zeuxippus Ware derivatives (*graffita arcaica*)

See also D. Papanikola-Bakirtzi (ed.), *Byzantine Glazed Ceramics: The Art of Sgraffito* (Athens, 1999), and her *Mesaionike efyalomene keramike tes Kyprou: Ta ergasteria Pafou kai Lapethou* (Thessalonike, 1996); D. Papanikola-Bakirtzis, E. Dauterman Maguire and Henry Maguire, *Ceramic Art from Byzantine Serres* (Urbana and Chicago, 1992); V. François, "Sur la circulation des céramiques byzantines en Méditerranée orientale et occidentale," in *La céramique médiévale en Méditerranée* (Aix-en-Provence, 1997), pp. 231–6; V. François and J.-M. Spieser, "Pottery and Glass in Byzantium," *EHB* 2, pp. 601–9. A ship loaded with Aegean Ware foundered off Kastellorizo in the early thirteenth century: G. Philotheou and M. Michailidou, "Plats byzantins provenant d'une épave près de Castellorizo," in V. Déroche and J.-M. Spieser, *Recherches sur la céramique byzantine, BCH Suppl.* (1989), pp. 173–6. On Sardis, see J. A. Scott and D. C. Kamilli, "Late Byzantine Glazed Pottery from Sardis," *Actes du XVe Congrès international d'études byzantines, Athens, 1976*, vol. II.2 (Athens, 1981), pp. 679–96.

[43] M. M. Lovecchio, "Commercio e ceramica bizantina in Italia," in Déroche and Spieser, *Recherches*, pp. 95–107.

[44] Papanikola-Bakirtzi, "Ergasteria," p. 50.

[45] J. Vroom, *After Antiquity: Ceramics and Society in the Aegean from the 7th to the 20th Century AC: A Case Study from Boeotia, Central Greece* (Leiden, 2003), p. 67. For imports of Protomaiolica from southern Italy and the Veneto in the second half of the thirteenth century and after, see C. K. Williams, "Frankish Corinth," *Hesperia* 62 (1993), pp. 15–35, and Th. Stillwell Mackay, "Byzantine and Frankish Pottery from Corinth," *Hesperia* 36 (1967), pp. 249–305.

which are influenced by Byzantine techniques and supplant Byzantine pottery in the Italian market. More generally, in Italy local production increases and replaces Byzantine imports. At first, potters in Venice, Savona and other places copied Byzantine ceramic types and even imported Byzantine potters. As their production fulfilled local demand, the importation of Byzantine pottery stopped in the middle of the thirteenth century. On the other hand, Italian ceramics such as Roulette Ware, Metallic Ware, Sgraffito Ware and Protomaiolica flooded the markets of Greece, Epiros, Corinth, Boeotia and other parts of the former Byzantine Empire. In this, Venetian and Genoese merchants, whose presence in Byzantine waters and lands was constantly increasing, have been rightly recognized as having played a major role. It is also probable that the Italian production acquired "exotic" status.[46] Thus, there was a shift in elite demand. The promising development of Byzantine pottery as an export item ended.

Accordingly, in the second half of the thirteenth and in the fourteenth century, the manufacturing and distribution of Byzantine pottery changes. There is no evidence of large, organized workshops, while pottery of varying quality is produced in many places, for example, St Symeon Ware in Sardis. Village production is a certainty. J. Lefort thinks he can distinguish family workshops of potters in the villages of Macedonia. Logically, local production must have reduced, to an unknown extent, the demand for ceramics imported from larger centers.

Distinctive glazed pottery was mass-produced in a number of places, throughout the Empire and its former territories in the second half of the thirteenth and the fourteenth centuries. Thessalonike and Serres, as well as Cyprus, which was firmly in Western hands, produced large quantities of pottery. Other centers too have been identified. Cherson and the Dobrudja, which in the past had imported Byzantine pottery, now produce ceramics with Byzantine and eastern influences; Serbia, still importing Byzantine ceramics in the thirteenth century, then developed its own production of similar wares. Corinth still produced pottery, but of simplified design. Other centers of production are Mikro Pisto, a village near Komotini in Thrace, Pergamon, Zichna, Gratini, Varna, Veliko Trnovo, Athens,

[46] S. Gelichi (ed.), *La ceramica nel mondo bizantino tra XI e XV secolo e i suoi rapporti con l'Italia* (Florence, 1993), p. 39; Vroom, *After Antiquity*, p. 167.

Sparta, Nicaea, the island of Lemnos, and perhaps Verroia, Thebes and Argos; the Cypriot production is well known (see Map 7).[47]

The pottery of this late period, with its standardized decoration, may have been produced in small workshops by a personnel with fewer technical skills and specialization than in the twelfth century.[48] The objects were smaller than in the previous period, and probably cheaper. Where the dissemination of the objects can be established, it is found to be relatively limited in space. The pottery of Nicaea, both champlevé and incised, both produced in the thirteenth and the early fourteenth centuries, had regional distribution.[49] Elaborate Incised Ware, probably made in Constantinople, was exported along the Black Sea coasts and, to a lesser degree, in western Asia Minor even into the fourteenth century. These are small luxury objects, and not very numerous.[50] Serres pottery has been found in Macedonia (including Serbian-held areas like Skopje, Melnik and Prilep), in Thessalonike, and, to a smaller degree, in Epiros and Corinth. Thessalonike pottery is found in various areas, including Corinth and Boeotia. All of this points primarily to regional trade, perhaps interregional to some extent. What is of interest, however, is the fact that as older centers of production, like Corinth, decline, new ones replace them; the case of Serres, whose production is dated to the second half of the thirteenth century and probably extends into the fourteenth, is particularly interesting, since Serres is not known as a center of manufacturing before this period.

The niche for Byzantine ceramics production in this period, after the explosion of Aegean and Zeuxippus Wares, appears to be part of the Byzantine domestic market, the Balkan hinterland and the Crimea. The market seems to have been a middle-level market, perhaps of landowners of moderate wealth, and similar strata of the urban population. In this market, Byzantine production was not supplanted by Italian wares.

---

[47] On all this, see the articles by N. Zekos and V. Binkić, in *VIIe Congrès International*, pp. 455–66 and 191–204 respectively, as well as I. Barněa and V. N. Zalesskaya in Déroche and Spieser, *Recherches*, pp. 131–42 and 143–9.

[48] Papanikola-Bakirtzi, "Ergasteria."

[49] V. François, "La céramique byzantine et ottomane," in B. Geyer and J. Lefort (eds.), *La Bithynie au Moyen Âge* (Paris, 2003), pp. 293–4.

[50] V. François, "Elaborate Incised Ware: une preuve du rayonnement de la culture Byzantine à l'époque paléologue," *BSl* 61 (2003), pp. 151–68.

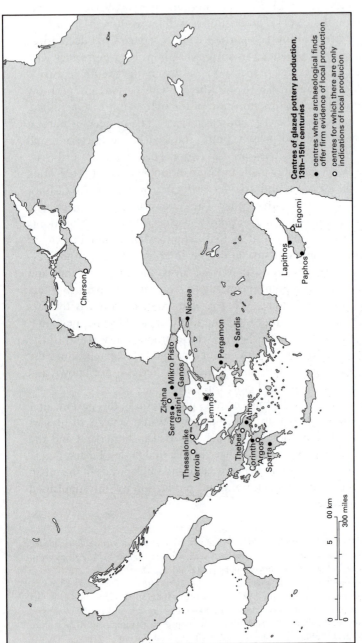

Map 7. Centers of glazed pottery production, thirteenth–fifteenth centuries (map by Demetra Papanikola-Bakirtzi)

● centers where archeological finds offer firm evidence of local production

○ centers for which there are only indications of local production

Glass

As far as glass production is concerned, the evidence is much more fragmentary, since the archeological record for this period is limited. It appears that the production of small glass objects persisted in Sardis, in the thirteenth and fourteenth centuries. Architectural glass (for window panes) has also been found in Sardis of the thirteenth century. [51] The "Glass Factories" of Corinth have been dated to this period by D. Whitehouse, but we have argued that the evidence better supports the original eleventh–twelfth-century dating. [52] Venetian documents permit a general assessment of the fate of Byzantine glass. In the thirteenth century, the glass industry was developing rapidly in Venice, under the protection of and regulation by the government. Venice's extensive trade network helped the industry. Glass cullet was imported from the eastern Mediterranean, as were soda ashes (from Syria) and alum, a necessary ingredient for the manufacturing of glass. [53] The import of glass objects into Venice and the export of technology were both forbidden. It is not surprising that glass was made for export to the East. Already in the late thirteenth century a glass-maker from Murano lists, among other things, a large case of glasses specifically for export to the Romania (i.e., the Byzantine and former Byzantine territories), which suggests specialized production catering to specific markets as, much later, Venice was to do for the Ottoman market. In 1279, the price of plain glass beakers was quoted by the thousand pieces, which certainly shows mass production. In 1345, a case of glassware was sent from Venice to Rhodes via Crete. Both Rhodes and Crete were in Western hands, Crete being a Venetian colony. While firm conclusions must await further archeological evidence, it would seem that the Byzantine glass industry declined and was replaced by imports from the active Venetian industry, which was assured of raw materials and also of markets for its products. If

[51] C. Foss and J. A. Scott, "Sardis," *EHB* 2, pp. 619–21; J. Henderson and M. Mundell Mango, "Glass at Medieval Constantinople: Preliminary Scientific Evidence," in G. Dagron and C. Mango (eds.), *Constantinople and its Hinterland* (Aldershot, 1995), p. 343.

[52] See above, Chapter IV; Williams, "Frankish Corinth," p. 22, n.9, introduces nuances to his argument

[53] D. Jacoby, "Raw Materials for the Glass Industries of Venice and the Terraferma, about 1370–about 1460," *Journal of Glass Studies* 35 (1993), pp. 65–90. Even Constantinopolitan clay was imported into Venice to make expensive crucibles: *ibid.*, pp. 78–9 (early fifteenth century).

the original dating of the Corinth glass workshops is correct, then we have a clear case of substitution: Corinthian glass exported into the Veneto and other parts of Italy in the earlier period influenced local production that replaced the Corinthian industry in the thirteenth–fourteenth centuries.[54]

Textiles

Major changes took place in the manufacturing of silk cloth after the Fourth Crusade. Most of the silk-cloth producing areas were lost to the Byzantine Empire: Thebes, Corinth, Patras, Euboea, even Constantinople until 1261. No other center emerged within Byzantine territory, not even in the Despotate of the Morea, to substitute for these losses.[55] In Asia Minor, there is some evidence that the city of Philadelpheia, an island in Turkish-occupied territory until its fall in 1390, produced silk cloth, but both quantity and distribution are unknown.[56] Some high-quality silk cloth was produced in Ottoman Anatolia, especially by the Armenian population of Erzıncan in eastern Turkey.[57] Bithynia flourished as a center of silk textile production only in the Ottoman period.

What happened to the centers of silk production in western Greece in instructive.[58] Some of them stopped producing silk cloth almost immediately: so, probably, Corinth. Others, like Euboea, and Andros, went through a transitional period during which they continued to manufacture silk cloth and exported it to the West. This period

---

[54] On this, see Laiou, "Venice as a Centre of Trade."

[55] D. Jacoby's assertion that Nicaea produced silk textiles into the Palaiologan period ("The Jews and the Silk Industry of Constantinople," in his *Byzantium, Latin Romania and the Mediterranean* (Aldershot, 2001), art. XI, 18–19) is based on the forced interpretation of a text which speaks only of "the art of weaving . . . at its finest." K.-P. Matschke, "Tuchproduktion und Tuchproduzenten in Thessalonike und in anderen Städten und Regionen des späten Byzanz," *Vyzantiaka* 9 (1989), pp. 56–9, mentions some minor production of ecclesiastical silks in Constantinople.

[56] H. Ahrweiler, "La région de Philadelphie au XIVe siècle (1290–1390) dernier bastion de l'hellénisme en Asie Mineure," AIBL, *Comptes rendus* (1983), p. 194; P. Schreiner, "Zur Geschichte Philadelpheias im 14. Jh. (1293–1390)," *OCP* 35 (1969), pp. 411–12; Matschke, "Tuchproduktion," pp. 56–9.

[57] K. Fleet, *European and Islamic Trade in the Early Ottoman State* (Cambridge, 1999), p. 97.

[58] D. Jacoby, "The Production of Silks in Latin Greece," in *Technognosia ste Latinokratoumene Ellada* (Athens, 2000), pp. 22–35.

was brief, lasting for one decade into the thirteenth century in the case of Andros, until later in the thirteenth century in Euboea. The Peloponnese continued to produce and export to the West a cheap, rough silk fabric called *koukoularikon* into the late thirteenth century. Thebes lasted longer as a center of production. Its artisans manufactured silk cloth, apparently of good quality, into the first part of the fourteenth century: it was exported to both Western Europe and Egypt as late as the 1320s, with sporadic exports to the West until 1380. However, even in the case of Thebes this production could not compete, certainly in quantity, perhaps in quality, in any case in marketability, with the new centers of the silk industry, Lucca and Venice in the first instance. Luccan manufacturing received an impetus in the twelfth century, and Venetian production began soon after 1204.[59]

As the manufacturing of silk cloth declined and then ceased, what increased was the export to Western Europe of the raw materials necessary for the industry. The Peloponnese, both Latin-occupied and Byzantine-held, was a great exporter of raw silk and kermes, the expensive red dye. The island of Andros, which had exported cloth in the twelfth century, now exported silk yarn. Silk and dyestuffs were exported from Patras, Modon, Coron, Monemvasia and the new busy port of Clarentza, while Byzantine territories like Epiros also exported raw silk as did Turkish Anatolia, way into the fourteenth century.[60] The Venetian silk industry made heavy use of these imports. It is also possible that there were technology transfers, in the form of skilled Byzantine silk workers who moved to Venice.[61] On the other hand, the Byzantines now imported silk cloth from the West. In the middle of the fourteenth century, the historian Nikephoros Gregoras complained of the habits of young

---

[59] On the above, see primarily the studies of D. Jacoby, assembled in *Byzantium*: "Silk Crosses the Mediterranean" (art. X), "Italian Migration and Settlement in Latin Greece: The Impact on the Economy" (art. IX); also, his "Silk Production in the Frankish Peloponnese: The Evidence of Fourteenth-Century Surveys and Reports," in *Travellers and Officials in the Peloponnese. Descriptions–Reports–Statistics in Honour of Sir S. Runciman* (Monemvasia, 1994), pp. 41–61 (repr. in his *Trade, Commodities, and Shipping in the Medieval Mediterranean* (Aldershot, 1997), art. XIV); "Dalla materia prima ai drappi tra Bisanzio, il Levante e Venezia: la prima fase dell'industria serica veneziana," in L. Molà, R. C. Mueller and C. Zanier (eds.), *La seta in Italia dal Medioevo al Seicento: dal baco al drappo* (Venice, 2000), pp. 265–304, esp. pp. 281 and 277.

[60] Fleet, *European and Islamic Trade*, p. 98; Jacoby, "Dalla materia prima," p. 275.

[61] Jacoby, "Dalla materia prima," p. 277.

fashionable men who appeared in Italian hats and "Persian" dress, or vice versa; he saw in this spendthrift attitude a cause of the decline of the Empire. One of his contemporaries complained of elite demand for foreign fabrics and Egyptian aromatics. By the middle of the fifteenth century, George Gemistos Plethon wrote, "it is a great evil for a society which produces wool, linen, silk, cotton, to be unable to fashion these into garments and instead to wear the clothes made in the lands beyond the Ionian Sea from wool produced in the Atlantic [area]."[62]

Thus, the Byzantine silk industry, which for centuries had been an important segment of its secondary production, ceased to exist. The decline and reorientation of elite demand certainly played a role in this. So also did the fact that the major centers of silk cloth production fell out of Byzantine hands, with the consequent loss of the infrastructures and accumulated knowhow. This combination of factors explains the fact that even the Byzantine state ceased to give silks as gifts to foreign potentates after 1204. However, it does not explain the decline or demise of the silk industries of Thebes and Corinth, to take two salient examples. The major reason for that is the growth of the silk industries in Italy. Demand for raw materials grew concomitantly, and as their export increased native industries were deprived of them.[63] The question is, why Western silk industries were more competitive, and why the economies of Byzantine territories, both in Byzantine and in Western possession, became geared toward the export of raw materials. The answer lies in the structure of distribution and trade. Western European markets were still expanding, and the market for luxury and semi-luxury products continued to expand even after the Black Death. At the same time, international trade in the Mediterranean was becoming dominated by the Italian maritime cities which controlled transportation and the communications networks and dictated the terms of trade.[64] One should not forget that Venice itself was one of the primary new centers of silk cloth production in Western Europe, while Genoa had, since the eleventh century, provided raw silk for the industries of Lucca. It was in the interest of these cities to sell raw materials to the new production centers and to market their production in Europe and the Near

---

[62] Gregoras III, p. 555; I. Ševčenko, "Alexios Makrembolites and his 'Dialogue Between the Rich and the Poor,'" *ZRVI* 6 (1960), p. 221; S. Lambros, *Palaiologeia kai Peloponnesiaka*, III (Athens, 1926), p. 263.

[63] This argument has been made by D. Jacoby.   [64] See pp. 202–4.

East. In any case, it was easier for Italian merchants to market Italian rather than Byzantine silk cloth in Italy and on the European continent. Finally, differentiated tastes in the West were best served by a combination of the sale of Western products that were substitutes for Byzantine ones, and the importation of luxury silks from Persia or the Far East, which continued until the middle of the fourteenth century. The Venetians also filled an earlier Byzantine niche, the market for lower-quality silks and mixed silks.[65] The existence of a broad spectrum of clients and an equally broad palette of products encouraged the growth of the Italian silk industry; technological innovations followed. As the production and distribution of Western silks increased, they became fashionable, and Byzantine demand followed the trend. This early form of economic "globalization," coupled with the relative decline of domestic demand, spelled the end of the Byzantine silk industry. The silk cloth production of Ottoman-held territories, with access to both Asia and Europe, and with a domestic market that was becoming enlarged, was virtually the only one to have resisted.

Woolen textiles are another case in point. They were certainly always produced in the Byzantine Empire in one form or another, but little is known about the forms of production beyond the household production that one may intuitively assume. In this period, some limited information appears. Household production, in villages, is occasionally seen to have a broader distribution. Apparently, some villages were well known for the production of heavy woolen mantles and carpets.[66] Some cities may have had a sizeable production of woolen cloth. The countryside around Serres had large flocks of sheep and goats. It is reasonable to suppose that their wool was turned into cloth in the city. Indeed, the accounts of a petty landowner and trader from Thessalonike (1355–7) show that he was conducting, between Thessalonike, the Chalkidike and Serres, trade in relatively small but not negligible quantities of cloth and grain. In the fifteenth century, the accounts of the Venetian Badoer mention a merchant (in cloth?) from Serres.[67] Mixed wool cloth was also produced in Thessalonike in the fourteenth century.[68]

---

[65] Jacoby, "Dalla materia prima," p. 293.

[66] S. Eustratiades, "Gregoriou tou Kypriou oikoumenikou Patriarchou epistolai kai mythoi," *Ekklesiastikos Pharos* 3 (1909), Letter 87; Matschke, "Tuchproduktion," p. 54.

[67] A. E. Laiou, "Koinonikes dynameis stis Serres sto dekato tetarto aiona," *Oi Serres kai e perioche tous apo ten archaia ste Metavyzantine koinonia*, Serres (1998), pp. 203–19.

[68] Matschke, "Tuchproduktion," pp. 71 ff.

Whatever the woolen cloth production of Byzantium, it is not in any way comparable to the rapidly developing industry all over continental Western Europe. This swallowed up the alum production of the eastern Mediterranean; and to serve its needs it also imported wool from Byzantium and other parts of the Near East. In return, the credit side of the trade balance between Western Europe and the eastern Mediterranean increasingly consisted of industrial goods, soap, for example, and, primarily and on a large scale, woolen cloth. Technological improvements made the production of woolen cloth possible on a mass scale and at cheap prices. While one should resist the urge to speak of dumping, it is a certainty that European woolen cloth filled the markets of the eastern Mediterranean, from Egypt to Ottoman Anatolia, to Crete. The Byzantine Empire was certainly an importer of Western woolens. In the late thirteenth century, woolen cloth for sale within the Byzantine Empire was one of the main items for which *commenda* contracts were made among the Genoese of Pera. French and Italian cloth was one of the most important commodities in the accounts of the Venetian merchant Giacomo Badoer in Constantinople, in the 1430s. Thessalonike was a major center of the redistribution of Western cloth, which was cut there and sold retail.[69] From there, the cloth was distributed to western Greece and the Balkans. The other center of redistribution was Ragusa, which functioned both as a re-exporter of Italian cloth and, especially after 1420, as exporter of its own cloth, much to the chagrin of Venetian merchants. Therefore, even in the regional market of western Greece and the Balkans it seems that Byzantine woolens, if they were marketed, were sold in relatively small quantities. They could not compete with Western woolens, at a time when the trade was a bulk trade, necessitating a large production, and the terms were dictated by Western merchants.[70]

The entire Byzantine textile sector, then, suffered from Western competition and the structure of Italian trade. It was reoriented

---

[69] A. E. Laiou, "E Thessalonike, e endochora tes kai o oikonomikos tes choros sten epoche ton Palaiologon," in *Vyzantine Macedonia 324–1430 m. Ch.* (Thessalonike, 1995), pp. 189, 191.

[70] Cyprus, conquered by Richard Lionheart and held by the Lusignan since 1192, constitutes a special case. Although it exported gold thread to the West, it also produced and exported camelot as well as a variety of silk cloth: A. Aristeidou, "E paragoge yfasmaton, alatiou kai zachares sten Latinokratoumene Kypro: technikes paragoges kai diadikasia emporiou," in *Technognosia*, pp. 50–6.

toward the export of raw materials (including cotton, of which no mention has been made here because our knowledge of the production of cotton cloth in the Byzantine Empire is exiguous), and the importation of Western manufactured goods. It has been argued that pre-industrial economies should not necessarily be considered "poor" when they are geared toward the export of food and raw materials and the import of manufactured goods; that this becomes a negative factor only when agriculture itself depends on the use of manufactured inputs and/or poor people begin to buy non-agricultural goods.[71] However, if one follows the idea that in pre-industrial societies intensive growth is partly dependent on an international market leading to a division of labor,[72] then surely the terms of trade and division of labor make all the difference: the real value added comes from manufacturing, and that, in this period, was firmly lodged in Western Europe. The terms of the export of raw materials were only partly in the hands of the economies of the eastern Mediterranean, and the growth of these economies, including the Byzantine one, was, to this extent, captive to the needs of others. Thus, neither manufacturing nor, as we shall see, trade, came to the rescue of the economy, whose agriculture had already perhaps reached its Malthusian limits, that is, declining returns per unit of land, and had made no adjustments to overcome them.

THE URBAN ECONOMY

Any discussion of the general traits of the urban economy must respect the chronological distinctions. A major change, as has already been stated, occurred in the period after 1348, with its sharp demographic characteristics. Since the urban economy is connected with both the development of the state and that of the agricultural economy, the second decade of the fourteenth century marks another important, though less all-encompassing break: before that, the Byzantine state still functioned fairly well, while afterwards the decentralizing process became accelerated, and insecurity became endemic. All of these factors affected the urban economy. While respecting these chronological differences, we may nevertheless distinguish some general traits.

---

[71] K. Pomeranz, *The Great Divergence* (Princeton, 2000), p. 261.
[72] See above, Chapter IV.

One general statement that can be made with some certainty is that the cities were small by the end of the period under discussion. Constantinople lost some population at the time of its conquest in 1204, and especially after the Black Death. By the time it fell to the Ottomans, in 1453, it had at most a population of 50,000. Thessalonike is reported to have had 40,000 souls in 1423. Monemvasia, the commercial city off the eastern coast of the Peloponnese, had reached its peak in the twelfth century with about 20,000 people. Pergamon is an exception, for it grew in the course of the late thirteenth and early fourteenth centuries because of the merging of different agglomerations, but it fell to the Turks in the 1320s.[73] Smallness of scale applies to the city populations as well.

Another general statement is that the entire period after the reconquest of Constantinople is characterized by a powerful trend toward city autonomy. In political terms, this means that progressively the cities of the Byzantine Empire developed into what have been called "mini Greek Orthodox states"; the cities and their immediate hinterland became isolated from the central government, and to some extent assumed responsibility for their own political fate and even their defense functions. The trend was accelerated in the period after 1340, but it was already evident in the earlier Palaiologan period. This phenomenon must not be seen as equivalent to the growth of city-states in parts of Western Europe. It was primarily a function of the need of cities to defend themselves against invaders, eventually the Ottomans. It is thus a phenomenon due to exogenous factors, and the fairly weak but nevertheless real development of urban institutions is an epiphenomenon.[74]

The trend toward city autonomy was to some extent fostered by the central government, not, perhaps, out of choice, but out of necessity. Since the times of the emperors of Nicaea, and through the 1320s,

---

[73] K. Rheidt, "The Urban Economy of Pergamon," *EHB* 2, p. 625.

[74] On these issues see E. Zachariadou, "Ephemeres apopeires gia autodioikese stis Ellenikes poleis kata ton XIV kai XV aiona," *Ariadne* 5 (1989), pp. 345–51; N. Oikonomidès, "Pour une typologie des villes 'séparées' sous les Paléologues," in W. Seibt (ed.), *Geschichte und Kultur der Palaiologenzeit* (Vienna, 1996), pp. 160–7; K.-P. Matschke, "Bemerkungen zu 'Stadtbürgertum' und 'stadtbürgerlichen Geist' in Byzanz," *Jahrbuch für Geschichte des Feudalismus* 8 (1984), pp. 265–85; L. Maksimović, "Charakter der sozial-wirtschaftlichen Struktur der spätbyzantinischen Stadt (13.–15. Jh)," *JOB* 31/1 (1981), pp. 149–88. On all that follows, see also A. E. Laiou, "Koinonia kai oikonomia (1204–1453)," in *Istoria tou Ellenikou Ethnous*, vol. 9 (Athens, 1979), pp. 214–43.

successive emperors granted to a number of cities charters and privileges that guaranteed them at the very least tax exemptions for their properties in the city and its immediate hinterland, and at most, as in the case of Ioannina in 1319, extensive judicial and administrative privileges. In all cases, these privileges were granted to cities as they came back under Byzantine control.[75] As political conditions worsened, the cities extended their independence of action. During the civil wars of the 1320s, the 1340s, and later, both sides fought for control of the cities. So did successive conquerors, since the cities and their countryside were units whose control should proceed in tandem.

All of this had important consequences for the urban economy. Constantinople and Thessalonike, because of their size and importance, are cases apart, as is Monemvasia for other reasons. The other cities have certain traits in common, although with a different mix from case to case. All cities had to provide for their defense; some, like Servia, had a strong defense aspect. An important characteristic of the late Byzantine city was the interpenetration of the agricultural and the urban economy. Landowners resident in the cities exploited the countryside. Inside the cities there were frequently gardens or even small fields that were cultivated: this is true also of Constantinople and Thessalonike, certainly in the last hundred years or so of the Byzantine Empire. Cities functioned as refuges in times of crisis; this reinforced the pre-existing phenomenon that part of the urban population worked in agricultural pursuits, as, in any case, they did in medieval and pre-modern Western cities as well. Ioannina in Epiros and Serres in Macedonia are among the cities with a strong agrarian character, centers of the distribution of agricultural products, and with a powerful aristocratic element actively engaged in the governance of the city.

All cities for which we have evidence had some secondary production and some trade. Both were, generally speaking, small-scale. There are, however, important elements of differentiation here. Constantinople had lost its special regime already in the twelfth century. But it remained an important commercial center. It therefore housed a significant population of merchants, shipowners and bankers, even into the first half of the fifteenth century, as may be seen from the

---

[75] See D. Kyritses, "The 'Common Chrysobulls' of Cities and the Notion of Property in Late Byzantium," *Symmeikta* 13 (1999), pp. 229–45.

account books of Giacomo Badoer, who was active in Constantinople between 1436 and 1439.[76] There were, as always, people who sold food and drink. There were also artisans and craftsmen who worked in the building industry or engaged in secondary production: soap-makers, smiths, barrel-makers, and so on. They had small shops, and their activities were geared to local consumption.[77]

Thessalonike is another city with special traits. It, too, was a major port, and an important center of inter-regional trade with western Greece and the western Balkans. It functioned almost as a relay station of Venetian trade; in any case, it was part of the Venetian trade subsystem.[78] It had an active construction industry, probably until the middle of the fourteenth century. Its population included a strong mercantile element and powerful seamen. In the late fourteenth century, its bishop, Isidore, listed, in his description of the non-aristocratic segments of the population, those who worked in agricultural labor, carpenters and possibly builders, and smiths. We also know that there were people who worked in the salines near the city. There was, of course, pottery, some woolen cloth production, and goldsmithing. But we do not know of many other manufacturing sectors. We may conclude that here, too, production was small-scale, and geared toward the consumption of the city and its region, with the exception of pottery and perhaps some woolen cloth.

Serres is an interesting case. At first glance, it would seem to fit the pattern of the city whose economy derives from its administrative functions, in other words, a "parasitic" city. It was the capital of the theme of Serres and Strymon after 1261, and great aristocrats, including John Kantakouzenos, had property there. In 1355, it became the

---

[76] The accounts have been published by U. Dorini and T. Bertelè, *Il libro dei conti di Giacomo Badoer* (Rome, 1956). On this, see T. Bertelè, "Il giro di affari di Giacomo Badoer," *Akten des XI. Internationalen Byzantinistenkongresses* (Munich, 1960), pp. 48–57; M. M. Shitikov, "Konstantinopolj i Venetsianskaja torgovlja v pervoij polovine XV v. po dannym knigi schetov Dzakomo Badoera," *VV* 30 (1969), pp. 50–1. See also the Index to the account book, G. Bertelè, *Il Libro dei Conti di Giacomo Badoer (Costantinopoli 1436–1440)* (Padova, 2002); on Badoer, see *Dizionario biografico degli Italiani*, 5 (1963), *s.v.* Badoer, Giacomo.

[77] N. Oikonomidès, *Hommes d'affaires grecs et latins à Constantinople (XIIIe–XVe siècles)* (Montreal, 1979), pp. 102–3, 111–13.

[78] The most recent work on Thessalonike is K.-P. Matschke, "Bemerkungen zur Stadtgeschichte Thessalonikes in spaetbyzantinischer Zeit," in L. R. Hoffmann (ed.), *Zwischen Polis, Provinz und Peripherie: Beiträge zur byzantinischen Geschichte und Kultur* (Wiesbaden, 2005), pp. 433–44.

capital of the local Serbian statelet, after the dissolution of the empire of Stefan Dushan. The fact that it had commercial exchanges with its hinterland has been remarked upon by scholars; its secondary production, in the textile sector, was noted some time ago;[79] its pottery production in the thirteenth and perhaps the fourteenth century gives us an example of an "administrative" city which is, at the same time, productive.

Monemvasia is a particular phenomenon among Byzantine cities and will be discussed in connection with trade.

There were sharp social and economic divisions in Byzantine cities, most evident in the fourteenth century. The cities were, generally speaking, under the political domination of the aristocracy. In the first half of the fourteenth century, however, the sources begin to place emphasis on the *mesoi*, the "middle" class, that middle lying between the very rich, who are identifiable with the landowning aristocracy, and the poor, who are small-scale traders and artisans, while at the very bottom are the destitute. The *mesoi* are identified as those who produce wealth and make it multiply (the manufacturers and merchants). In a famous text, *The Dialogue between Rich and Poor*, the relatively big merchants and skilled artisans are seen to be quite rich, but still in a position inferior to that of the aristocracy.[80] This stratification of the urban populations was rather new, and did not last long. After the troubles of mid-century, the Byzantine aristocracy, increasingly deprived of its lands, began to engage in commerce and banking, and the special designation of the *mesoi* lapsed.[81]

One of the major events of mid-century was the great civil war of 1341–54. In its origins a dynastic dispute, the civil war quickly acquired social dimensions especially in certain cities of Macedonia and Thrace: Constantinople itself, Thessalonike above all, but also Didymoteichon, Adrianople and Vizye. In these cities, the seamen, the merchants and to some degree the bankers (in Constantinople) contested the political monopoly of the aristocrats and, in Thessalonike, tried to take it into their own hands. The aristocracy, with the help of Serbian and Turkish allies, emerged as winners from this

---

[79] Laiou, "Koinonikes dynameis," pp. 203–19.

[80] The author is Alexios Makremvolites who wrote in the middle of the fourteenth century: see Ševčenko, "Alexios Makrembolites," pp. 219–25.

[81] The most cogent description of this development may be found in Oikonomidès, *Hommes d'affaires*, pp. 114 ff.

contest. But they lost much of their wealth to the Serbs and, in the long run, to the Ottomans.

The civil war, especially as it developed in Thessalonike, Constantinople and Vizye, forms part of the history of rebellions and urban revolutions that took place all over Western Europe in the fourteenth century: the revolution of 1339 in Genoa, which brought to power Simone Boccanegra as representative of the *popolo grasso*, the rebellion of the Ciompi in Florence in 1378, the cities of Flanders throughout the century. In the Byzantine cities, the merchants and manufacturers were too weak and the aristocracy too powerful for an urban rebellion to succeed; besides, even in Western Europe the power of the commercial and manufacturing elite was primarily economic, and found political expression only rarely.

The main differences between the urban economy in the Palaiologan period and that of the eleventh and twelfth centuries are clear. The cities of the later period are smaller, but have a more independent existence. Their economy therefore has to accommodate the needs of the population: it revolves around provisioning and the production of manufactured goods for local consumption. Pottery seems to be the only item which is produced for larger markets, which are regional. This is the meaning of dispersion of production: there are many small centers of artisanal production, including rural ones, but no major centers. The city economies also had a strong commercial sector focused on trade in agricultural products and on participation in the commercial networks organized by the Venetians and the Genoese, as will be seen below. What is missing is the relatively large-scale production of glass, textiles and pottery that characterized the urban economies in the period of growth. At that time, urban production supplied the demand of a large Byzantine public and that of part of an international market. In the Palaiologan period, with the important exception of the commercial sector, the cities regressed toward the model of an economy based on local consumption.

EXCHANGE

The creation of a Mediterranean trade system

In the course of the thirteenth century, the activities of Italian (and other Western European merchants) in the eastern Mediterranean expanded dramatically, so that by the second half of the century, certainly by its end, it is possible to speak of a Mediterranean trading system progressively dominated by Italians, especially Venetians and Genoese, with Pisa playing an active role until 1284. The areas involved include, in the eastern Mediterranean, all former Byzantine territories, Syria and Palestine, and to a lesser extent Egypt. The trading system affected more than distribution: the pull of demand and the mechanisms developed by the Italian city-states became structuring factors for manufacturing and for primary production that were geared, in certain areas, to the demands of an international market.[82] In other words, demand became international, and supply was to some extent oriented toward it.

The Byzantine economy of exchange was very active during this entire period, although it is more visible after the recovery of Constantinople in 1261, partly as a result of the state of the documentation. Never before was there such intensive mercantile activity or so many people involved in trade in one way or another. In virtually all of its aspects mercantile activity was greatly influenced by the ubiquitous presence of Western merchants in cities large and small and even in the countryside, as well as by the existence of the Italian-dominated international market, in which the Byzantine Empire was integrated.[83] These two overarching facts framed the structure of the Byzantine market and the activities of Byzantine merchants. A third important factor is a major shift in the trade partners of Byzantium: the role of the Arab states declined drastically, while that of the Italian states increased.

---

[82] On this see Laiou-Thomadakis, "The Byzantine Economy," pp. 177–222.

[83] This section follows, for the most part, the analysis in the following works: K.-P. Matschke's publications, starting with his seminal "Zum Charakter des byzantinischen Schwarzmeerhandels im 13. bis 15. Jh.," in *Wissenschaftliche Zeitschrift, Karl-Marx-Univ., Leipzig, Gesch. und Sprachwiss.,* 19/3 (1970), pp. 447–58; see also his "Byzantinische Politiker und byzantinische Kaufleute im Ringen um die Beteiligung am Schwarzmeerhandel in der Mitte des 14.Jh.," *Mitteilungen des bulgarischen Fosrchunginstitutes in Österreich,* 2/VI (1984), pp. 75–90, and his synthesis, "Commerce, Trade, Markets, and Money, Thirteenth-Fifteenth Centuries," *EHB* 2, pp. 771–806; Laiou, "The Byzantine Economy," and "The Greek Merchant of the Palaeologan Period: A Collective Portrait," *Praktika tes Akademias Athenon,* 57 (1982), pp. 97–132 (reprinted in her *Gender, Society and Economic Life,* art. VIII); Oikonomidès, *Hommes d'affaires.* Specific reference to these works will rarely be made hereafter. For the more general presence of Venetians and Genoese in the formerly Byzantine territories and the Black Sea see F. Thiriet, *La Romanie vénitienne au Moyen-Âge,* 2nd edn. (Paris, 1975) and M. Balard, *La Romanie génoise,* 2 vols. (Rome, 1978).

The presence of Western merchants in all territories that had formerly belonged to the Byzantine Empire and beyond them, in Lesser Armenia, in the crusader states, even, to a smaller degree, in Egypt, is well established and needs no further elaboration; its impact will be examined below. The creation of an international market, although a concept now accepted by historians of Mediterranean trade, nevertheless should be briefly described. In general terms, it refers to the interconnected trade system that linked, for about the century during which the Pax Mongolica lasted (*c*.1250–*c*.1350), a huge area starting from China and including the Middle East, the eastern Mediterranean, Italy and continental Europe.[84] Here, however, we use the term in a more restricted sense, to describe the system that involved the eastern Mediterranean and Italy in the first instance. We mean by it an allocation device, characterized by the functioning of supply and demand mechanisms that result in a fairly uniform price formation, once transportation costs have been compensated for; by the existence of widely accepted or convertible currency as well as banking, and by the existence of efficient techniques for acquiring and disseminating economic information. The most important trait, however, is division of labor.

Most of these conditions existed in the eastern Mediterranean in this period. Specifically regarding the supply and price of wheat, it seems that the Black Sea region, Turkish Asia Minor and Crete functioned as a vast area where supplies were interchangeable, and the price of wheat tended to revert to normal after disruptions produced by acute crises, mostly political.[85]

The division of labor is the factor that is the most clearly discernible. The eastern Mediterranean, globally speaking, became an area which exported to the West raw materials and alimentary products, while it imported from the West manufactured products, primarily woolen cloth. From the eastern Mediterranean also were re-exported the spices and other luxuries of the Eastern trade. There are many nuances that one could bring to this statement: for example, Ottoman Asia Minor and Egypt not only imported textiles but also exported them. So did Cyprus which, in the later Middle Ages,

[84] On this, see J. Abu-Lughod, *Before European Hegemony: The World System*, AD 1250–1350 (New York–Oxford, 1989).

[85] E. Zachariadou, "Prix et marchés des céréales en Romanie (1343–1405)," *Nuova rivista storica* 61(1977), pp. 291–306, reprinted in her *Romania and the Turks* (London, 1985), art. IX.

became a major exporter of sugar as well. Yet as a general observation it remains true. To the extent that this was an international market, local economies responded to a greater or lesser degree to international demand; this was mediated by Venetian, Genoese and other merchants who ruled the waves and had access to the Western markets. The effect on the local economies differed from place to place. Syrian agriculture, for example, was geared toward the production of cotton and sugar, both in high demand in the West.[86]

Along with the crusader states, it was the Byzantine Empire that felt most strongly the effects of this division of labor. The reasons are many. The very fact of the occupation of large parts of the former Byzantine Empire by Westerners, for varying periods of time, gave Western merchants, at first the Venetians, then the Genoese and then others, a highly privileged position which did not end with the Byzantine recovery of territories. Secondly, the importance of the Black Sea, both as a wheat-exporting area and as a series of outlets for the products of the Eastern trade, heightened the interest of Western powers in this area, as well as in Constantinople through whose straits the ships had to pass. The opening of the Black Sea to Western merchants was one of the most important results of the Fourth Crusade in the economic realm. The Venetians profited at first, but after 1261 the Genoese had the upper hand, although others were active there as well. It is striking that already in the late thirteenth century the Genoese, ostensibly allies of the Byzantines, were trying with every means at their disposal, including violence, to hinder the activities of Byzantine merchants in the Black Sea, as well as contesting the presence of the Byzantine fleet which was patrolling there.[87] It is also instructive that Bithynia, which until 1204 had functioned as a productive hinterland of Constantinople, became integrated in the international Black Sea trade network, both while it was still Byzantine and, much more so, under the Ottomans.[88]

Furthermore, the commercial dominance of Westerners in the eastern Mediterranean was in considerable part founded upon privileges granted them by the various political authorities. Among those,

---

[86] E. Ashtor, *Levant Trade in the Later Middle Ages* (Princeton, 1983), pp. 24–5.

[87] A. E. Laiou, "Monopoly and Privilege: The Byzantine Reaction to the Genoese Presence in the Black Sea," in L. Balletto, ed., *Oriente e Occidente tra medioevo ed età moderna: studi in onore di Geo Pistarino* (Genoa, 1977), pp. 675–6.

[88] M. Gerolymatou, "Le commerce, VIIe–XVe siècle," in Geyer and Lefort, *La Bithynie*, pp. 48 ff.

Byzantium and the crusader states were the ones least capable of resisting the blackmail of the powers that held sway on the seas, and therefore the privileges granted in these areas were the most extensive.[89]

Markets and products old and new, domestic and international

The division of labor meant that new products became important export items to the West. Grain had been a protected commodity in the Byzantine Empire, at least in theory. In practice, some grain seems to have been exported by Venetians in the twelfth century, but the quantities cannot have been important. Western demand was not yet high, the Byzantine market may well have absorbed most of the (increased) production, and there was not yet an integrated Mediterranean market, with product specialization and adequate mechanisms that could match supply to demand across large regions.[90] All of these conditions changed in the course of the thirteenth century. Grain from the Black Sea became important for the Genoese market in the late 1250s, and remained so thereafter. The Venetians, in their own name or through the Ragusans, imported grain from Macedonia and western Greece and their colony in Crete, as well as from Turkish Asia Minor and the Black Sea. Wheat was massively bought in the Crimea. It was also collected in smaller quantities all along the Black Sea coasts, where sometimes it was brought by Greek merchants, and reloaded on large ships; Pera, the Genoese colony in Constantinople, was an important relay station. Byzantine landlords, including the imperial family, remained active in this trade until the end. Western merchants also bought directly from farmers. The first Palaiologan emperors made an effort to impose state control on the export of this important commodity. Wheat, iron and salt, in fact, were the only three products for which any effort was made to re-establish something resembling the old policy of the *kekolymena*. Yet the prohibitions were not enforced.

Another new item of trade was slaves. This did not affect the Byzantine economy much, since most of the slave traders were

---

[89] On privileges, see pp. 207–9.

[90] A. E. Laiou, "Monopoly and Privileged Free Trade in the Eastern Mediterranean (8th–14th Century," in *Chemins d'outre-mer: études d'histoire offertes à Michel Balard* (Paris, 2004), pp. 519 ff.

Western, especially Genoese, but also Venetians and Greeks from Italian-dominated areas. The great slave markets were situated along the northern coast of the Black Sea, although Asia Minor and other areas also were places where slaves could be bought, while the islands of Rhodes and Crete (held by the Venetians) were major centers for this trade.[91]

On the luxury side, there was mastic, an aromatic gum much in demand. There was an in-built monopoly here, since the tree only grows on the island of Chios, off the coast of Asia Minor at about the height of Phocaea. It became a Genoese monopoly after the conquest of the island by the *mahona* of Chios, in 1346.[92]

The new conditions also meant new markets and marketplaces. The new markets were the Western European ones, although there was also active trade within the regions of the eastern Mediterranean. The trade of the old markets for Byzantine products, Syria, Palestine, and Egypt, for example, had passed into the hands of the Italians, although there is evidence of Byzantine merchants in Egypt in the late thirteenth century. Traditional marketplaces competed with new ones. Constantinople remained a major port. Its importance for the Eastern luxury trade declined after the 1350s, when the end of the Pax Mongolica reoriented trade routes toward Egypt, but was never extinguished.

Thessalonike too functioned as a major marketplace. But whereas in the twelfth century the city had collected products and merchandise from Western Europe, the Balkans, Greece, Syria and Egypt, its commerce was reoriented in the course of the thirteenth and fourteenth centuries. Italian and other Western European manufactured products certainly reached the city. The Syrian trade did not reach it. Neither, more interestingly, did the Bulgarian trade.[93]

---

[91] The classic work on slavery in this period is C. Verlinden, *L'esclavage dans l'Europe médiévale*, 2 vols. (Bruges, 1955).

[92] The *mahona* was a Genoese institution: a chartered private company, charged by the state with taking a specific action, and rewarded with state revenues (or what would otherwise have been state revenues). In the case in point, the *mahona* was organized in order to conquer Chios, and was rewarded with the revenues of the island.

[93] The statement of Demetrios Kydones, that before the 1340s Thessalonike was a commercial city frequented by merchants from all over the world must be discounted as patriotic exaggeration on the part of a man who was contrasting the glories of the city before the civil war to the disasters wrought by the "popular" party in the course of it: *Monodia occisorum Thessalonicae*, PG 109, col. 641.

Communications had something to do with this last development. Land communications with Constantinople and through it with the eastern Balkans were at the mercy of wars, civil wars and invasions: the major roadway, the Via Egnatia, was open until the 1320s, then progressively became less accessible until, in the 1340s and after, it was no longer used except perhaps by troops. Communications with Constantinople were henceforth by sea, a different kettle of fish altogether in terms of the movement of people, animals and merchandise. Merchants from Thessalonike to the Black Sea areas are few and far between. Instead, Thessalonike was a nodal point in a commercial subsystem consisting of western Greece, Epiros, Serbia, the Dalmatian coast, Ragusa and Venice. Herein lies the most important explanation of the reorientation of Thessalonian trade. Incorporated in the Italian-dominated system, the city, by reason of geography first and politics eventually, formed part of the Venetian trade network, and had few contacts with the Genoese one, which was centered on the Black Sea and the north-eastern Aegean.[94]

By the early fourteenth century, Venice and Genoa had created in the old Byzantine territories commercial subsystems each of which was dominated by one or the other of these powers, although the domination was never complete and was constantly contested. Both old marketplaces and new ones must be seen in the context of these subsystems and the needs of international commerce. In the Venetian-dominated system, western Greece enters the commercial record. Durrazzo (Dyrrachium) and Avlona are "old" marketplaces, since they had been active since the eleventh century. Arta, Naupaktos, and other, smaller cities were new marketplaces. Wheat, salt and meat were important exports from these areas. The city of Ioannina had a considerable mercantile element, most probably trading in grain and animal products.[95] The Peloponnese, whether occupied by Westerners or by Byzantines, formed part of the subsystem, and had an active trade, in large part tied to Venetian interests. Crete and the Venetian-occupied islands of the Aegean belonged to the same subsystem. Modon, Coron, Clarentza, Candia (Chandax) are only the best-known of the new ports/marketplaces.

---

[94] Laiou, "E Thessalonike," pp. 183–94.
[95] E. A. Zachariadou, "Paragoge kai emporio sto despotato tes Epeirou," in *Praktika Diethnous Symposiou gia to Despotato tes Epeirou* (Arta, 1992), pp. 87–93.

The Genoese subsystem was located in the Eastern part of the Empire. It was more powerfully contested than the Venetian one, in part because Genoa did not have territorial ownership on much of it, but in part also because some of the most important commercial areas were located here. The Venetians, and, for a short period, the Byzantines, wanted and got access to the Black Sea. The Trapezuntine ports, on the Asia Minor coast of the Black Sea, were marketplaces where both Venetians and Genoese were active. Constantinople was home to the merchants of both cities, although the Venetian quarters in Constantinople formed less highly developed a colony than the semi-autonomous Genoese settlement in Pera (Galata).

Genoese dominance resulted in the appearance of a number of marketplaces that may have been older but acquired new importance. After the middle of the fourteenth century, Caffa, the major Genoese base in the Black Sea, was insecure because of problems with the Tatars. A number of smaller ports in the Danube Delta, Chilia, Licostomo and others, sprang up in partial replacement of Caffa; they exported primarily wheat to Pera and thence to Genoa. Chios and Phocaea formed part of the subsystem. In the first part of the fifteenth century, as Caffa declined, Chios became the fulcrum of Genoese trade with the eastern Mediterranean.[96]

There was intense trading activity within each of the two subsystems, as networks of merchants were established, connecting native traders, as well as Venetians or Genoese respectively, to each other within broad geographic areas. However, the subsystems were not impermeable. There was competition between the two major sea powers, which at times became intense, leading to open warfare; warfare that became more acute and more merciless in the second half of the fourteenth century, when economic crisis engulfed the Mediterranean and caused states to fight savagely for dwindling resources.

Markets and privileges

Indeed, new approaches toward international trade were established in the course of the thirteenth century, soon after the Fourth Crusade, and governed trade thereafter. While the controls exercised by Byzantine governments in the past lapsed for the most part, this was

[96] J. Heers, *Gênes au XVe siècle: civilisation méditerranéenne, grand capitalisme, capitalisme populaire* (Paris, 1971).

international trade which took place among states, and thus it still depended, to a degree, on inter-state institutional arrangements. In other words, Byzantine emperors were still asked to and did give trade privileges to the Italian city states and eventually to others, Barcelona, for example, as of course did most other nearly states of the eastern Mediterranean, for example the Seljuks or the Mamluks.

Both Venice and Genoa, as the strong players in the area, pursued a policy with a double aim: to acquire for themselves what they called freedom of the sea (*libertas maris*), that is, privileged trade conditions, monopolies if possible, and to impose adverse conditions on everyone else; clearly two competing aims when more than one state is involved. These policies are evident in the Byzantine Empire and most powerfully in Constantinople and the Black Sea area. Here, the Genoese tried to keep the sea closed to everyone else. The Venetians fought for freedom of trade (meaning, for safeguarding their own presence there). The Byzantine merchants entered the fray for a short while in the 1340s, when Tatar attacks on Caffa weakened the position of the Genoese. The War of the Straits ensued (1351–5), and the peace treaties included clauses which limited Venetian and Byzantine access to the Black Sea. Eventually, relative freedom of access returned, although the Genoese predominance was preserved.

In such conditions, this was a commercial world in which relations between the Italian maritime cities and the Byzantine Empire were based on privilege. Venice and Genoa, and others after them and to a lesser degree, acquired complete access to all markets, freedom to trade in all items except for salt, iron, and grain under certain conditions, and mastic (until the Genoese occupation of Chios), and freedom from customs duties. Thereafter, they sought to have their privileges extended to their clients: Greeks who acquired Venetian or Genoese citizenship, Greek mariners on Italian ships, and even Byzantine subjects in their transactions with Venetian merchants. Privileges provided the institutional base on which Italian dominance rested.

The new attitude and the extensive grant of privileges changed the conditions of trade within the Byzantine Empire. A protected domestic market no longer existed except, for a while, and unsuccessfully, for grain. With no restrictions on trading activity, the competitive edge belonged to those with privileges. As a result, a number of Byzantine individuals or institutions or communities sought and received privileged terms of trade in one form or another. Among the privileges belonged the right to a "monopoly," although it is counter-intuitive to discuss this in the same breath as the privileges that seem to promote freedom of trade. In the internal market, a "monopoly" describes the right of an individual or institution to pre-empt the sale of commodities: selling one's own stock before others may sell theirs limits the supply for a time and creates favorable prices for the seller. Byzantine officials exercised such a right, although it is not clear whether they did so with the permission of the emperor or not. In 1408, in any case, Manuel II forbade the monopoly of wine by the officials of Thessalonike, saying that he disapproved of the practice; but the prohibition was issued at the specific request of the competition, the monks of Mount Athos.[97] Regional rulers held such a right, as, for example, did Thomas Preljubovitch, Despot of Ioannina in Epiros (1366/7–84) on the sale of wine, wheat, meat, cheese, fruit and fish; sometimes he ceded it to his officials.[98] State officials or privileged individuals also had a limited monopsony right: they could buy alimentary products before other buyers, without, in theory, having the right to resell them. In theory also, they were not to buy at a lower than market price, but of course monopsony, even limited to a brief period, has that effect in general, and had it then.[99] All of these practices skewed the market in agricultural commodities.

Certain Byzantine merchants or sellers acquired trade privileges in this period. Some monasteries received the right to trade freely with ships of specified tonnage, without paying customs dues. Such exemptions were acquired by great monasteries already in the twelfth century. The merchants of Monemvasia, both those of the city itself and those of its colony in Pegai, in Asia Minor, are a category unto themselves. Their city's economy was based on trade, primarily maritime, but also on land. In that, it was not unlike Venice: both had, at this time, rather a small territory, both were oriented toward the sea. Monemvasiot merchants plied their trade in their natural hinterland,

---

[97] A. Mošin, "Prostagma tsara Manuila II Paleologa Svetogortsima," *Srpska Kraljevska Akademija, Spomenik* 91 (1939), p. 166.

[98] Laiou-Thomadakis, "The Byzantine Economy," p. 209; Zachariadou, "Production," p. 93.

[99] P. Magdalino, "An Unpublished Pronoia Grant of the Second Half of the Fourteenth Century," *ZRVI* 18 (1978), p. 157; L. Burgmann and P. Magdalino, "Michael VIII on Maladministration," *Fontes Minores* VI (1984), p. 382, on a much misunderstood text; P. J. Alexander, "A Chrysobull of the Emperor Andronicus II Palaeologus in Favor of the See of Kanina in Albania," *Byz* 15 (1940–1), pp. 181–3.

the Peloponnese, in the Aegean, in Constantinople and the Black Sea, and all along the coast of Thrace. They were also active in markets where they engaged in land trade, both in the Peloponnese itself and in the interior of Thrace. They had the reputation of being fearless seafarers. They were also fearless pirates, for piracy, in this period, was thriving, feeding as it does on active maritime commerce.

Successive Byzantine emperors granted the merchants of Monemvasia a series of privileges, including either complete exemption from or a drastic reduction of the *kommerkion*. Their privileges were thus a replica of those of the Venetians, except that the Monemvasiots had, as far as we know, no restrictions on the purchase and export of grain, for example. Of course, their activities did not extend beyond the waters of the Aegean and the Black Sea: they do not appear in Western markets, so to that extent their role is far from comparable to that of the Venetians or the Genoese. Monemvasia also had a form of self-government.

Freedom of trade in the Byzantine Empire in this period, then, was not what one would understand by the term today. The end of control of almost all aspects of international trade by the Byzantine government did create conditions in which goods and merchants circulated more freely; the market was liberalized. Competitiveness, however, was governed not only by economic factors, such as access to sources of supply and demand, or economies of scale, or knowhow, but also on institutional factors. The merchants in the least competitive position were those with no privileges: individuals, mostly Byzantines, who for one reason or another could not piggyback on the privileges of foreign or domestic merchants.

The question arises, whether the developments described here were beneficial to the Byzantine economy and the Byzantine merchant. That the Byzantine state lost by them is clear and certain. To the extent that the commercial activity was untaxed, the fisc gained nothing from it, and lost revenues that it had collected in the past.

Merchants and bankers

The problem regarding the Byzantine merchant is more complicated. There is no question that international trade was more active than ever before during the period under question, at least until the general crisis of the mid-fourteenth century. Western demand, and the ability of the Venetians, the Genoese and others to create mechanisms that made this demand effective, led to intensification of commerce. It has been argued that the weakening of the central government and of the integrating role of Constantinople created a better climate for provincial initiatives and investment.[100] An early fifteenth-century rhymed chronicle encapsulates this position in a compelling manner: "The whole region opened up/land as well as sea/the roads were cleared, the routes widened/all men became rich, the great and the poor."[101]

The Byzantine merchant of the Palaiologan period is highly visible in the sources, especially but not only the notarial documents of Venice, Genoa and Ragusa. The documentation becomes rich starting with the late thirteenth century. Furthermore, Greeks from the Latin-occupied parts of the former Byzantine Empire were very active in trade; this is very much the case with the Greeks of Crete and Rhodes, but also of other areas.[102] The activities of this second category of merchants will not be examined here, although there is promising work to be done on the networks they established.

As far as the "Byzantine" Greeks and those of the Black Sea coasts are concerned, certain important traits are clearly discernible. Fragmentary Byzantine documentation shows the existence, throughout the period, of merchants of limited means and activity, who dealt mostly in agricultural products. There were also people who lived in the cities, who were engaged in trade, and who owned vineyards of a size that permits the conclusion that they produced for the market.[103]

Such merchants must have been very numerous, trading locally or engaged in regional trade of foodstuffs and cloth. Some of them would have carried out their activities quite independently of

---

[100] See C. Morrisson, "L'ouverture des marchés après 1204: un aspect positif de la IVe croisade?" in A. E. Laiou (ed.), *Urbs capta: The Fourth Crusade and its Consequences; La Quatrième Croisade et ses conséquences* (Paris, 2005), pp. 227–30.

[101] G. Schirò (ed.), *Cronaca dei Tocco di Cefalonia di Anonimo* (Rome, 1975), p. 448 refers to western Greece during the rule of Carlo Tocco (d. 1429).

[102] For Crete, see A. E. Laiou, "Venetians and Byzantines: Investigation of Forms of Contact in the Fourteenth Century," *Thesaurismata* 22 (1992), pp. 29–43; for the activities of Greeks from the Latin-held areas in Cyprus, see D. Jacoby, "Greeks in the Maritime Trade of Cyprus around the Mid-Fourteenth Century," in *Kypros–Venetia: Koines istorikes tyches* (Venice, 2002), pp. 59–83.

[103] For the documentation, see P. Schreiner, *Texte zur spätbyzantinischen Finanz- und Wirtschaftsgeschichte in Handschriften der Biblioteca Vaticana* (Vatican City, 1991), pp. 33 ff. (this trader also dealt in soap); the case of Basil Krasinos, in Laiou, *Mariage*, pp. 158–67; the case of Theodore Karavas, discussed above.

Western merchants. Our documentation, however, heavily although not exclusively Italian, highlights the Byzantine merchant whose activities are intimately and inextricably linked with the trading networks established by the Venetians and the Genoese. In the eastern subsystem, we find, from the late thirteenth century onward, Byzantine merchants from Constantinople and then, increasingly in the course of the fourteenth century, from the Black Sea areas or from Thrace, who conduct their business with or through the Genoese. They are, with some exceptions, people with small or in any case limited capital, who enter into business arrangements, among them *commenda* contracts and exchange contracts, with Genoese merchants. Some reside in Genoese colonies, including Caffa.

They sail in relatively small ships. They deal mostly in grain of various kinds, which they transport as far as the Genoese colony of Pera and no further. The movement of merchandise from Pera to Genoa is done on Genoese ships. The Byzantines therefore feed the Genoese grain trade. The presence of these merchants becomes much more visible in the 1340s and the 1360s, partly as an accident of documentation but partly also because the grain trade perhaps changed form after the troubles with the Tatars of the Crimea, and became more dependent on numerous smaller sources of supply. By the late fourteenth and early fifteenth centuries, again a period of political crisis (Constantinople was blockaded by the Ottomans in 1394–1402, and Timurlane's invasions disrupted the trade of the Trapezuntine coast), some merchants were sailing over longer distances, into the Aegean and Chios. A few ventured into southern Russia and Wallachia, to buy furs among other things, a new and interesting departure for Byzantine traders.

By that time too, the profile of the Byzantine merchant of Constantinople had changed. The civil war that ended in 1354 had deprived many aristocratic families of their landed possessions, while the demographic problems and the constant wars and invasions had made land unprofitable. Byzantine aristocrats, therefore, turned to trade, and members of some of the most important families are among the merchants of Constantinople in the late period. This is a very significant departure for the Byzantine aristocracy. But high social status did not change the terms under which they did business. Their activities were intimately tied to those of the Genoese and the Venetians. The accounts of Giacomo Badoer are full of the names of Byzantine aristocrats. Greeks form 27 per cent of the merchants in his account book; in terms of the value of their transactions, they account for 25 per cent of goods purchased and 9.5 per cent of the goods sold to Badoer. They engage mostly in retail trade. There are also Greek bankers, also belonging to great families. This is an important pointer to the position of the Greeks in the trade system. They supplied the great commerce dominated by Venetians and Genoese, and they engaged in activities that supported this commerce: currency exchange, deposits and so on. Their knowledge of local conditions and personalities, as well as languages, gave them an advantageous position from which they served Italian interests well. Byzantine merchants did not set the conditions of or the framework for trade or banking activity.

This intimate connection was sometimes reinforced by family ties. The de Draperiis family of men of affairs was among the richest in Pera. They were connected by marriage to the important Palaiologos and Livadarios families, and they bought and exported grain produced on imperial estates.[104] By the very late period, the comprador nature of the activities of Greek businessmen becomes personified in the Notaras family. Merchants, members of the petty aristocracy of Monemvasia, the Notaras relocated to Constantinople in the 1340s. The first important member of the family, George Notaras, engaged in trade in the Black Sea and the northern Aegean, in close collaboration with the Genoese. His son acquired shares in the Venetian public debt and in the *compere* of Caffa and Pera. His grandson, Loukas Notaras, held the highest office, that of *grand doux* in the last Byzantine government. Loukas' fortune was securely invested in the public debt of Venice and Genoa, and he held both Genoese and Venetian citizenship.[105] He is nevertheless best known for the statement attributed to him just before the fall of Constantinople to the Ottomans in 1453: "It would be better to see the Turkish turban rule in the center of the City than the Latin mitre."[106]

---

[104] On the Draperio family, see T. Ganchou, "Autonomie locale et relations avec les Latins à Byzance au XIVe siècle: Ioannès Limpidarios/Libadarios, Ainos et les Draperio de Péra," *Chemins d'outre-mer: études d'histoire sur la Méditerranée médiévale offertes à Michel Balard* (Byzantina Sorbonensia 20) (Paris, 2004), pp. 353–74.

[105] Th. Ganchou, "Le rachat des Notaras après la chute de Constantinople ou les relations 'étrangères' de l'élite byzantine au XIVe siècle," in *Migrations et diasporas méditerranéennes (Xe–XVIe siècles)* (Paris 2002), pp. 149–229; K.-P. Matschke, "The Notaras Family and its Italian Connections," *DOP* 49 (1995), pp. 59–72.

[106] V. Grecu (ed.), *Ducas, Istoria Turco-Bizantina* (Bucharest, 1958), p. 329; H. J. Magoulias (transl.), *Doukas and the Fall of Byzantium to the Ottomans* (Detroit, 1975), p. 210.

In the western subsystem, although there were several differences, the role of the Greek merchant was substantially the same. Here, Thessalonike was the centre; its role, when political circumstances did not strangle it, was primarily to collect the products of the hinterland for export to Venice, and serve as a center of distribution of Western imports. This, too, was the role of the merchants of western Greece, from the Peloponnese up the Dalmatian coast and the Macedonian and Serbian hinterland. Local trade was thriving, and to a considerable but non-quantifiable extent it was tied to the needs of Italian commerce.

Such, then was the role of the Byzantine merchants and bankers. Their activities were the rivulets that fed the great rivers of Italian commerce, and they were relegated to a service role. Many made a living out of this role, and a few people gained considerable fortunes. The fact that they controlled neither communications nor the money markets nor the information mechanisms placed limits on their activities. The full effect of these limitations may be seen in the events of the 1340s. There was, at the time, a merchant group in Constantinople, powerful and wealthy through trade in the Black Sea. The problems faced by the Genoese in the Crimea in the 1340s allowed these merchants to expand their activities significantly. They seem to have done a heavy trade in grain. Eventually, there was full-scale war with Genoa, which ended in the defeat of the Byzantines. The desire of the Genoese to virtually forbid the access of the Byzantines to the Black Sea was not fulfilled, but the cost of the war was so heavy for this merchant class that large-scale Byzantine mercantile activity in the Black Sea is not attested from that time on.

Only a few Byzantines were able to make beneficial use of the possibilities offered by international commerce to extend their activities in ways that foretell the future. The activities of some Byzantines in Russia and Vallachia are an early harbinger of the extensive networks that Greeks would establish in these lands. The establishment of some Greeks in Bruges are an early form of the successful Greek colonies in European cities, especially in Central Europe.[107] Both events took place in the fifteenth century. Both developments would flourish during the period of Ottoman domination.

As for the Byzantine economy generally, it profited from all these developments insofar as active trade stimulated production, and

---

[107] For the events, see Matschke, "Commerce, Trade," pp. 793, 798–9.

insofar as part of the population gained a living from trade. It lost to the extent that its structure was determined by the needs of others. It had a large agricultural sector and an active economy of exchange. What was missing was manufacturing on a large scale and for the large European or Eastern markets where the money was made. The Byzantine economy lost revenues in the secondary sector, in maritime transport, and in tax revenues. Here the impact of Western penetration was most destructive.

MONETARY DEVELOPMENTS[108]

In the long run, the conquest of Constantinople in 1204 entailed a major disruption of the monetary situation in the Byzantine world.[109] Through the twelfth century, a unified currency had prevailed in the Empire; foreign coins were not accepted and Byzantine gold played an important role in international trade. Starting from the mid-thirteenth century, foreign coins increasingly penetrated local circulation, which became more and more fragmented. From the fourteenth century, Western gold currencies dominated Mediterranean exchanges, while Byzantium was left with a silver *hyperpyron* and poor petty coins of very restricted circulation. This turnaround was not an instant process, as we will see, before we outline on the one hand the transformation of the Byzantine coinage and its shift

[108] Fundamental for the subject are: M. F. Hendy, *Catalogue of the Byzantine Coins in the Dumbarton Oaks Collection and in the Whittemore Collection*, 4 *(1081–1261)* and P. Grierson, *ibid.*, vol. 5 *(1258–1453)* (Washington, 1999) (hereafter, *DOC*). See the detailed reviews by C. Morrisson in *Revue historique* 306/2 (2004), pp. 398–411, and by C. Morrisson and S. Bendall in *Revue numismatique* 157 (2001), pp. 471–93.

[109] Following the policy outlined above (p. 169), regarding the Byzantine world in this period we will not deal here with the contemporary coinages in the broader region, on which the reader is referred to D. M. Metcalf, *Coinage in South-Eastern Europe (820–1396)* (London, 1979), to the chapter by Grierson in *DOC* 4, pp. 32–9, and to the classic G. Schlumberger, *Numismatique de l'Orient latin* (Paris, 1882, repr. Graz, 1954), not entirely superseded by the excellent 2nd edition of D. M. Metcalf, *Coinage of the Crusades and the Latin East in the Ashmolean Museum Oxford* (London, 1995). On Serbian coinage, the standard reference is V. Ivanišević, *Novcartsvo srednjovekovne Srbije* (Belgrade, 2001) (with extensive summary in English). For south Italian coinages circulating in the Aegean, see Ph. Grierson and L. Travaini, *Medieval European Coinage*, vol. XIV, *South Italy* (Cambridge, 1998). For Turkish coinages, see Ş. Pamuk, *A Monetary History of the Ottoman Empire* (Cambridge, 2000).

from gold to silver, and, on the other hand, the opening of the Byzantine monetary market and its fragmentation into smaller areas of circulation.

The partition of the Empire into various successor states led of course to the creation of regional, "national," coinages which, while proclaiming their identity by iconographic devices, retained the previous imperial tradition with only minor adaptations in the metal content. One adaptation was the abandonment of the previous gold/silver alloy for the *trikephalon*, which became a pure silver coin, the other was the final shift to a pure copper alloy for the *stamenon*. The Empire of Nicaea issued the entire series of denominations, including gold. In spite of the imperial ambitions of the Despots of Epiros, the mint of Thessalonike was content with silver *trikephala*, abundant issues of copper *stamena* and minor quantities of *tetartera* and half-*tetartera*. The Despotate of Epiros struck only rare issues of electrum and *stamena*. The Bulgarian state issued rare *hyperpyra* and more *stamena* only after Ivan Asen II's victory over Theodore Komnenos-Doukas in 1230. The Serbian ruler Stefan Radoslav (1228–34) issued an even rarer *trikephalon* in his fortress of Ras. In the Empire of Trebizond, the first coins were *stamena* of Andronikos I (1222–35), followed by electrum *trachea* of Manuel I (1238–63). All these continued the Byzantine tradition of the twelfth century. The copying of John II Komnenos' *hyperpyra* by John III Vatatzes of Nicaea (1228–54), and the fact that *trikephala* were often called *manuelati* or *manoelata*, whether they were issues of Manuel I Komnenos or not, show how the model and prestige of the previous coinage persisted. This might be considered a political stance, but it was also of an economic nature.

That the Byzantine model was inescapable can be deduced from the fact that the Latin empire of Constantinople never introduced Western elements in its coins as it did on its bilingual seals, for fear that they would not be accepted by the public. The Latin empire's elusive coinage was a purely imitative one. It included perhaps *hyperpyra* (the *perperi latini* listed later by Pegolotti) and consisted mainly of billon *stamena*, containing just 0.15 per cent silver, which imitated loosely the issues of emperors of the twelfth and thirteenth centuries, and introduced a few new iconographical types of Latin origin. However, this "post-Komnenian" monetary *koine*, so to speak, was of limited duration, as will be seen below.

After 1261, the restored empire of the Palaiologoi was the only state that maintained the Byzantine tradition of a trimetallic monetary system. Its Balkan neighbours (Serbians or Bulgars) now imitated mainly the Western silver grosso, while in Anatolia the Turkomans and the Ottomans relied on small silver coins (*aqçe*/aspers) and copper *manghirs*. The Palaiologan system itself had to adapt to include Western-inspired denominations in the early fourteenth century, and underwent a complete upheaval in 1367 with the creation of the silver *hyperpyron* system. This is best understood with the help of the following table (Table 5.1):

The adaptation of the early fourteenth century consisted of the replacement of the silver concave *trikephalon* by a coin which imitated the Venetian grosso and was called both *doukaton* (= coin of the doge) and *basilikon* (= imperial coin) and of the introduction of a billon (base silver) coin on the model of the *denier tournois* of Frankish Greece. A more important evolution was on its way, namely, the steady weakening of the gold *hyperpyron*, which the historian George Pachymeres sums up and explains with great precision:

The *nomisma* was debased because of need. At first, under John [III] Doukas the refined gold of *nomismata* amounted to two-thirds of their weight [i.e., 16 carats], and this situation continued under his successor. Then, under Michael [VIII], after the recovery of the City, because of the expenses then necessary, not least with regard to the Italians, he [Michael] . . . reduced the measure of gold by a carat, so that the total of 24 units [carats] fell to a ratio of 15 to 9 [of alloy]. Later, when he was succeeded [by Andronikos II], it amounted to 14 [of gold] compared with 10 [of alloy], and now [*c*.1308] the purity is said to be mixed by half [i.e. 12 of gold compared with 12 of alloy] . . .[110]

All of Pachymeres' figures agree with the data found in the section on the alloy of gold coins in Francesco Balducci Pegolotti's manual of trade. Pegolotti relied on touchstone and fire assays that the merchants took great care to practice.[111] The figures are also confirmed by modern chemical analyses (see Fig. 2).[112] The causes of

[110] George Pachymeres, *Relations historiques*, II, *Livres IV-VI*, CFHB 24.2, ed. A. Failler (Paris, 1984), p. 540.

[111] L. Travaini, *Monete, mercati e matematica: le monete medievali nei trattati di aritmetica e nei libri di mercatura* (Rome, 2003) (with commented abstracts of such coin lists, and references). On Pegolotti and Byzantine coins, see Grierson and Hendy, *DOC*.

[112] C. Morrisson et al., *L'or monnayé* (Paris, 1985), and C. Morrisson, J.-N. Barrandon and S. Bendall, "Proton Activation and X-ray Fluorescence Analysis: An Application to the Study of the Alloy of Nicaean and Palaeologan Hyperpyra," in W. A. Oddy and M. Archibald (eds.), *Metallurgy in Numismatics*, vol. 2 (London, 1988), pp. 23–39.

Table 5.1 *The Byzantine monetary system in the thirteenth–fifteenth centuries*

a – THE POST-KOMNENIAN SYSTEM (1204–1304)

GOLD	SILVER		COPPER	
Hyperpyron nomisma	Nomisma trachy aspron (trikephalon)	Carat / keration (money of account)	Aspron trachy (stamenon)	Tetarteron
(~4.3g 75 % to 50 % Au)	(~4.3g 95 % Ag)		(~4.3g)	(~2.2g)
1	12	(24)	288	576

b – THE WESTERNIZED PALAIOLOGAN SYSTEM (1304–67)*

GOLD	SILVER		BILLON	COPPER	
Hyperpyron nomisma	Basilikon (argyrion or doukaton)	Half-basilikon	Tornese / politikon	Stamenon trakhion	Assarion / tetarteron
(~4.3g 60 % to 50 % Au)	(~2g 94 % Ag)	(~1.3–1g 6 % to 2 % Ag)	(0.7 g ~22.5 % Ag)	(~4.2g)	(~2.1g)
1	12	24	96	384	768(?)

c – THE SILVER HYPERPYRON (STAVRATON) SYSTEM (1367–1453)*

| Hyperpyron nomisma (money of account) | SILVER | | | Carat / keration kokkion (money of account) | COPPER | |
	Stavraton (stravato)	Half-stavraton	Doukatopoulon duchatelo / aspron		Tornese tournesion	Folaro
	(~8g 95 % Ag)	(~4.4g 95 % Ag)	(~1.1g 95 % Ag)		(~2.4g)	(~0.8g)
1	2	4	16	(24)	192	576(?)

* Sources for the coins' values and names will be found in C. Morrisson, "Les Noms de monnaies des Paléologues," in W. Seibt (ed.), *Geschichte und Kultur der Palaeologenzeit* (Vienna, 1996), pp. 151–62.

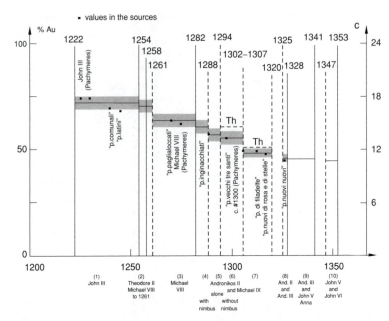

Figure 2. The debasement of the *hyperpyron*, 1222–1354
(C. Morrisson, *EHB* 2, Ch. 42, fig. 4)

Dots indicate the values in carats given by Pachymeres and Pegolotti (the coin names given by the latter are shown vertically). Shaded areas show the range of value from analyses. "Th" and the dotted lines below it are the slightly higher values measured on *hyperpyra* attributed to Thessalonike.

the debasement adduced by the Byzantine historian are indisputable. The relationship between strains on imperial finances and the various stages of the debasement process can even be established in close detail.[113] The quantities struck declined progressively in the 1320s and, after 1353, gold coins ceased being struck altogether in Byzantium. The thousand-year old history of the *solidus-nomisma* or bezant had come to an end.[114]

---

[113] The classic study by D. Zakythinos, *Crise monétaire et crise économique à Byzance du XIIIe au XVe siècle* (Athens, 1948), reprinted in his *Byzance: état, société, économie* (Variorum, 1973), art. XI.

[114] John V Palaiologos struck a gold florin in 1354, known from a unique coin in the Bibliothèque Nationale. If it was anything other than a ceremonial coin, it did not last long in any case. It can be related to the equally rare imitations of the florin struck in the Aegean at the same time by the emir of Aydin.

Even if finances were exhausted, the Byzantines' adaptability was not, and in 1367 an entirely new system based on silver was introduced. This was a complete and double reversal from the previous situation when the Western currency was primarily silver and the Byzantine was gold. Since the second half of the thirteenth century, the West had "returned to gold" and, as will be seen below, in the fourteenth century Venetian gold issues came to dominate the long-distance trade of the eastern Mediterranean.[115] The *hyperpyron* was now only a money of account. Its value could be paid by two big silver coins, called *stavrati* or *stravati* (coins with a cross) in the sources, a reference to their prototype, the double *carlino* or *gigliato* of the Angevins of Naples with its ornate cross.[116] These coins, equivalent to twice the weight of fine metal in the last *hyperpyra* at a 1:9 gold:silver ratio, were supplemented by two divisions of 1/2 and 1/4, and two small copper coins. Thus, the Byzantine range of denominations was still broad and could meet different levels of transactions, as documented in the accounts of Giacomo Badoer.[117]

Another important difference with the situation prevailing before 1204 (and perhaps preserved in Nicaea) lies in the *organization of minting*. The Constantinopolitan mint[118] (or mints) had changed from a directly managed imperial workshop into one which could accept bullion or coins brought by private individuals, and was probably farmed out from the mid-14th century onwards.[119] The revenues of the mint were surely considered important by the state as is shown by the claim made in 1258 by Michael VIII to a share in the *kommerkion* and *khrysepseteion* (gold smelting, and minting installation)

[115] In R. S. Lopez' famous words: "Settecento anni fa: il ritorno all'oro nell'Occidente duecentesco," *Rivista storica italiana* 65 (1953), pp. 19–55, 161–98 (shorter English version: "Back to Gold, 1252," *Economic History Review* 2nd series 9 (1956), pp. 219–40); P. Spufford, *Money and its Use in Medieval Europe* (Cambridge, 1988), pp. 132–86, 267–88; F. C. Lane and R. C. Mueller, *Money and Banking in Medieval Venice* (Baltimore, Md., 1985), pp. 314–18, 326–32, 347.

[116] According to P. Grierson's astute interpretation in *DOC* 5.1, pp. 28–31.

[117] Above, n. 76.

[118] We know nothing about the provincial mints of the Palaiologan period: Thessalonike, active till around 1370 and possibly Monemvasia or Mystra under Manuel II, according to the recent identification by J. Baker, "A Coinage for Byzantine Morea," *Revue numismatique* 162 (2006), pp. 395–416. Temporary striking in fourteenth-century Philadelphia is by no means certain.

[119] K.-P. Matschke, "Münzstätten, Münzer und Münzprägung im späten Byzanz," *Revue numismatique* 152 (1997), pp. 191–210.

of the Constantinople mint. The extreme variety in types of copper coinage, characteristic of post-1204 issues, points also to possible regular changes (on an annual or pluri-annual, trimestrial, basis) yielding seignorage profit on forced exchange, like the Western *renovationes*. The numerous privy marks on the *hyperpyra* have also led to similar speculation which cannot yet be proven. Many of them also designated the moneyers in charge.[120] This evolution of coinage production and its context illustrate the decisive role that Western money, particularly Italian, played in the circulation in the eastern Mediterranean, to which we now turn.

The rupture created in 1204 determined two radical changes in *monetary circulation*: on the one hand, a greater fragmentation into several regional monetary areas that depended on various new political entities resulted in a multiplicity of coins and weights and an increase in transaction costs. On the other hand, the exclusive use of Byzantine currency in imperial territory ended, while exactly the reverse evolution was taking place in the West, where certain states were imposing the exclusive circulation of their coinage. The opening of the monetary market had major consequences: following trade, the Italian "hard" currencies in gold and silver which were more stable and more abundant than Byzantine specie came to dominate exchanges.

In the first half of the thirteenth century, the *hyperpyron* had remained the currency of high-value transactions and long-distance trade in the Byzantine world, as evidenced by Romanian, Bulgarian, and Greek hoards. In Venetian territories, it was chosen as a money of account; in Sicily, the augustal of Frederick II Hohenstaufen was struck at the *hyperpyron* standard of $20\frac{1}{2}$ carats. The *hyperpyron* was fairly widespread until the 1320s and is still mentioned 50 years after it had ceased being struck.[121] But the steady decline in its fineness sapped its value in terms of the gold ducat of Venice, created in 1282, and the ducat replaced it in long-distance trade from the 1350s onward. The worsening financial situation of the Empire was compounded by the international monetary context of the "re-globalized" Mediterranean economy. Different gold to silver

---

[120] Grierson, *DOC* 5.1, pp. 63, 231; Hendy, *DOC* 4.1, pp. 112–21. Various estimates of the possible rhythm of these changes have been proposed in several articles by S. Bendall.

[121] See the summaries and brief quotations assembled in T. Bertelè, *Moneta veneziana e moneta bizantina* (Florence, 1973), pp. 38–58.

ratios in Byzantium and the Islamic world on the one hand, and Western Europe on the other entailed constant exports of metal and coins among these three zones. They resulted in the double reversal of the monetary systems, which we saw above.[122]

The gold ducat was not the only, nor the first Venetian coin to penetrate the monetary circulation in Byzantium. The silver ducat or grosso, created in 1194 as a multiple of the debased *denier* of insufficient value, reached the southern Balkans in the 1270s, where it replaced the English *esterlins* and the French or Frankish *deniers tournois*, introduced after 1204. Later on, it spread to Bulgaria and Thrace. Many Athonite documents mention cases of *hyperpyra* paid in "Venetian ducats" or in "ounces of ducats" until the mid-fourteenth century, when the shortage of silver in Venice put an end to this export. In Asia Minor and in the Balkans, the Ottoman aspers (*aqçe*) accompanied the Turkish advance. In fact, all these currencies were replacing the Byzantine coinage because it had become too unreliable and was insufficient in quantity.

The resulting circulation was a mix of local monetary markets for petty or small coinages (the *stavraton* did not find its way out of the immediate hinterland of Constantinople) with an "international" one where several renowned hard currencies coexisted: though dominant, the Venetian ducat was at par with Florentine florins or Genoese gold ducats, and the silver ducat was represented not only by the Venetian coin, but also by its many imitations, Serbian, Bulgarian, etc. The widespread variety of imitations, such as those of the gold ducat or the *gigliato* by Turkish and other states, shows the disruption of the minting monopoly that had prevailed before 1204 and the "competitive debasement" to which states resorted in order to gain the highest profit from seignorage. Now Byzantium was out of this game, as Gemistos Plethon bitterly complained in 1420: "it is truly absurd to employ these foreign copper pieces [probably the Venetian "colonial" *tornesello*] which are also bad coins, for which others reap the profit, whereas we, for our part, retain only the ridicule."[123]

---

[122] See A. M. Watson, "Back to Gold – and Silver," *Economic History Review 2nd series* 20/1 (1967), pp. 1–34; Spufford, *Money and its Use*; F. C. Lane, "Exportations vénitiennes d'or et d'argent de 1200 à 1450," in J. Day (ed.), *Études d'histoire monétaire* (Lille, 1984), pp. 32–3; J. Day, "The Levant Trade in the Middle Ages," *EHB* 2, pp. 807–14; J. Day, "A Note on Monetary Mechanisms, East and West," *EHB* 3, pp. 967–72.

[123] P. Lambros (ed.), *Palaiologeia kai Peloponnesiaka* (Athens, 1923), vol. III, p. 262.

A WEAK STATE ABANDONS THE ECONOMY

All elements of this heading hold true for the period after the 1340s, that is, for the last century or so of the existence of the Byzantine Empire; the state was, then, virtually dissolved. They are somewhat less true for the period between the 1320s and the 1340s, and progressively less true the farther back one goes in time. Yet the factors that led to the dissolution of the state can be perceived clearly during the reign of the first two Palaiologoi (1261–1328). After the 1340s, the state abandoned any semblance of its traditional role.

Policies and degrees of freedom

The Greek splinter states created after 1204 saw themselves as the continuators of the Komnenoi. In terms of the history of the economy, the question one must ask is to what degree they continued to structure the economy, and to be major players on the economic scene. Little is known about the Despotate of Epiros and the Empire of Trebizond in this respect, for lack of studies that would elucidate such issues. The policies of the emperors of Nicaea, in Asia Minor, are clearer. There is no question that the state here played a structural role. The hostility of Nicene emperors to international trade was specifically directed toward the West, despite treaties with the Venetians; John III Vatatzes passed sumptuary laws forbidding the use of foreign luxury goods.[124] The Nicene state, heir to large and now lordless tracts of land, was centered on agriculture. For the first time, considerable investments were made in the management of imperial estates, and encouragement was given to other large landlords to do the same.

The first two Palaiologan emperors, Michael VIII and Andronikos II, also had what may be termed an economic policy. They had a state apparatus that needed revenues, a foreign policy that entailed expenses, and imperial officials who enriched themselves through the performance of their duties.[125] The two emperors exercised a heavy fiscality, making use of regalian rights that had been instituted by the Komnenian emperors, and imposing extraordinary taxes to meet the expenses of recovering lost territories and defending the ones they had.[126] But they undermined their own policy by making

[124] Gregoras I, p. 43.   [125] Matschke, "Commerce, Trade," pp. 773–5.
[126] See above, and A. E. Laiou, "Le débat sur les droits du fisc et les droits régaliens au début du 14ᵉ siècle," *REB* 58 (2000), pp. 97–122.

even greater grants of privileges than earlier emperors. Extensive grants of territory and privileges to private individuals, cities and monasteries, even when some regalian rights were safeguarded, correspondingly reduced the economic power of the state. Michael VIII allowed *pronoia* lands to become hereditary, reinforcing this trend. On whom did the heavy fiscality fall? Clearly, on an ever-reduced tax base, which could less and less support the traditional needs of the state. A similar situation, in effect if not in intent, obtained with the privileges granted to Italian city-states. Byzantine emperors exercised a theoretical authority in economic matters when they granted commercial privileges. But their overall policy defies economic or fiscal logic. They lost revenues by making the Italians tax-exempt and allowing the Genoese a quasi-autonomy in their colony in Pera. At the same time, they charged in Constantinople a *kommerkion* of 10 per cent, the highest in the eastern Mediterranean. The Genoese collected fiscal revenues (customs duties of 2 per cent) as well as commercial benefits from Pera. The result, predictably, was that merchants went through Pera rather than through Constantinople, and the fiscal revenues from trade became picayune, without reducing the burden on non-privileged Byzantine merchants. A Byzantine historian wrote that, at about the middle of the fourteenth century, the Byzantine part of Constantinople collected 30,000 gold coins (debased, of course) a year from customs duties, whereas the Genoese in Pera had 200,000.[127] In 1347/8, John VI Kantakouzenos tried to remedy this situation by reducing the *kommerkion* to 2 per cent, the same rate as in Pera. But it was much too late by then. Clearly, in the long run the policy of fiscal harshness touching fewer and fewer people, combined with grants of privileges to more and more groups, is untenable. And so it proved to be.

In the course of the civil wars and the period that followed, the grant of privileges accelerated, and so did the deleterious results. The dissolution of the state proceeded apace, especially when the Ottomans, as a result of the great civil war that ended in 1354, established themselves in Europe.

The institutional support that the Byzantine state had traditionally given to economic activity was reduced to vanishing point by the last decades of the existence of the state. Certainly, the state did not integrate the domestic market any more; indeed, by the late thirteenth century, the domestic market as an integrated unit ceased

[127] Gregoras II, p. 841.

to exist, and was dissolved into the Italian-dominated international trade system. In terms of defense, the central state still and always retained the duty to provide for it. But at the local level defense was exercised by local strongmen of one sort or another, with the complicity or active encouragement of the state. The multiplication of towers, erected by individuals or monasteries, to provide refuge for peasants and others, and perhaps to store crops, is a visible sign of this devolution of authority.[128] The Byzantine state really retained only the possibility of defending its diminishing territory through diplomacy, a task which, it must be admitted, it carried out rather effectively for a long time.

A unified and trustworthy currency had been one of the comparative advantages of the Byzantine economy until the late twelfth century. This advantage was lost, as the territories of the Byzantine Empire saw the proliferation of Western, especially Venetian, coins used for transactions even among Byzantines, from the second half of the thirteenth century. By the late fourteenth century, coins of Byzantine issue circulated only in Constantinople and its hinterland. Thus the integrating role of the Byzantine coinage, with the attendant benefits for the Byzantines, was lost. Only legislation retained its traditional role, more or less; but new legislation with general applicability (as opposed to privileges) was rarely issued in the Palaiologan period.

The role of the state in the economy, then, was greatly reduced. The role of Constantinople was also reduced, since the functions it had filled in the past either disappeared, or changed. It is not even the case that Constantinople set fashion, and therefore elite demand, any more. That role seems to have devolved to Italy.

Not only was the role of the state reduced, it also changed fundamentally. Perhaps the most important action that only the state could still perform was to create institutional regulations affecting the conditions of trade. The grant of privileges, to Byzantines or foreigners, was the contribution of the Byzantine state to the developing trade system. This was a considerable prerogative, constantly reduced by being given away.

---

[128] A number of agglomerations whose main purpose was defense was created by Byzantine emperors in the period until the late 1320s; towers dotted the countryside; the fortifications of other cities were strengthened. For an example of the latter activity, in the small but strategically located city of Khrysoupolis in the Strymon Delta, see A. Dunn, "The Survey of Khrysoupolis, and Byzantine Fortifications in the Lower Strymon Valley," *JÖB* 32/3 (1982), pp. 605–14.

Others filled the void thus created. To some extent, the role of the state was replaced by that of the monasteries: certainly, monasteries and the Church generally now became the largest landowner, as the state had been in the past. But the most important part was played by the Italian city-states: it was they who integrated the politically weak and decentralized areas into an economic system. Economics worked where politics did not, until the Ottomans re-established political integration.

Ideology

The ideological discourse regarding economic matters becomes somewhat incoherent in this period, in the sense that two schools of thought and practice, with widely different implications, which had always coexisted, emerge more sharply now. It is perhaps to be expected that the state and its officials can be credited with rather limited action with a consistent ideological base, except for the efforts to re-establish state monopolies and to exercise regalian rights. It is, rather, from the pen of theologians, jurists and one philosopher that the two different positions emerge.

One set of attitudes continues trends that were in force in the twelfth century. It is represented by the writings of Thomas Magistros (Theodoulos Monachos) in the early fourteenth century and Nicholas Kavasilas later in that century. They place emphasis on private property and the importance of safeguarding it. This is a medieval defense of private property: what both are trying to safeguard against is the actions of the fisc, which endangered privileges and lands that as often as not had been granted by the state itself, the *pronoia*, for example, as well as ecclesiastical property. A more general argument, made by Kavasilas, that if private goods are not secure from state action people will stop working, so production will come to an end, has a good liberal air about it, but for all its general aspect it arises from specific and limited concerns.[129]

More interesting is the development of the protection afforded by the legislation on *laesio enormis*, a trend that is very much in line with the eleventh and twelfth centuries. In practice, the protection lapsed. Sales contracts of the thirteenth and fourteenth century frequently have the form of combined sale and donation, which safeguards the

---

[129] On this and what follows, see A. E. Laiou, "Economic Concerns and Attitudes of the Intellectuals of Thessalonike," *DOP* 57 (2003), pp. 205–23.

price against any subsequent contestation that might have been based on the legislation on pre-emption and on *laesio enormis*.[130] In the same period, a clause is inserted in the contracts by which the seller renounces all legal protections afforded him by the laws on *laesio enormis*. Thus, freedom of exchange remains untrammeled. When, in the middle of the fourteenth century, the great jurist Constantine Harmenopoulos wrote the legal compilation *Hexabiblos*, which had a very long life, he essentially did away with the protection afforded to those who sold at an exceedingly low price. The combined effect of all this was to make inoperative any definition of the just price other than the one that makes it equivalent to the market price. One might say that we have here an acceptance, by these individuals and in this respect, of the economic mechanisms of their day. At the very end of the fourteenth century, the Patriarchal tribunal of Constantinople, which also judged cases involving contracts, seems to have retained the memory of the older tenor of the legislation regarding extreme damage, and with it the notion of just price; on the other hand, it did not regard economic need as creating a presumption of force that annuls contracts.

A different set of ideological statements can be described as regressive, traditional or rigorist, depending on one's viewpoint. They all seek to reinstitute state controls according to the principle that the state has the right and duty to intervene in the economic process in order to serve the greater good of safeguarding justice in exchange and promoting social justice. This position emerged with clarity in moments of crisis, of which there were many. In the early fourteenth century, the Patriarch of Constantinople, Athanasios I, wrote urgent letters to the emperor regarding the famine then raging in Constantinople. He reminded the ruler that "the particular function of the imperial power is the exercise of justice," including the economic protection of the population, and that there was a just price and a just profit. He asked the emperor to take measures to stop the stockpiling of grain, and to regulate the price of grain and bread.[131]

Lending at interest became a topic of debate in mid-fourteenth-century Thessalonike, in the wake of the disasters and

---

[130] A. E. Laiou, "E diamorfose tes times tes ges sto Vyzantio," *Vyzantio, kratos kai koinonia: mneme Nikou Oikonomide* (Athens, 2003), pp. 344–6.

[131] A.-M. Maffry Talbot, *The Correspondence of Athanasius I Patriarch of Constantinople* (Washington, D.C., 1975), letters 93, 100, 106.

impoverishment brought about by civil wars and invasions. Three different important figures each in his own way adopted a hostile attitude toward lending at interest. The theologian Nicolas Kavasilas was the most vocal in this respect. He condemned lending at interest unequivocally and, uncharacteristically for Byzantium, contested the civil laws that permitted it to laymen. His argumentation was less interesting than that of the twelfth-century canonists, and far less interesting than that of Western theologians ever since Saint Thomas Aquinas, but it was presented with passion. The eminent jurist Constantine Harmenopoulos, and the less eminent but nevertheless very influential Matthew Vlastares, who produced a compendium of civil and ecclesiastical law, presented the civil laws that permitted lending at interest. But by slightly misrepresenting or misplacing the pertinent laws, they introduced a strong legal bias against interest-bearing loans. This is the first time, since the late ninth century, that such attitudes found their way into the legislation.[132]

George Gemistos Plethon, who lived in Mistra in the first half of the fifteenth century (d.1452), was a Platonist, who, among other things, wrote on political economy. His writings argue for the introduction of reforms that would create an economy very unlike what existed in his time. His ideal state was based on agriculture; industry and commerce had a subordinate and not very honorable place. He argued for the use value of land: it was a common good, to be used by anyone who could make it productive. Agricultural production should be equally shared by capital, labor and the security forces. In terms of international economic relations, he raised the concept of self-sufficiency to the macroeconomic level. Imports of necessities would be permitted, but exports would only be allowed in very specific situations, and with a tariff of 50 per cent. The use of money was discouraged, and international trade would ideally take place by barter. All of this was radical, and it was coherent. But it negated all contemporary realities, and sought refuge in a closed, self-sufficient, protectionist system. It was an extreme reaction to the open, international markets of the period, and to the position that the Byzantine lands (much reduced by now) had in it.[133] Interestingly, his ideas

[132] The fact that Harmenopoulos and Kavasilas had more "modern" positions regarding just price and private property is an example of the lack of coherence we have mentioned.

[133] Of course, Plethon's Platonism was important in the development of his ideology. There is a large bibliography on Plethon, mostly with interpretations that differ

have close parallels to the position of the "literati" in the famous debate on salt and iron, which had taken place in the Chinese court many centuries earlier (in 81 BC). In both cases, commercial expansion had apparently created great social and economic inequalities, which made some people search for a lost self-sufficient agricultural paradise.[134]

from this one. Apart from C. M. Woodhouse's *George Gemistos Plethon: The Last of the Hellenes* (Oxford, 1986), the interested reader should consult the works of S. P. Spentzas and Ch. P. Baltoglou.

[134] E. M. Gale (transl.), *Discourses on Salt and Iron: A Debate on State Control of Commerce and Industry* (Taipei, 1967), passim.

VI

THE BYZANTINE ECONOMY AS EXEMPLAR; THE BYZANTINE AND THE WESTERN MEDIEVAL ECONOMIES

·

The Byzantine Economy as Exemplar

Throughout its long history the Byzantine Empire had a mixed and complex economy. The state played a role whose importance and weight varied depending on the development of production. But it was never the sole economic actor, and it never operated in an environment where economic processes were suspended. In other words, market forces always operated, with greater or lesser impact. In the period immediately following the seventh-century crisis, the presence of the state and its fiscality was paramount. Even then, however, basic economic laws functioned: thus, when, in 769, Constantine V ordered the payment of base taxes in cash, the markets were flooded with agricultural products whose price plummeted. Until some time in the tenth century, the state was the major motor force; it set in motion monetary circulation, for example, by collecting much of the added value of agricultural production and paying it out in public works and salaries to officials and soldiers. Once that had been done, though, money and merchandise circulated through market channels, although to a varying degree depending on the economic sector and area. Liberalization, in the sense of a greater autonomy of the markets, including the land market, began in stages in the course of the tenth century and continued through the eleventh and twelfth, while after that it took a particular form, since it occurred within the conditions created by an Italian-dominated Mediterranean economy. The state still played an important role, whose specificities have been discussed in the appropriate chapters. This economic system, whose variations are such that they invite the conclusion that there are several systems succeeding each other, was characterized by coherence, functionality and flexibility, until it was disaggregated because of both structural problems and the international economic situation, sometime in the middle of the fourteenth century.

In the tenth century, the system that had evolved since the aftermath of the seventh-century crisis reached its maturity. It looks well structured. Agriculture, manufacture and commerce had been developing slowly but surely, in a secular trend of controlled growth. The state had increasingly guaranteed safety and put into effect policies that promoted stability. One is the village community, which was much more than a fiscal invention, functioning as a structuring mechanism that allowed peasants to collectively assure the productive capacity of the land and also to increase it, through land clearance. Another is the effort to prevent accumulation of land or resources in the hands of individuals, thus ensuring a sort of social justice, although perhaps hampering rapid economic growth. Another still is the oversight of manufacturing and trade in Constantinople, though not, it seems, in the provinces. The policies were grounded in and further promoted a specific ideological stance as to the social and economic role of the state.

The system outlined above was coherent but not free of tensions. At the time when it mattered, the state had provided security and stability. But the growth thus engendered created new opportunities for landlords, artisans, traders, and some peasants. By the tenth century, the rise in production, accompanying demographic growth, and the multiplication of towns and cities created favorable conditions for internal trade, and was one of the factors that led the elite to seek the accumulation of resources. At the same time, elite demand for luxury and semi-luxury products grew, and was at the base of the growth of regional manufactures. Specialized production of pottery, glass and textiles took place in a number of cities. Trade, both regional and international, quickened, and that before the appearance of Western merchants. New possibilities of enrichment appeared, both in agricultural and other production and through exchange. Government regulations were, as a result, relaxed, both in the countryside and, it would seem, in the cities. A significant part of agricultural production took place on large estates, which became important players in the countryside. Trade was freer than before, even though the privileges granted to Western merchants remind us that we are dealing with a medieval, not a modern concept of the freedom of trade. Ideology, too, evolved, to accommodate the pursuit of profit and to insist on the sanctity of contracts. The state remained a major actor, but the role of other actors increased considerably, so that the system now in effect differed considerably from the earlier one.

In the realm of economics, the tenth-century system did not collapse. It evolved into a different one that conformed to evolving realities. This flexibility was to a considerable extent facilitated by state action. However, the political system, extractive and authoritarian in the twelfth century, gave rise to internal tensions and showed itself incapable of holding the Empire together. Such was the situation in 1204.[1]

The thirteenth century continued to be a period of economic growth in certain sectors. As the power of the state was reduced, especially after the late thirteenth century and catastrophically after the 1340s, the importance of other economic actors rose commensurately. However, this is far from an example of a liberal or neo-liberal paradise. The reduced size and economic weight of the state eventually disaggregated the "national" market, although not the regional or local markets. At the same time, international developments worked to the disadvantage of the Byzantine economy. In an increasingly internationalized commercial world, economic power was in the hands of those who controlled commerce. Progress in commercial techniques, shipping, banking, manufacturing became rapid in parts of Western Europe in the thirteenth century and after. In this world, Byzantine products could not compete, and the Byzantine economy itself became, to some degree, ancillary. Thus, Byzantium entered in a weakened state the pan-European crisis of the 1340s, and, faced also with the expansionary Ottoman state, had fewer powers of recovery. Individuals prospered, but the system finally failed, in the last century of the existence of the Byzantine state.

The failure of the last hundred years cannot obscure the achievements of the centuries that preceded it. The Byzantine economy was

---

[1] M. Hendy has reached a similar conclusion in his "'Byzantium, 1081–1204:' The Economy Revisited, Twenty Years On," in Hendy, *The Economy, Fiscal Administration and Coinage of Byzantium* (Northampton, 1989), art. III, p. 48. We disagree, however, with his concept of a state-dominated economy even in the twelfth century.

strong and successful for a very long time. Indeed, it is probably the most successful example of a mixed economy in the European Middle Ages. This is a statement which would have surprised Byzantinists of the past. The realization that the economy was flourishing in the eleventh and twelfth centuries is a discovery of the last few decades; that some sectors continued to grow in the thirteenth, a still more recent scholarly position. As for the fact that it was a mixed economy, with all that implies, although a few voices have mentioned it in the past, the most common position has been that this was a highly protectionist economy, with overwhelming state intrusion, and that there was a conflict between state action and market forces, the existence of one virtually excluding the other.

Scholars have argued that "protectionism" was good (it ensured the survival of the state) and that it was bad (it sapped the dynamism of the economy, and made Byzantine merchants sedentary and unable to function outside their cocoon). Much of this is colored, explicitly or implicitly, by post-nineteenth century evaluations of the economic success or failure of state-dominated systems or the "free market." That the Byzantine economy was a mixed one is an observable fact, as we hope to have demonstrated. The evaluation of this fact can be helped to some extent by present-day development and growth theory, some practitioners of which recognize a positive role as well as "failures" (that is, limitations) in both state intervention and the market. The contribution of the state in guaranteeing security and safety, creating infrastructures, safeguarding institutional mechanisms, offering legal guarantees and, in modern societies, promoting health, education, and research is generally recognized. The "failures" of state intervention revolve around the potential rigidity of planning, the inability to respond quickly to changed conditions, the stifling of initiative and the possibility of domination by narrow interest groups. The benefits of the market are thought to be the liberation of private initiative, flexibility, quick adjustment to changing business conditions. The "failures" lie in the fact that no market is perfect; in the possibility of monopolistic markets; in the fact that individuals or institutions may have poor information, or may respond in ways that are not beneficial.[2] Above all, there is the possibility that the impersonal market creates economic and social inequalities,

[2] N. Stern, "The Economics of Development: A Survey," *Economic Journal* 99 (1989), p. 616.

sometimes beyond what each society will tolerate.[3] The categoriza-
tion and the vocabulary are modern, but some of the major aspects
of the two systems existed in the past, and indeed some were articulated in the famous debate on iron and salt, in China, in the first
century BC.[4]

If one looks at medieval realities, one will find elements of the
advantages and disadvantages of both systems in the Byzantine economy. But the fact is that for a long time, for seven hundred years, if one
begins with the seventh century, the combination of state action and
private enterprise was felicitous, the advantages of both outweighing
the flaws. Byzantium was prosperous through the twelfth century,
indeed more prosperous than most parts of Western Europe, with a
higher standard of living and probably a higher basic literacy than in
the West.[5] It was a system that, far from being immutable, proved
itself to be flexible, preserving for a long time the fragile equilibrium
between growth and stability. To that extent, it is an exemplar of a
successful mixed economy, as impressive an achievement as Byzantine
art.

The Byzantine and the Western medieval economies

Discussions of the Byzantine economy almost always compare it,
explicitly or implicitly, with the economies of Western Europe in
the Middle Ages. Comparisons are sometimes drawn for the wrong
reason: Western Europe eventually developed capitalism, and thus
becomes a model against which all other economies are examined,
and usually found wanting. This, in our view, is a historiographical and methodological error. There are, however, other, more solid

---

[3] For the most recent statement regarding the positive role of state action, in conjunction with the market, see J. E. Stiglitz and A. Charlton, *Fair Trade for All: How
Trade Can Promote Development* (Oxford, 2005), esp. pp. 11–40.

[4] On this, see Introduction, p. 3.

[5] For the promotion of basic literacy by the state, see N. Oikonomidès, "Literacy in
Thirteenth-Century Byzantium: An Example from Western Asia Minor," in J. S.
Langdon, S. W. Reinert, J. S. Allen and Ch. P. Ioannides (eds.), *TO EΛΛHNIKON:
Studies in Honor of Speros Vryonis, Jr.* (New York, 1993), pp. 223–65. For a comparison between Byzantium, England and continental Europe in the twelfth century,
arguing that the Byzantine Empire was the richest part of Europe, and at the upper
limits of the European GDP, see J. Luiten Van Zanden, "Cobb-Douglas in pre-
modern Europe: Simulating Early Modern Growth," Working Paper, International
Institute of Social History University of Utrecht (May 2005), pp. 17–18.

reasons to attempt the comparison. Both Byzantium and parts of Western Europe came out of the Late Roman system and the crisis it underwent. The Roman heritage included legal concepts, laws, and structures, retained in Byzantium, recovered in the West, while a shared Christianity had a powerful input into economic ideology. Long-term factors such as climate and land are common to the Mediterranean areas. Byzantium and Western Europe were, at various times, in contact, and, beginning in the eleventh century, the economic contacts became intense. There are also structural elements shared by Western and Byzantine systems.

Any comparison must avoid the fallacy of the "model." There are other pitfalls, too, the most important of which is to think that there was one Western European medieval economy. "Western" Europe shifted in terms of geography as various areas were eventually adopted or forced into the religious, cultural and economic framework originally elaborated in Francia or in Rome. Most importantly, the Carolingian core expanded northward and eastward, into the lands bordering the North and Baltic seas. Furthermore, economic historians of the Middle Ages have made it abundantly clear that regional economies were of the utmost importance in this fragmented world. There are, therefore, many Western economies. There is little point in picking and choosing parts of Europe to compare: whereas Byzantine agrarian development might look like that of Italy, the role of the state would be closer to that of the German or the Anglo-Norman state. Nor is it possible to trace developments in various European regions over time and compare each to Byzantium. One may make comparisons of specific developments or concepts, or periods, and to some extent this has been done.[6] At the more general level, one may compare structures and study dynamics, or the effects of major events, economic or other. One may also discuss the different sets of possibilities for economic growth and development in the medieval economies in question.[7]

---

[6] C. Wickham has done this successfully on a number of occasions. See, for example, his "Overview: Production, Distribution and Demand, II," in I. L. Hansen and C. Wickham (eds.), *The Long Eighth Century* (Leiden–Boston–Cologne, 2000), pp. 345–77.

[7] References to the vast bibliography on the various Western European economies will be made very sparingly. An excellent synthesis of the scholarship as it stood a decade ago may be found in P. Contamine, M. Bompaire, St. Lebecq and Jean-Luc Sarrazin, *L'économie médiévale* (Paris, 1993).

Strikingly, there is a broad chronological coincidence in economic developments from the seventh century until some time in the thirteenth.[8] The early period of crisis is a general phenomenon, although much less acute in Francia and northern Europe, which had not suffered from the Justinianic plague as southern lands had done. Underpopulation, however, was general, as was the simplification of economic structures and the low degree of economic differentiation. Because of regional differences, the recovery came at different points. It began early in the northern parts of Europe, starting at any point between 550 and 650. It came late in the western Mediterranean and Italy, sometime around 850. In Byzantium, it is evident already in the late eighth century: the existence of the state and institutions, the survival of some cities and exchange had prevented fragmentation and facilitated recovery.[9] The modalities of recovery, however, exhibit certain similarities overall. Demographic and agricultural recovery go hand in hand. Still generally speaking, once recovery starts, there is a broad upward trend, with periods of interruption and regression, as in those parts of Western Europe that were subject to Norman invasions in the course of the ninth century and to Magyar raids in the first half of the tenth. In Byzantium there does not seem to have been an interruption to the secular trend, unless the paucity of the sources obscures temporary crises. Broadly speaking, then, there is a general upward trend, with acceleration in the eleventh and twelfth centuries. A break in the pattern comes in the thirteenth century, when, as we have seen, developments diverged. The mid-fourteenth century crisis affected all of Europe and the Near East, although it did so differentially. When recovery began in Western Europe late in that century, the Western economies had become much more complex and much more dynamic than the Byzantine one.

---

[8] This has already been noted by J. Lefort and J.-M. Martin for agriculture, in relation to the northern coast of the western Mediterranean (J. Lefort, J.-M. Martin, "L'organisation de l'espace rural: Macédoine et Italie du Sud (Xe–XIIIe siècle)," in V. Kravari, J. Lefort and C. Morrisson (eds.), *Hommes et richesses dans l'Empire byzantin*, II (Paris, 1991), p. 260), and A. Harvey more generally: *Economic Expansion in the Byzantine Empire 900–1200* (Cambridge, 1989), pp. 259–62; cf. P. Toubert, "Byzantium and the Mediterranean Agrarian Civilisation," *EHB* I, pp. 385–6.

[9] See Wickham, "Overview," pp. 373 ff. and Contamine et al., *L'économie*, pp. 49–60. Cf. M. McCormick, *Origins of the European Economy, Communications and Commerce AD, 300–900* (Cambridge, 2001), p. 791.

The similarities in chronology demand an explanation. They are due in part to the similarity of structures and factors of growth. In all areas, agriculture was preponderant as an economic activity, no surprise in a pre-industrial society. It was a labor-intensive activity, and so demographic patterns played an important role: the period of growth in all areas goes in tandem with population growth, until the early fourteenth century. Agricultural activity and human settlement were helped by the "little climatic optimum," which began sometime in the ninth century, lasted until the late thirteenth century, and had beneficial effects on all European areas.[10] Polyculture is equally a general phenomenon in pre-industrial European agriculture, especially in the Mediterranean regions. Still, a certain regional specialization came in early, whatever the original cause: whether the impulse came from the expansion into new lands and the different resource endowments of large estates, as has been suggested for parts of Western Europe,[11] or from the needs of the state and a large *metropolis*, as well as the existence of towns, as in the Byzantine Empire.

The modalities of agricultural development and growth differ significantly. In Western Europe, especially in the north-west, but also in Italy in the mid-tenth century and after, these developments took place in the framework of the large estate. In Byzantium, the village structure and an economy based on small farms and villages were very old,[12] whereas in Western Europe the concentration of the population into villages was a development of the Middle Ages, coming at different points in different areas.[13] In Byzantium, the first stages of growth took place in the framework of the village, further structured by the state which was pursuing its own fiscal needs.

---

[10] For the effects in Byzantium, see B. Geyer, "Physical Factors in the Evolution of the Landscape and Land Use," *EHB* 1, pp. 42–3.

[11] A. Verhulst, *The Carolingian Economy* (Cambridge, 2002), pp. 60, 101–2; P. Toubert, "La part du grand domaine dans le décollage économique de l'Occident (VIIIe–Xe siècles)," in his *L'Europe dans sa première croissance: de Charlemagne à l'an mil* (Paris, 2004), p. 83; D. C. North and R. P. Thomas, *The Rise of the Western World: A New Economic History* (Cambridge, 1973), p. 26.

[12] A. E. Laiou, "The Byzantine Village (5th–14th Century)," in J. Lefort, C. Morrisson and J.-P. Sodini (eds.), *Les villages dans l'Empire byzantin, IVe–XVe siècle* (Paris, 2005), pp. 36 ff.

[13] C. Wickham, "The Development of Villages in the West, 300–900," and B. Cursente, "Les villages dans l'Occident médiéval (IXe–XIVe siècle)," both in Lefort et al., *Villages*, pp. 54–69 and 71–88 respectively.

Eventually, as we have seen, in Byzantium too the large estate became the important structuring factor. It was a different large estate from that in the West. The Byzantine Empire never knew the Carolingian system of the bipartite manor, with a large domanial reserve under direct cultivation, and peasant tenures.[14] In Byzantium, the domanial reserve was always small, except perhaps on imperial estates, and small-scale exploitation by peasant households was always the dominant form. Even here, however, there are intriguing convergences, for in the West, with the major exception of England, the units of land under direct cultivation started decreasing in size in the middle of the ninth century, a very slow evolution that apparently continued throughout the Middle Ages.[15] It has been argued that the small peasant tenure is a rational economic decision even for landlords, at a time of demographic growth and a time also when no large economies of scale were possible in agriculture.[16] The same economic logic underlies the slow reduction of imperial estates in Byzantium. If small tenures make economic sense, then one might argue that the Byzantine system of small-scale exploitation was, in fact, an advantageous one.

A major difference lies in the fact that the Byzantine Empire did not develop the *seigneurie banale*, with the charges on men and activities (the use of mills, or ovens, for example) that became so important for the revenues of estate owners in Western Europe. Such a development was doubtless hindered by the strong presence of the state. On the other hand, the Byzantine estate owners developed, in the eleventh century, sophisticated systems of accounting, estate management, and reinvestment, quite unknown in the West. Also due to the persistence of the state is the higher monetization of the agrarian economy and the consequent existence of salaried labor much earlier than in Western Europe, where it begins to play an important role in the later Middle Ages.[17] Thus, broad similarities in response to demographic and climatic factors reveal, under closer examination, rather important specificities which are connected with different power structures; this should be sufficient warning against economic determinism.

---

[14] On this, see Verhulst, *The Carolingian Economy*, pp. 33 ff.
[15] Toubert, "La part du grand domaine," pp. 95 ff.; Contamine et al., *L'économie*, pp. 157 ff., 225 ff., 361 ff.
[16] Toubert, "La part du grand domaine," pp. 95 ff.
[17] Toubert, "Byzantium and the Mediterranean Agrarian Civilization," pp. 389–91.

Insofar as the urban economy is concerned, there is chronological coincidence in the growth of number and size of cities. There are also functional similarities: exchange between the city and the countryside plays a role in economic differentiation and growth everywhere; cities are or become important centers of manufacturing. The chronological coincidence is interesting, and simple to explain at a first level: increase of population, production and productivity makes possible the congregation of people in urban agglomerations or proto-cities, and stimulates exchange which leads to further urban growth. The growing needs of administration work in the same direction. However, the differences are much greater than in the agricultural economies, and at a deeper level the phenomenon is much too complex to discuss here. Furthermore, the study of the origins of towns in Western Europe is an ongoing pursuit, while that of Byzantine towns needs further systematic investigation.[18] Of interest to Byzantine history is the growing consensus that in north-western Europe before the year 1000 there were proto-urban centers, with a combination of artisanal, commercial and agricultural activities.[19] This places in proper perspective the fact that early Byzantine towns also had a variety of functions including defense and ecclesiastical and administrative ones. The significant difference is that the great estate did not play the important role in commerce and in the formation of urban agglomerations that it did in the West; the state played that role. In the beginnings of the period of economic recovery, there is little sign in Byzantium of the siting of manufacturing in the manorial setting, as there was in Carolingian Europe.[20] True, there was, in the late ninth century, a lady in the Peloponnese whose vast estates may have produced silk cloth and woolen carpets, but this is a single piece of information; and it is possible that the production took place in the city of Patras.

[18] R. Hodges, *Dark Age Economics: The Origins of Towns and Trade AD 500–1000* (London, 1989); R. Hodges and B. Hobley, *The Rebirth of Towns in the West, AD 700–1050,* Council for British Archaeology, Research Report 68 (1988); H. Clarke and B. Ambrosiani, *Towns in the Viking Age* (Leicester, 1996); A. Verhulst, *The Rise of Cities in Northwest Europe* (Cambridge, 1999); H. K. Schultze, "Grundherrschaft und Stadtentstehung," in K. Flink and W. Janssen (eds.), *Grundherrschaft und Stadtenstehung am Niederrhein* (Klever Archiv 9) (Cleves, 1989), pp. 9–22.

[19] A. Verhulst, "Marchés, marchands et commerce au Haut Moyen Âge dans l'historiographie récente," *Mercati et mercanti nell'alto medioevo: l'area Euroasiatica et l'area Mediterranea* (Spoleto, 1993), pp. 41–3.

[20] Verhulst, *The Carolingian Economy*, pp. 72 ff.

The Byzantine Empire, ruralized as it became in the wake of the seventh-century crisis, never ceased to have towns that functioned both as administrative centers and as centers of at least low-level exchange; the urban expansion, observable in the tenth century and after, did not arise ex nihilo.[21] Towns existed, they had markets, money circulated in them, and most archeological and textual evidence of manufacturing places this activity in towns. The advances of archeology, which now allow us to speak of Byzantine cities as centers of production already in the late eighth and ninth centuries, increasingly so in the tenth–twelfth centuries, have removed a fictional difference between Byzantine and Western cities. In fact, Byzantine production, which is urban and with greater specialization, appears more advanced than the polyvalent domanial production of Western Europe in the early medieval period. In the late Middle Ages, however, the existence of large manufacturing and commercial cities in Flanders and Italy is one of the markers of the divergent development of East and West. Finally, the existence of a *megalopolis* throughout Byzantine history, with all its implications, is a phenomenon that Western medieval Europe would not experience for a long time. So, if one ignores Constantinople, the function of Western and Byzantine cities in, let us say, the twelfth century, is very similar, but the origins and the dynamic differ very considerably.

Economic growth, both in Byzantium and in Western Europe, also involved an acceleration of exchange. Scholars have different and varied views on the importance of trade in pre-industrial economies, and specifically in medieval economies. Different opinions also exist on the relative importance of town–country exchange and regional trade versus international trade or of the role of bulk trade and luxury trade. They cannot be summarized here. Of importance to us is that in Western medieval historiography the concept of a Commercial Revolution, eloquently argued by R. S. Lopez,[22] has given way to an understanding of the slow process of the development of exchange, in which both professional merchants (especially in Italy) and agents of manorial lords played a role.[23] The merchant, whose origins may

---

[21] Northern Italy too had a certain urban continuity: see B. Ward-Perkins, "The Towns of Northern Italy: Rebirth or Renewal?" in Hodges and Hobley, *The Rebirth*, pp. 16–27.

[22] R. S. Lopez, *The Commercial Revolution of the Middle Ages* (Englewood Cliffs, N.J., 1971).

[23] Verhulst, "Marchés, marchands," pp. 23–43.

well have been manorial, became progressively more professional in the eleventh century. In Byzantium, of course, no manorial origin can be conceived. However, there is evidence, in the seventh and eighth centuries, of imperial officials who also functioned as merchants, their commercial activity being tied to their office in an oligopolistic way, although the pursuit of that activity was subject to economic possibilities and laws.[24] New research has established the existence of exchange in Byzantium, throughout the medieval period, and the uninterrupted existence of professional merchants, whose role increased in the tenth century and after. It is now clear that provincial merchants played an important role, which was not controlled by the state, and that merchants became rich and powerful in the eleventh and twelfth centuries. The trajectory of merchants and exchange in the period through the twelfth century is similar in East and West. The origins and modalities of trade and merchants were different. And so was their development: in the later Middle Ages, neither the large-scale enterprises of a few Italian or northern commercial houses, nor the long-range trade of Westerners can be found in the Byzantine Empire, for reasons that have been discussed. In this context, it is worth noting that the development of trade is not always universally beneficial, as the experience of the Byzantine economy of the later period indicates.

The role of money in medieval economies is a difficult area. There are very significant differences within Western Europe itself, differences both chronological and geographical, depending on the status of regional economies and on the power of the various states. It can only be reiterated here that the Byzantine Empire throughout most of its history, with the exception of the last century or so, had a unitary monetary system, guaranteed by the government, which facilitated exchange considerably and reduced the cost of transactions. That "dollar of the Middle Ages"[25] was one of the comparative advantages of the Byzantine economy. The relative monetization of the Byzantine agrarian economy because of the payment of tax in coin has already been stressed, even as the

---

[24] N. Oikonomidès, "Silk Trade and Production in Byzantium from the Sixth to the Ninth Century: The Seals of Kommerkiarioi," *DOP* 40 (1986), pp. 33–53. On the debate regarding this article, see above, Chapter III, p. 80.

[25] The term was coined by R. S. Lopez, "The Dollar of the Middle Ages," *Journal of Economic History* 11 (1951), pp. 209–34 (= Lopez, *Byzantium and the World Around it: Economic and International Relations* (London, 1978), art. VII).

viscosity of monetary circulation dependent on fiscality has been recognized.[26]

Economic ideology exhibits the same pattern of broad similarity and important differences. The Byzantines had an institutional advance of over 300 years in comparison to the West. They developed the practice of partnership with proportional gains and losses at least as early as the eighth century; its Western equivalent, the *colleganza* or *commenda* is first documented in Venice in the late eleventh century – a Byzantine advance of no mean importance. In Byzantium, the development probably had nothing to do with an effort to avoid the opprobrium of lending at interest, as has been argued for Western Europe. Attitudes toward lending at interest show how non-economic factors can influence economic behavior and legislation. Both Byzantine and Western theologians opposed lending at interest, on similar religious arguments. But in Byzantium civil law prevailed, and as a result, interest-bearing loans were not forbidden to laymen except for a very brief period in the ninth century. That banking did not develop in Byzantium in the form it acquired in Western Europe is due to reasons other than the attitude toward loans.

As similarities and differences between the Byzantine economy and various Western European economies become apparent, the former no longer looks strange, exotic, or an aberration, and becomes a part of the European economic universe. In this development, the adoption of similar epistemological approaches by scholars has been significant. To take but one example, the role of demand in all these economies has been recognized by scholars of both broad areas as an important factor in economic development. Chris Wickham has made elite demand an explanatory tool, while already in 1989 Alan Harvey had entitled one of the chapters of his important book "The Pattern of Demand."[27] Once historians use the same analytical tools, similarities and differences are brought to the fore. Elite demand is important in pre-industrial societies, and especially in the sectors of international exchange (whether trade or gift) and secondary production, although the demand for expensive agricultural goods also affects the rural economy.

[26] Toubert, "Byzantium and the Mediterranean Agrarian Civilisation," p. 387; A. E. Laiou, "Use and Circulation of Coins in the Despotate of Epiros," *DOP* 55 (2001), pp. 207–15.
[27] Wickham, "Overview," passim; Harvey, *Expansion*, Chapter 5.

The investigation of patterns of demand has proved fruitful for the study of the Byzantine economy. It has also underlined, yet again, a major difference with most parts of Western Europe. Especially in the Early and High Middle Ages, elite demand in most parts of Western Europe means primarily the demand (and the purchasing power) of the aristocracy, eventually of the feudal aristocracy. In Byzantium, for a long time demand was concentrated in the state and the ruling class which was state-derived and state-oriented: the officialdom, civil, military and ecclesiastical. That had a powerful impact on both production and distribution. The changing nature of elite demand also influenced economic development: as the aristocracy became more firmly established, as their territorial and revenue base increased, so demand rose. The city populations eventually came to exercise effective demand, especially for semi-luxury goods like ceramics and textiles, and even special wines and cheeses. The production of semi-luxury goods proved to be a dynamic sector of the economy everywhere in Europe, whether that was Flemish, French, Italian and eventually English woolen cloth or fustians, or half-silks, or pottery and glass. It also was, for a time, an important sector in Byzantine production and exchange. In prestige goods, Byzantium had the upper hand until both the political and the economic power of the state declined, in the thirteenth century.

The linkage of production, distribution and consumption would seem to be intuitive. Yet in the otherwise fruitful theoretical concern with forms of exchange – economic and non-economic, gift exchange versus commercialized exchange – and in the theoretical discussions regarding the appropriateness or otherwise of economic analysis of ancient and medieval societies, production and distribution have become disjointed.[28] Much of the discussion focuses on exchange, without engaging the process of production which, on the other hand, has been much discussed by both Marxist and neoclassical economic historians. The disjunction has fortunately been questioned, and Western medievalists now investigate the entire economic process.[29] In Byzantine historiography, the separation has been

---

[28] J. Moreland, "Concepts of the Early Medieval Economy," in Hansen and Wickham, *The Long Eighth Century*, pp. 1–34, esp. pp. 18 ff., "An Economy without Production." For an overview of the various theoretical approaches, see A. E. Laiou, "Economic and Non-Economic Exchange," *EHB* 2, pp. 681–96.

[29] For example, Toubert, "La part du grand domaine," has discussed the expansion of the manor in terms not only of production but also of distribution. Similar

less acute, partly for lack of theoretical discussion; however, the systematic linkage between production and distribution has appeared relatively recently in the bibliography, in the works of A. Harvey and J. Lefort among others.

The Byzantine Empire had an integrated economy, given a degree of cohesion by the state. It functioned, for a long time, as a large economic whole, with an important domestic market. In terms of resources and achievement, it was either superior to or could compete very successfully with any European economy, until the late twelfth century. However, Western Europe had certain fundamental advantages whose import took hold beginning with the twelfth century. One was the existence of vast, resource-rich and potentially productive areas in the north-eastern and central parts: what became eastern Germany, the Baltic lands, and Hungary. The persistent colonization of these territories, starting as the Carolingian state declined, and continuing with special forcefulness in the twelfth and thirteenth centuries, not only relieved population pressures but also created new resources by stimulating agricultural production and trade in the north-eastern areas. This was a very great economic advantage. In the Byzantine Empire, there was land clearance locally, as there was, of course, in Western Europe. Some new lands in eastern Asia Minor may have been reclaimed in the eleventh century. But there were no great spaces into which to expand, and that important aspect of Western history has no counterpart in Byzantium.

Another important resource which became available to Western Europeans but not to Byzantines was the renewal of sources of metal supplies. The extraction of iron increased spectacularly in the eleventh and twelfth centuries. The opening of silver mines in Goslar in the tenth century, and then, in the twelfth century, in many places, of which Saxony is perhaps the best known, increased the stock of metal available for monetary use. In Byzantium, there is no evidence of discovery of major new mines; indeed, with the loss of Asia Minor, many of the mineral resources were no longer available to the Byzantines. The spectacular expansion of Serbia in the fourteenth century, in the wake of the exploitation of the silver and gold mines of Novo

concerns run through the works of A. Verhulst and the collective work of Contamine et al., *L'économie*. See also J. Moreland, "The Significance of Production in Eighth-Century England," in Hansen and Wickham, *The Long Eighth Century*, pp. 69–104.

Brdo, highlights the importance of the availability of large quantities of silver.[30]

Large-scale colonization and the discovery of new resources increased the endowments of various areas of Western Europe. Just as important, indeed fundamental, was the eventual linkage of two areas of Europe that were well along in terms of economic growth: the northern areas and the Mediterranean. They had, of course, been in contact before.[31] But over time, contacts became systematic, large-scale and constant. For the land route, the role of the fairs of Champagne in the twelfth century needs no elaboration. By sea, the Genoese sent their first ships to Flanders in the 1270s, and the Venetians were not far behind. In 1291, some intrepid Genoese merchants tried to reach India by circumnavigating Africa. From the late thirteenth century on, these cities organized regular annual voyages to Flanders. Whereas it would probably be an exaggeration to speak of economic integration, it is nonetheless a fact that this linkage promoted the exchange of differentiated commodities and merchandise over a vast area. In the meantime, Italian merchants had created a Mediterranean trade system. All of this created a dynamic with immense possibilities. The development of manufacturing, the spread of commercial and banking techniques, even the opening of the Atlantic took place in a Europe that was in closer economic contact than ever before. Not all areas developed; and the system had many tensions and points of weakness, as the problems of the mid-fourteenth century showed. But in this Europe, the Byzantine economy occupied a peripheral position.

This ultimate divergence is not explicable in economic terms alone. The pattern of Western expansion, one where the conquest of new lands and new markets was carried out by a combination of military and economic means, was foreign to Byzantium, where economic activity outside the state did not depend on force of arms, the conquest of Bulgaria always excepted. An array of political, military and cultural factors have to be taken into account for a proper understanding of this difference. In any case, it has been shown here that agriculture continued to grow, and trade flourished in Byzantine lands in the thirteenth century and part of the fourteenth. The real failure was political in the first instance.

---

[30] On mines, see Contamine et al., *L'économie*, pp. 180, 197, 250 ff.
[31] McCormick's *Origins of the European Economy* has made this abundantly clear.

Advances in both Western medieval and Byzantine history have made these two areas look more like each other than they did a few decades ago. Interestingly, the comparison we attempted here was made between economies at a higher level of complexity or development than historians would have thought until recently. This is true especially of the early period, for which Western medievalists now propose a much more robust economy than many of their predecessors. Some Byzantinists have also started to see that the "Dark Ages," a designation that should not be used, were not so very dark; and the eleventh and twelfth centuries have been rehabilitated in Byzantine historiography. Nevertheless, each economy has to be evaluated in its own terms, and comparison has its limits. The Byzantine economy was far from backward, and the fallacy must be avoided of evaluating it against the eventual rise of capitalism in Western Europe. After all, industrial capitalism did not develop until the late eighteenth century, and its development was neither continuous nor inevitable.[32] When one looks at the Byzantine economy on its own terms and in its own time, the judgement must be that this was a flexible and dynamic economy, which was successful in terms of growth but also provided some important needs of the people: basic necessities, and often a surplus; relative safety; relatively good communications; even a fairly extensive basic literacy, that is, all the factors which today are recognized as constituting true economic development.

[32] K. Pomeranz, *The Great Divergence: China, Europe and the Making of the Modern World Economy* (Princeton and Oxford, 2000).

SELECT BIBLIOGRAPHY

———————— • ————————

This bibliography includes the titles of books and articles that are most pertinent to the subject at hand. Articles which have been included in a volume of the author's collected studies are not cited here in their original form. In the text, we provide the original title and publication details of the article, and direct the reader to the appropriate volume of collected studies. A similar policy has been followed with articles in Symposia volumes. Individual chapters of the *Economic History of Byzantium* (A. E. Laiou, editor-in-chief) are mentioned, with their authors, in the text, but not in the Bibliography. While this is not the best possible choice, it is optimal given the restrictions created by the small size of the volume.

Under Primary Sources, we include not all the sources that underlie the text, but only those specifically cited therein.

PRIMARY SOURCES

P. J. Alexander, "A Chrysobull of the Emperor Andronicus II Palaeologus in Favor of the See of Kanina in Albania," *Byzantion* 15 (1940–1), pp. 167–207

Archives de l'Athos (Paris, 1945–2006): publication of medieval documents preserved in the monastic archives of Mount Athos, with abstracts and comments; 15 vols. publ. to date

W. Ashburner, "The Farmer's Law," *Journal of Hellenic Studies* 30 (1910), 85–108 (Greek text) and 32 (1912), pp. 68–95 (English translation)

Athanasios I of Constantinople: A.-M. Maffry-Talbot (ed.), *The Correspondence of Athanasios I Patriarch of Constantinople* (Washington, D.C., 1975)

Attaleiates, Michael: I. Bekker (ed.), *Michaelis Attaleiote Historia* (Bonn, 1853)

Badoer, Giacomo: U. Dorini and T. Bertelè, *Il libro dei conti di Giacomo Badoer* (Rome, 1956)

G. Bertelè, *Il libro dei conti di Giacomo Badoer (Costantinopoli 1436–1440) Complemento e indici*, (Padova, 2002): index

Benjamin bar Jonah of Tudela: M. V. Adler (transl.), *The Itinerary of Benjamin of Tudela* (Malibu, 1983)

L. Burgmann and P. Magdalino (eds.), "Michael VIII on Maladministration," *Fontes Minores* VI (1984), pp. 377–90

Chomatianos, Demetrios: G. Prinzing (ed.), *Demetrii Chomateni ponemata diaphora* (Berlin, 2002)

Choniates, Michael: S. Lambros (ed.), *Michael Akominatou tou Choniatou ta sozomena*, 2 vols. (Athens, 1879–80; reprint Groningen, 1968)

Choniates, Niketas: J. L. van Dieten (ed.), *Historia*, 2 vols. (Berlin–New York, 1975)

Constantine VII Porphyrogennetos: J. F. Haldon (ed.), *Three Treatises on Imperial Military Expeditions* (Vienna, 1990)

Doukas: V. Grecu (ed.), *Ducas, Istoria Turco-Bizantina* (Bucharest, 1958)

H. J. Magoulias (transl.), *Doukas and the Fall of Byzantium to the Ottomans* (Detroit, 1975)

Gregoras, Nikephoros: L. Schopen and I. Bekker (eds.), *Nicephori Gregorae byzantina historia*, 3 vols. (Bonn, 1829–55)

al-Idrisi: J.-A. Jaubert (ed.), *La géographie d'Edrisi*, 2 vols. (Paris, 1836–40; reprint Amsterdam, 1975)

Kosmas Indikopleustes: W. Wolska-Conus (ed.), *Topographie chrétienne*, 5 vols. (Paris, 1968–73)

Kydones, Demetrios: *Monodia occisorum Thessalonicae*, PG 109, 639–52

S. Lambros, *Palaiologeia kai Peloponnesiaka*, vol. 3 (Athens, 1926)

Leo VI: J. Koder (ed.), *Das Eparchenbuch Leons des Weisen* (Vienna, 1991)

P. Noailles and A. Dain, *Les Novelles de Léon VI le Sage* (Paris, 1944)

Leo the Grammarian: I. Bekker (ed.), *Leo Grammaticus* (Bonn, 1842)

E. McGeer, *The Land Legislation of the Macedonian Emperors: Translation and Commentary* (Toronto, 2000)

F. Miklosich and J. Müller, *Acta et diplomata graeca medii aevi sacra et profana*, 6 vols. (Vienna, 1860–90)

C. Morrisson, "La Logarikè: réforme fiscale et réforme monétaire sous Alexis Ier Comnène" (= C. Morrisson, *Monnaies et finances*, art. VI)

A. Mošin, "Prostagma tsara Manuila II Paleologa Svetogortsima," *Srpska kraljevska Akademija, Spomennik*, 91 (1939), pp. 164–7

M. Nystazopoulou-Pelekidou, *Eggrafa Patmou*, II: *Demosion Leitourgon* (Athens, 1980)

Pachymeres, Georgios: A. Failler (ed.), *Georges Pachymérès, Relations historiques*, II: *Livres IV–VI*, CFHB 24.2, 5 vols. (Paris, 1984–)

Peira: I. and P. Zepos, *Jus Graecoromanum*, IV (Athens, 1931)

M. Pozza and G. Ravegnani (eds.), *I trattati con Bisanzio 992–1198* (Venice, 1993)

Psellos, Michael: E. Renauld (ed.), *Chronographie* (Paris, 1926–28: reprint, 1967)

Procopius, *History of the Wars*: H. B. Dewing (transl.), *Procopius*, vols. 1–5 (Cambridge, Mass., 1914–40)

G. Schirò (ed.), *Cronaca dei Tocci di Cefalonia di Anonimo* (Rome, 1975)

P. Schreiner, *Texte zur spätbyzantinischen Finanz- und Wirtschaftsgeschichte in Handschriften der Biblioteca Vaticana* (Vatican City, 1991)

Skylitzes continuatus: E. T. Tsolakes (ed.), *He Synecheia tes Chronographias tou Ioannou Skylitse* (Thessalonike, 1968)

Skylitzes, Ioannes: H. Thurn (ed.), *Ioannis Scylitzae Synopsis historiarum* (Berlin–New York, 1973)

B. Flusin and J.-C. Cheynet (transl.), *Empereurs de Constantinople* (Paris, 2003)

Theophanes: C. de Boor (ed.), *Chronographia*, 2 vols (Leipzig, 1883–5)

C. Mango and R. Scott (transl.), *The Chronicle of Theophanes Confessor* (Oxford, 1997)

Theophanes Continuatus: I. Bekker (ed.), *Theophanes continuatus* (Bonn, 1838)

Timarion: R. Romano (ed.), *Timarione* (Naples, 1974)

Travaini, L. (ed.), *Monete, mercati e matematica: le monete medievali nei trattati di aritmetica e nei libri di mercatura* (Rome, 2003)

Vita of Saint Philaretos: M. H. Fourmy and M. Leroy (eds.), "La vie de Saint Philarète," *Byzantion* 9 (1934), pp. 85–167

Zonaras, Ioannes: M. L. Dindorf and M. Buettner-Wobst (eds.), *Epitome historiarum*, 3 vols. (Leipzig, 1868–97)

SECONDARY WORKS

Abu-Lughod, J., *Before European Hegemony: The World System, AD 1250–1350* (New York–Oxford, 1989)

Ahrweiler, H., *Byzance et la mer* (Paris, 1967)

Angelidi, C. G. (ed.), *To Vyzantio orimo gia allages* (Athens, 2004)

Angold, M., "The Shaping of the Medieval City," *Byzantinische Forschungen* 10 (1985), pp. 1–38

Angold, M. (ed.), *The Byzantine Aristocracy, IX–XIII Centuries* (Oxford, 1984)

Archaiologika tekmeria viotechnikon engatastaseon kata te Vyzantine epoche, 50s-150s aionas (Athens, 2004)

Arnaldi, G., and Cavallo, G. (eds.), *Europa medievale e mondo bizantino: contatti effettivi e possibilità di studi comparati* (Rome, 1997)

Ashtor, E., *A Social and Economic History of the Near East in the Middle Ages* (London, 1976)

— *Levant Trade in the Later Middle Ages* (Princeton, 1983)

Bagnall, R., *Later Roman Egypt: Society, Religion, Economy and Administration* (Aldershot, 2003 (collected studies))

— *Egypt in Late Antiquity* (Princeton, 1993)

Bakirtzis, Ch., *Vyzantina Tsoukalolagena* (Athens, 1989)

Balard, M., "Amalfi et Byzance (Xe–XIIe siècles)," *Travaux et Mémoires* 6 (1976), pp. 85–96

— *La Romanie génoise*, 2 vols. (Rome, 1978)

Barcelò, M. and Sigaut, F. (eds.), *The Making of Feudal Agricultures* (Leiden–Boston–Cologne, 2004 (Transformation of the Roman World 14))

Belke, K. F. et al. (eds.), *Byzanz als Raum: zu Methoden und Inhalten der historischen Geographie des oestlichen Mittelmeerraumes* (Vienna, 2000)

Bertelè, T., "Il giro di affari di Giacomo Badoer," *Akten des XI. Internationalen Byzantinistenkongresses* (Munich, 1960), pp. 48–57

— *Moneta veneziana e moneta bizantina* (Florence, 1973)

Birot, P., *La Méditerranée et le Moyen Orient*, 2nd edn., 2 vols (Paris, 1964)

Boehlendof-Arslan, B., *Die glasierte byzantinische Keramik aus der Türkei* (Istanbul, 2004)

Brandes, W., *Die Städte Kleinasiens im 7. und 8. Jahrhundert* (Berlin, 1989)

— *Finanzverwaltung in Krisenzeiten: Untersuchungen zur byzantinischen Administration im 6.–9. Jahrhundert* (Frankfurt, 2002)

Brogiolo G. P., Gauthier, N. and Christie, N. (eds.), *Towns and their Territories between Late Antiquity and the Early Middle Ages* (Leiden–Boston–Cologne, 2000 (Transformation of the Roman World 9))

Brogiolo, G. P. and Ward-Perkins, B. (eds.), *The Idea and Ideal of the Town between Late Antiquity and the Early Middle Ages* (Leiden–Boston–Cologne, 1999 (Transformation of the Roman World 4))

Bryer, A., "The Question of Byzantine Mines in the Pontos: Chalybian Iron, Chaldian Silver, Koloneian Alum and the Mummy of Cheriana," *Anatolian Studies* 32 (1982), pp. 133–50

Cavanaugh, W. et al. (eds.), *Continuity and Change in a Greek Rural Landscape: the Laconian Survey*, I (London, 2002)

Charanis, P., *Studies in the Demography of the Byzantine Empire* (London, 1972 (collected studies))

Christie, N. (ed.), *Landscapes of Change: Rural Evolutions in Late Antiquity and the Early Middle Ages* (Aldershot, 2004)

Cipolla, C., *Before the Industrial Revolution*, 3rd edn. (London, 1993)

— *Money, Prices and Civilization in the Mediterranean World* (New York, 1967)

Claude, D., "Der Handel im westlichen Mittelmeer während des Frühmittelalters," *(Abhandl. der Akad. d. Wiss. in Göttingen. Phil.-hist. Kl. III, n. 144 = Untersuchungen zu Handel und Verkehr der vor- und frühgeschichtlichen Zeit in Mittel- und Nordeuropa*, vol. II (Göttingen, 1985)

Contamine, P., Bompaire, M., Lebecq, S. and Sarrazin, J.-L., *L'économie médiévale* (Paris, 1993)

Cutler, A., "Gifts and Gift Exchange as Aspects of the Byzantine, Arab, and Related Economies," *Dumbarton Oaks Papers* 55 (2001), pp. 247–78

Dagron, G. and Mango, C. (eds.), *Constantinople and its Hinterland* (Aldershot, 1995)

Davidson, G. R., "A Medieval Glass Factory at Corinth," *American Journal of Archaeology* 44 (1940), pp. 297–327

— *Corinth,* vol. XII: *The Minor Objects* (Princeton, 1952)

Déroche, V. and Spieser, J.-M., *Recherches sur la céramique byzantine* (*BCH* Suppl., Athens, 1989)

Dunn, A. "The Exploitation and Control of Woodland and Scrubland in the Byzantine World," *Byzantine and Modern Greek Studies* 16 (1992), pp. 235–98

— "The *Kommerkiarios,* the *Apotheke,* the *Dromos,* the *Vardarios* and *The West,*" *Byzantine and Modern Greek Studies* 17 (1993), pp. 3–24

Durliat, J., *De la ville antique à la ville byzantine: le problème des subsistances* (Rome, 1990 (see also R. Delmaire's review in *Antiquité Tardive* 1, (1993), pp. 253–57))

E autokratoria se krise (?): to Vyzantio ton endekato aiona (1025–1081)(The Empire in Crisis (?): Byzantium in the 11th Century (1025–1081)) (Athens, 2003)

E Vyzantine Mikra Asia (Byzantine Asia Minor (6th–12th centuries)) (Athens, 1998)

First Anatolian Glass Symposium, April 26th–27th, 1988 (Istanbul 1990)

Fleet, K., *European and Islamic Trade in the Early Ottoman State* (Cambridge, 1999)

Foss, C., *History and Archaeology of Byzantine Asia Minor* (Aldershot, 1990 (collected studies))

— *Cities, Fortresses and Villages of Byzantine Asia Minor* (Aldershot, 1996) (collected studies))

François, V., "Elaborate Incised Ware: une preuve du rayonnement de la culture Byzantine à l'époque paléologue," *ByzantinoSlavica* 61 (2003), pp. 151–68

Garnsey, P., Hopkins, K. and Whittaker, C. R. (eds.), *Trade in the Ancient Economy* (London, 1983)

Gelichi, S. (ed.), *La ceramica nel mondo bizantino tra XI e XV secolo e i suoi rapporti con l'Italia* (Florence, 1993)

Gerstel, S. and Lauffenberger, J. (eds.), *A Lost Art Rediscovered: The Architectural Ceramics of Byzantium* (Baltimore, 2001)

Gerstel, S., Munn, M. et al., "A Late Medieval Settlement at Panakton," *Hesperia* 72 (2003), pp. 147–234

Geyer, B. and Lefort, J. (eds.), *La Bithynie au Moyen Âge* (Paris, 2003)

Giardina, A. (ed.), *Società romana e impero tardoantico*, 4 vols. (Rome–Bari, 1986)

Gill, M. A. V., *Amorium Reports, Finds I: The Glass (1987–1997)* (Oxford, 2002)

Goitein, S. D., *A Mediterranean Society*, vol. 4 (Berkeley–Los Angeles, 1983)

Grierson, P., *Dark Age Numismatics* (London, 1979)

— *Later Medieval Numismatics* (London, 1979 (collected studies))

— *Catalogue of the Byzantine Coins in the Dumbarton Oaks Collection and in the Whittemore Collection,* II *(610–717)* (Washington, D.C., 1968); III *(717–1081)* (Washington, D.C., 1973); V *(1258–1453)* (Washington, D.C., 1999)

Guillou, A., *Culture et société en Italie byzantine (VIe-XIe siècle)* (London, 1978)

Haldon, J., "Military Service, Military Lands and the Status of Soldiers: Current Problems and Interpretations," *Dumbarton Oaks Papers* 47 (1993), pp. 1–67

— *Byzantium in the Seventh Century: The Transformation of a Culture* (Cambridge–New York, 1990)

— *The State and the Tributary Mode of Production* (London, 1993)

Hansen, I. L. and Wickham, C. (eds.), *The Long Eighth Century: Production, Distribution and Demand* (Leiden, 2000 (Transformation of the Roman World, 11))

Harrison, R. M. (ed.), *Excavations at Saraçhane in Istanbul* (Princeton, 1992)

Harvey, A., *Economic Expansion in the Byzantine Empire 900–1200* (Cambridge, 1989)

Hendy, M. F., *Coinage and Money in the Byzantine Empire (1081–1261)* (Washington, D.C., 1969)

— *Studies in the Byzantine Monetary Economy* (Cambridge, 1985)

— *The Economy, Fiscal Administration and Coinage of Byzantium* (Northampton, 1989 (collected studies))

— *Catalogue of the Byzantine Coins in the Dumbarton Oaks Collection and in the Whittemore Collection,* IV *(1081–1261)* (Washington, D.C., 1999)

Hodges, R. and Whitehouse, D., *Mahomet, Charlemagne et les origines de l'Europe* (Paris, 1996; updated edition of the original *Mohammed, Charlemagne and the Origins of Europe* (London, 1983))

Hommes et richesses dans l'empire byzantin, I (IVe–VIIe siècle) (Paris, 1989); II *(VIIIe–XVe siècle)* (Paris, 1991)

Jacoby, D., *Société et démographie à Byzance et en Romanie latine* (London, 1975 (collected studies))

— "Raw Materials for the Glass Industries of Venice and the Terraferma, about 1370–about 1460," *Journal of Glass Studies* 35 (1993), pp. 65–90

— *Trade, Commodities and Shipping in the Medieval Mediterranean* (Aldershot, 1997 (collected studies)).

— "Byzantine Trade with Egypt from the Mid-Tenth Century to the Fourth Crusade," *Thesaurismata* 30 (2000), pp. 25–77

Jacoby, D. "Dalla materia prima ai drappi tra Bisanzio, il Levante e Venezia: la prima fase dell'industria serica veneziana," in Molà, L., Mueller, R. C. and Zanier, C. (eds.), *La seta in Italia dal Medioevo al Seicento: dal baco al drappo* (Venice, 2000), pp. 265–304

— *Byzantium, Latin Romania and the Mediterranean* (Aldershot, 2001 (collected studies))

Jameson, M. H., Runnels, C. M. and van Andel, T. H., *A Greek Countryside: The Southern Argolid from Prehistory to the Present Day* (Stanford, 1994)

Jones, A. H. M., *The Later Roman Empire 284–602: A Social, Economic and Administrative Survey*, 3 vols. (Oxford, 1964)

Kaplan, M., *Les hommes et la terre à Byzance du VIe au XIe siècle: propriété et exploitation du sol* (Paris, 1992)

Kazanski, M., Nercesian, A. and Zuckerman, C. (eds.), *Les centres protourbains russes entre Scandinavie, Byzance et Orient* (Paris, 2000)

Kazhdan, A. P., "Vizantiiski goroda v vii–xi vekah," *Sovetskaya Arheologyia*, 21 (1954), pp. 164–83

Kazhdan, A. and Epstein, A. W., *Change in Byzantine Culture in the Eleventh and Twelfth Centuries* (Berkeley–Los Angeles–London, 1985)

Kazhdan, A. and Talbot, A.-M. (eds.), *The Oxford Dictionary of Byzantium* (Oxford, 1986) (cited throughout as *ODB*)

Kehoe, D. P., *The Economics of Agriculture on Roman Imperial Estates in North Africa* (Göttingen, 1988)

Kingsley, S. and Decker, M. (eds.), *Economy and Exchange in the East Mediterranean during Late Antiquity* (Oxford, 2001)

Koder, J., *Der Lebensraum der Byzantiner: Historisch-geographischer Abriss ihres mittelalterlichen Staates im östlichen Mittelmeerraum* (Vienna, 2001; updated and revised Greek edition, *Vyzantio os choros: Eisagoge sten istorike geographia tes Anatolikes Mesogeiou ste Vyzantine Epoche* (Thessalonike, 2005)

Kontoura-Galake, E. (ed.), *Oi skoteinoi aiones tou Vyzantiou (7os–9os ai.) (The Dark Centuries of Byzantium)* (Athens, 2001)

La céramique médiévale en Méditerranée (Aix-en-Provence, 1997)

Laiou-Thomadakis, A. E., *Peasant Society in the Late Byzantine Empire* (Princeton, 1974)

Laiou, A. E., "Venice as a Center of Trade and of Artistic Production in the Thirteenth Century," *Atti del XXIV Congresso del Comitato Internazionale di storia dell'arte, sez. 2* (Bologna, 1982), pp. 11–26

— "Händler und Kaufleute auf dem Jahrmarkt," in Prinzing, G. and Simon, D. (eds.), *Fest und Alltag in Byzanz* (Munich, 1990) pp. 53–70

— *Gender, Society and Economic Life in Byzantium* (London, 1992 (collected studies))

— *Mariage, amour et parenté à Byzance aux XIe–XIIIe siècles* (Paris, 1992)

— "Byzantine Traders and Seafarers," in Vryonis, S. (ed.), *Byzantium and the Sea* (New York, 1993), pp. 77–96

— "Koinonike dikaiosyne: to synallattesthai kai to euemerein sto Vyzantio" *Praktika tes Akademias Athenon*, 74 (1999), pp. 103–30

— "*Nummus parit nummos*: l' usurier, le juriste et le philosophe à Byzance," in *Académie des Inscriptions et Belles-Lettres, Comptes rendus* (Paris, 1999), pp. 583–604

— "Methodological Questions Regarding the Economic History of Byzantium," *Zbornik Radova Vizantološkog Instituta* 39 (2001/2), pp. 9–23

— "Economic Concerns and Attitudes of the Intellectuals of Thessalonike," *Dumbarton Oaks Papers* 57 (2003), pp. 205–23

— "Monopoly and Privileged Free Trade in the Eastern Mediterranean (8th–14th Century)" in *Chemins d'outre-mer: Études d'histoire sur la Méditerranée médiévale offertes à Michel Balard* (Paris, 2004), pp. 511–26

Laiou, A. E. (editor-in-chief), *The Economic History of Byzantium from the Seventh through the Fifteenth Century*, 3 vols. (Washington, D. C., 2002) (cited throughout as *EHB*)

Laiou, A. E. (ed.), *Urbs capta: The Fourth Crusade and its Consequences; La quatrième croisade et ses conséquences* (Paris, 2005)

Laiou, A. E. and Mottahedeh, R. (eds.), *The Crusades from the Perspective of Byzantium and the Muslim World* (Washington, D.C., 2001)

Laiou, A. E. and Simon, D., "Eine Geschichte von Mühlen und Mönchen: Der Fall der Mühlen von Chandax," *Bollettino dell'Istituto di Diritto Romano*, 3rd ser., 30 (1992), pp. 619–76

Laiou, A. E. and Simon, D. (eds.), *Law and Society in Byzantium, Ninth–Twelfth Centuries* (Washington, D.C., 1994)

Lal, D., *Unintended Consequences: The Impact of Factor Endowments, Culture, and Politics on Long-Run Economic Performance* (Cambridge, Mass., 1998)

Lane, F. C. and Mueller, R. C., *Money and Banking in Medieval and Renaissance Venice* (Baltimore, 1985)

Lavan, L. and Bowden, W. (eds.), *Theory and Practice in Late Antique Archaeology* (Leiden–Boston, 2003)

Lefort, J., *Société rurale et histoire du paysage à Byzance* (Paris, 2006 (collected and revised studies))

Lefort, J., Morrisson, C. and Sodini, J.-P. (eds.), *Les Villages dans l'empire byzantin (IVe–XVe siècle)* (Paris, 2005)

Lemerle, P., *Cinq études sur le XIe siècle byzantin* (Paris, 1977)

— *The Agrarian History of Byzantium from the Origins to the Twelfth Century* (Galway, 1979)

Liebeschuetz, W., *The Decline and Fall of the Roman City* (Oxford, 2001)

Lightfoot, C. S., "Byzantine Anatolia: Reassessing the Numismatic Evidence," *Revue numismatique* 158 (2002), pp. 229–39

— "Trade and Industry in Byzantine Anatolia – The Evidence from Amorium," *Dumbarton Oaks Papers*, 59 (2006), pp. 173–81.

— "Glass Finds at Amorium," *Dumbarton Oaks Papers* 59 (2006), pp. 173–181
— "The Survival of Cities in Byzantine Anatolia: The Case of Amorium," *Byzantion* 68 (1998), pp. 56–71

Lilie, R.-J., *Handel und Politik: zwischen dem byzantinischen Reich und den italienischen Kommunen Venedig, Pisa und Genua in der Epoche der Komnenen und der Angeloi, 1081–1204* (Amsterdam, 1984)

Lock, P. and Sanders, G. D. R. (eds.), *The Archaeology of Medieval Greece* (Exeter, 1996)

Lopez, R. S., *The Commercial Revolution of the Middle Ages* (Englewood Cliffs, N.J., 1971)
— *Byzantium and the World around it* (London, 1978 (collected studies))

Loungis, T., "E exelixe tes Vyzantines poles apo ton 40 sto 120 aiona," *Vyzantiaka* 16 (1996), pp. 32–67

Magdalino, P., *The Empire of Manuel I Komnenos* (Cambridge, 1993)
— *Constantinople médiévale* (Paris, 1996)
— *L'orthodoxie des astrologues: la science entre le dogme et la divination à Byzance (VIIe–XIVe siècle)* (Paris, 2006)

Maguire, H. (ed.), *Materials Analysis of Byzantine Pottery* (Washington, D.C., 1997)

Mango, C., *Le développement urbain de Constantinople, IVe–VIIe siècle* (Paris, 1985)

Maniatis, G. C., "The Domain of Private Guilds in the Byzantine Economy, Tenth to Fifteenth Centuries," *Dumbarton Oaks Papers* 55 (2001), pp. 339–69
— "Organization, Market Structure, and Modus Operandi of the Private Silk Industry in Tenth-Century Byzantium," *Dumbarton Oaks Papers* 53 (1999), pp. 263–332

Marin, B. and Virlouvet, C. (eds.), *Nourrir les cités de Méditerranée: antiquité–temps modernes* (Paris, 2003)

Matschke, K.-P., "Zum Charakter des byzantinischen Schwarzmeerhandels im 13. bis 15. Jahrhundert," *Wissenschaftliche Zeitschrift der K.-Marx Universität Leipzig*, 19 (1970), pp. 447–58
— "Byzantinische Politiker und byzantinische Kaufleute im Ringen um die Beteiligung am Schwarzmeerhandel in der Mitte des 14. Jh.," *Mitteilungen des bulgarischen Forschungsinstitutes im Österreich*, 2 (1984), pp. 75–95
— "Tuchproduktion und Tuchproduzenten in Thessalonike und in anderen Städten und Regionen des späten Byzanz," *Vyzantiaka* 9 (1989), pp. 68–84
— "Zum Anteil der Byzantiner an der Bergbauentwicklung und an den Bergbauerträgen Südosteuropas im 14. und 15. Jahrhundert," *Byzantinische Zeitschrift* 84/5 (1991/2), pp. 49–71

McCormick, M., *Origins of the European Economy: Communications and Commerce AD 300–900* (Cambridge, 2001)

McDonald, W. A., Coulson, W. E. and Rosser, J., *Excavations at Nichoria in Southern Greece* (Minneapolis, 1983)

Mercati e mercanti nell'altomedioevo (Settimana di Studi sull'alto medioevo XL) (Spoleto, 1993)

Metcalf, D. M., *Coinage in South-Eastern Europe 820–1396* (London, 1979)

— *Coinage of the Crusades and the Latin East in the Ashmolean Museum Oxford* (London, 1995)

Morrisson, C., *Monnaie et finances à Byzance; Analyses, techniques* (Aldershot, 1994 (collected studies))

Morrisson, C. (ed.), *Le monde byzantin, 1: (330–641)* (Paris, 2004)

Morrisson, C., Barrandon, J.-N., Brenot, C., Callu, J.-P., Halleux, R. and Poirier, J., *L'or monnayé I: De Rome à Byzance* (Paris, 1985)

Morrisson, C., Popović, V., Ivanišević, V., et al., *Les trésors monétaires byzantins des Balkans et d'Asie Mineure (491–713)* (Paris, 2006)

Moschonas, N. G. (ed.), *Money and Markets in the Palaeologan Era* (Athens, 2003)

Muthesius, A., *Studies in Byzantine and Islamic Silk Weaving* (London, 1995)

North, D. C. and Thomas, R. P., *The Rise of the Western World: A New Economic History* (Cambridge, 1973)

Oikonomides, N., *Hommes d'affaires grecs et latins à Constantinople (XIIIe–XVe siècles)* (Montreal, 1979)

— *Fiscalité et exemption fiscale à Byzance (IXe–XIe Siècles)* (Athens, 1996)

— *Social and Economic Life in Byzantium* (Aldershot, 2004 (collected studies))

— *Society, Culture, and Politics in Byzantium* (Aldershot, 2005 (collected studies))

Oikonomides, N. (ed.), *Byzantium in the Twelfth Century* (Athens, 1991)

Ostrogorskij, G., *Pour l'histoire de la féodalité byzantine* (Brussels, 1954)

— *Quelques problèmes d'histoire de la paysannerie byzantine* (Brussels, 1956)

Pamuk, Ş., *A Monetary History of the Ottoman Empire* (Cambridge, 2000)

Panella, C., "Merci e scambi nel Mediterraneo tardoantico," in Momigliano, A. and Schiavone, A. (general eds.), *Storia di Roma*, vol. 3, *L'età tardoantica*, part 2, *I luoghi e le culture*, ed. by A. Carandini, Cracco-Ruggini, L. and Giardina, A. (Torino, 1993), pp. 613–97

Papanikola-Bakirtzi, D., "Ergasteria efyalomenes keramikes sto Vyzantino kosmo," in *VIIe Congrès international sur la céramique médiévale en Méditerranée* (Athens, 2003), pp. 45–66

— *Mesaionike efyalomene keramike tes Kyprou: ta ergasteria Pafou kai Lapithou* (Thessalonike, 1996)

Papanikola-Bakirtzi, D. (ed.), *Byzantine Glazed Ceramics: The Art of Sgraffito* (Athens, 1999)

— *Byzantinon diatrophe kai mageireiai* (Thessalonike, 2005)

— *Everyday Life in Byzantium* (Athens, 2002)

Papanikola-Bakirtzis, D., Dauterman Maguire, E. and Maguire, H., *Ceramic Art from Byzantine Serres* (Urbana–Chicago, 1992)

Parker, A. J., *Ancient Shipwrecks of the Mediterranean and the Roman Provinces* (Oxford, 1992)

Philippe, J. *Le monde byzantin dans l'histoire de la verrerie* (Bologna, 1970)

Piéri, D., *Le commerce du vin oriental à l'époque byzantine (Ve–VIIe siècles): le témoignage des amphores en Gaule* (Beyrouth, 2005)

Pitarakis, B., "Mines anatoliennes exploitées par les Byzantins: recherches récentes," *Revue Numismatique* 153 (1989), pp. 141–85

Pomeranz, K., *The Great Divergence: China, Europe and the Making of the Modern World Economy* (Princeton, 2000)

Praktika diethnous synedriou gia to Despotato tes Epeirou (Arta, 1992)

Pryor, J. H., *Geography, Technology and War: Studies in the Maritime History of the Mediterranean* (Cambridge, 1988)

Russell, J., "Late Ancient and Medieval Population," *Transactions of the American Philosophical Association*, n.s., 48, 3 (1958), pp. 1–152

Sanders, G. D. R., "An Overview of the Chronology for 9th to 13th Century Pottery at Corinth," in *VIIe Congrès international sur la céramique médiévale en Méditerranée* (Athens, 2003), pp. 35–44

Shitikov, M. M., "Konstantinopolj i Venetsianskaja torgovlja v pervoj polovine XV v. po dannym knigi schetov Džakomo Badoera," *VV* 30 (1969) pp. 46–63

Smyrlis, K., *La fortune des grands monastères byzantins (fin du Xe–milieu du XIVe siècle)* (Paris, 2006)

Spufford, P., *Money and its Use in Medieval Europe* (Cambridge, 1988)

Stahl, A. M., Zecca, *The Mint of Venice in the Middle Ages* (Baltimore, 2000)

Stathakopoulos, D. Ch., *Famine and Pestilence in the Late Roman and Early Byzantine Empire: A Systematic Survey of Subsistence Crises and Epidemics* (Aldershot, 2004)

Stiglitz, J. E., A. Charlton, *Fair Trade for All: How Trade Can Promote Development* (Oxford, 2005)

Svoronos, N., *Etudes sur l'organisation intérieure, la société et l'économie de l'empire byzantin* (London, 1973 (collected studies))

— "Remarques sur les structures économiques de l'empire byzantin au XIe siècle," *Travaux et Mémoires* 6 (1976), pp. 49–67

Tate, G., *Les campagnes de la Syrie du Nord* (Paris, 2002)

Teall, J. L., "Byzantine Agricultural Tradition," *Dumbarton Oaks Papers* 25 (1971), pp. 35–59.

— "The Grain Supply of the Byzantine Empire, 330–1025," *Dumbarton Oaks Papers* 13 (1959), pp. 87–190

Technognosia ste Latinokratoumene Ellada (Athens, 2000)

Thiriet, F., *La Romanie vénitienne au Moyen-Âge*, 2nd edn. (Paris, 1975)

Toubert, P., *Les structures du Latium médiéval*, 2 vols. (Rome, 1973)

— *L'Europe dans sa première croissance: de Charlemagne à l'an mil* (Paris, 2004)

Verhulst, A., *The Carolingian Economy* (Cambridge, 2002)

Verlinden, C., *L'esclavage dans l'Europe médiévale*, 2 vols. (Bruges, 1955)

VIIe Congrès international sur la Céramique médiévale en Méditerranée (Athens, 2003)

Vroom, J., *After Antiquity: Ceramics and Society in the Aegean from the 7th to the 20th Century AC: A Case Study from Boeotia, Central Greece* (Leiden, 2003)

Vryonis, S., Jr., *Byzantium: Its Internal History and Relations with the Muslim World* (London, 1971) (collected studies)

— *The Decline of Medieval Hellenism in Asia Minor and the Process of Islamization from the Eleventh through the Fifteenth Century* (Berkeley, 1971)

Watson, A. M., *Agricultural Innovation in the Early Islamic World: The Diffusion of Crops and Farming Techniques, 700–1100* (Cambridge, 1983)

Whitehouse, D., "Glassmaking at Corinth: A Reassessment," in *Ateliers de verriers: de l'Antiquité à la période pré-industrielle* (Rouen, 1991), pp. 73–82

Wickham, C., *Framing the Early Middle Ages: Europe and the Mediterranean 400–800* (Oxford, 2005)[1]

Williams, Ch. K., "Frankish Corinth," *Hesperia* 62 (1993), pp. 15–35

Zachariadou, E., *Romania and the Turks* (London, 1985 (collected studies))

Zakythinos, D., *Crise monétaire et crise économique à Byzance du XIIIe au XVe siècle* (Athens, 1948; repr. in idem, *Byzance: état, société, économie* (London, 1973 (collected studies))

Zuckerman, C., *Du village à l'Empire: autour du registre fiscal d'Aphroditô* (Paris, 2004)

Zuckerman, C. (ed.), *La Crimée entre Byzance et les Khazars (VIIe –IXe siècle)* (Paris, 2006)

---

[1] This important and massive volume appeared too late for us to be able to take it into due account.

INDEX

———— • ————

Cambridge Medieval Textbooks

Already published

Germany in the High Middle Ages c. 1050–1200
HORST FUHRMANN

The Hundred Years War:
England and France at War c. 1300–c. 1450
CHRISTOPHER ALLMAND

Standards of Living in the Later Middle Ages:
Social Change in England, c. 1200–1520
CHRISTOPHER DYER

Magic in the Middle Ages
RICHARD KIECKHEFER

The Papacy 1073–1198: Continuity and Innovation
I. S. ROBINSON

Medieval Wales
DAVID WALKER

England in the Reign of Edward III
SCOTT L. WAUGH

The Norman Kingdom of Sicily
DONALD MATTHEW

Political Thought in Europe 1250–1450
ANTONY BLACK

The Church in Western Europe from the Tenth to the Early
Twelfth Century
GERD TELLENBACH
Translated by Timothy Reuter

The Medieval Spains
BERNARD F. REILLY

England in the Thirteenth Century
ALAN HARDING

Monastic and Religious Orders in Britain 1000–1300
JANET BURTON

Religion and Devotion in Europe c. 1215–c. 1515
R. N. SWANSON

Medieval Russia, 980–1584
JANET MARTIN

The Wars of the Roses: Politics and the Constitution in England,
c. 1437–1509
CHRISTINE CARPENTER

The Waldensian Dissent: Persecution and Survival, c. 1170–c. 1570
GABRIEL AUDISIO
Translated by Claire Davison

The Crusades, c. 1071–c. 1291
JEAN RICHARD
Translated by Jean Birrell

A History of Business in Medieval Europe, 1200–1550
EDWIN S. HUNT, JAMES MURRAY

Medieval Economic Thought
DIANA WOOD

Medieval Scotland
A. D. M. BARRELL

Roger II of Sicily
A Ruler between East and West
HUBERT HOUBEN
Translated by Graham A. Loud, Diane Milburn

The Carolingian Economy
ADRIAAN VERHULST

Women in Early Medieval Europe, 400–1100
LISA M. BITEL

Southeastern Europe in the Middle Ages, 500–1250
FLORIN CURTA

The Jews of Medieval Western Christendom, 1000–1500

ROBERT CHAZAN